THE FATHERS
OF THE CHURCH

A NEW TRANSLATION

VOLUME 2

THE FATHERS OF THE CHURCH

Founded by
LUDWIG SCHOPP

EDITORIAL BOARD

ROY JOSEPH DEFERRARI
The Catholic University of America
Editorial Director

RUDOLPH ARBESMANN, O.S.A.
Fordham University

BERNARD M. PEEBLES
The Catholic University of America

STEPHAN KUTTNER
The Catholic University of America

ROBERT P. RUSSELL, O.S.A.
Villanova College

MARTIN R. P. MCGUIRE
The Catholic University of America

ANSELM STRITTMATTER, O.S.B.
St. Anselm's Priory

WILFRID PARSONS, S.J.
Georgetown University

JAMES EDWARD TOBIN
Queens College

GERALD G. WALSH, S.J.
Fordham University

SAINT AUGUSTINE

CHRISTIAN INSTRUCTION
translated by
John J. Gavigan, O.S.A.

ADMONITION AND GRACE
translated by
John Courtney Murray, S.J.

THE CHRISTIAN COMBAT
translated by
Robert P. Russell, O.S.A.

FAITH, HOPE AND CHARITY
translated by
Bernard M. Peebles

THE CATHOLIC UNIVERSITY OF AMERICA PRESS
Washington, D. C.

NIHIL OBSTAT:

        JOHN M. FEARNS, S.T.D.
        CENSOR LIBRORUM

IMPRIMATUR:

        ✠ FRANCIS CARDINAL SPELLMAN
        ARCHBISHOP OF NEW YORK

August 13, 1947

Library of Congress Catalog Card No.: 66-20314

Copyright, 1947 by
THE CATHOLIC UNIVERSITY OF AMERICA PRESS, INC.

All rights reserved
Second Edition 1950
Reprinted, 1966
Reprinted, 1985
Reprinted, 1992
First paperback reprint 2002
ISBN 0-8132-1318-5
ISBN-13: 978-0-8132-1318-7

CONTENTS

CHRISTIAN INSTRUCTION
Introduction 3
Text 19

ADMONITION AND GRACE
Introduction 239
Text 245

THE CHRISTIAN COMBAT
Introduction 309
Text 315

FAITH, HOPE AND CHARITY
Introduction 357
Text 369

INDEX 473

CHRISTIAN INSTRUCTION

(De doctrina Christiana)

Translated

by

JOHN J. GAVIGAN, O.S.A., Ph.D.
Villanova College

NIHIL OBSTAT:
> THOMAS F. ROLAND, O.S.A.
> CENSOR DEPUTATUS

IMPRIMI POTEST:
> VERY REV. MORTIMER A. SULLIVAN, O.S.A.
> PRIOR PROVINCIALIS

NIHIL OBSTAT:
> JOSEPH A. M. QUIGLEY
> CENSOR LIBRORUM

IMPRIMATUR:
> ✠ D. CARDINALIS DOUGHERTY
> ARCHIEPISCOPUS
> PHILADELPHIENSIS.

September 5, 1945

INTRODUCTION

TO INTRODUCE St. Augustine's *Christian Instruction* we can hardly do better than translate the chapter of his own *Retractations* in which, while correcting certain errors, the author relates why and under what circumstances the former work was written:[1]

When I became aware that the books on Christian Instruction were incomplete, I chose to finish them, rather than leave them in such a condition and pass on to the revision of other works. I therefore completed the third book, which had been written up to the point where a reference from the Gospel is made concerning the woman who hid leaven 'in three measures of flour until all of it was leavened.' I also added the last book and completed the work in four books. The first three of these help to an understanding of the Scriptures, while the fourth instructs us how to present the facts which we have comprehended. However, in the second book, referring to the author of the book which many call the Wisdom of Solomon, I have learned since then that it was not a certainty that Jesus the son of Sirach wrote this book, as well as the Book of Ecclesiasticus, as I had stated, and I have discovered that it is more probable that he is not the author of this book. Moreover, when I said, 'The authority of the Old Testament is terminated by

---

1 *Retractationes* 2.4.30.

these forty-four books,' I was referring to the Old Testament according to the general practice by which the Church speaks of it; however, the Apostle appears to designate as the Old Testament only that which was promulgated on Mount Sinai. Furthermore, my memory deceived me in the statement that I made that Saint Ambrose, because of his information on the chronology of historical matters, had settled a subject of debate, holding that Plato and Jeremias were living at the same time. What that bishop stated about this matter can be read in the book which he wrote on the Sacraments or on Philosophy. The present work begins as follows: 'There are several norms.'

Since the reader will have an opportunity himself to study the three passages in which the author pointed out his errors of statement or fact,[2] this discussion of the passage from the *Retractations* will be confined to the problem of dating the two stages in the composition of the *De doctrina Christiana*. Both stages, it will be noticed, fall within the period of St. Augustine's episcopate, towards the end of which he set himself, in the *Retractations,* to list his principal writings and apply to them that candid self-criticism which is so characteristic.

This task, as he states, he interrupted in order to complete the *De doctrina Christiana,* which he found he had left unfinished near the end of Book 3 (sect. 35). The importance which the author attached to this work may be judged from his determination to interrupt the *Retractations* in order to complete it. Since the latter was finished in A.D. 427, it is fair to conclude that, at some time in that or the previous year, the end of the third book of the *De*

---

2 See this translation 2.8.13 (two passages) and 2.28.43.

doctrina Christiana and all of the fourth were written. Independent evidence confirms this dating.³

Both external and internal evidence make it possible to place the composition of the first part of the work in 396 or 397. Since in the *Retractations,* where St. Augustine enumerated his writings in an approximate chronological order, the *De doctrina Christiana* follows the *De agone Christiano* of 396 or 397,⁴ it is not likely to be of an earlier date. A passage in Book 2 (2.40.61) leads to a result which is consistent with the above conclusion and fixes a lower limit. Here, in listing deceased ecclesiastical writers who had employed the rich legacy of pagan culture —one of the most influential and most quoted passages in the work—St. Augustine omitted the name of St. Ambrose, whose style, with that of St. Cyprian (who *is* duly mentioned), is so highly commended in Book 4. This would imply that St. Ambrose was still alive. As this writer died 4 April 397, the first part of the *De doctrina Christiana* must have been completed prior to that date—and, as is seen, not much earlier. It does not appear that this early part of the work was published separately.⁵

To supplement St. Augustine's own analysis of the purpose and content of the work, it may be noted that Books 1 and 2 treat of the subjects, sacred and profane, whose

---
3 See below, 4.24.53. This passage dates, as an event of about eight years earlier, St Augustine's part in quelling the riot at Caesarea in Mauretania, an episode of the important visit he made there in 418.
4 For a discussion of the date of this work, see below, p. 309f.
5 From the fact that St. Augustine, in the *Contra Faustum* (22.91) of ca. 400 quotes *De doctr. Christ.* 2.40.60, it was argued that the author had published the first part of the work prior to this date. This opinion was subsequently abandoned by the distinguished scholar who originated it. For the details see Vernon J. Bourke, *Augustine's Quest of Wisdom* (Milwaukee 1945) 146 n. 43.

study forms a necessary preparation to the proper reading and interpretation of the Bible. While modern educational theory may hold that St. Augustine is over-rigid in fixing limits to the study of the liberal arts, no one could deny that it is no mean instruction he prescribed to the would-be student of the Bible. Book 3 deals with the subjects now called hermeneutics, the interpretation of the Scriptures, and forms the most important early Latin treatise in the field. It would appear that St. Augustine was prompted to his task partly by the publication not long before of the *Book of Rules* of the Donatist Tyconius, the earliest extant Latin treatise dealing with Biblical hermeneutics. While St. Augustine made some adverse criticism of the Donatist's work, he commended it for the most part, setting out its contents in detail and quoting certain passages verbatim.[6] St. Augustine could be a just critic of others as well as of himself.

In Book 4 the author deals with the manner in which the Christian teacher was to expound the truths of religion. It is substantially a manual of homiletics. While the former teacher of rhetoric disclaimed any intention of supplying the rhetorical precepts taught in the secular schools,[7] he had hardly been able to keep his promise. Had the rhetorical writings of Cicero, the *Auctor ad Herennium,* and Quintilian been lost—to mention only a few of the pagan authors upon whom St. Augustine certainly or probably drew—a large part of their doctrinal content could be recovered from Book 4 of the *De doctrina Christiana*.[8] Of special

---

6 See below, 3.30.42ff.

7 See below, 4.1.2.

8 The dissertation of Sister Mary Thérèse Sullivan (see Bibliography) is a convenient work in which to assess St. Augustine's reliance on pagan rhetorical writers. See especially her Index Locorum (203-205) and

and independent value are the chapters[9] in which St. Augustine offered extended passages from Scripture and from St. Cyprian and St. Ambrose to illustrate the three styles of eloquence distinguished by ancient rhetorical theory.

Even for the reader who has no special interest in Biblical studies, the work is far from valueless. Passages, sometimes extended, of high dogmatic value abound, as do others which contribute to the understanding of St. Augustine's teachings on Christian morality.

Both the essential and accidental merits of the work were not lost on future generations. Its influence was extensive and long-lived and was brought into play both through the dissemination of the book itself and the use made of it by such men as Cassiodorus and Hrabanus Maurus. The former (d. ca. 585) at once highly commended it in his *Institutions* and, although he adopted a different plan of organization, used it as a model for that work. Hrabanus Maurus (d. 856) drew heavily upon it in Book 3 of the *De institutione clericorum*. In the later Middle Ages, St. Bonaventure and St. Thomas assigned it a due importance. Book 4 of the *De doctrina Christiana* was among the first works of St. Augustine to be printed. About a decade after the Gutenberg Bible, two editions (Strasburg, Mainz) appeared under the title, *De arte praedicandi*.

The judgment passed upon the *De doctrina Christiana* by its seventeenth-century Benedictine editors is well de-

---

Tables 8-13. Her references to ancient writers have greatly enriched the annotations in Book 4 of the present translation. Since Sister Mary Thérèse cites abundant parallels from Quintilian, the statement of a later writer (H.-I. Marrou, *Saint Augustin* 48) that St. Augustine appears not to have read Quintilian is difficult of acceptance.

9 See below 4.20.39ff.

served: 'a work in conformity with the dignity of the subject, wrought with scholarly care and surely not unworthy of a place at the front of the Bible along with the Prefaces of St. Jerome.'

Since no recent critical edition of the Latin text exists, the present translation has been based, for Book 1-3, on the edition of Vogels (substantially reproducing the Benedictine edition, but with a few emendations); for Book 4, on the revised text of Sister Mary Thérèse Sullivan. For the New Testament quotations the rendering published in 1941 under the patronage of the Episcopal Committee of the Confraternity of Christian Doctrine has been used; for quotations from the Old Testament, the source has been the Douay-Reims Bible. Certain changes have been made when necessitated by the Latin text of the *De doctrina Christiana*, in which St. Augustine frequently drew on a text somewhat different from the Vulgate.

SELECT BIBLIOGRAPHY

Texts:

> J. P. Migne, *Patrologia Latina* 34 15ff. (reprinting the seventeeth-century Benedictine (Maurist) edition).
>
> H. J. Vogels, *S. Aurelii Augustini de doctrina christiana, in Florilegium patristicum*, Fasc. 24 (Bonn 1930).
>
> Sister M. Thérèse Sullivan, ... *De doctrina Christiana liber quartus* (The Catholic University of America Patristic Studies 23, Washington 1930). Revised text, with introduction and translation.

Translations:

> J. F. Shaw, in *The Works of Saint Augustine, A New Translation* 9 edited by Marcus Dods (Edinburgh 1892).
>
> Sigisbert Mitterer, O.S.B., in *Bibliothek der Kirchenväter* 49 München 1925; reprinted 1932).
>
> See also Sullivan above.

Other works:

W. J. V. Baker and C. Bickersteth, *Preaching and Teaching according to St. Augustine* (London 1907).

Sister M. Inviolata Barry, *St. Augustine the Orator* (Washington 1924).

R. J. Deferrari, 'St Augustine's Method of Composing and Delivering Sermons,' *American Journal of Philology* 43 (1922) 97-123, 193-219.

J. B. Eskridge, *The Influence of Cicero upon Augustine in the Development of his Oratorical Theory for the Training of The Ecclesiastical Orator* (Menasha, Wis. 1912).

H. I. Marrou, *Saint Augustin et la fin de la culture antique* (Paris 1938).

CONTENTS

Prologue

BOOK ONE

Chapter	Page
1 The treatment of Scripture, which should be undertaken with the help of God, depends upon discovering and explaining its meaning	27
2 The definition of things and signs	28
3 The classification of things	29
4 What is meant by enjoyment and use	29
5 God the Trinity, the Object we are to enjoy	30
6 How God is ineffable	31
7 All understand God as the Being who cannot be surpassed in excellence	32
8 Since God is unchangeable Wisdom, He should be preferred to everything	33
9 Everyone knows that unchangeable Wisdom should be esteemed above that which is changeable	34
10 The soul must be cleansed to see God	34
11 Incarnate Wisdom is the model for cleansing our soul	34
12 How the Wisdom comes to us	35
13 The Word was made flesh	36
14 How the Wisdom of God healed man	36
15 Our faith is sustained by the Resurrection and Ascension of Christ and animated by His Judgment	37
16 The Church as body and spouse of Christ is purified by Him with afflictions which act as medicine	38

Chapter	Page
17 Christ has opened up the way to our heavenly country by forgiving our sins	39
18 The keys entrusted to the Church	39
19 The death and resurrection of body and soul	40
20 Some rise again, not for life but for punishment . . .	40
21 More on the resurrection of the body	40
22 We must enjoy God alone	41
23 Man does not need a commandment to love himself and his own body—his love of himself is inordinate . .	42
24 No one hates his own flesh, not even those who rebel against it	44
25 Although we are to love something more than our bodies, we are not, however, to hate our bodies	45
26 A commandment has been given concerning the love of God and our neighbor and also of ourselves . . .	46
27 The order of love	47
28 To whom we must give assistance when we cannot help everyone or even two persons	48
29 We must pray and strive that all may love God . . .	48
30 All human beings and the very angels are our neighbors	49
31 God does not enjoy us, but uses us	52
32 How God uses man	52
33 How one should enjoy man	53
34 Christ is the first road to God	54
35 The plenitude and end of the Scripture is the love of God and our neighbor	56
36 The interpretation of Sacred Scripture may be erroneous, but it is not mendacious nor dangerously deceptive, provided that it is capable of establishing charity— Yet, the translator who errs in this way must be corrected	56

Chapter	Page
37 There is much danger in faulty interpretation	58
38 Charity remains forever	58
39 The man who has been provided with faith, hope and charity does not need Scripture	59
40 What kind of reader Scripture requires	60

BOOK TWO

1 The nature and kinds of signs	61
2 The class of signs to be discussed in this book	62
3 Words hold the most important place among signs	63
4 The origin of writing	64
5 The diversity of languages	64
6 Why the obscurity of Scripture in regard to tropes and figures is useful	65
7 The steps to wisdom: first, fear; second, piety; third, knowledge; fourth, fortitude; fifth, counsel; sixth, cleansing of the heart; seventh grade, or termination, wisdom	66
8 The canonical books	69
9 How we should devote ourselves to the study of Scripture	71
10 It happens that Scripture is not understood because the signs are either unknown or obscure	72
11 To remove an ignorance of signs, a knowledge of languages, especially Greek and Hebrew, is essential	73
12 The diversity of translations is useful. How the error of translators came from ambiguous terms	74
13 How a defect of translation may be corrected	76
14 The source from which we must draw a knowledge of unknown words and expressions	78
15 The Latin Itala version and the Greek Septuagint are recommended	79
16 The knowledge of languages and of things is a help to the understanding of figurative signs	81

Chapter	Page
17 The origin of the fable of the nine Muses	86
18 Profane writers should not be rejected if they have said anything worthwhile	87
19 We find two kinds of learning among the pagans	87
20 Some sciences which men have originated are full of superstition—The witty saying of Cato	88
21 The superstitions of astrologers	89
22 Observation of the stars to learn about the course of life is futile	91
23 Why we must reject the knowledge of the composers of horoscopes	92
24 The alliance and contract with demons in the superstitious use of things	94
25 In human practices that are not superstitious, some are unnecessary, while others are useful and indispensible	95
26 Which practices of men should be avoided and which should be chosen	97
27 Some of the sciences which men have not instituted help us to a knowledge of the Scriptures	97
28 The extent to which history is a help	98
29 The extent to which a knowledge of animals, plants, and especially of the stars, contributes to our knowledge of the Scriptures	100
30 How the mechanical arts contribute to this same end	102
31 How dialectics aid us—Sophisms	102
32 The truth of logical sequences has not been instituted by men, but only observed by them	104
33 True conclusions can be drawn from false propositions, and false conclusions from true propositions	105
34 It is one thing to know the principles governing conclusions, another to know the truth of propositions	106
35 The science of definition and division is not false even though it may be applied to errors. The definition of falsehood	107

Chapter	Page
36 The principles of eloquence are true, although sometimes they are used to persuade us of things that are false	107
37 The usefulness of rhetoric and dialectic	108
38 The science of numbers has not been instituted by men, but only discovered by them from the nature of things	109
39 To which of the sciences mentioned above we should give our attention, and our intention in doing so—Human laws	110
40 We must turn to our own advantage anything profitable that the pagans have said	112
41 What disposition of soul the duty of sacred Scripture demands.—The properties of hyssop	114
42 A comparison of Sacred Scripture with profane literature	116

BOOK THREE

1 A summary of the preceding books and the aim of the following one	117
2 How we must remove ambiguity arising from punctuation	117
3 How ambiguity arising from punctuation may be explained.—The difference between a question for information and a rhetorical question	120
4 How ambiguity of style may be rendered intelligible	123
5 It is a miserable slavery to take the figurative expressions of Scripture literally	124
6 The slavery of the Jews under useful signs	125
7 The slavery of the pagans under useful signs	126
8 The Jews were freed from the slavery of signs in one way, the Gentiles in another	127
9 Who is oppressed by the slavery of signs and who is not.—Baptism.—Holy Eucharist	128
10 How we may learn whether a passage is figurative. A general rule.—Charity.—Lust.—Vice.—Crime.—Prudence.—Kindness	129

Chapter	Page
11 The rule concerning those passages which suggest harshness and still are referred to the person of God or of the saints	131
12 The rule concerning words and deeds that are seemingly sinful in the opinion of the inexperienced but which are attributed to God or the saints.—Deeds are judged according to circumstances	132
13 A continuation of the same argument	134
14 The delusion of those who think that justice does not exist of itself	134
15 The rule to be observed in figurative expressions . . .	135
16 The rule for didactic passages	136
17 Some commands are given to everyone in general, while others are given to separate individuals	137
18 We must consider the time when a thing was either commended or permitted	138
19 The evil judge others according to their own character	139
20 In any mode of life the good resemble one another . .	140
21 David, although he fell into adultery, was far from the intemperance of the licentious	141
22 The rule concerning passages of Scripture where certain deeds of good men contrary to the morals of today are praised	142
23 The rule concerning passages where the sins of great men are recorded	143
24 The nature of the expression must be considered before everything else	143
25 The same word does not have the same meaning everywhere	144
26 Obscure passages must be explained from clearer ones	146
27 Nothing prevents the same passage from having various interpretations	147
28 An uncertain passage is explained more safely by means of other passages of Scripture than by reason . . .	147

Chapter	Page
29 A knowledge of tropes is essential	148
30 The rules of Tyconius, the Donatist, are considered	150
31 The first rule of Tyconius	152
32 The second rule of Tyconius	153
33 Third rule of Tyconius.—It can otherwise be called 'On the Spirit and the Letter,' the title I used	154
34 Fourth rule of Tyconius	155
35 Fifth rule of Tyconius	160
36 Sixth rule of Tyconius	162
37 Seventh rule of Tyconius	165

BOOK FOUR

1 The aim of this work is not to submit rules of rhetoric	168
2 It is proper for the Christian teacher to use the art of rhetoric	169
3 At what age or by what method the principles of rhetoric can be learned	169
4 The duty of a Christian teacher	172
5 It is more important that the Christian orator speak wisely than that he speak eloquently. How he can attain this	173
6 Wisdom is joined with eloquence in the sacred authors	175
7 By offering examples, he teaches beautifully that genuine eloquence exists in the Sacred Scriptures and that it clings to wisdom like an inseparable companion.—Examples are proposed from the Epistles of St. Paul and from the Prophet Amos.—Another example of salutary eloquence from Amos 6.1	177
8 The obscurity of sacred writers may be eloquent, but it should not be imitated by Christian teachers	187
9 With whom and how we are to discuss things that are hard to understand	188
10 The desire for clearness in speaking	189
11 A person who is trying to teach must, therefore, speak clearly but not inelegantly	192

Chapter	Page
12 According to Cicero in *De Oratore*, the object of the orator is to teach, to please, and to persuade.—How he should fulfill these three	192
13 We must persuade hearts especially in speaking	195
14 We must attend to attractiveness of style according to the nature of the discussion	195
15 The Christian teacher should pray before preaching	197
16 Although God forms teachers, the rules of teaching are not imposed unnecessarily by men	198
17 The three kinds of eloquence relate to teaching, pleasing and persuading	201
18 The Christian orator is always concerned with a sublime subject	201
19 We must use a different style of speaking for different subjects	204
20 Examples from the sacred writing: first, of the subdued style; next, of the moderate style; and finally of the grand style; these three from the Epistles of Saint Paul	205
21 Examples of the three styles of speaking selected from the teachers of the Church (Cyprian and Ambrose)	214
22 The delivery should be varied with every kind of style	221
23 How the style of speaking should be intermingled	223
24 What effect the grand style of speaking produces	224
25 For what purpose the moderate style of speaking is properly used	225
26 In any style of speaking the orator should aim at being listened to with understanding, pleasure and persuasion	227
27 The man whose life corresponds to his teaching is listened to with greater docility	229
28 We must be anxious about truth, rather than about our words.—What this dispute about words means	231
29 We should not blame a preacher who delivers in public a speech written by a more experienced speaker	232
30 The preacher should offer prayer to God beforehand	234
31 Augustine apologizes for the length of the book	235

CHRISTIAN INSTRUCTION

Prologue

THERE ARE several norms for expounding Scripture. These I am convinced can be profitably presented to those devoted to the study of this subject, so that they may benefit, not only by acquiring knowledge from others who have unveiled the mysteries of sacred writings, but by disclosing these mysteries to others themselves. I am undertaking to transmit these principles to those who are able and willing to grasp them, if only God our Lord will not refuse to supply me as I write with the same help which He usually grants me when I reflect upon this matter. Before I begin this, I think that I should reply to those who will censure these principles, or who would do so if I did not pacify them first. But if some, even after this, find fault, at least they will not influence others, whom they could influence unless they were previously fortified and equipped, nor will they entice them from beneficial study to the indolence of ignorance.

(2) Some will censure my work because they have failed to comprehend those principles of which I shall treat. Others, when they have desired to employ the principles which they have learned and have endeavored to explain the Sacred Scriptures according to these principles, but have failed to disclose and elucidate what they want, will think that I have labored uselessly; and, because they themselves have not been aided by this work, will think

that no one could profit from it. The third category of critics comprises those who either actually interpret Scripture well, or seem to in their own estimation. These observe, or think they observe, that they have gained the ability to explain sacred writings, although they have studied none of the regulations of the sort that I have now determined to recommend. Accordingly, they will protest that those principles are essential to no one, but that whatever is convincingly revealed about the obscurities of those writings could be achieved more effectively by divine assistance alone.

(3) Briefly answering all those who do not comprehend the matters about which I am writing, I make this statement: I should not be criticized because they do not understand, just as they should not become enraged at me if, wishing to see the waning moon, the new moon, or some barely distinguishable star which I was indicating with my finger, they did not have sufficiently keen vision to see even my finger. In fact, those who cannot discern the obscure points of Sacred Scripture, even after studying and learning these rules, would believe that they could indeed see my finger, but could not see the stars which it was extended to indicate. Consequently, these two groups ought to refrain from criticizing me and beg that vision be granted them from heaven. For, if I can lift my finger to indicate something, I cannot on the other hand illumine the eyes of individuals to see either my act of indicating or that subject to which I am anxious to direct attention.

(4) However, there are some who boast about the grace of God, and pride themselves upon the fact that they appreciate and are able to interpret Sacred Scripture without rules such as I have undertaken to propose, and for

that reason they consider unnecessary what I have planned to write. These persons should moderate their anxiety, so that, although they may well be glad for the wonderful grace of God, they may still keep in mind that they have learned these matters through men or books. They should not be despised by Antony, the saintly Egyptian hermit, simply because he, without any knowledge of reading, is said to have memorized the Sacred Scripture by merely hearing it and to have penetrated its meaning by profound reflection. Nor should they be scorned by that foreign Christian slave, about whom we learned not long ago from very eminent and reliable persons. Although no one taught him how to read, he acquired proficiency by praying that the secrets might be disclosed to him. After three days' prayer he received the answer to his petition, with the result that he astounded the spectators by reading at sight the book they handed him.

(5) If anyone believe that these accounts are false, I am not going to argue violently about it. Certainly, since my case deals with Christians who rejoice that they understand Sacred Scripture without human instruction (and if this is so, they rejoice in a true and by no means insignificant blessing), they must concede that any one of us has learned his own language simply from hearing it habitually from childhood, and that we have acquired a knowledge of any other language—Greek, Hebrew, or any one of the others similarly—either by hearing them or by some person's instruction. Now then, are we to admonish all our brethren not to train their children in these subjects, since in a single instant the Apostles,[1] filled with grace by the coming of the Holy Ghost, spoke in the tongues of all

---
1 Acts 2.1ff.

peoples; or are we to admonish anyone who has not enjoyed such privileges to think that he is not a Christian or to doubt that he has received the Holy Ghost? On the contrary, let whatever should be acquired through human means be acquired humbly, and let anyone who is instructing another pass on to him whatever he has received[2] without haughtiness or grudging. Let us not tempt Him whom we have believed,[3] lest, deceived by such cunning of the Devil and by our own stubbornness, we may even decline to go to church to listen to the Gospel itself or to learn about it, or to refuse to read a book, or to pay attention to a reader or a preacher, but expect, as the Apostle says, to be caught 'up to the third heaven . . . whether in the body or out of the body,'[4] and there hear 'secret words that man may not repeat,' or there see the Lord Jesus Christ[5] and learn the Gospel from Him rather than from men.

(6) We should guard against such presumptuous and perilous snares. Instead, we should reflect that the Apostle Paul himself,[6] even though he was thrown to the ground and instructed by the divine Voice from heaven, was nevertheless sent to a human being to receive the sacraments and be united to the Church. We should also consider that the centurion Cornelius,[7] though an angel informed him that his prayers had been heard and his alms regarded with approval, was still sent to Peter to be guided and not only to receive from him the sacraments, but also to learn what he was to believe in, hope for, and love. All these

---

2 Wisd. 7.13; 1 Cor. 11.23.
3 2 Tim. 1.12.
4 2 Cor. 12.2,4.
5 1 Cor. 9.1.
6 Acts 9.3ff.
7 Acts 10.1ff.

things might well have been accomplished by an angel, but human nature would have been lowered in dignity if God had seemed unwilling to transmit His word to men through human means. Indeed, how would there be truth in the statement, 'for holy is the temple of God, and this temple you are,'[8] if God did not grant replies from a human temple, but announced from heaven through angels all the learning which He desired to have imparted to men? Then charity itself, which unites men to one another with the bond of unity, would have no way of joining and almost fusing souls with each other, if men learned nothing from other men.

(7) Again, the Apostle did not send to an angel the eunuch[9] who failed to comprehend what he read in the prophet Isaias. What he did not understand was not taught him by an angel, nor was it revealed to him by divine inspiration. He sat with him and explained in human terms and language what had been veiled in that passage of Scripture. God spoke to Moses,[10] did he not? Yet Moses very prudently and humbly yielded to the advice of his father-in-law, foreigner though he was, with regard to governing and directing such a mighty nation. For he realized that, from whatever intellect right counsel proceeded, it should be attributed not to him who conceived it but to Him who is the Truth, the immutable God.

(8) Finally, whoever glories in understanding by the grace of God whatever things are obscure in the Scriptures, although he has not been guided by any principles, believes correctly indeed (and it is true) that that ability is not his

---
8 1 Cor. 3.17.
9 Acts 8.26ff.
10 Exod. 18.14ff.

own as if it came into existence from him, but it was committed to him from heaven (for thus he seeks the glory of God and not his own). But, when he reads and understands without anyone's explanation, why does he try to explain to others? Instead, why does he not send them to God so that they also may understand, not through human agency, but by His teaching within their souls? Of course, he is afraid that he may hear from the Lord:[11] 'Wicked servant, thou shouldst have entrusted my money to the bankers.' Therefore, just as these individuals instruct others either orally or by their writings in matters they understand, I certainly should not be criticized by them if I, too, teach not only the points which they understand, but also the principles they observe in order to come to an understanding. Nevertheless no one should consider anything his own except, perhaps, falsehood,[12] since all truth comes from Him who has said:[13] 'I am the Truth.' For what have we that we have not received? But, if we have received it, why do we boast as if we had not received it?[14]

(9) He who reads written matter to listeners pronounces what he understands. But, he who teaches reading does so that others will also learn how to read; yet, both transmit what they have been taught. So also, he who explains to his hearers the thoughts which he understands in Sacred Scripture acts like one who in the office of reader pronounces the words which he understands. On the other hand, he who teaches how to understand is like a person teaching reading. It is his task to teach reading

---

11 Cf. Matt. 25.26,27.
12 John 8.44.
13 John 14.6.
14 1 Cor. 4.7.

in such a way that the man who knows how to read has no need of another reader, when he comes upon a book, to tell him what is written in it. Similarly, the person who has accepted the principles which we are trying to propose, when he comes upon any obscurity in books, observes certain rules, as he did in reading, and does not require another person as interpreter to lay open for him whatever is obscure. Rather, by following certain indications, he may arrive at the hidden meaning himself, without any false step, or, at least, will not fall into the foolishness of misguided thought. Therefore, although it may be clear enough in this work itself that no one can in justice criticize this undertaking of mine which is intended to be useful, nevertheless, it seemed fitting to answer any objectors in a preface such as this. This, then, presented itself to me as the starting point of the course I propose to follow in this book.

BOOK ONE

Chapter 1

THE ENTIRE treatment of the Scriptures is based upon two factors: the method of discovering what we are to understand and the method of teaching what has been understood. I shall discuss first the method of discovery and then the method of teaching. This is a worthy and laborious task, and, though it should prove hard to accomplish, I fear that I am rash enough to undertake it. Indeed, I should be, if I were relying solely upon myself. However, since all my confidence of finishing this work depends upon Him from whom I have already received much inspiration through meditation, I need not fear that He will cease to grant me further inspiration when I shall have begun to employ that which He has already granted. Everything which is not exhausted by being given away is not yet owned as it ought to be, so long as we hold on to it and do not give it away. 'For,' He has said:[1] 'He that hath to him shall be given.' Therefore, He will give to those who already have; this is, He will increase and heap up[2] what He has given, when they dispense with generosity what they have received. There were five loaves of bread and, on another occassion, seven loaves, before they were distributed to the hungry multitude.[3] Afterwards, although the hunger of

---
1 Matt. 13.12.
2 2 Cor. 9.10.
3 Matt. 14.17ff.; 15.34ff.

so many thousands was satisfied, they filled baskets and baskets. And so, just as that bread increased after it was broken, the Lord has now granted me the thoughts which are necessary for beginning this work, and they will be increased by His inspiration when I have begun to dispense them.[4] As a result, I shall not only suffer no poverty of thought in this ministry of mine, but shall even exult in a remarkable abundance of ideas.

Chapter 2

(2) All teaching is concerned with either *things* or *signs*. But things are learned by means of signs. I have defined a thing in the accurate sense of the word as that which is not used to *signify* something, for example, wood, stone, animal or others of this kind. But I do not include that tree which we read that Moses cast into bitter waters to take away their bitterness,[1] nor that stone which Jacob placed under his head,[2] nor that ram which Abraham sacrificed instead of his son.[3] These are indeed things, but they are also symbols of other things. There are other signs whose whole usefulness consists in signifying. Words belong to this class, for no one uses words except to signify something. From this is understood what I designate as signs, namely, those things which are employed to signify something. Therefore, every sign is also a thing. For, whatever is not a thing is absolutely nothing, but not every thing is also a sign. So, in this division of things and signs, when I speak of things, I shall do so in such a way that, although some of them can be used to

---

4 2 Cor. 9.6ff.

1 Exod. 15.25.
2 Gen. 28.11.
3 Gen. 22.13.

signify, they will not disturb the division according to which I am treating first of things and then of signs. We must keep in mind, in regard to things, that the point to be considered now is what they are, not what other thing, aside from themselves, they signify.

Chapter 3

(3) There are, then, some things which are to be enjoyed, others which are to be used, others which are enjoyed and used. Those which are to be enjoyed make us happy. Those which are to be used help us as we strive for happiness and, in a certain sense, sustain us, so that we are able to arrive at and cling to those things which make us happy. But, if we who enjoy and use things, living as we do in the midst of both classes of things, strive to enjoy the things which we are supposed to use, we find our progress impeded and even now and then turned aside. As a result, fettered by affection for lesser goods, we are either retarded from gaining those things which we are to enjoy or we are even drawn away entirely from them.

Chapter 4

(4) To enjoy anything means to cling to it with affection for its own sake. To use a thing is to employ what we have received for our use to obtain what we want, provided that it is right for us to want it. An unlawfully applied use ought rather to be termed an abuse. Suppose, then, we were travelers in a foreign land, who could not live in contentment except in our own native country, and if, unhappy because of that traveling abroad and desirous of ending our wretchedness, we planned to return home, it would be necessary to use some means of transportation, either by land or sea, to

enable us to reach the land we were to enjoy. But, if the pleasantness of the journey and the very movement of the vehicles were to delight us and turn us aside to enjoy the things which we ought, instead, merely to use, and were to confuse us by false pleasure, we would be unwilling to end our journey quickly and would be alienated from the land whose pleasantness would make us really happy. Just so, wanderers from God[1] on the road of this mortal life, if we wish to return to our native country where we can be happy,[2] we must use this world,[3] and not enjoy it, so that the 'invisible attributes' of God may be clearly seen, 'being understood through the things that are made,'[4] that is, that through what is corporeal and temporal we may comprehend the eternal and spiritual.

Chapter 5

(5) The proper object of our enjoyment, therefore, is the Father, Son, and Holy Ghost, the Same who are the Trinity, one supreme Being, accessible to all who enjoy Him, if, indeed, He is a thing and not rather the Cause of all things, or, perhaps, both Thing and Cause. It is not easy to find a term which appropriately defines such great excellence, unless it is better to say that this Trinity is one God from whom, through whom, and in whom all things exist.[1] Thus, there are Father, Son, and Holy Ghost. Each of these individually is God. At the same time They are all one God. Each of Them individually comprises the fullness of divine

---

1 2 Cor. 5.6.
2 Heb. 11.14.
3 1 Cor. 7.31.
4 Rom. 1.20.

---

1 Rom. 11.36.

substance. At the same time They are all only one Substance. The Father is neither the Son nor the Holy Ghost; the Son is neither the Father nor the Holy Ghost; the Holy Ghost is neither the Father nor the Son. The Father is only the Father; the Son, only the Son; the Holy Ghost, only the Holy Ghost. All Three have the same eternity, the same immutability, the same majesty, the same power. In the Father resides unity, in the Son equality, and in the Holy Ghost the perfect union of unity and equality. These three qualities are all one because of the Father, all equal because of the Son, and all united because of the Holy Ghost.

Chapter 6

(6) Have I spoken or given utterance to anything worthy of God? On the contrary, I realize that I have done nothing but wish to speak. But, if I have spoken anything, it is not what I wanted to say. How am I aware of this, unless God is ineffable? What I have said would not have been said, if it had been ineffable. For this reason God should not be spoken of even as ineffable, because, when we say this word, we are saying something about Him. There is some contradiction of terms, since, if that is ineffable which cannot be spoken of, a thing is not ineffable which can be called ineffable. We should guard against this contradiction of terms by silence, rather than attempt to reconcile them by discussion. Yet God, although we can say nothing worthy of Him, has accepted the tribute of our human voice and has wished us to rejoice in His praise in our own language. This is the reason why He is called *Deus*. In reality, He is not recognized in the sound of those two syllables, but He causes all those who share the Latin language, when this sound reaches their ears, to ponder over His most excellent and immortal nature.

Chapter 7

(7) When the one God of gods[1] is thought of, even by those who believe in, invoke, and worship other gods 'whether in heaven or on earth,'[2] He is considered in such a way that the very thought tries to conceive a nature which is more excellent and more sublime than all others. Men are indeed influenced by diverse goods, some by those which are concerned with the senses of the body, others by those which affect the intellectual quality of the mind. Consequently, those who have surrendered to the bodily senses think that the sky, or what they see so radiant in the sky, or the world itself is the God of gods. Or, if they attempt to go beyond the world, they visualize something luminous and conceive it as infinite or of that shape which seems most pleasing in their vague imagining. Or they think of it in the form of the human body, if they prefer that to other things. However, if they do not think there is one God of gods, but rather many or innumerable gods of equal rank, they still attribute to each one the form of body that seems most excellent in their own minds. Those who by means of their intellect strive to visualize what God is, place Him above not only all visible and corporeal natures, but even all intellectual and spiritual natures, above all changeable things. All men engage in contest over the excellence of God, and no one can be found to believe a being is God if there is any being more excellent. Hence, all men agree that He is God whom they esteem above all other things.

---

1 Ps. 49.1.
2 1 Cor. 8.5.

Chapter 8

(8) Since all who reflect upon God think of a living Being, only those who think of Him as Life itself can form an opinion of God that is not unworthy and absurd. Whatever bodily shape presents itself to their minds, they determine that it is life which makes it animate or inanimate and esteem the animate above the inanimate. They realize that the living body itself—however resplendent it may be with brilliance, remarkable in size, or distinguished by its beauty—is one thing, while the life by which it is animated is another. Moreover, because of its incomparable dignity, they esteem that life above the mass which is nourished and animated by it. Then they strive to look upon life itself. If they find it to be vegetative life without feeling, such as trees have, they prefer a sentient life to it, for example, that of cattle; and in turn, to this latter they prefer intelligent life, such as that of man. When they have seen that even this life is still changeable, they are compelled to prefer something unchangeable to it, that very Life, in fact, which is not sometimes foolish and at other times wise, but is rather Wisdom itself. For a wise mind, that is, one that has attained wisdom, was not wise before it attained it; but Wisdom Itself was never unwise, nor can It ever be. If men did not perceive this, they would not, with the utmost trust, esteem an unchangeably wise life above a changeable one. Indeed, they see that the very rule of truth, according to which they claim the unchangeable life is better, is itself unchangeable. They do not perceive this rule anywhere except beyond their own nature, since they perceive that they are changeable beings.

Chapter 9

(9) No one is so shamelessly foolish as to say: 'How do you know that an unchangeably wise life should be preferred to a changeable one?' For, the very point that he is inquiring about—how I know—is universally and unchangeably evident for all to see. He who does not see this is just like a blind man in the sunlight who derives no benefit at all, even though the brightness of light, so clear and so close at hand, pours into the very sockets of his eyes. But, he who sees the light of truth and flees from it is one who has caused the keenness of his mind to become dulled through association with carnal shadows. So then, men are driven back from their native country by the contrary breezes of bad habits, as it were, and eagerly seek after inferior and less estimable things than the One which they acknowledge is better and more excellent.

Chapter 10

(10) Since we are to enjoy to the full that Truth which lives without change and since, in that Truth, God the Trinity, the Author and Founder of the universe, takes counsel for the things which He has created, the mind must be cleansed in order that it may be able to look upon that light and cling to it when it has seen it. Let us consider this cleansing as a sort of traveling or sailing to our own country. We are not brought any closer to Him who is everywhere present by moving from place to place, but by a holy desire and lofty morals.

Chapter 11

(11) We would not be able to do this, unless Wisdom Himself deigned to share even such great weakness as ours

and show us the way to live according to human nature, since we ourselves are human. But, because we act wisely when we come to Him, He was thought by proud men to have acted foolishly when He came to us. When we come to Him we grow stronger; He was regarded as weak when He came to us. But, 'the foolishness of God is wiser than men, and the weakness of God is stronger than men.'[1] Therefore, although He Himself is our native land, He made Himself also the Way[2] to that native land.

Chapter 12

Whereas He is everywhere present to the healthy and pure interior eye, He deigned to appear even to the fleshly eyes of those who have weak and unclean vision. Since, in God's wisdom, the world could not know God by 'wisdom,' it pleased God by the foolishness of preaching to save those who believe.[1]

(12) Therefore, He is said to have come to us, not by traveling through space, but by appearing to mortals in human flesh. He came, then, to that place where He already was, because He was in the world and the world was made by Him.[2] But, because of their eagerness to enjoy the creature in place of the Creator, men have been conformed to this world[3] and have been fittingly called 'the world.' Consequently, they did not know Wisdom, and, therefore, the Evangelist said:[4] 'the world knew Him not.' And so, in God's

---
1 1 Cor. 1.25.
2 John 14.6.

---
1 1 Cor. 1.21.
2 John 1.10.
3 Rom. 12.2.
4 John 1.10.

wisdom, the world could not know God by 'wisdom.' Why, then, did He come, since He was really here, except that it pleased God by the foolishness of preaching to save those who believe?

Chapter 13

How did He come, except that 'the Word was made flesh, and dwelt among us'?[1] Just as in speaking: In order that what we have in our mind may penetrate to the mind of our listener through his ears of flesh, the word which we carry in our heart becomes a sound and is called speech. Nevertheless, our thought is not changed to the same sound. Remaining entire in itself, it takes on the nature of speech, by means of which it may penetrate his ears; yet it does not incur any deterioration in the change. Just so, the Word of God, although unchanged, was made flesh, in order that He might dwell among us.

Chapter 14

(13) Just as medical care is the road to bodily health, so this Care has received sinners to heal them and make them strong again. And as physicians bind up wounds in an orderly and skillful manner, so that even a certain beauty may join the usefulness of the bandage, so the medicine of Wisdom, by assuming humanity, accommodated Himself to our wounds, healing some by opposite remedies and others by like remedies. A physician, in treating an injury to the body, applies certain opposites, as cold to hot, wet to dry; in other cases he applies like remedies, as a round bandage to a circular wound or an oblong bandage to an oblong

---

1 John 1.14.

wound, not using the same bandage for every limb, but adapting like to like. Likewise, the Wisdom of God, in healing humanity, has employed Himself to cure it, since He is both the physician and the medicine. Therefore, because man fell through pride, He has applied humility to cure him. We were deceived by the wisdom of the serpent, but we are freed by the foolishness of God. Furthermore, just as that which was called wisdom was really foolishness in the case of those who despised God, so that which is called foolishness is wisdom for those who vanquish the devil. We abused our immortality, and, as a result, died; Christ used His mortality well, and so we live. The disorder began in the corrupted soul of a woman; salvation came from the untainted body of a woman. There is another example of the use of opposites in the fact that our vices are cured by the example of His virtues. But, it was as if He were applying like bandages to our limbs and wounds when, as a man born of a woman, He saved men deceived by a woman; as a mortal He rescued mortals; by His death He freed the dead. Instruction will unfold many other uses of contrary and like remedies in Christian medicine to those who ponder them more carefully and are not hurried away by the necessity of completing a task they have undertaken.

Chapter 15

(14) Indeed, our belief in the Resurrection of our Lord from the dead and His Ascension into heaven sustains our faith with great hope. For this belief shows us forcibly how willingly He who had the power to take it up again[1] laid down His life for us. What great confidence, then, inspires the hope of the faithful when they consider what great things

---
1 John 10.18.

He who is so great suffered for men who were not yet believers.² When He is expected from heaven as the Judge of the living and the dead, He strikes great fear into the negligent, with the result that they devote themselves to earnest effort and long for Him by leading a saintly life, instead of dreading His coming because of their wicked lives. What words can tell or what thought can conceive the reward which He will give at the last day, when He already has given so great a measure of His spirit for our consolation in this journey, in order that, in the midst of the adversities of this life, we may have such great trust in Him and love of Him whom we do not yet see? Moreover, He has granted to each of us the special graces³ requisite for the upbuilding of His Church, so that we will do what He has indicated should be done, not only without complaint, but even with joy.⁴

Chapter 16

(15) For the Church is 'His body,'¹ and is also spoken of as His spouse,² as Apostolic teaching shows us. Therefore, He consolidates His body, although it is composed of many members which do not have the same functions,³ by the bond of unity and charity—its health, so to speak. In addition, He disciplines it now and cleanses it with certain afflictions which act as medicines, so that, when it has been drawn forth from this world⁴ to eternity, He may join to

---

2 Rom. 5.8.
3 Rom. 12.6.
4 1 Peter 4.10.

1 Eph. 1.23.
2 Eph. 5.23ff.
3 Rom. 12.4.
4 Gal. 1.4.

Himself as His spouse 'the Church not having spot or wrinkle or any such thing.'[5]

Chapter 17

(16) Besides, we are on a road which is concerned not so much with the traversing of space as with the affections of the heart, a road which was shut off by the malice of our past sins, as if by a thorny edge. Then, what more generous or more merciful thing could He do, who was willing to abase Himself for us as the Way by which we might return to Him, than forgive us all our sins, after we had transformed our lives, and, by being crucified for us, blot out the severely enjoined decrees against our return to Him?

Chapter 18

(17) Therefore, He granted these 'keys' to His Church, so that whatever it might loose upon earth would be loosed in heaven, and whatever it might bind on earth would be bound also in heaven.[1] That is to say: Whoever in His Church did not believe that his sins were forgiven him, they were not forgiven, but whoever believed and turned aside from them by repentance, having placed himself in the bosom of the Church, would be healed by the same faith and repentance. Whoever does not believe that his sins can be forgiven him becomes worse by his despair when he doubts the fruit of his conversion, as if there remained nothing better for him than to be sinful.

---
5 Eph. 5.27.

---
1 Matt. 16.19

Chapter 19

(18) Just as there is a certain death of the soul, a forsaking of one's former life and habits, which comes about through repentance, so the death of the body is also a releasing of the principle that previously animated it. Further, as the soul, after repentance, by which it destroys its former evil habits, is changed for the better, so, after that death which we all owe because of the bond of sin, we must believe and hope that the body will be entirely changed for the better at the time of the resurrection. For, it cannot happen that flesh and blood can obtain any part in the kingdom of God,[1] but 'this corruptible body, must put on incorruption and this mortal body must put on immortality.'[2] The body will not cause any annoyance, because it will not suffer any want; it will be animated by a happy and perfected spirit in complete peace.

Chapter 20

(19) But, the soul of one who does not die to this world and begins to be fashioned according to the image of Truth is drawn, by the death of the body, into a more serious death and will be restored to life, not in order to change to a heavenly home, but to undergo punishment.

Chapter 21

Faith maintains this principle and we must believe it: Neither the soul nor the human body suffers complete annihilation; the wicked arise again for punishment beyond imagination, while the good rise again for everlasting life.[1]

---

1 Cor. 15.50.
2 1 Cor. 15.53.

1 Matt. 25.46.

Chapter 22

(20) Consequently, in all these things the only ones which are to be enjoyed are those which we have mentioned as eternal and unchangeable. The other things are to be used that we may be able to arrive at a complete enjoyment of the former. We who enjoy and use other things are things ourselves. Man is a noble being created to the image and likeness of God,[1] not insofar as he is housed in a mortal body, but in that he is superior to brute beasts because of the gift of a rational soul. Hence, the great question is: whether men ought to enjoy themselves or merely use themselves, or whether they may do both. We have been commanded to love one another,[2] but the question is: whether man is to be loved by man for his own sake or for another reason. If he is loved for his own sake, we are enjoying him; if he is loved for another reason, we are using him. But, it seems to me that he should be loved for another reason. For, if a thing is to be loved for itself, we find in it the happiness of life, the hope of which consoles us in the present time, although we do not yet possess the reality. Yet, 'cursed is the man who places his hope in man.'[3]

(21) No one ought to enjoy himself, if you observe clearly, because he should not love himself for his own sake, but because of Him whom he ought to enjoy. For, man is most excellent at that time when his whole life tends toward the unchangeable Life and clings to Him with all its affection. However, if he loves himself for his own sake, he does not refer himself to God, but, since he has turned to

---
1 Gen. 1.27.
2 John 15.12,17.
3 Cf. Jer. 17.5.

himself, he is not turned toward something unchangeable. On that account, he does not enjoy himself perfectly, because he is better when he clings entirely and is bound to the unchangeable Good than when he is inclined from It even toward himself. Therefore, if you ought to love yourself, not for your own sake, but on account of Him who is the most fitting object of your love, no other man should be angered if you love him also for the sake of God. This has been divinely ordained as the rule of love; for He said:[4] 'Thou shalt love thy neighbor as thyself,' but God 'with thy whole heart, and with thy whole soul, and with thy whole mind.' Consequently, you direct all your thoughts, your whole life, and all your intellect to Him from whom you have those very things which you devote to Him. When He said, 'with thy whole heart, and with thy whole soul, and with thy whole mind,' He left no part of our life which could be empty and, as it were, give place to the desire to enjoy any other thing. Whatever else comes to our attention to be loved is to be carried along to that place to which the whole torrent of our love rushes. Thus, whoever loves his neighbor rightly ought to stress this point with him, so that he, too, may love God with his whole heart, his whole soul, and his whole mind. For, thus loving him as himself, he refers all the love of himself and the other to that love of God which suffers no trickle to be led off from Itself by those whose diversion Its own volume might be lessened.

Chapter 23

(22) We are not to love everything which we are to use, but only those things which either by a certain association with us are accountable to God, as a man or an angel, or

---

[4] Lev. 19.18; Deut. 6.5; Matt. 22.39-37.

which, related to us, require the grace of God through us, as our body. For, assuredly, the martyrs did not love the wickedness of those who persecuted them, yet they used it to win God. There are, then, four kinds of things to be loved: first, that which is above us; second, ourselves; third, that which is equal to us; fourth, that which is below us. Concerning the second and fourth no rules have to be given. For, however far a man errs from the Truth,[1] there remains in him a love of himself and of his own body. For his soul, fleeing from the unchangeable Light, the Sovereign of all things, does this in order that it may control itself and its own body; hence, it cannot do anything else except love itself and its own body.

(23) Moreover, it thinks it has gained something important if it is able to rule over its fellows also, that is, over other human beings. For it is characteristic of a depraved mind to seek after and claim as its due what is owed properly to God alone. Such love of one's self is better termed hatred. For, it is unjust to wish what is below oneself to serve one, when one refuses to serve a superior Being, and it has been truly said:[2] 'he that loveth iniquity hateth his own soul.' Likewise, the soul becomes weak and is tortured by the mortal body. It loves that mortal body by necessity, and is weighed down by its corruption. For, immortality and incorruption of the body result from the health of the soul, but the health of the soul consists in cleaving very tenaciously to something better, that is, to the unchangeable God. But, when it exerts itself to rule even over those who are naturally on a level with it, that is, even its fellow men, its pride is utterly intolerable.

---
1 2 Tim. 2.18.
2 Ps. 10.6.

Chapter 24

(24) Consequently, no one hates himself; there has never been any dispute on this point with any sect. Neither does anyone hate his own body, for, what the Apostle said is true: 'No one ever hated his own flesh.'[1] Some are entirely deceived, because they say that they would rather be without bodies altogether. They do not hate their own body, but rather its corruptions and its weight. So, they do not wish to be without a body, but to have an incorrupt and agile body. They think that is not a body which is incorrupt and agile, because they think something of that sort is a spirit. But, even if some seem to persecute their bodies by restraint and labor, those who do this according to reason are striving not to rid themselves of their bodies, but rather to possess them, subjected to reason and ready for all necessary work. They are striving, by a certain laborious warfare[2] on the part of the body itself, to quench those passions which have a bad effect upon the body, that is, those habits and inclinations of the soul which bend it toward the enjoyment of lesser goods. They are not destroying themselves, but are taking care of their own good health.

(25) But, those who do this in the wrong way make war upon their bodies, as if they were their natural enemies. They are deceived in their understanding of this passage:[3] 'The flesh lusts against the spirit, and the spirit against the flesh; for these are opposed to each other.' The Apostle said this because of the unsubdued sensual appetite against which the spirit strives, not to destroy the body, but, by thoroughly

---
1 Eph. 5.29.
2 2 Cor. 10.4.
3 Gal. 5.17.

mastering its concupiscence and its perverse inclinations, to make it subject to the spirit, as the natural order demands. Since, after the resurrection, the body is to live immortally in perfect peace, completely subject to the spirit, so also in this life we must keep in mind that the carnal appetite is to be changed for the better and is not to resist the spirit with its inordinate inclinations. Until this is accomplished, 'the flesh lusts against the spirit, and the spirit against the flesh.' The spirit does not struggle because of hatred, but for dominion, because it desires that what it loves should be subjugated to something better. The flesh does not resist because of hatred, but because of the bond of habit which has descended to it from its progenitors and has grown deeply rooted by the law of nature. In subduing the flesh, the spirit strives to dissolve the disordered agreements of bad habits and to establish the peace of good ones. Yet, not even those who, misled by a false belief, detest their own bodies would be prepared to lose one eye, even without feeling any pain, and even if just as much sense of sight would remain in the one as there was before in both, unless something which had to be given precedence should compel it. By this example and also by similar instances, it is satisfactorily pointed out to those who seek the truth with unbiased minds how true was that statement of the Apostle in which he declares: 'For no one ever hated his own flesh.' And he also added:[4] 'on the contrary he nourishes and cherishes it, as Christ also does the Church.'

Chapter 25

(26) Man must be instructed, therefore, about the manner of loving, that is how he should love himself so that

---
[4] Eph. 5.29.

he may help himself. To doubt that he loves himself and is desirous of doing good to himself is folly. Yet, he must be instructed how to love his body, in order that he may take care of it reasonably and wisely. It is an incontestable fact that a man loves his own body and is anxious to preserve it well and unimpaired. Yet, a man can love something more than the health and soundness of his own body. Many have been known to undergo suffering and even loss of some of their limbs willingly, in order to secure other things which they loved better. It should not be said that a person does not love the health and well-being of his own body simply because he loves something else more. Even the miser, although he loves money, buys himself bread. When he does this, he gives away the money which he loves so much and wishes to amass, but he does so because he puts a higher value upon the health of his body which the bread sustains. It is unnecessary to discuss at greater length a matter that is so obvious, yet very often the errors of the wicked compel us to do this.

Chapter 26

(27) There is, then, no necessity for commanding us to love ourselves and our own bodies, because we love what we are—and also what is below us, yet belongs to us—by an indisturbed law of nature which extends even to brute beasts, for, even animals love themselves and their own bodies. It remained only to impose commandments upon us concerning God who is above us and our neighbor who is beside us. 'Thou shalt love the Lord thy God,' He said, 'with thy whole heart, and with thy whole soul, and with thy whole mind,' and thou shalt love thy neighbor as thyself. On these two commandments depend the whole Law and

the Prophets.'[1] Now the purpose of this charge is charity,[2] a two-fold love, of God and our neighbor. But, if you consider yourself in your entirety, your soul and body, and your neighbor in his entirety, his soul and body (for man is composed of soul and body), no class of objects to be loved has been omitted in these two commandments. Since the love of God has precedence, and since the measure of that love has been so defined that all other loves are to fuse in Him, it seems that no mention has been made about our love of ourselves. But, when it is said: 'Thou shalt love thy neighbor as thyself,' at once it is clear that our love of ourselves has not been overlooked.

Chapter 27

(28) Now, he lives a just and holy life who appraises things with an unprejudiced mind. He is a person who has a well-regulated love and neither loves what he ought not, nor fails to love what he should. He does not love more an object deserving only of lesser love, nor love equally what he should love either more or less, nor love either more or less what he should love equally. Every sinner, insofar as he is a sinner, should not be loved, and every man, insofar as he is a man, should be loved for the sake of God, but God is to be loved for His own sake. And, if God is to be loved more than any man, each one ought to love God more than himself. Thus, another man should be loved more than our own bodies, because all those things are to be loved for the sake of God; another man can enjoy God with us, whereas our bodies cannot, because the body lives through the soul, by which we enjoy God.

---

1 Matt. 22.37-40.
2 1 Tim. 1.5.

Chapter 28

(29) Everyone must be loved equally; but, when you cannot be of assistance to all, you must above all have regard for those who are bound to you more closely by some accident, as it were, of location, circumstances, or occasions of any kind. For instance, suppose you had an abundance of something which you felt obliged to give to someone who did not have it, and were not able to give it to two persons. If two people came to you, neither of whom held precedence over the other, either because of want or any relationship to you, you could do nothing more just than decide by lot to which one you should give what you were unable to give to both. So, in the case of your fellow-men; since you cannot take care of all of them, you must decide by lot in proportion as each one can claim a closer connection with you at that time.

Chapter 29

(30) Of all who can enjoy God with us, we love some whom we help, some by whom we are helped, some whose assistance we stand in need of and whose wants we relieve, some on whom we neither bestow any benefit nor expect that they should bestow any upon us. Nevertheless, we ought to desire that they all love God with us, and all the assistance which we either give them or receive from them must be directed toward that one purpose. In the theaters, places of wickedness, if a man has a fondness for some actor and enjoys his acting as a great, or even as the greatest, good, he likes all who share this fondness with him, not on their own account, but because of the one whom they like in common. The more ardent he is in his

own affection for that actor, the more he strives in every possible way to have more people like him, and is all the more anxious to show him off to more people. When he sees anyone somewhat unenthusiastic, he stirs him up as much as he can by his praise of the actor. If he chances upon someone who opposes him, he is greatly vexed at his dislike for the object of his affections and strives in every way he can to remove the feeling. How should we act who are united by the love of God, the enjoyment of whom constitutes our happy life, from whom all who love Him receive their existence and their love of Him, of whom we have no fear at all that, once known, He could fail to satisfy anyone? He wishes to be loved, not for any benefit to Himself, but that He may grant to those who love Him an everlasting reward, that is, Himself whom they love. Hence it is that we love even our enemies. We do not fear them, since they are unable to snatch from us that which we love; instead, we feel compassion for them, because the more they hate us the farther they sever themselves from Him whom we love. If they would be reconciled to Him, they would have to love Him as the Supreme Good and us as sharers of such a great blessing.

Chapter 30

(31) At this point there arises some question concerning the angels. They are happy because they enjoy Him whom we desire to enjoy and, in proportion as we enjoy Him in this life as 'through a mirror' or 'in an obscure manner,'[1] we endure our exile more patiently and are more eager to end it. It is reasonable to ask whether the love of the angels is affected by those two commandments. Now, the

---
1 1 Cor. 13.12.

Lord Himself in the Gospel and Saint Paul the Apostle point out that He who commanded us to love our neighbor excepted no human being. When he, to whom He had mentioned these two commandments and said that on them depended the whole Law and the Prophets, questioned Him, saying: 'And who is my neighbor?' the Lord related that a certain man, going down 'from Jerusalem to Jericho,' fell 'among robbers' and, having been seriously wounded by them, was left beaten and half-dead. He explained that no one was his neighbor except the man who had shown himself merciful to him by rescuing and caring for him. And the man who had asked the question acknowledged that this was so, when he was asked. The Lord said to him, 'Go and do thou also in like manner,'[2] evidently that we might understand that he is our neighbor to whom it is our duty to show mercy if he be in need of it, or to whom it would be our duty to show it if he were in need. It follows that he is also our neighbor who in his turn must perform this same office for us. For, the term 'neighbor' connotes a relation to something, and no one can be a neighbor except to someone who is a neighbor to him. Who, then, does not see that no one has been excepted to whom we may deny the duty of mercy? The rule was extended even to our enemies by the Lord, when He said:[3] 'Love your enemies, do good to those who hate you.'

(32) The Apostle Paul also teaches this when he says:[4] 'For "Thou shalt not commit adultery; Thou shalt not kill; Thou shalt not steal; . . . Thou shalt not covet"; and if there is any other commandment, it is summed up in this

---
2 Luke 10.25ff.
3 Matt. 5.44.
4 Rom. 13.9,10.

saying, "Thou shalt love thy neighbor as thyself." Love does no evil to a neighbor.' Therefore, whoever is of the opinion that the Apostle was not enjoining commands concerning every human being is compelled to suggest that it did not seem a sin to the Apostle if someone committed adultery with the wife of either a non-Christian or his enemy, or killed him, or coveted his property—but this idea is very foolish and very wicked. If it is madness to suggest this, then it is clear that every human being must be regarded as our neighbor, because we must not do evil to anyone.

(33) And so, if he is rightly said to be our neighbor to whom we must show the service of mercy, or by whom it must be shown to us, it is clear that the holy angels are also included in this command by which we are ordered to love our neighbor. Such great services of mercy have been done to us by them, as we easily observe in many places of the Sacred Scriptures. In accordance with this teaching, God Himself, our Lord, wished Himself to be called our neighbor. For the Lord Jesus Christ meant that He Himself was the one who gave help to the man lying half-dead upon the road, beaten and left by the robbers.[5] And the Prophet said in prayer:[6] 'As a neighbor and as an own brother, so did I please.' But, since the divine nature is far superior and above our human nature, the precept by which we are to love God is distinct from our love of our neighbor. He shows mercy to us because of His own Goodness, while we show mercy to one another because of God's goodness; that is, He has compassion on us so that we may enjoy Him completely, while we have compassion on another that we may completely enjoy Him.

---

5 Luke 10.33.
6 Ps. 34.14.

Chapter 31

(34) Therefore, it still seems vague to say that we fully enjoy a thing which we love for its own sake and that we should only enjoy a thing which can make us happy, but should use other things. God loves us and Holy Scripture often mentions His love for us.[1] How does He love us: to use us or to enjoy us? If He enjoys us, He needs a benefit that is ours—something no sane man would say, because He Himself is our every good, or else it comes from Him.[2] To whom is it bewildering or doubtful that light has no need of the brightness of those things which it has illuminated? The Prophet speaks most clearly:[3] 'I have said to the Lord, 'Thou art my God, for Thou hast no need of my goods.' Consequently, He does not enjoy us, but uses us. If He neither enjoys nor uses us, I cannot discover how He loves us.

Chapter 32

(35) He does not use anything, however, in the same way that we do. We apply the use we make of creatures to our purpose of completely enjoying the goodness of God, but God applies His use of us to His own goodness. Since He is good, we exist. Inasmuch as we exist, we are good. Besides, since He is also just, we are not evil without fear of punishment; inasmuch as we are evil, to that extent is our existence diminished. He is the first and greatest existence, who is utterly unchangeable and who could say most perfectly:[1] 'I am Who am, and Thou shalt say to them, "He Who

---

1 Rom. 5.8; John 3.16.
2 James 1.17.
3 Ps. 15.2.

---

1 Exod. 3.14.

is hath sent me to you." ' As a result, the other things which exist could not exist except by Him, and these things are good insofar as they have received the ability to be. Therefore, God refers that use which He is said to make of us to our benefit, not to His benefit, but only to His goodness. When we show pity on someone or are mindful of his interests, we do so for, and with an eye to, his benefit. But, somehow or other, our own advantage becomes a consequence, since God does not leave without a reward that mercy which we expend upon one who needs it. Our greatest reward is that we may enjoy Him perfectly and that all of us who enjoy Him may perfectly enjoy one another in Him.

Chapter 33

(36) If we find this enjoyment in ourselves, we delay upon the road and place the hope of our happiness in a man or in an angel. The proud man and the proud angel claim this for themselves and rejoice that the hope of others is founded upon them. On the other hand, the holy man and the holy angel refresh us, even when we are exhausted and desirous of resting and remaining in them, with what they have received from God, either for us or for themselves. In this way they compel us, refreshed now, to go to Him in the enjoyment of whom we are happy together with them. Even the Apostle proclaims: 'Was Paul crucified for you? Or were you baptized in the name of Paul?'[1] and 'Neither he who plants is anything, nor he who waters, but God who gives the growth.'[2] And the angel instructs the

---
1　1 Cor. 1.13.
2　1 Cor. 3.7.

man who is adoring him that he should rather adore God, that Master under whom he himself is also a fellow-servant.[3]

(37) When you enjoy a man in God, you enjoy God rather than the man. For you enjoy Him by whom you are made happy and you will rejoice that you have come to Him in whom you place the hope that you may come. Accordingly, Paul said to Philemon:[4] 'Yes, indeed, brother! May I enjoy thee in the Lord!' If he had not added 'in the Lord' and had said only 'May I enjoy thee,' he would have placed in him the hope of his happiness. Yet, 'to enjoy' is very close to saying 'to use with delight.' When that which is loved is close at hand, it is inevitable, also, that it bring pleasure with it. If you pass beyond this pleasure and refer it to that end where you are to remain forever, you are using it; it would not be correct, but an error, to say you are enjoying it. If you cling to it and place the goal of all your joy in it as a permanent abode, then you ought with truth and correctness to be said to enjoy it. And this we must not do, except in regard to the Holy Trinity, the greatest and unchangeable Good.

Chapter 34

(38) Consider how, although Truth Himself and the Word, by whom all things were made,[1] was made flesh that He might dwell among us,[2] the Apostle still says:[3] 'And even though we knew Christ according to the flesh, yet now we know Him so no longer.' Since He wished not only to

---
3 Apoc. 19.10; 22.9.
4 Philem. 20.

---
1 John 1.3.
2 John 1.14.
3 2 Cor. 5.16.

show Himself as the reward of those who have arrived at Him, but also, to those who were only coming to the beginning of their journey, to show Himself as the way, He willed to assume human flesh. So there is also this verse:[4] 'The Lord created me in the beginning of His ways,' so that those who wished to come might begin from Him. Therefore, although the Apostle was still walking on the way and following God who was calling him to the crown of a heavenly vocation, still, 'forgetting what is behind, and straining forward to what is before,'[5] he had already passed beyond the beginning of the journey and was no longer in need of it. However, all those who are desirous of arriving at truth and abiding forever in eternal life must begin and advance upon the journey, starting from Him. For, He has said:[6] 'I am the way, and the truth, and the life,' and this means: everyone comes through Me, arrives at Me, and dwells in Me forever. When we come to Him, therefore, we come also to the Father,[7] for an equal is recognized through a person to whom he is equal. The Holy Ghost unites and, so to speak, cements us, so that we may dwell forever in the highest unchangeable Good. Accordingly, we understand how nothing ought to hold us back on the way, since the Lord Himself, inasmuch as He deigned to be our way, did not wish to hold us on the way, but wished to have us pass along it, lest we cling feebly to temporal things, even though they were taken up and borne by Him for our salvation. Let us, rather, run quickly through them, in order that we may deserve to make progress and attain to Him who has

---

4 Prov. 8.22.
5 Cf. Phil. 3.13.
6 John 14.6.
7 John 14.9.

freed our nature from the things of time and placed it at the right hand of the Father.

Chapter 35

(39) Therefore, the summary of all that has been said since we began our discussion of *things* is that we are to realize that the plenitude and the end of the law and of all Sacred Scripture is the love[1] of a thing which is to be enjoyed and the love of another thing which can enjoy that first thing with us, since there is no need for a precept that each one is to love himself. In order that we might know this and be able to do it, there was created by Divine Providence, for our salvation, the whole temporal dispensation which we ought to use, but not with any permanent affection and pleasure. Ours should rather be like the transitory pleasure felt toward the road, or conveyances, or any other means to an end. Or it may be possible to express more fittingly this love we are to have for the things by which we are carried along for the sake of the end toward which we are carried.

Chapter 36

(40) Whoever, then, appears in his own opinion to have comprehended the Sacred Scriptures, or even some part of them, yet does not build up with that knowledge the twofold love of God and his neighbor, 'has not yet known as he ought to know.'[1] Yet, if anyone has derived from them an idea that may be useful to him in building up this love, but has not expressed by it what the author whom he

---
1 Rom. 13.10; 1 Tim. 1.5.

---
1 1 Cor. 8.2.

is reading demonstrably intended in that passage, he is not erring dangerously nor lying at all. For, inherent in lying is the will to speak falsehoods. We find many persons who wish to lie, but no one who wishes to be deceived. Therefore, since a man deceives with knowledge, but is deceived through ignorance, it is sufficiently evident, in any one instance, that he who is deceived is better than he who lies, since it is better to suffer injustice than to commit it.[2] Everyone who lies acts unjustly, and, if lying ever seems useful to anyone, it is possible that injustice sometimes seems useful to him. No liar preserves faith in that about which he lies. He wishes that he to whom he lies may have faith in him, but he does not preserve this faith by lying to him. Every breaker of faith is unjust. Therefore, either injustice is sometimes useful (a thing which is impossible) or lying is always hurtful.

(41) Whoever understands in the Sacred Scriptures something other than the writer had in mind is deceived, although they do not lie. Yet, as I began to say, if he is deceived in an interpretation by which, however, he builds up charity (which is the end of the precept[3]), he is deceived in the same way as is someone who leaves the road through error, but makes his way through the field to the place where the road also leads. Nevertheless, he must be corrected and must be shown how it is more advantageous not to leave the road, lest by a habit of deviating he may be drawn into a crossroad or even go the wrong way.

---

2 1 Peter 3.17.
3 1 Tim. 1.5.

Chapter 37

By rashly asserting something which the author did not intend, he frequently runs into other passages which he cannot reconcile to that interpretation. If he agrees that these latter are true and definite, then the opinion which he had formed concerning the former cannot be true, and it happens, in some way or other, that by loving his own opinion he begins to be more vexed at Scripture than at himself. If he allows this error to creep in, he will be utterly destroyed by it. 'For we walk by faith and not by sight.'[1] Faith will totter, if the authority of Sacred Scriptures wavers. Indeed, even charity itself grows weak, if faith totters. If anyone falls from faith, it is inevitable that he also falls from charity. For, he cannot love what he does not believe exists. But, if he both believes and loves, by leading a good life and by obeying the commandments of good morals, he gives himself reason to hope that he may arrive at that which he loves. And so 'there abide faith, hope, and charity, these three'[2] which all knowledge and all prophecy serve.

Chapter 38

(42) But the vision which we shall see takes the place of faith and that blessedness to which we shall attain takes the place of hope, but charity will be all the more increased as those former die away. If by faith we love what we do not yet see, how much more shall we love when we have begun to see? If through hope we love what we have not yet attained, how much more shall we love when we have attained it? There is this difference between temporal goods

---
1 2 Cor. 5.7.
2 1 Cor. 13.1ff.

and eternal goods, that something temporal is loved more before we have it, but becomes worthless when it has come into our possession. It does not content the soul, whose true and appointed abode is eternity. But, an eternal good is loved more ardently when we have obtained it than it was when we were seeking it. No one who desires it can value it higher than inherently it is worth, with the result that it would become worthless to him when he discovers that it was less than his valuation of it. But, however highly anyone may value it while he was coming to it, he will find it more valuable when he has obtained it.

Chapter 39

(43) And so, a man who relies upon faith, hope, and charity and resolutely holds fast to them does not need the Scriptures, except to teach others. And many by means of these three virtues live in solitude without the Sacred Scriptures. It seems to me that in them is already exemplified the saying:[1] 'Whereas prophecies will disappear, and tongues will cease, and knowledge will be destroyed.' Yet, by these devices, so to speak, such a great building of faith, hope, and charity has risen in them that, holding on to something perfect—perfect, of course, insofar as it is possible in this life—they do not seek after those things which are only partially so.[2] For, in comparison with the life to come, no just or holy man has a perfect life here. Hence, the Apostle says:[3] 'There abide faith, hope, and charity, these three; but the greatest of these is charity'; since, even when we have attained to the eternal goods, although the other two die

---

1 1 Cor. 13.8.
2 1 Cor. 13.10.
3 1 Cor. 13.13.

away, charity will remain forever, increased and more firmly established.

Chapter 40

(44) Therefore, when anyone recognizes that 'the end of the precept is charity from a pure heart and a good conscience and faith unfeigned,[1] and proposes to refer his whole comprehension of Sacred Scriptures to these three virtues, he may approach the interpretation of those books fearlessly. For, when he spoke of 'charity,' the Apostle added 'from a pure heart,' so that nothing would be loved except that which ought to be. He joined to it 'a good conscience' for the sake of our hope, because a person upon whom the anxiety of a bad conscience is weighing despairs of attaining that which he has faith in and loves. Third, he said 'and faith unfeigned.' For, if our faith is untainted by falsehood, then we do not feel affection for what we ought not to love; by living rightly, we hope that our hope may not be deceived in any way.

I have wished to speak of matters concerning faith only insofar as I considered them of benefit for the time being, because much has been said already in other works, either by other writers or by me. And so, let this be the limit of this book. As for the rest, I shall treat of signs, as far as God gives me inspiration.

---

1 1 Tim. 1.5.

BOOK TWO

Chapter 1

WHEN I was writing about things, I began with a forcible reminder that one should only consider in them what they are in themselves, even when they are signs of something else. But now, when I come to the treatment of signs, one should not consider in them what they are, but rather direct his attention to the fact that they are signs, namely, that they signify something. A sign is a thing which, apart from the impression that it presents to the senses, causes of itself some other thing to enter our thoughts. For example, at the sight of a footprint, we think that the animal whose track it is has passed this way; at the sight of smoke, we learn there is a fire nearby; at the sound of a living voice, we direct our attention to the idea in that person's mind; at the sound of a trumpet, soldiers know whether to advance or retreat, or whether the action requires them to do something else.

(2) Some signs are natural; others are conventional. Natural signs are those that, independently of any purpose or desire of being a sign of anything except themselves, cause something else to be recognized. Such is the case when smoke indicates fire. It is not a will to signify that causes this. Rather, through observation and attention to our experiences we learn that fire is near at hand, even when only the smoke

is visible. The footprint of a passing animal also belongs to this category. The face of an angry or sad person indicates his state of mind, although this may not be the intention of the person who is angry or sad. Every other operation of the mind is revealed by the testimony of our facial expression, even when we are not endeavoring to betray it. But it is not my aim to treat here of this type of signs. However, since it has a place in my division of the subject, I could not disregard it entirely; it is sufficient to have alluded to it to this extent.

Chapter 2

(3) Conventional signs are those which living creatures give to one another. They thus indicate, as far as possible, either the operations of their minds or anything perceived by sense or intellect. The only reason we have for indicating by signs is that we may call forth and transfer to another's mind what is in our mind as we give the sign. I intend, therefore, to examine and treat of this type of signs, insofar as it pertains to men. This I do because even the signs communicated by inspiration which are included in Holy Scripture were disclosed to us by the men who wrote them. Even beasts have certain signs among themselves by which they reveal the desires they feel. After the cock finds food, he gives a sign with his voice to the hen to hurry to him; and the dove calls his mate or is called by her by cooing. We are accustomed to observe many such signs. Whether these, such as the expression or outcry of a man in pain, conform to the operation of the mind with no intention of giving a sign, or whether they are given for the specific purpose of signifying, is another issue. It has no reference to

the matter under discussion and I am omitting it from this work as irrelevant.

Chapter 3

(4) Of the symbols by which men express their ideas to one another, some involve the sense of sight; many, the sense of hearing; and a very few, the other senses. When we nod, we are giving a sign only to the eyes of the person whom we desire through this sign to make a sharer of our will. Some express ever so much by the movements of their hands. Actors by the motions of all their limbs give certain signs to those who understand and, in a certain sense, speak to their eyes. Banners and military standards make known through the eyes of the intention of the leaders. All these signs are like visible words. But, as we have said, there are more which have to do with hearing and these are principally expressed in words. The trumpet, the flute, and the harp often produce not only a pleasing sound, but also one full of meaning. All these signs are very infrequent, in contrast to words. Words have gained, by far, a pre-eminence among men for expressing whatever operations of the mind a person might desire to reveal. The Lord, it is true, gave a sign by means of the perfume of the ointment with which His feet were anointed.[1] He made known through taste what He intended in the Sacrament of His Body and Blood.[2] And when the woman was healed by touching 'the tassel of His cloak,'[3] the act signified something. But, an incalculable number of signs by which men convey their ideas are based upon words. I could express in words all those signs of the

---

1 John 12.3-7; cf. Aug. *Tract. in Joan.* 50.7.
2 Matt. 26.29.
3 Matt. 9.21; cf. Aug. *De cons. Ev.* 2.20.50.

kinds I have mentioned briefly, but I would not at all be able to make words clear by those signs.

Chapter 4

(5) Since, after words have reverberated upon the air, they pass away and last no longer than the sound they make, signs of words have been provided by means of letters. In this manner voice-sounds are presented to the eye, not through themselves, but through certain characteristic signs. Those signs could not be the same for all nations, because of the sin of human dissension, in which each one seizes the first place for himself. An evidence of this pride is that tower raised up to heaven where impious men merited the just penalty of having not only their minds, but also their tongues, confounded.[1]

Chapter 5

(6) The result was this. Although Sacred Scripture, which heals such grave maladies of human hearts, began from one language,[1] by which it could be spread abroad through the whole world at the proper time, it was scattered far and wide by the various languages of translators, and only thus became known to the nations for their salvation. In reading it, men are desirous only of discovering the thoughts and intentions of those by whom it was written. Through these in turn they discover the will of God, according to which we believe such men spoke.

---
1 Gen. 11.1ff.

---
1 The reference is to Hebrew; cf. Aug. *De civ. Dei* 16.43.3.

Chapter 6

(7) Those who read indiscreetly are deceived by numerous and varied instances of obscurity and vagueness, supposing one meaning instead of another. In some passages they do not find anything to surmise even erroneously, so thoroughly do certain texts draw around them the most impenetrable obscurity. I am convinced that this whole situation was ordained by God in order to overcome pride by work and restrains from haughtiness our minds which usually disdain anything they have learned easily. There are holy and perfect men by whose lives and example the Church of Christ rids those who come to her of superstition and incorporates them with herself through the imitation of these good men. These good and truly faithful servants of God, ridding themselves of wordly cares, have come to the holy laver of baptism, and arising from it, produce by the infusion of the Holy Ghost the fruit of a two-fold charity: a love of God and of their neighbor. Why is it, then, I ask, that, when anyone asserts these facts, he affords less charm to his listener than when he explains with the same interpretation that text from the Canticle of Canticles where the Church is alluded to as a beautiful woman who is being praised: 'Thy teeth are as flocks of sheep, that are shorn, which come up from the washing, all with twins, and there is none barren among them'?[1] Does one learn anything more than when he hears that same thought phrased in the simplest words, without the aid of this simile? But, somehow or other, I find more delight in considering the saints when I regard them as the teeth of the Church. They bite off men from their heresies and carry them over to the body of the Church,

---
1 Cant. 4.2.

when their hardness of heart has been softened as if by being bitten off and chewed. With very great delight I look upon them also as shorn sheep that have put aside wordly cares, as if they were fleece. Coming up from the washing, that is, the baptismal font, all bear twins, that is, the two precepts of love, and I see no one destitute of that holy fruit.

(8) But it is hard to explain why I experience more pleasure in this reflection than if no such comparison were derived from the Sacred Books, even though the matter and the knowledge are the same. This is another question. However, no one is uncertain now that everything is learned more willingly through the use of figures, and that we discover it with much more delight when we have experienced some trouble in searching for it. Those who do not find what they are seeking are afflicted with hunger, but those who do not seek, because they have it in their possession, often waste away in their pride. Yet, in both cases, we must guard against discouragement. The Holy Ghost, therefore, has generously and advantageously planned Holy Scripture in such a way that in the easier passages He relieves our hunger; in the ones that are harder to understand He drives away our pride. Practically nothing is dug out from those unintelligible texts which is not discovered to be said very plainly in another place.

Chapter 7

(9) Primarily, we must be led by the fear of God that we may recognize His will, what He orders us to seek after and what we must flee from. It is inevitable that this fear should awaken reflection upon our mortal nature and the death that will be ours. By it all our emotions of pride are

fastened to the wood of the cross, as it were, by nailing our flesh. Then we must become gentle through piety. We ought not to protest against Holy Scripture, either when we understand it and it is attacking some of our faults, or when we do not understand it and think that we ourselves could be wiser and give better advice. In this latter case we must rather reflect and believe that what is written there is more beneficial and more reasonable, even if hidden, than what we could know of ourselves.

(10) After those two steps of fear and piety we come to the third step, that of knowledge, which I have now begun to discuss. Everyone devoted to the study of the Holy Scriptures trains himself in this. In them he will find nothing else except that God must be loved for His own sake, and our neighbor for the sake of God; and to love God with his whole heart, and with his whole soul, and with his whole mind, and his neighbor as himself;[2] that is, that our entire love of our neighbor as also of ourselves is to be referred to God. I treated of these two precepts in the previous book when I was discussing things. It is inevitable, then, that at first, each one should discover in the Scriptures that he has been enmeshed by the love of this world, that is, of temporal things, and has been far separated from such a great love of God and of his neighbor as Scripture itself prescribes. Then, truly, that fear with which he meditates upon the judgment of God and that piety through which he must needs believe in and yield to the authority of the Holy Books should force him to mourn over himself. That knowledge of a good hope causes a man to be not boastful, but sorrowful. In this disposition he begs, through unceasing

---
1 Isa. 11.2,3; Matt. 5.3ff.
2 Matt. 22.37,39.

prayers, the consolation of divine assistance, that he may not be crushed by despair. He thus begins upon the fourth step, that of fortitude, where he hungers and thirsts for justice. In this state he withdraws himself from every deadly pleasure of passing things. In turning aside from these, he turns toward the love of eternal things, namely, the unchangeable Trinity in Unity.

(11) When, as well as he can, he has observed this gleaming from a distance, and has plainly perceived that he cannot bear that light because of the weakness of his vision, he is at the fifth step, that is, in the counsel of mercy. Here he cleanses sordid thoughts from his soul, which is somehow confused and annoying to him because of its craving for inferior things. It is here that he zealously practices the love of his neighbor and perfects himself in it. Now, full of hope and spiritually vigorous, when he has attained even to the love of his enemy, he rises to the sixth step. There he cleanses the sight itself which can see God, so far as He can be seen by those who die to this world as far as they can. They see in proportion to the extent that they die to this world, but, insofar as they live to it, they do not see. And so, although the splendor of that light begins to appear more definite now, and is not only more endurable, but even more pleasant, it is still said to be seen 'through a mirror in an obscure manner.'[3] This is because we walk more 'by faith' than 'by sight' while 'we are exiled'[4] in this life, although 'our citizenship is in heaven.'[5] At this level, however, he so cleanses the eye of his heart that he does not prefer or compare even his neighbor to the Truth, and therefore, not him-

---
3 1 Cor. 13.12.
4 2 Cor. 5.6ff.
5 Phil. 3.20.

self either, since he does not so exalt the one he loves as himself. Therefore, that holy man will be so sincere and clean of heart that he will not be turned away from truth, either through a desire of gratifying men or through an intention of evading whatever inconveniences disturb this life. Such a child of God mounts to Wisdom, which is the last and seventh step, and this he fully enjoys with perfect calm and serenity. For, 'the fear of the Lord is the beginning of wisdom.'[6] From that fear until we arrive even at Wisdom, it is through these steps that we make our way.

Chapter 8

(12) Let us now turn our attention to that third step which I have determined to discuss and reflect upon as the Lord may prompt me. The most intelligent investigator of Sacred Scriptures will be the man who has in the first place read them all and obtained a knowledge of them. Perhaps he has not yet acquired the knowledge of understanding; yet, he may have some grasp of them through reading, at least with respect to those which are called canonical Scriptures. For, fortified by the belief of truth, he will read the others more securely, that they may not preoccupy a weak mind, nor, deluding it with dangerous lies and imaginations, prejudice it against a wholesome understanding. In the canonical Scriptures he should follow the authority of the majority of Catholic Churches, among which are surely those that have deserved to have apostolic sees and receive epistles. He will keep to this method in canonical Scriptures, therefore preferring those which are accepted by all Catholic Churches to those which some do not accept. Among those

---

6 Ps. 110.10; Eccli. 1.16.

which are not accepted by all, let him favor those which the greater number of more eminent churches accept, rather than those upheld by a minority of churches of less authority.[1] If he discovers that some are accepted by the greater number of churches and others by the more important ones, although he cannot discover this easily, I believe the authority in the two cases should be considered as equal.

(13) The whole canon of the Scriptures on which I maintain that this consideration should depend is contained in these books: the five of Moses, that is, Genesis, Exodus, Leviticus, Numbers, and Deuteronomy; one book of Josue; one of Judges; a little book which is called Ruth, which seems rather to pertain to the beginning of Kings; then four books of Kings and two of Paralipomenon, which do not follow them in thought, but, as it were, are collaterally joined and proceed together with them. These are the books of history which contain a connected narrative of the times and have an orderly arrangement. There are others, histories of a different order which are not united to the aforementioned order or to one another, such as the books of Job, Tobias, Esther, Judith, the two books of the Machabees, and the two of Esdras. These last two follow the orderly history up to its termination in the books of Kings and Paralipomenon. Then the Prophets, in which there are one book of the Psalms of David and three of Solomon: Proverbs, the Canticle of Canticles, and Ecclesiastes. As to the two books, one of which is entitled Wisdom and the other Ecclesiasticus, these are said to have been Solomon's, because of a certain likeness of style. Yet Jesus the son of Sirach

---

[1] Cf. Concil. Hipponense A.D. 393, Can. 38; also Concil. Carthag. A.D. 397, Can. 47.

is asserted most consistently to have written them.² However, they must be counted among the prophetical books, because they have deserved recognition for their authority. The rest are the books which are properly termed Prophets, twelve separate books of the Prophets, which are connected with one another and are considered as one, since they have never been separated. These are the names of the prophets: Osee, Joel, Amos, Abdias, Jonas, Micheas, Nahum, Habacuc, Sophonias, Aggeus, Zacharias, and Malachias. Then the four major prophets: Isaias, Jeremias, Daniel, and Ezechiel. The authority of the Old Testament is contained in these forty-four books.³ The authority of the New Testament rests in the following: the four books of the Gospel, according to Matthew, Mark, Luke, and John; the fourteen Epistles of Paul the Apostle; to the Romans, two to the Corinthians, to the Galatians, to the Ephesians, to the Philippians, two to the Thessalonians, to the Colossians, two to Timothy, to Titus, to Philemon, and to the Hebrews; two Epistles of Peter; three of John; one of Jude; and one of James; the Acts of the Apostles in one book; and one book of the Apocalypse of John.

Chapter 9

(14) In all these books those who fear God and are meek in their devotion seek the will of God. The first care of this task and endeavor, as I have said, is to know these books. Although we may not yet understand them, nevertheless, by reading them we can either memorize them or become somewhat acquainted with them. Then, those things which are clearly asserted in them as rules, governing either life or belief, should be studied more intelligently and

---
2 See Introduction, p. 3.
3 See Introduction p. 3f.

more attentively. The more anyone learns about these, the more capable of discernment he is. For, among those things which have been clearly expressed in the Scriptures, we discover all those which involve faith and the rules of living, namely, hope and charity, of which I treated in the previous book. Then, after a certain intimacy with the language of the Holy Scriptures has been achieved, we should begin to uncover and examine thoroughly those passages which are obscure, selecting examples from clearer texts to explain such as are more obscure, and allowing some proofs of incontestable texts to remove the uncertainty from doubtful passages. In this endeavor the memory is of very great value. If this is wanting, it cannot be imparted by these precepts.

Chapter 10

(15) Things which have been written fail to be understood for two reasons; they are hidden by either unknown or ambiguous signs. These signs are either literal or figurative. They are literal when they are employed to signify those things for which they were instituted. When we say *bos* we mean an ox, because all men call it by this name in the Latin language just as we do. Signs are figurative when the very things which we signify by the literal term are applied to some other meaning; for example, we say *bos* and recognize by that word an ox to which we usually give that name; but again, under the figure of the ox, we recognize a teacher of the gospel. This is intimated by Holy Scripture, according to the interpretation of the Apostle, in the text:[1] 'Thou shalt not muzzle the ox that treads out the grain.'

---

1 Deut. 25.4; 1 Cor. 9.9; 1 Tim. 5.18.

Chapter 11

(16) A knowledge of languages is an efficacious cure for an ignorance of literal signs. Men who know the Latin language, whom I have now begun to teach, have need of two others in order to understand the Sacred Scriptures. These are Hebrew and Greek, by which they may turn back to the originals if the infinite variances of Latin translators cause any uncertainty. And yet, in these books we may often come upon Hebrew words that have not been translated, such as *Amen, Alleluia, Raca, Hosanna,* and some others. Some of these, although they could have been translated, have been kept unchanged, like *Amen* and *Alleluia,* because of their holier authority. Some, on the other hand, are not considered capable of being translated into another language, such as the other two which I specified. There are some expressions in certain languages which cannot pass over into the usage of another language through translation. This occurs especially with interjections; these words indicate an impulse of the mind, rather than any part of reasoned thought. The two last are cited as such, for they maintain that *Raca* is the expression of an indignant person, and *Hosanna* of a person who is rejoicing. However, an understanding of the languages named is indispensable, not because of these few examples, which are very easy to observe and investigate, but because of the variances of translators, as I mentioned. For we can enumerate those who have translated the Scriptures from Hebrew to Greek, but the Latin translators are innumerable. In the first ages of the faith, when a Greek text came into the possession of anyone who considered himself slightly capable in both languages, he attempted to translate it.

Chapter 12

(17) In fact, this diversity has helped rather than impeded understanding, if readers would only be discerning. A close study of a number of texts frequently has clarified some of the more obscure phrases, for instance that of the Prophet Isaias which one translator expresses:[1] 'And do not despise the domestics of thy seed'; while another interprets it thus:[2] 'And despise not thy own flesh.' Each one confirms the other, for the one is interpreted from the other. 'Flesh' can be understood in its literal sense, and this one could believe that he has been warned not to despise his own body, and figuratively, 'the domestics of thy seed' could be taken to mean Christians who, together with us, have been given spiritual birth from the same seed, the Word. However, after we have compared the opinions of the translators, a more probable meaning occurs to us. The precept, literally, is not to despise one's relations, because, when we associate 'domestics, of the seed' with 'flesh,' relations come particularly to mind. That, I think, is the source of the Apostle's statement:[3] 'In the hope that I may provoke to jealousy those who are my flesh, and may save some of them.' By this he means, through zealously imitating those who had believed, they themselves might also believe. For, he designates the Jews his own flesh because of his blood-relationship to them. Likewise, that text of the Prophet Isaias:[4] 'If ye will not believe, ye shall not understand,' has also been translated:[5] 'If you will not believe, you shall not continue.'

---

1 Isa. 58.7 (ancient version).
2 Isa. 58.7 (Vulgate version).
3 Rom. 11.14.
4 Isa. 7.9 (ancient version).
5 Isa. 7.9 (Vulgate version).

It is open to question which one of these conforms to the literal meaning, unless we read the texts in the original language. However, something valuable in both is impressed upon those who read with understanding. It is difficult for translators to become so different from one another that they do not converge by some resemblance. Now, the essence of knowledge is the eternal Vision, while faith nourishes us as babes, upon milk, in the cradles of earthly things (for now 'we walk by faith and not by sight.'[6] If, however, we do walk by faith, we shall not be able to arrive at sight, which does not vanish, but continues through our intellect once cleansed by our union with the Truth. Therefore it is that one translator says: 'If ye will not believe, ye shall not understand,' and the other declares: 'If you will not believe, you shall not continue.'

(18) Frequently, a translator who does not understand the sense very well is led astray by an obscure expression in the original language. He therefore translates it with a meaning which is utterly foreign to that of the writer. For example, some texts have: 'Their feet are sharp to shed blood.' *Oxus* in Greek means both 'sharp' and 'swift.' So, he who translated as 'Their feet are swift to shed blood,'[7] recognized the true meaning; the other, drawn in the opposite direction by an equivocal term, made a mistake. Such translations are not ambiguous; they are erroneous, and there is a great difference between the two things. For we must be taught not how to understand such texts, but rather how to rectify them. On this account, because in Greek *móschos* means 'calf,' some did not know that *moscheúmata* are 'transplantings,' and they have translated it as 'calves.' This

---
6 2 Cor. 5.7.
7 Rom. 3.15 (Ps. 13.3).

mistake has crept into so many texts that it can hardly be found written otherwise. Yet, the sense is very apparent, since it is clarified by the words which follow. It is more consistent to say 'Bastard slips shall not take deep root'[8] than to speak of calves. Calves walk upon the earth with their feet and do not hold fast to it by roots. Other expressions in this passage defend this interpretation.

Chapter 13

(19) The meaning which the various translators attempt to give, each in accordance with his own skill and opinion, is not obvious unless it is studied in the language which is being translated. Very often, also, a translator, unless he is a very learned man, deviates from the sense of the author. Accordingly, we must either strive after a mastery of those languages from which Holy Scripture is translated into Latin or we must use the translations of those who have adhered unduly to the actual words. It is not that such translations are adequate, but through them we may detect the looseness or error of others who have preferred to conform to the meaning rather than to the actual words in translating. Often times they translate, not only individual words, but even whole phrases which cannot be translated at all into a customary Latin expression, if we are desirous of preserving the idiom of the ancients who spoke Latin. These expressions sometimes take nothing from our comprehension. However, they do irritate those who find more charm in things when in their signs a certain appropriate correctness is preserved. What is called a solecism is nothing but a combination of words contrary to the rule used by the ancients who spoke

---

8 Wisd. 4.3.

with any authority. It does not concern a seeker after truth whether we say *inter homines* or *inter hominibus* [among men]. Likewise, what else is a barbarism but a word either spelled or pronounced other than was the custom of those who spoke Latin before our time? Whether *ignoscere* [forgive] is pronounced with a long or a short third syllable is not much of a worry to a man begging God to forgive his sins in whatever way he can utter that word. What is purity of language, therefore, but the preservation of the idiom, supported by the authority of the earlier speakers?

(20) The weaker men are, the more they are annoyed by this. And they are weak in proportion as they wish to appear learned, not in the knowledge of the things by which we may be instructed, but rather in a knowledge of signs. Through this knowledge it is very easy to become proud, since even the knowledge of things often raises up our pride,[1] unless it be curbed by the yoke of the Master. To one who understands, what harm comes because a passage is written this way: *Quae est terra in qua isti insidunt super eam, si bona est an nequam, et quae sunt civitates in quibus ipsi inhabitant in ipsis?*[2] ['Of what sort is the land in which those people dwell, whether it is good or bad, and what manner of cities there are in which they live.'] I consider that this is rather the expression of a foreign language than that it has any more profound significance. There is also that text which we are now unable to take away from the chant of the faithful: *Super ipsum autem floriet santificatio mea*[3] ['But upon him shall my sanctification flourish']. Assuredly, this detracts nothing from the sense, but a more instructed reader would rather

---

1 1 Cor. 8.1.
2 Cf. Num. 13.20; cf. Aug. *Locut. in Heptat.* 4.35.
3 Ps. 131.18.

have this corrected so that we would say not *floriet,* but *florebit.* Moreover, nothing prevents this revision except the custom of the chanters. These defects, then, can be easily overlooked by anyone who is unwilling completely to avoid them, for they do not at all detract from a sound meaning. Then, there is that text of the Apostle:[4] '*Quod stultum est Dei, sapientius est hominibus; et quod infirmum est Dei, fortius est hominibus*' [For the foolishness of God is wiser than men, and the weakness of God is stronger than men']. Suppose someone had wished to preserve the Greek idiom in this text and had said *Quod stultum est Dei, sapientius est hominum, et quod infirmum est Dei, fortius est hominum.* The attention of a watchful reader would certainly go on to the truth of the passage, but someone rather slow of comprehension would either not understand it at all or else would interpret it the wrong way. For, such a phrase is not only incorrect in the Latin language, but it even tends to obscurity, so that it might seem that the foolishness or the weakness of men is wiser or stronger than God's. And yet, even that phrase *sapientius est hominibus* [is wiser than men] is not untainted by ambiguity, although it is exempt from solecism. It is not clear whether *hominibus* is dative plural or ablative plural, except through a recognition of its meaning. Accordingly, it would be better expressed: *sapientius est quam homines* and *fortius est quam homines.*

Chapter 14

(21) I shall speak about ambiguous signs later on. Now I am discussing unknown signs, of which there are two forms insofar as they apply to words. Obviously, an unknown word or an unknown expression causes the reader to be

---
4 1 Cor. 1.25.

perplexed. If these come from foreign languages, we must ask about them from men who use those languages, or learn the languages, if we have the time and the ability, or study a comparison of the various translators. If we are unfamiliar with some words or expressions of our own language, they become known to us through repeated usage in reading or hearing them. Indeed, the best things for us to memorize are those classes of words or expressions which we do not know. Thus, we may be able easily, by the assistance of our memory, to study and acquire a knowledge of them, either when a more educated man whom we may question happens along, or when we come upon a text such that, either by the preceding or the following context or both, it indicates the import or meaning of that which we did not understand. Yet, so powerful is the effect of habit even in learning, that those who have in a certain sense been nourished and reared in the Holy Scriptures wonder more at other expressions, and consider them less perfect Latin than the ones they have learned in the Scriptures, but which are not found in Latin authors. Here also the multitude of translators is a very important aid, when they have been considered and debated upon by a comparison of texts. However, avoid all that is positively false. For, in correcting texts, the ingenuity of those who desire to know the Sacred Scriptures should be exercised principally in such a way that uncorrected passages, at least those coming from a single source of translation, yield to those that have been rectified.

Chapter 15

(22) In the case of translations themselves, however, the Itala[1] is to be preferred to the others, since it combines

---

1 What ancient version St. Augustine intended as the *Itala* (Italian) is

greater precision of wording with clearness of thought. In emending any Latin translations, we must consult the Greek texts; of these, the reputation of the seventy translators[2] is most distinguished in regard to the Old Testament. These translators are now considered by the more learned Churches to have translated under such sublime inspiration of the Holy Ghost that from so many men there was only one version. According to tradition and to many deserving of our trust, these men, while translating, were isolated from one another in separate cells. Nevertheless, nothing was discovered in the work of anyone of them which was not discovered in the others expressed in the same words and the same arrangement of words. Who, then, would venture to put anything on a level with this authority; still less, esteem anything better? But, if they consulted one another so that one version was produced by the united treatment and opinion of all of them, even then it is certainly not reasonable or proper for any one man, regardless of his knowledge, to presume to reform the common opinion of so many older and more learned men. Therefore, even if we discover something in the Hebrew original other than they have interpreted it, it is my opinion that we should yield to the divine direction. This guidance was accomplished through them so that the books which the Jewish nation refused to transmit to other nations, either because of reverence or jealousy, were revealed so far ahead of time, with the aid of the authority

---

not altogether clear. For a discussion of the problem and for St. Augustine's Biblical text, see Hugh Pope, O.P., *The Catholic Student's 'Aids' to the Study of the Bible* I (New York 1936) 216-218, also Dom D. de Bruyne, O.S.B., in *Miscellanea Agostiniana* II (Rome 1931) 521-606.

2 I.e., the Septuagint; cf. Pope, *op. cit.* I 184-192.

of King Ptolemy, to those nations who would believe through our Lord. It may be that they translated according to the manner in which the Holy Ghost, who directed them and caused them all to speak the same words, decided was adapted to those persons. Yet, as I said before, a comparison of those translators, also, who have adhered more persistently to the actual words is often efficacious in interpreting a thought. As I began to say then, the Latin texts of the Old Testament should be corrected, if they need correction. They ought to follow the model of the Greek texts, and especially the version of those who, although seventy in number, are declared to have translated with complete agreement. Moreover, there is no doubt that the books of the New Testament, if there is any confusion resulting from the differences in Latin translations, ought to defer to the Greek texts, especially the ones that are found in the Churches of greater and more diligent learning.

Chapter 16

(23) However, in reference to figurative expressions, if, by chance, the reader is caused perplexity by any unknown signs, he must decipher them partly through a knowledge of languages, partly through a knowledge of things. The pool of Siloe,[1] where the Lord ordered the man whose eyes He had smeared with clay made of spittle to wash his face, is applicable in some degree as an analogy and unquestionably alludes to some mystery. Nevertheless, if the Evangelist had not explained that name from an unknown language, such an essential implication would be hidden from us. So also, many Hebrew names which have not been interpreted by the authors of those books unquestionably have no small

---

1 John 9.7; cf. Aug. *Tract. in Joan.* 44.2.

power to help toward explaining the obscurities of the Scriptures, if someone is able to translate them. Some men, expert in that language, have rendered a truly valuable service to succeeding ages by having interpreted all these words apart from the Scriptures and by having given the meanings for *Adam, Eve, Abraham,* and *Moses,* and also for the interpretation of the name of places like *Jerusalem, Sion, Jericho, Sinai, Lebanon, Jordan,* or whatever other names in that language are unknown to us. Because these have been revealed and translated, many figurative passages in the Scriptures are interpreted.

(24) In addition, an imperfect knowledge of things causes figurative passages to be obscure; for example, when we do not recognize the nature of the animals, minerals, plants, or other things which are very often represented in the Scriptures for the sake of an analogy. It is well known that a serpent exposes its whole body, rather than its head, to those attacking it, and how clearly that explains the Lord's meaning when He directed us to be 'wise as serpents.'[2] We should, therefore, expose our body to persecutors, rather than our head, which is Christ.[3] Thus, the Christian faith, the head so to speak, may not be killed in us, as it would be if, preserving our body, we were to reject God! There is also the belief that, having forced itself through a small opening in disposing of its old skin, the serpent gains renewed vigor. How well this agrees with imitating the wisdom of the serpent and stripping off the 'old man'[4] that we may put on the new, as the Apostle expresses it; and we must strip it off passing through narrow places, since the Lord

---

2 Matt. 10.16.
3 Eph. 4.15.
4 Eph. 4.22ff; Col. 3.9.

says: 'Enter by the narrow gate.'⁵ A knowledge of the nature of the serpent, therefore, explains many analogies which Holy Scripture habitually makes from that animal; so a lack of knowledge about other animals to which Scripture no less frequently alludes for comparisons hinders a reader very much. The same is true of an ignorance of minerals and plants, or whatever is held fast by roots. Knowledge of the carbuncle, which glitters in darkness, also illumines many obscure passages of these books wherever it is proposed for the sake of comparison, and an ignorance of the beryl or the diamond frequently closes the doors to understanding. Is it easy to comprehend that everlasting peace is signified by the olive branch which the dove, returning, brought back to the ark,⁶ in no other way than through our knowledge that the smooth surface of oil is not readily marred by a different liquid and that the olive tree itself is always in leaf. Indeed, many, through an ignorance of hyssop—not knowing its potency, either for purifying the lungs or, as it is said, for penetrating rocks with its roots, although it is a little, unpretentious plant—cannot discover at all why it has been said:⁷ 'Thou shalt sprinkle me with hyssop, and I shall be cleansed.'

(25) An ignorance of numbers is the reason why many things expressed figuratively and mystically in the Scriptures are not understood. Certainly a sincere nature cannot help being concerned about the significance of the fact that Moses, Elias, and the Lord Himself fasted forty days.⁸ The figurative perplexity of this act is solved only by a knowledge and

---

5 Matt. 7.13.
6 Gen. 8.11.
7 Ps. 50.9; cf. Aug. *Enarr. in ps.* 50.12.
8 Exod. 24.18; 3 Kings 19.8; Matt. 4.2.

study of this number. It is composed of four times ten; as it were, the knowledge of all things joined together by time. The course of the day and year are accomplished through the number four; the days are carried through in intervals of hours: morning, noon, evening, and night; the years, by the spring, summer, autumn, and winter months. But, while we are living in time, we must abstain and fast from all pleasure in time because of the eternity in which we hope to live; although, by the passage of time, that very doctrine of despising temporal things and striving for eternal goods is recommended to us. Further, the number ten symbolizes the knowledge of the Creator and the creature. For a trinity is present in the Creator, while the number seven signifies the creature, by reason of his life and body. In the case of his life, there are three Commandments to love God with our whole heart, our whole soul, and our whole mind;[9] with regard to the body, there are four very discernible elements of which it is composed. So, while the number ten is being impressed upon us in the sense of time, that is, multiplied by four, we are being instructed to live virtuously and temperately, free from the delights of time—in other words, to fast for forty days. This instruction comes from the Law, exemplified by Moses, from the prophecies, exemplified by Elias, and from the Lord Himself. He, as if claiming the testimony of the Law and the prophets, revealed Himself on the mount between those two to His three watching and wondering disciples.[10] The next question is: How the number fifty, which is especially sacred in our religion because of Pentecost, proceeds from forty; also, how this number mul-

---

9 Matt. 22.37.
10 Matt. 17.3.

tiplied by three[11]—because of the three periods of time (before the Law, under the Law, and under grace) or, because of the Name of the Father, the Son, and the Holy Ghost, eminently increased by the Holy Trinity Itself—is applied to the mystery of the most Holy Church and equals the hundred and fifty-three fishes which were caught in the net cast 'on the right side' after the Resurrection of the Lord. And so, certain mysteries of comparison are expressed in the Sacred Books in many other numbers and arrangements of numbers, which are hidden from readers because of their ignorance of numbers.

(26) An ignorance of certain elements of music also encloses and conceals many other things. A certain author[12] has beautifully interpreted some figurative passages from the dissimilarity between the psaltery and the harp.[13] It is also reasonable that learned men strive to discover whether the psaltery with its ten chords is dependent upon any musical law requiring only that number of strings, or, if it is not, whether that number itself should be regarded as all the more sacred because of the Ten Commandments. Just so, if there would be any question about this number, it should be ascribed to the Creator and the creature, because of the number ten itself as explained above. That number of forty-six years required for the building of the Temple, which is related in the Gospel,[14] has a certain musical sound. Applied to the formation of the Lord's body (because of which He mentioned the Temple), it constrains some heretics to acknowledge that the Son of God has

---

11 John 21.11,6.
12 Cf. *Brev. in psalmos* (G. Morin, *Anecdota Maredsolana* III.2 312).
13 Ps. 32.2; Ps. 91.4.
14 John 2.20.

clothed Himself not with a counterfeit, but with a truly human, body. Indeed, in many places in the Sacred Scriptures we discover both number and music alluded to with respect.

Chapter 17

(27) We must not approve of the superstitions of the pagans who taught that the nine Muses were the daughters of Jupiter and Memory. Varro disproves these errors and I know of no one among the ancients more learned or diligent in such matters. He says that a certain state (I do not remember the name) made an agreement with three artists each for three statues of the Muses to present as an offering in the temple of Apollo. There was one condition, however, that it would choose and buy, in preference to all others, the statues of whichever of the artists had fashioned the most beautiful ones. It turned out that the artists all produced works equally beautiful and that all nine satisfied the state. Therefore, all were purchased to be enshrined in the temple of Apollo. He declares that the poet Hesiod later ascribed names to them. Consequently, Jupiter did not produce the nine Muses, but three workmen chiseled three statues each. Besides, that state had not arranged for three because it had witnessed them in dreams or because such a number of Muses had shown themselves to any of the inhabitants. It did so because it was easy to observe that all sound which is the material of songs is by nature three-fold. It is caused either by the voice, as in the case of those who sing from their throats without an instrument, or by the breath, as in playing trumpets or flutes, or by striking, as is true of harps, drums, or any other instruments which produce tone through percussion.

Chapter 18

(28) Whether Varro's story is true or not, we should not avoid music because of pagan superstition, if we can take from it anything useful for comprehending the Sacred Scriptures. But, let us not maintain that we are attending to their theatrical frivolities to see if there is anything about harps and other instruments which would aid in comprehending spiritual things. We should not ignore literature because Mercury is reputed to be its presiding deity. Nor, because they have consecrated temples to Justice and Virtue and have chosen to adore in stone what should be carried in the heart, must we therefore shun justice and virtue. On the contrary, every good and true Christian should understand that wherever he discovers truth it is the Lord's. Considering and discerning this truth, he will repudiate their superstitious fables, even in their religious writings. He will deplore and guard against men who 'although they knew God, did not glorify Him as God or give thanks, but became vain in their reasonings and their senseless minds have been darkened. For while professing to be wise they have become fools, and they have changed the glory of the incorruptible God for an image, made like to corruptible man and to birds and to four-footed beasts and creeping things.'[1]

Chapter 19

(29) In order that we may develop this whole subject more accurately, for it is especially necessary, there are two kinds of learning which affect pagan morals. One is a knowledge of those things which men have set up; the

---
[1] Rom. 1.21-23.

other, of those things which they have observed were the work of time or were divinely originated. That which is based upon human institutions is partly superstitious and partly not so.

Chapter 20

(30) Whatever has been conceived by men for fashioning and worshipping idols is superstitious, since it concerns the worship of a created thing, or some part of it, as God, or else concerns communications and certain arrangements and pacts with demons about portents. Included as such are the works of the magical arts, which the poets are wont to mention rather than teach. The books of the soothsayers and diviners are in this class, but, as it were, with more presumptuous falsity. To this category belong also all amulets and charms, of which the science of medicine also disapproves, whether these involve enchantments, or certain signs called 'characters,' or the hanging, attaching, or even in a way the dancing of certain objects, not in relation to the bodily condition, but according to certain portents either obscure or evident. These are more leniently termed 'physics,' that they may seem as if they were not involved in superstition, but only profiting by nature. Instances of these are earrings hung at the top of each ear, or small rings of ostrich bone worn on the fingers, or telling a person with hiccups to hold the left thumb in the right hand.

(31) In addition, there are thousands of the most absurd rules to follow should a limb tremble, or a stone or dog or child come between friends walking arm-in-arm. That practice which treads upon a stone as if it were a destroyer of friendship is less offensive than the one which strikes a

harmless child a box on the ear if he runs between two people walking together. But it is only fitting that sometimes the dogs avenge the children. Some people are often so superstitious that they even dare to strike a dog that has run between them, but not without paying the penalty. Sometimes the dog sends his smiter quickly away from a ridiculous practice to a real physician. Other practices like this are: to tread upon the sill when you cross in front of your house; to go back to bed if you sneeze while putting on your shoes; to return home if you stumble on your way to a certain place; to be more disturbed by the premonition of a future calamity than concerned about the present damage if mice gnaw at your clothing. This is the origin of Cato's humorous response when he was consulted by a certain man who told him that his shoes had been gnawed away by mice. Cato answered that that was not a marvel, but that it would certainly have been one if the shoes had eaten the mice.

Chapter 21

(32) We must not segregate from this class of dangerous superstition those men who used to be called *genethliaci* [composers of horoscopes] because of their concern with birthdays, but are now commonly called *mathematici* [astrologers]. These might search after and sometimes even trace out the exact location of the stars at the time of anyone's birth. Yet, when they try to foretell from that source either our actions or the effects of them, they stray very far from the truth and offer a wretched slavery to unlearned men. For, whenever a free man enters the home of an astrologer like this, he pays money in order that he may leave as the slave of Mars or Venus, or of all the stars. Those who were

the first to make this mistake and have transmitted it to succeeding ages have attached to these stars names, either of beasts, because of resemblances, or of men, to pay deference to those men. This is not strange, for, even in rather recent times, the Romans tried to dedicate to the glory and name of Caesar the star which we now call Lucifer.[1] Perhaps this would have happened and passed on to posterity, except that his ancestor Venus had previously taken possession of this title. Moreover, she could not transfer to her heirs by any law what she had never owned nor desired to own while alive. Where there was a place vacant or one not consecrated in honor of some dead ancestor, the usual course of action in such matters was taken. Instead of Quintilis and Sextilis, we have named these months July and August in honor of Julius Caesar and Augustus Caesar; so, anyone who wishes can easily understand that the stars in former times followed their courses in the sky without these present names of theirs. Since these men were dead, their descendants were either forced by royal authority or influenced by human conceit to honor their memory. By attaching their names to the stars, they thought they were elevating the dead men themselves to heaven. But, whatever men may call them, they are stars which God has created and regulated as He wished. They have an undeviating course which separates and differentiates the seasons.[2] It is easy to notice this motion and its progress at the birth of a person through the directions invented and written down by those whom Holy Scripture denounces in these words:[3] 'For if they were able to know so much as to make a judgment

---
1 Verg. *Eclog.* 9.47.
2 Gen. 1.14.
3 Wisd. 13.9.

of the world: how did they not more easily find out the Lord thereof?'

Chapter 22

(33) A desire to foretell from such observation the character, actions, and fortunes of human beings is a grave error and deceitful folly. In fact, those who have learned about such matters that really should be forgotten disprove this superstition. These wretched men observe the location of the stars, which they call constellations, at the time of the birth of the one about whom they are being consulted by persons even more wretched. Now, it is possible that twins be born in such swift succession that no interval of time between them can be perceived and noted in the movements of the constellations. For this reason, it is inevitable that some twins have the same constellations, although they do not have equal experiences, either in their accomplishments or in their sufferings. Instead, they frequently undergo such unequal fortunes that one has a very happy life, and the other a very unhappy one. We have learned that Esau and Jacob were born twins in such a way that Jacob, who was born second, was discovered holding on with his hand to the foot of his brother who preceded him.[1] Certainly the day and hour of the birth of these two could not be noted in any other way except that they would both have the same constellation. Yet, Scripture, now well known in the language of every nation, is a witness to the great difference in the characters, deeds, labors, and destinies of these two men.

---

1 Gen. 26.25.

(34) It is irrelevant to say that the smallest and shortest moment of time which separates the birth of twins is of very great importance in nature and in the extraordinary swiftness of the heavenly bodies. Even though I concede that it may be very important, yet it cannot be discovered by an astrologer in the constellations by whose contemplation he declares that he foretells destinies. Consequently, he does not find this difference in the constellations, since he must inspect the same ones whether he is consulted about Jacob or about his brother. What good is it to him, then, that there is a difference in the sky which he is rashly and carelessly blaming, if there is not a difference in the chart which he examines assiduously, but to no purpose? Therefore, those beliefs which also result from the arrangement of certain signs of things by human audacity must be placed in the same category as contracts and agreements with demons.

Chapter 23

(35) It follows from this that, by a certain secret judgment of God, men avid for evil things, in just punishment of their own desires, are handed over to be mocked and deceived. Those who mock and deceive them are the fallen angels, to whom, in accordance with the decree of divine Providence and God's most excellent disposition of human affairs, the lower part of the world has been subjected. Because of these illusions and deceptions, it happens that many past and future events are revealed by these superstitious and dangerous methods of divination, and come to pass just as they are predicted. Many happen in conformity with the observations of those who honor these superstitions. Enmeshed by them, they become more curious and entangle themselves more and more in the manifold subtleties of a

very dangerous error. For our benefit Holy Scripture has not silently passed over this kind of fornication of the soul; neither has it so frightened the soul away from it as to maintain that such practices should not be used because their teachers utter falsehoods. Rather, it says:[1] 'Even if what they predict to you should come to pass, do not believe them.' Simply because the ghost of the dead Samuel predicted truths to King Saul,[2] sacrileges such as those which called up that apparition should be no less detestable. In the Acts of the Apostles, although the woman with the divining spirit gave true evidence to the Lord's Apostles, the Apostle Paul did not show mercy to the evil spirit for that reason. Instead, he cleansed the woman by denouncing and driving out the demon.[3]

(36) Therefore, a Christian must completely reject and shun all the arts of a superstition like this. They are either worthless or sinful. Their origin is in some pernicious union of men and demons as the established agreement of a faithless and dishonorable friendship. The Apostle says: not 'that an idol is anything, but that what they sacrifice, they sacrifice to devils, and not to God; and I would not have you become associates of devils.'[4] Moreover, what the Apostle has said concerning idols and the sacrifices which are offered to their honor must be understood in connection with all imaginary signs. It is these that attract us either to the veneration of idols or to the worship of a created thing and its parts as God, or relate to the use of charms and other observances. They have not been universally ordained by God to develop

---

1 Cf. Deut. 13.1-3.
2 1 Kings 28.17.
3 Acts 16.16.
4 1 Cor. 10.19,20.

the love of God and our neighbor. Rather, they destroy the hearts of unhappy creatures through their own individual longing for temporal things. In all these sciences, therefore, we must dread and avoid association with demons, who strive, along with the Devil their leader, solely to block and cut off our way back home. Not only have men resolved upon vain and deceitful omens concerning the stars which God created and set in order. In regard also to things that are born or to situations originating from some exercises of divine Providence, many of them, whenever they happened to notice anything unusual (for example when a mule bore young, or lightning struck an object), have made conjectures of their own and committed them to writing as if rules.

Chapter 24

(37) All these omens are effective only to the extent that they have been agreed upon with the demons through presumption of mind, like some language possessed in common. Yet, they are all laden with a destructive curiosity, tormenting solicitude, and a fatal slavery. They were not noticed because they had any value, but they became significant because they were noticed and marked out as signs. For this reason they have different meanings for different people, according to their opinions and suppositions. Those evil spirits, wishing to deceive, procure for each such signs as those which they observe have ensnared him through his own suspicions and agreements. For example, the same letter X, which is written in the form of a cross, has one meaning among the Greeks and another among the Latins. This is not because of its nature, but because of agreement and common accord as to its meaning. Consequently, anyone who understands both languages would not use this letter in writing to

a Greek with the same meaning as he would if he wrote to a Latin. *Beta,* although it is pronounced the same way, is to the Greeks the name of a letter, but it is a vegetable to the Latins. From the two syllables of *lege* a Greek takes one meaning, a Latin another. Consequently, just as all these signs impress men's minds according to the common agreement of each one's own community and, because there is a diversity of agreement, they impress people differently. Therefore, men did not agree upon them because they intrinsically possessed their meaning; they have a meaning because men have agreed upon them. So, too, those signs which are the basis of an evil alliance with demons are significant according to each person's ideas. The usage of the augurs illustrates this very clearly. Both before and after they observe the omens, they are careful not to observe the flight or listen to the cries of birds, whose actions are insignificant signs unless the opinion of the observer agrees with them.

Chapter 25

(38) After these superstitions have been severed and eradicated from the mind of a Christian, we must examine human practices that are not superstitious. By this I mean those that have not been arranged with demons but with men themselves. All practices which have meaning among men, simply because they have decided that they should, are human ordinances. Some of these are unnecessary and excessive; others are useful and indispensable. Suppose the signs made by actors while dancing had a natural meaning, and not one derived from the arrangement and agreement of men. Then, in ancient times the public crier would not have narrated to the people of Carthage, while the panto-

mime was dancing, what meaning the dancer intended to convey. (Many old men still remember this practice and I used to listen to their recital of it.) This is plausible. Even now, if someone unacquainted with such trifles enters the theater, unless the meaning of these movements is explained to him, he wastes his attention upon them. However, everyone strives for some similarity in making signs, so that the signs themselves may resemble the things they indicate as much as possible. But, since one thing may be like another in many ways, such signs are not consistent among men, unless common agreement approves them.

(39) In the case of paintings, statues, and other imitative works of this nature, however, especially those of skilled artists, no one seeing the likenesses errs in identifying the originals. This entire group must be considered among the unnecessary institutions of men, except when it is important to know in regard to any one them, why, where, when, or under whose authority it was produced. Finally, the thousands of imagined fables and falsities, whose untruths charm men, are human institutions. Nothing should be judged more characteristic of men and derived from themselves than whatever is deceitful and mendacious.[1] But, the useful and indispensable institutions of men with men include all the differences that seemed proper in dress and adornment of the body in order to differentiate sex and dignity; the numerable kinds of signs without which human society either is not managed at all or is not managed skillfully; also whatever weights and measures, stamping and weighing of coins are proper to each state and nation, and other practices of this kind. If these had not been the arrangements of men,

---

1 John 8.44.

they would not have been different for different nations. They also would not be altered in separate nations themselves, according to the judgment of their own rulers.

(40) A Christian, however, is certainly not to shun this whole division of human institutions which are helpful for the necessary intercourse of life. Instead, he should even give a sufficient degree of attention to them and remember them.

Chapter 26

Some human institutions are imperfect semblances and in some way likenesses of real things. Those which concern alliance with demons must be completely cast off and abhorred, as I have said; those which men use with other men must be adopted, as far as they are not excessive and unnecessary. These are, especially, the forms of letters, without which we cannot read, and a sufficient diversity of languages, of which I treated previously. In this class also are shorthand characters; those who are familiar with them are now properly called shorthand writers. These are useful forms of knowledge and they are not learned in a forbidden manner or connected with any superstition. Nor do these forms weaken us through any excess, provided that they engross our attention only to the extent that they are not a hindrance to the nobler things which they ought to help us acquire.

Chapter 27

(41) But we must not consider as human arrangements, everywhere we learn about them, those things which men have recorded, not because they organized them, but because they recognized them either as the work of time or the

dispositions of divine Providence. Some of these affect the senses of the body; others, the reason. But, those which are reached by the senses we either believe after they have been explained to us, or observe after they have been shown to us, or interpret after we have experienced them.

Chapter 28

(42) Therefore, whatever that science called history teaches us about the order of past events is a very important help to us. Through it we are aided in understanding the Sacred Books, even though we learn it outside the Church through our study as children. We often seek information on many points by using the Olympiads and the names of the consuls. An ignorance of the consulship in which the Lord was born and of that in which He suffered has caused some to make the mistake of believing that He suffered His Passion when He was forty-six years old. This is because the Jews maintained that the temple, which was a figure of His Body, was in the process of being built for that number of years.[1] We know from the authority of the Gospel that He was baptized when He was about thirty years old.[2] It is possible for us to compute how many years He lived after that from the sequence of His actions. Yet, in order that no shadow of doubt may come from any other source, we determine it more plainly and more accurately by comparing the history of the pagan nations with the Gospel. It will then be obvious that there was some reason for the statement that the temple was in building for forty-six years; since that number cannot be related to the Lord's age, it may be concerned with a more hidden teaching about the human

---

1 John 2.20; cf. Ps. Cypr. *De monte Sina et Sion* 4; Lact. *Div. Inst.* 4.18.4.
2 Luke 3.23.

body. For, with this body the only Son of God, through whom all things were made,³ did not disdain to clothe Himself for our sake.

(43) In connection with the usefulness of history, to pass over the Greeks, what a troublesome controversy our Ambrose has settled for the readers and devoted followers of Plato! They slanderously dared to say that all the maxims of the Lord Jesus Christ, which they are forced to respect and acclaim, were learned by Him from the works of Plato, since it cannot be denied that Plato lived a long time before the human coming of the Lord. When that renowned bishop learned from his study of pagan history that, in the time of Jeremias, Plato had traveled to Egypt while the prophet was there, did he not prove that it was more probable that Plato had been initiated into our literature through Jeremias? As a result, he was capable of teaching and writing those things which are justly held in esteem.⁴ Not even Pythagoras himself, from whose disciples these men claim that Plato learned theology, lived before the time of the literature of the Hebrew nation. It was in this people that the worship of one God originated, and from it the Lord came 'according to the flesh.'⁵ So, through a study of dates, it is much more credible that those men obtained from our literature anything they said that was noble and truthful, rather than that the Lord Jesus Christ learned from the works of Plato, which it is the utmost madness to suppose.

(44) Further, when the past arrangements of men are recounted in historical narration, we must not consider

---

3 John 1.3.
4 See Introduction, p. 4
5 Rom. 9.4-5.

history itself among those human institutions. For, things which have now passed away and cannot be revoked must be considered to be in the order of time, whose Creator and Administrator is God. It is one thing to relate what has been done, but another to teach what should be done. History reports honestly and profitably what has been accomplished. On the other hand, books of the soothsayers and all similar writings endeavor to teach what should be done or heeded, with the presumption of an instructor and not with the reliability of a guide.

Chapter 29

(45) There is also a kind of narration similar to description, which reveals to the inexperienced not past events, but present circumstances. In this class is included everything that has been written about the location of places and the natures of animals, trees, plants, minerals, and other bodies. I spoke about this class before and taught that this knowledge is valuable in explaining the mysteries of the Scriptures, not that they are to be employed according to certain signs like charms or devices of some superstition. That type I have already distinguished from this lawful and unrestricted kind. It is one thing to say: 'If you drink the juice crushed from this herb, your stomach will not pain you'; and quite another to say: 'If you hang this herb around your neck, your stomach will not pain you.' In the first instance, a suitable and salutary mixture is recommended; in the second, a superstitious token deserves censure. And yet, where there are no enchantments, invocations, or characters, we can ask these questions. Is the object which is tied or fastened in any way to the body for the restoration of its health efficacious by virtue of its own nature? (If so, we may use this remedy unrestrictedly.)

Or, does it succeed because of some signifying bond? The more effectually this seems to do good, all the more cautiously should the Christian beware of it. But, when we do not know the reason for the efficacy of a thing, the intention for which it is used is important so far as concerns the cure or alleviation of bodies, whether in medicine or in agriculture.

(46) However, it is not narration, but rather description, that gives us a knowledge of the stars, of which Scripture mentions very few. Where the course of the moon, which is even regularly used in annually commemorating the Lord's Passion, is well known to many people, only a very few know either well or accurately the rising, setting, or other movements of the rest of the stars. This knowledge in itself, although it does not imply a connection with a superstition, nevertheless helps our treatment of the Sacred Scriptures only a little and practically not at all. It is more of an obstacle, because our application to it is useless. Also, since it is allied to the extremely dangerous fallacy of those who utter foolish prediction, it is more profitable and more virtuous to despise it. Besides a description of present circumstances, this science includes something similar to a narration of past events as well, because from the present location and movement of the stars we can, according to rule, trace even their past courses. It also includes consistent inferences about future events that are not suspiciously ominous, but rather accurately calculated. We may not attempt to learn anything from them about our own deeds and their consequences, like the absurdities of the composers of horoscopes, but only what relates to the stars themselves. When anyone who makes calculations about the moon has discovered its size today, he can assert how large it was as many years before as you like, or how large it will be in so

many years from now. In the same way, those who are experienced in calculating the stars are accustomed to reply about any of them. I have revealed my opinion about this whole division of knowledge so far as its use is concerned.

Chapter 30

(47) Of the other arts, some are concerned with fashioning something which endures as an effect of the laborer's work, such as a house, a bench, a dish, or anything else of this nature; others display a sort of assistance to God in His works, like medicine, agriculture, and government; there are others whose whole purpose is action, as dancing, running, and wrestling. In all these arts, experience causes us to infer the future from the past. For, no skilled worker in these arts moves his limbs in any operation without uniting the remembrance of past events to his hopes for future ones. In this life we are to apply our knowledge of these arts in a superficial and cursory fashion, so that we do not devote ourselves to them (unless, perhaps, some obligation requires it, and I am not discussing this point now). We do apply ourselves, however, that we may appreciate them. Thus, we will not be completely unaware of what Scripture wishes to suggest when it introduces figurative expressions from these arts.

Chapter 31

(48) There are left, now, those institutions which concern not the senses of the body, but the intellect, where the sciences of reasoning and of numbers have the mastery. The science of reasoning is very valuable in penetrating and answering all kinds of disputed points which are found in

the sacred writings. However, there we must beware of an inclination to wrangle and a certain puerile pretension of deluding our opponent. There are many deceitful conclusions of reasoning called sophisms. These so closely resemble true ones that they mislead not only stupid persons, but even those who are quick of apprehension, when they are not carefully attentive. For instance, a certain person stated this premise to the man to whom he was talking: 'You are not what I am.' The other agreed, because the statement was partly true, or because the one was subtle, while the other was guileless. Then the first man continued: 'I am a man.' When the other agreed to this also, he concluded: 'Therefore, you are not a man.' As far as I can judge, Holy Scripture abominates this type of deceptive conclusions, according to the passage which says:[1] 'He that speaketh sophistically, is hateful.' However, a manner of speaking which is not deceptive, but still strives after verbal embellishments in more abundance than is suitable for seriousness, is also called sophistical.

(49) There are also correct modes of reasoning which result in false ways of thinking because they are the logical consequences of the fallacy of the person with whom one is disputing. These conclusions are drawn by a good and learned man so that the person, of whose error they are the consequence, blushing over them, may abandon that error. For if he wishes to maintain it, he is also inevitably compelled to hold to those conclusions which he censures. For instance, the Apostle was not introducing true conclusions when he said:[2] 'Neither has Christ risen,' and also: 'vain then is our preaching, vain too is your faith,' and so on with others.

---
[1] Eccli. 37.23.
[2] 1 Cor. 15.13,14.

These are all entirely false, because Christ has risen and the preaching of those who announced this truth was not vain, and neither was the faith of those who believe it vain. Those false conclusions were reasonably linked to that proposition which maintained that there was no resurrection of the dead. Since these conclusions were true on condition that the dead do not rise, when they have been rejected as false, the consequence will be the resurrection of the dead. Therefore, since there are true conclusions not only of truthful, but also of false, propositions, it is easy to learn the real nature of logical sequence even in those schools which are outside the Church. However, the true nature of propositions must be traced out in the Sacred Books of the Church.

Chapter 32

(50) However, the true nature of logical conclusions has not been arranged by men; rather they studied and took notice of it so that they might be able either to learn or to teach it. It is perpetual in the order of things and divinely ordained. The person who relates the chronological order of events does not arrange it himself; the person who makes known the location of places and the natures of animals, plants, or minerals, does not reveal things instituted by men; and he who describes the stars and their movements is not describing his own or any other man's creation. So, too, the man speaks very truthfully who says: 'When the conclusion is false, it is inevitable that the proposition also is false.' But he himself does not cause it to be true; he only shows that it is. The quotation I gave from the Apostle Paul originates from this rule. The proposition was that there was no resurrection of the dead; those whose error the Apostle wished to destroy maintained this. The necessary conclusion

of that proposition which said that there was no resurrection of the dead was: 'Neither has Christ risen.' But this conclusion is false, for Christ has risen; therefore the proposition is invalid. But, the proposition was that there is no resurrection of the dead. Therefore, there is a resurrection of the dead. This whole syllogism is stated briefly as follows: 'If there is no resurrection of the dead, neither has Christ risen. But Christ has risen; therefore, there is a resurrection of the dead.' Men have not established, but only expressed, this principle, that, when the consequence is invalidated, the proposition is also necessarily disproved. This rule applies to the logical truth of conclusions, but not to the absolute truth of principles.

Chapter 33

(51) However, in the discussion about the resurrection, the rule of the conclusion and the judgment reached in the conclusion are true. There is authenticity of conclusion from invalid propositions in this way: We may assume that someone has agreed: 'If a snail is an animal, it has a voice.' Since he concedes this, when it has been demonstrated that the snail has no voice, the conclusion is that the snail is not an animal, because, when the conclusion is illogical, the proposition is also illogical. This judgment is unsound, but the logical sequence of the conclusion from the false premise is sound. In the same way the integrity of a proposition is intrinsically valid, but the integrity of the conclusion emanates from the belief or concession of the person with whom one is disputing. Therefore, as I said before, an incorrect conclusion may be inferred by means of a sound logical sequence, so that he whose fallacy we are anxious to rectify may regret that he has proposed premises whose

logical conclusions he perceives he must reject. Now, it is easily recognized that just as there can be logical conclusions from invalid propositions, so also can there be untenable conclusions from valid propositions. Assume that someone has advanced the proposition: 'If that man is just, he is good'; and when this was conceded, he then joined the minor proposition: 'But he is not just.' When this also was conceded, he brought forward the deduction: 'Therefore, he is not good.' Even though all those assertions are true, the authority of the conclusion is not valid. The invalidation of the premise does not necessarily involve the invalidation of the conclusion, as was the case when the negation of the conclusion unavoidably entailed that of the premise. It is correct to say: 'If he is an orator, he is a man.' But, if we negate the proposition and say: 'But he is not an orator,' the logical conclusion will not be: 'Therefore, he is not a man.'

Chapter 34

(52) Therefore, it is one thing to know the rules governing logical sequences, another to know the truth of propositions. In regard to sequences, we learn the nature of a logical, an illogical, and an inconsistent sequence. 'If he is an orator, he is a man' is a logical sequence; 'If he is a man, he is an orator' is an illogical sequence; and 'If he is a man, he is a quadruped' is an inconsistent sequence. Here, then, we form an opinion with regard to the sequence itself. However, in regard to the validity of propositions, we must judge the propositions themselves and not their logical sequence. But, when doubtful propositions are joined in a sound sequence to valid and reliable ones, it is inevitable that they themselves become incontestable. When some people have learned the true nature of logical sequences, they boast

as much as if it were the true nature of propositions. On the other hand, some, who maintain a valid proposition, erroneously have a low opinion of themselves because they do not know the principles of consequence. Yet, he who knows that there is a resurrection of the dead is a better man than the one who knows that it is a consequence that Christ has not risen, if there is no resurrection of the dead.

Chapter 35

(53) The science of definition, division, and partition, although it may often be employed even in fallacies, is not false itself; neither was it instituted by men, but was discovered in the reason of things. Poets have customarily used it for their fables; false philosophers and even heretics, that is, false Christians, for their false beliefs. Nevertheless, nothing on that account causes it to be untrue that in definition, division, and partition there is to be included nothing which does not apply to the subject, nor is anything which does apply to be excluded. This principle is true, even though the things being defined or divided may not be true. Even falsehood itself is defined by saying that it is the representation of a thing which actually in one way or another is not as it is represented. This definition is true, although falsehood cannot be true. We can also divide falsehood by saying that there are two kinds. The one consists of things that cannot be true at all, the other of things which are not true, although they could be. If someone say that seven and three are eleven, what he says cannot be true at all. But, if someone declares that it rained, say, on January first, even though it actually did not, still, what he says could have happened. Therefore, the definition and division of falsities can be completely true, although falsehoods themselves certainly are not true.

Chapter 36

(54) There are also certain principles of a more abundant kind of disputation, which is called eloquence. Although they can be employed in convincing us of falsehood, nevertheless, they themselves are true. Since they can be employed also in the service of truths, the power itself is not culpable, but the bad faith of those who misuse it is. Men did not ordain that a demonstration of regard would win over a listener, or that a brief and intelligible narration easily makes the impression at which it aims, and that its variety holds its listeners intent without any tedium. There are also other rules of this kind which are still true, whether they are employed with false or true motives. And these rules are true to the extent that they cause something to be either known or believed, or influence men's minds either to seek it or avoid it. Men discovered that these rules existed, rather than ordained that they should exist.

Chapter 37

(55) When this lesson is learned, we should apply it rather to revealing a matter we have understood than to the actual understanding of it. That science of conclusions, definitions, and divisions is a very important aid to understanding, provided that men do not make the mistake of imagining that they have learned the true nature of a happy life when they have learned those principles. Yet, it frequently happens that men more easily understand the matters for which those principles are learned than the very difficult and irritating teachings of those principles. For instance, some one is desirous of giving rules for walking. He admonishes you not to raise the foot behind you until you have put down

the other foot. Then he explains in details how you ought to move the sockets of your knee-joints. The facts he is telling you are true, and you cannot walk in any other way. Men walk more easily, however, by doing these things than they notice them as they are doing them, or understand the directions they hear. On the other hand, people who cannot walk trouble themselves much less about rules which they cannot apply through actual experience. So, an intelligent man frequently perceives more quickly that a conclusion is not valid than he learns the principles of it, while a stupid person does not perceive the fallacy, but still less does he comprehend the principles governing it. In all these principles the very semblances of truth often charm us more than they help us, either in disputing or in drawing conclusions, except, perhaps, that they cause our talents to be exercised more; if only they do not also cause those who have learned these principles to be more disposed to evil and pride, so that they either delight in deceiving others through a sophistical manner of speaking and specious questioning, or believe they have obtained something important and therefore set themselves above noble and upright men.

Chapter 38

(56) Certainly it is clear to even the most stupid person imaginable that the science of numbers was not ordained by men, but rather investigated and learned by them. Virgil[1] wanted the first syllable of *Italia* long, not short as the ancients pronounced it, and he made it so. No one can decide, however, merely because he desires it, that three times three are not nine, or do not form a square, or are not

---

1 Verg. *Aen.* 1.2.

the triple of the number three, or are not one and one half times six, or that they are the double of some number, since odd numbers do not have a half. Therefore, whether numbers are regarded in themselves or in their application to the principles of figures, sounds, or other movements, they have unchangeable rules. These were not ordained by men in any way, but were learned through the intelligence of clever men.

(57) Yet, whoever esteems all these things so highly that he wants to speak boastfully of himself among unlearned men, instead of trying to learn the source of the truth of things which he has seen are true, or the source of the truth and immutability of those which he has learned are immutable, or in advancing from the bodily appearance to the human mind, has found out that it is inconstant, sometimes learned, sometimes ignorant, but still established between Immutable Truth above it and the other changeable things below it; whoever, I say, acts in this manner and does not refer everything to the praise and love of the one God, from whom he knows that everything has come into existence, may seem to be erudite, but he can by no means be considered wise.

Chapter 39

(58) It seems to me, therefore, that it would be advantageous to instruct eager and talented young men, who fear God and strive for a happy life, that they should not rashly presume to study any sciences taught outside the Church of Christ in order to seize upon a happy life. They should rather decide upon them prudently and cautiously. Some sciences ordained by men are variable because of the diverse purposes of their authors, and obscure because of the notions of those who are in error. Should they find such,

they should completely repudiate and abhor them, especially if their authors or those in error have also formed any alliance with demons through certain pacts and agreements about signs. They should also discard the study of the unnecessary and excessive creations of men. However, because of the necessity of this life, they should not disregard those humans institutions which are of value for intercourse with their fellow men. Among the other sciences found among the pagans, however, I consider nothing beneficial except the history of either past or present events, the study of matters which concern the bodily senses, to which I would add the experiences and inferences of the useful mechanical arts, and also the sciences of reasoning and of numbers. In all these we must maintain the principle: 'Nothing in excess,'[1] but especially in those studies which, since they concern the bodily senses, occur in time and are restricted by localities.

(59) Now, some scholars have accomplished the task of interpreting, apart from their context, all the words and names in Hebrew, Syriac, Egyptian, or any other language found in the Sacred Scriptures which had been left there untranslated. Eusebius produced a history of past events because of the disputed points in the Sacred Books which demand its use. Consequently, just as these men, in matters of this kind, have made it unnecessary for a Christian to exert himself in many studies for a few facts, I believe the same thing could be done now, if there were someone capable who could be induced to devote a truly beneficial service to the advantage of his brethren. He could classify whatever unfamiliar places, animals, plants, trees, stones, metals, or other objects to which Scripture alludes. Then,

---

[1] Ter. *Andr.* 61.

after he has arranged them by classes, he should write down his explanations. He can do the same thing with regard to numbers, so that he would write down the explanation of the system of only those numbers which Holy Scripture mentions. Some of these tasks, or perhaps all of them, have been achieved already. I discovered that many, which I did not surmise, have been elaborated and written down by virtuous and learned Christians, but, either because of the multitudes of the indifferent or because of the works of the envious, they lie hidden. I do not know whether this could be done with the science of reasoning, but it seems impossible to me, because this is interwoven like strings through the whole text of the Scriptures. For this reason, it is more of a help to readers in solving and explaining ambiguities, about which I shall speak later, than in learning about unknown signs, which I am considering now.

Chapter 40

(60) Furthermore, if those who are called philosophers, especially the Platonists, have said things by chance that are truthful and conformable to our faith, we must not only have no fear of them, but even appropriate them for our own use from those who are, in a sense, their illegal possessors. The Egyptians not only had idols and crushing burdens which the people of Israel detested and from which they fled, but they also had vessels and ornaments of gold and silver, and clothing, which the Israelites leaving Egypt secretly claimed for themselves as if for a better use. Not on their own authority did they make this appropriation, but by the command of God,[1] while the Egyptians themselves, without

---
1 Exod. 3.22; 11.2; 12.35.

realizing it, were supplying the things which they were not using properly. In the same way, all the teachings of the pagans have counterfeit and superstitious notions and oppressive burdens of useless labor, which anyone of us, leaving the association of pagans with Christ as our leader, ought to abominate and shun. However, they also contain liberal instruction more adapted to the service of truth and also very useful principles about morals; even some truths about the service of the one God Himself are discovered among them. These are, in a sense, their gold and silver. They themselves did not create them, but excavated them, as it were, from some mines of divine Providence which is everywhere present, but they wickedly and unjustly misuse this treasure for the service of demons. When the Christian severs himself in spirit from the wretched association of these men, he ought to take these from them for the lawful service of preaching the Gospel. It is also right for us to receive and possess, in order to convert it to a Christian use, their clothing, that is, those human institutions suited to intercourse with men which we cannot do without in this life.

(61) For, what else have many noble and loyal members of our faith done? Do we not perceive with what an abundance of gold, silver and clothing that very eloquent teacher and blessed martyr, Cyprian, was loaded when he left Egypt? with what an abundance Lactantius was enriched, and Victorinus, Optatus, Hilary, and innumerable Greeks, not to speak of men who are still living? That most obedient servant of God, Moses himself, was the first to do this, and it was written of him that he 'was instructed in all the wisdom of the Egyptians.'[2] The superstitious custom of

---

2 Acts 7.22.

the pagans, especially at that time when, striking at the yoke of Christ, it was persecuting the Christians, would never have bestowed upon all these men sciences which it considered profitable, if it had supposed they were going to convert them to the worship of the one God, in order that the false worship of idols might be rooted out. But, they gave their gold, silver, and garments to the people of God who were leaving Egypt, not knowing how the things which they were giving would yield to 'the obedience of Christ.'[3] What happened in the exodus is undoubtedly a figure that signified the present. I assert this without prejudice to another understanding, either equal or better.

Chapter 41

(62) When the student of the Holy Scriptures, after being instructed in this manner, begins his examination of them, he should not fail to reflect upon that observation of the Apostle:[1] 'Knowledge puffs up, but charity edifies.' In that way he will realize that, although he leaves Egypt a rich man, still, unless he has observed the passover, he cannot be saved. Besides, 'Christ. our passover has been sacrificed.'[2] The most important lesson this sacrifice teaches Christians is the one that He Himself proclaimed to those whom He saw laboring as in Egypt under Pharaoh:[3] 'Come to me, you who labor and are burdened, and I will give you rest. Take my yoke upon you, and learn from me, for I am meek and humble of heart; and you will find rest for your souls.

---

3 2 Cor. 10.5.

1 1 Cor. 8.1.
2 1 Cor. 5.7.
3 Matt. 11.28-30.

For my yoke is easy, and my burden light.' To whom was He speaking, except to the meek and humble of heart, whom knowledge does not puff up, but whom charity edifies? Therefore, they are to bear in mind that those who celebrated the passover at the time through figures and shadows, when they were commanded to mark their door-post with the blood of the lamb, marked them with hyssop.[4] This is a mild and humble plant, but has very strong and penetrating roots. So, 'being rooted and grounded in love,' we may be able 'to comprehend with all the saints what is the breadth and length and height and depth,'[5] that is, the Cross of the Lord. Its breadth is signified by the transverse beam on which the hands are extended; the length from the ground to that crossbar is where the whole body from the hands down is fastened; the height, from the cross-bar up to the top which is near the head; the depth is that part which is concealed, driven into the earth. In this Sign of the Cross the whole Christian life is defined: to perform good works in Christ and cling to Him perseveringly, to aspire to heavenly goods, and not to profane the Sacraments. Cleansed by means of this action, we shall be able 'to know Christ's love which surpasses knowledge,' by which He is equal to the Father, through whom all things were made in order that we 'may be filled unto all the fullness of God.'[6] There is also a cleansing power in hyssop, lest the breast, arrogant because of the knowledge which puffs up, should boast haughtily about the riches carried away from Egypt. So the Psalmist says:[7] 'Thou shalt sprinkle me with hyssop, and I shall be cleansed. Thou shalt wash me, and I shall be made whiter than snow. To my hearing Thou

---

[4] Exod. 12.22.
[5] Eph. 3.17,18.
[6] Eph. 3.19.
[7] Ps. 50.9,10.

shalt give joy and gladness.' Then he continues in the following words to show that a cleansing from pride is signified by the hyssop: 'and the bones that have been humbled shall rejoice.'

Chapter 42

(63) Yet, all the knowledge gathered from the works of the pagans, however useful it is, when it is compared to the knowledge of Sacred Scriptures, is as inferior as the abundance of gold, silver, and clothing, which the Israelites carried out of Egypt with them, is in comparison with the wealth which they afterwards acquired at Jerusalem, especially during the rule of King Solomon.[1] Whatever a man has learned apart from Scripture is censured there, if it is harmful; if it is useful, he finds it there. And, although everyone may have found there everything which he learned profitably somewhere else, he will discover there, in much greater profusion, things which he can learn nowhere else at all, except in the admirable profundity and surprising simplicity of the Scriptures alone. Therefore, when unfamiliar signs do not ensnare the reader provided with this instruction—meek and humble of heart, easily brought under the yoke of Christ and weighed down by His light burden, grounded, rooted, and built up in love, beyond the power of knowledge to puff him up—let him advance to the study and thorough investigation of the ambiguous signs in the Scriptures. In the third book, I shall begin to say about these signs whatever our Lord will deign to grant me to say.

---

1 3 Kings 10.14ff.

BOOK THREE

Chapter 1

A MAN who fears God carefully searches for His Will in the Holy Scriptures. Gentle in his piety, so that he has no affection for wrangling; fortified by a knowledge of languages, that he may not be perplexed over unknown words and modes of expression; protected also by an appreciation of certain indispensable things, that he may not be unaware of the power and nature of those which are employed for the sake of analogy; aided, too, by the integrity of the texts which an intelligent accuracy in correction has assured;—let him approach, thus trained, to the investigation and explanation of the obscurities of the Scriptures. As a consequence, he will not be deceived by ambiguous signs, so far as I can teach him. It is possible, however, that, because of the stature of his genius or the clarity of his greater inspiration, he may laugh at, as being childish, those ways which I intend to show him. However, as I began to say, one who has such a disposition of soul that he is able to learn from me, as far as I can teach him, will understand that the ambiguity of Scripture consists in either literal or figurative use of words. I defined these classes in the second book.

Chapter 2

(2) When literal words cause Scripture to be ambiguous, our first concern must be to see that we have not punctuated

them incorrectly or mispronounced them. Then, when a careful scrutiny reveals that it is doubtful how it should be punctuated or pronounced, we must consult the rule of faith which we have learned from the clearer passages of the Scriptures and from the authority of the Church. I said enough about this matter when I discussed things in the first book. If both meanings or even all of them, if there should be several, sound obscure after recourse has been had to faith, we must consult the context of both the preceding and the following passage to ascertain which of the several meanings indicated it would consent to and permit to be incorporated with itself.

(3) Now, consider some examples. Some heretics punctuate a certain passage thus: *In principio erat verbum et verbum erat apud Deum et Deus erat,* so that the next sentence would be, *Verbum hoc erat in principio apud Deum* ['In the beginning was the Word and the Word was with God and God was.' 'This Word was in the beginning with God']. They are unwilling to acknowledge that the Word is God. This, however, must be shown to be false according to the rule of faith, which teaches us to say of the equality of the Holy Trinity:[1] *Et Deus erat verbum;* then to add: *Hoc erat in principio apud Deum.* ['and the Word was God.' 'He was in the beginning with God'].

(4) There is an obscurity of punctuation that is not opposed to faith through either interpretation and must therefore be determined from the context itself in this statement of the Apostle:[2] 'And I do not know which to choose. Indeed I am hard pressed from both sides—desiring to depart and

---

1 John 1.1.2.
2 Phil. 1.23,24.

to be with Christ, [for this is] a lot by far the better; yet to stay on in the flesh is necessary for your sake.' It is doubtful whether we are to understand *ex duobus concupiscentiam habens* ['desiring two things'] or *Compellor autem ex duobus* ['Indeed I am hard pressed from both sides'], that we may add *concupiscentiam habens dissolvi et esse cum Christo* ['desiring to depart and to be with Christ']. But, since the following words are *multo enim magis optimum* ['a lot by far the better'], it is clear that he is saying that he desires what is better, so that, although he is hard pressed from both sides, he recognizes a desire for one, but a need for the other: that is to say, a desire to be with Christ, and a necessity to stay on in the flesh. This ambiguity is decided by one word which follows and which is translated *enim* ['for']. The translators who have taken away that particle have been more influenced by the opinion that he appeared to be not only hard pressed from both sides, but that he also desired both. Consequently, we must punctuate this way: *Et quid eligam ignoro. Compellor autem ex duobus* ['And I do not know which to choose. Indeed I am hard pressed from both sides']. There follows this mark of punctuation: *concupiscentiam habens dissolvi et esse cum Christo* ['desiring to depart and to be with Christ']. And, as if he were asked why he had more of a desire of this, he says: *multo enim magis optimum* ['for this is by far the better lot']. Then, why is he hard pressed from two sides? Because there is a necessity for his staying on; so he adds this: *manere in carne necessarium propter vos* ['to stay on in the flesh is necessary for your sake'].

(5) But, when the ambiguity can be explained neither through a principle of faith nor through the context itself, there is nothing to prevent our punctuating the sentence

according to any interpretation that is made known to us. This is a case in the letter to the Corinthians:[3] 'Having therefore these promises, beloved, let us cleanse ourselves from all defilement of the flesh and of the spirit, perfecting holiness in the fear of God. Make room for us. We have wronged no one.' As a matter of fact, it is uncertain whether we should read: *Mundemus nos ab omni coinquinatione carnis et spiritus* ['Let us cleanse ourselves from all defilement of the flesh and of the spirit'], as in the passage:[4] 'that she may be holy in body and in spirit,' or whether we should read: *Mundemus nos ab omni coinquinatione carnis* ['Let us cleanse ourselves from all defilement of the flesh']. In this case, the next sentence would be: *Et spiritus perficientes sanctificationem in timore Dei, capite nos* ['And perfecting holiness of spirit in the fear of God, make room for us']. Such ambiguities of punctuation, then, are subject to the reader's judgment.

Chapter 3

(6) The same principles which I proposed for uncertain punctuations must also be followed for undetermined pronunciations. For these, also, unless the excessive negligence of the reader prevents it, are corrected either by the rules of faith or by the preceding or succeeding context. Or, if neither of these is employed in correcting, they will still remain undetermined, but in such a way that, no matter how the reader pronounces them, he will not be to blame. For, if faith, by which we believe that God will not call His elect to account and that Christ will not condemn His elect, did not restrain us, we might pronounce the passage: 'Who shall

---

[3] 2 Cor. 7.1,2.
[4] 1 Cor. 7.34.

make accusation against the elect of God?' in such a way that what follows this question is like an answer: 'It is God who justifies.' There would, then, be another question: 'Who shall condemn?' and the answer would be: 'It is Christ Jesus who died.'[1] Since it is utter folly to believe this, we shall pronounce it in such a way that the first sentence will be a question for information and the second a rhetorical question.[2] The ancients maintained that the difference between an ordinary question and a rhetorical question was that many replies are possible to an ordinary question, but to a rhetorical question the reply is either 'No' or 'Yes.' Accordingly, we shall pronounce this passage in such a way that, after the ordinary question: 'Who shall make accusation against the elect of God?' what follows will be pronounced interrogatively: 'Is it God who justifies?' so that the answer 'No' is implied. In the same way we should inquire: 'Who shall condemn?' And again we reply interrogatively: 'Is it Christ Jesus who died: yes, and rose again, He who is at the right hand of God, who also intercedes for us?' so that the answer 'No' is implied in both these questions. However, there is that other passage:[3] 'What then shall we say? That the Gentiles who were not pursuing justice have secured justice.' If, after the question: 'What then shall we say?' the following answer were not added: 'That the Gentiles who were not pursuing justice have secured justice,' the following context would not be in harmony. I do not see how it can be determined with what inflection we are to pronounce that

---

1 Rom. 8.33,34.
2 *Percontatio* and *interrogatio*. For a classical treatment on the former, cf. Quintilian *Inst. or.* 9.1.29; 9.2.6; on the latter, cf. *id.* 9.2.15; 9.3.98; cf. also Cicero *De or.* 3.53.203, quoted by Quintilian in the first passage here noted.
3 Rom. 9.30.

question of Nathaniel's:[4] 'Can anything good come out of Nazareth?' Should it be said with the tone of one who asserts, so that 'out of Nazareth' is the only thing that involves a question, or should the whole thing be expressed with the uncertainty of one who questions? However, neither meaning hampers our faith.

(7) There is uncertainty, also, in the doubtful sound of syllables, and this certainly concerns pronunciation. For example, we have this quotation:[5] 'My bone [*os meum*] is not hidden from Thee, which Thou hast made in secret.' It is not apparent to the reader whether he should pronounce *os* with a short vowel or a long one. If he makes it short, it is the singular of *ossa* ['bones']; if he makes it long, it is the singular of *ora* ['mouths']. Such matters can be decided, however, by an investigation of the original language. In Greek it was expressed not *stóma* ['mouth'], but *ostéon* ['bone']. As a consequence, the ordinary idiom of speech is often more helpful in expressing a thought than learned diction is. In fact, I would prefer it expressed as a barbarism: *Non est absconditum a te ossum meum,* rather than have it be less intelligible because it is purer Latin. Sometimes the dubious sound of a syllable is determined by a similar word referring to the same meaning. For instance, there is that statement by the Apostle:[6] 'Concerning these I warn you [*praedico*] as I have warned you [*praedixi*], that they who do such things will not attain the kingdom of God.' If he had said only: *quae praedico vobis* ['Concerning these I warn you'], and had not added: *sicut praedixi* ['as I have warned you'], we would not know, unless we had resorted

---
4 John 1.46.
5 Ps. 138.15.
6 Gal. 5.21.

to the original text, whether the middle syllable in *praedico* should be long or short. It is evident that it should be pronounced long, however, because he did not say *sicut praedicavi*, but *sicut praedixi*.⁷

Chapter 4

(8) We must consider in the same way not only difficulties like these, but also obscurities which are not concerned with punctuation or pronunciation. Such an obscurity is found in the Epistle to the Thessalonians:¹ *Propterea consolati sumus fratres in vobis* ['We have accordingly found comfort in you, brethren']. It is uncertain whether *fratres* ['brethren'] is in the vocative or the accusative case.² Neither of these is opposed to faith, but, in the Greek language, these cases are not alike in form; so, when that text has been examined, the case of *fratres* is found to be vocative. But, if the translator had been willing to say: *Propterea consolationem habuimus, fratres, in vobis,* his translation would not have been so literal, but there would have been less uncertainty about the meaning. Or, of course, had he added *nostri,* practically no one would have doubted that the word was vocative case, when he heard: *Propterea consolati sumus, fratres nostri, in vobis.* However, it is rather dangerous to venture this. It has been done in that passage to the Corinthians in which the Apostle says:³ *Quotidie morior, per vestram gloriam, fratres, quam habeo in Christo Jesu* ['I

---

7 *Praedico,* with a short middle syllable, would mean 'publish' or 'commend.'

---

1 Thess. 3.7.
2 With *fratres* taken in the accusative, the meaning would have been: 'We have accordingly comforted the brethren among you.'
3 1 Cor. 15.31.

die daily, I affirm it, by the very pride that I take in you, brethren, in Christ Jesus']. One translator has said: *Quotidie morior, per vestram juro gloriam,* because in Greek a word of adjuration is evident without any ambiguous sound. Consequently, so far as the books of the Sacred Scriptures are concerned, it is very seldom and with great difficulty that we can discover an ambiguity in literal words that cannot be explained either by the context, from which we discover the purpose of the authors, by a comparison of translators, or by an examination of the original language.

Chapter 5

(9) The obscurities of figurative words, which I must discuss next, require extraordinary attention and persistence. First of all, we must be careful not to take a figurative expression literally. What the Apostle said has reference to this: 'The letter kills, but the spirit gives life.'[1] When a figurative expression is understood as if it were literal, it is understood carnally. And nothing is more appropriately named the death of the soul[2] than that which causes the quality in the soul which makes it superior to beasts (that is, its intelligence) to be subjected to the flesh by a close conformity to the literal sense. A man who conforms to the literal meaning considers figurative words as if they are literal and does not transfer what is signified by a literal word to its other sense. If he hears about the Sabbath, for example, he thinks only of one day out of the seven which are repeated in continuous sequence. When he hears of sacrifice, his thoughts do not rise above the usual sacrifices of victims of the flocks and the fruits of the earth. It is a wretched slavery of soul, indeed, to be

---
1 2 Cor. 3.6.
2 Rom. 8.5,6.

satisfied with signs instead of realities, and not be able to elevate the eye of the mind above sensible creation to drink in eternal light.

Chapter 6

(10) Nevertheless, this slavery of the Jewish people was far different from the usual one of other nations, since the Jews were indeed subjected to temporal things, but in such a way that the one God was honored in all these things. And, although they observed the symbols of spiritual things instead of the things themselves, unaware of what they represented, they yet considered it a settled fact that by such servitude they were pleasing the one God of all, whom they did not see. The Apostle wrote that this subjection is like that of little children under a tutor.[1] And so, those who adhered stubbornly to such symbols could not tolerate the Lord's disdain for those things when the time of their revelation had come. For that reason, their leaders stirred up malicious accusations that He healed on the Sabbath, and the people, bound to those signs as if to realities, did not believe that He, Who was unwilling to give heed to the signs as they were observed by the Jews, either was God or had come from God.[2] Those who believed and of whom the first Church at Jerusalem was composed, however, have clearly shown how great a benefit it was to have been so guarded under a tutor that the symbols, which had been imposed temporarily upon those in servitude, bound to the worship of the one God who made heaven and earth the belief of those who respected those symbols. In the temporal and carnal sacrifices and symbols, even though they did not know how

---
1 Gal. 3.24f; 4.1.
2 John 9.14ff.

to interpret them in a spiritual sense, they had learned to worship the one, eternal God, and were very close to spiritual things. For this reason, they were so docile to the Holy Ghost that they sold all their possessions and laid the price of them 'at the feet' of the Apostles to be distributed to the needy,[3] and they dedicated themselves entirely to God as a new temple, of which the old temple they were honoring was an earthly figure.

(11) It has not been recorded that any churches of pagan nations did this, because those who had as their gods idols made by hand had not been found so near[4] the truth.

Chapter 7

If at any time any of them tried to explain those images as symbols, they applied them to the worship and veneration of a created thing. For what good it is to me that the representation of Neptune, for instance, should not be esteemed as a god itself, but only as a signification of the entire ocean or even all other waters which gush forth from springs? He is represented in this way by one of their poets who says (if I recall correctly):[1] 'O, Father Neptune, whose hoary temples crowned resound with the roaring sea, from whose beard eternally flows the vast ocean, and in whose hair wander the rivers.' This pod shakes rattling beans inside an agreeable husk. Yet, this is not food for men, but for swine.[2] He who knows the Gospel knows what I am maintaining. For, what

---

3 Acts 4.34f.
4 Eph. 2.17.

---

1 The author of these lines is not known.
2 Luke 15.16.

good is it to me that the statue of Neptune is represented with that meaning, except, perhaps, that I would not worship either representation? For no statue, nor even the entire sea, is God to me. Still, I acknowledge that those who regard the creations of men as gods have descended to lower depths than those who deify the creations of God. We, on the contrary, have been taught to love and worship the one God[3] who made all these things, the likeness of which others nations venerate either as gods or as symbols and images of gods. Hence, we know that it is carnal slavery to observe a symbol ordained as a benefit instead of the thing itself which it was arranged to symbolize. How much worse is it, then, to be satisfied with symbols arranged for unprofitable things, instead of with the things themselves? If you correlate these symbols to those things which are indicated by them and devote your mind to the worship of these, you will still not be liberated from the oppression and garb of a carnal slavery.

Chapter 8

(12) For this reason, Christian liberty took those whom it discovered subject to useful signs, those who were discovered near[1] it, in a sense, and interpreting the symbols to which they had been subjugated, made them free by elevating them to the realities of which those are but signs. Of such men the Churches of the faithful Israelites were composed. For those whom it discovered subject to unprofitable signs, however, it not only repealed their humiliating labor under such signs, but even canceled those very symbols and set them all aside. In this way, the pagans were converted from

---
3 Deut. 6.5.

1 Eph. 2.17.

the debasement of a multitude of false gods, which Holy Scripture often and accurately terms fornication, to the worship of the one God. They were not now to become subject to useful signs, but rather to train their intellects in the spiritual discernment of them.

Chapter 9

(13) He who produces or worships any symbol, unaware of what it means, is enslaved to a sign. On the other hand, he who either uses or esteems a beneficial sign, divinely established, whose efficacy and meaning he knows, does not worship this visible and transitory sign; he worships rather that reality, to which all such symbols must be ascribed. Besides, such a man is spiritual and free even during the period of his slavery, when it is not yet advisable to unveil to his mind, carnal as it is, those signs by whose yoke it is to be completely subdued. Such spiritual men as these were the patriarchs, prophets, and all those among the people of Israel, through whom the Holy Ghost gave us the remedies and comforts of the Scriptures. At present, since the evidence of our freedom has been made so clearly apparent in the Resurrection of the Lord, we are not burdened with the heavy labor of even those signs which we understand now. The Lord Himself and apostolic tradition have transmitted a few observances, instead of many, and these are very easy to fulfill, very venerable in their meaning, and most sublime in practice. Examples of these are the sacrament of Baptism and the celebration of the Body and Blood of the Lord. When anyone who has been instructed observes these practices, he understands to what they refer, so that he does not venerate them in a carnal slavery, but rather in a spiritual liberty. Besides, as it is a humiliating infirmity to conform

to the letter and be satisfied with symbols, instead of the realities represented by them, so it is sad delusion on our part to interpret symbols in a useless way. However, a person who does not understand what a symbol means, but still knows that it is a symbol, is not oppressed with slavery. It is preferable even to be subject to unknown but useful signs, rather than, by interpreting them incorrectly, to release one's neck from the yoke of slavery only to entangle it in the snares of delusion.

Chapter 10

(14) To this precept, in accord with which we are careful not to consider a figurative or transferred form of speech as if it were literal, we must also add another: That we are not to attempt to interpret a literal expression as if it were figurative. Therefore, I must first point out the method of making sure whether a passage is literal or figurative. In general, that method is to understand as figurative anything in Holy Scripture which cannot in a literal sense be attributed either to an upright character or to a pure faith. Uprightness of character pertains to the love of God and of our neighbor; purity of faith, to the knowledge of God and our neighbor. Further, everyone's hope is in his own conscience, so far as he knows that he is advancing in the love and knowledge of God and his neighbor. All these things I discussed in the first book.

(15) Since human nature is inclined to appraise sins not by the measure of their malice, but, instead, by the measure of its own customs, it often happens that a man considers as reprehensible only those acts which the men of his own country and age usually protest against and denounce; and

he holds as acceptable and commendable only those allowed by the usage of those with whom he lives. The result is that, if Scripture either teaches something which is at variance with the custom of its listeners, or censures what is not at variance, they consider it a figurative expression, provided that the authority of its word has a hold upon their minds. But, Scripture commands only charity, and censures only lust, and in that manner moulds the character of men. Also, if a belief in some fallacy has impregnated their minds, men consider whatever Scripture has maintained differently as figurative. But it teaches only the Catholic faith in relation to things past, future, and present. It is a history of the past, a prediction of the future, and a delineation of the present. All these are effective in cultivating and invigorating charity and in vanquishing and destroying lust.

(16) I define charity as a motion of the soul whose purpose is to enjoy God for His own sake and one's self and one's neighbor for the sake of God. Lust, on the other hand is a motion of the soul bent upon enjoying one's self, one's neighbor, and any creature without reference to God. The action of unbridled lust in demoralizing one's own soul and body is called vice; what it does to harm another is called crime. These are the two classes of sin as a whole, but vices are first. When these have weakened the soul and brought it to a kind of destitution, it leaps into crimes in order to eliminate impediments to its vices or procure help for them. Likewise, what charity does for one's own benefit is utility; what it does for our neighbor's good is called kindness. In this case, utility leads the way, for no one can give another a benefit from a supply which he does not have. The more the power of lust is destroyed, the more the power of charity is strengthened.

Chapter 11

(17) Whatever harshness and apparent cruelty in deed and word we read of in the Holy Scriptures as used by God or His saints is efficacious in destroying the power of lust. If it speaks plainly, we must not refer it to another significance as if it were a figurative expression. This passage from the Apostle is an example:[1] 'Thou dost treasure up to thyself wrath on the day of wrath and of the revelation of the just judgment of God, who will render to every man according to his works. Life eternal indeed He will give to those who by patience in good works seek glory and honor and immortality; but wrath and indignation to those who are contentious, and who do not submit to the truth but assent to iniquity. Tribulation and anguish shall be visited upon the soul of every man who works evil; of Jew first and then of Greek.' This is spoken to those who refused to conquer lust and are being destroyed along with it. However, when the power of lust is destroyed in a man whom it used to dominate, this passage is clear:[2] 'And they who belong to Jesus Christ have crucified their flesh with its passions, and desires.' Even in these instances some figurative words are employed, for instance, the 'wrath' of God and 'crucified.' Yet, there are not so many nor are they used in such a way that they conceal the meaning and create an allegory or an obscurity, which I term properly a figurative expression. On the other hand, consider the following, spoken to Jeremias:[3] 'Lo, I have set thee this day over the nations, and over kingdoms, to root up, and to pull down, and to waste, and to destroy.'

---

[1] Rom. 2.5-9.
[2] Gal. 5.24.
[3] Jer. 1.10.

Undoubtedly, the whole expression is figurative and must be attributed to that purpose which I have mentioned.

Chapter 12

(18) The things which seem almost wicked to the unenlightened, whether they are only words or whether they are even deeds, either of God or of men whose sanctity is commended to us—these are entirely figurative. Their latent kernels of meaning must be extracted as food for charity. Now, anyone who makes use of perishable things with more restraint than is characteristic of those among whom he lives is either temperate or superstitious. On the contrary, anyone who uses them in such a way that he exceeds the limits customary with the good men among whom he lives is either expressing something by signs or is sinful. For, in all such cases, it is not the use of the things, but the lust of the one who is using them, that is at fault. Under no circumstances would any reasonable person imagine that the Lord's feet were anointed with precious ointment by the woman[1] for the same reason that was customary for sensual and dissolute men whose banquets were such that we loathe them. In that case the good odor[2] is the good reputation which each one will possess by the works of good life, as long as he follows the footsteps of Christ, and, as it were, anoints His feet with very precious ointment. Hence, what is frequently sinful in other persons is a symbol of some sublime truth in the person of God or a prophet. Certainly union with an adulteress is one thing in the case of corrupt morals, but it is another in the case of the prophesying of the prophet

---

[1] John 12.3; Luke 7.37.
[2] 2 Cor. 2.15.

Osee.³ If it is shameful to strip the body at banquets of the drunken and lascivious, it is not for that reason sinful to be naked in the baths.

(19) Consequently, we must prudently take into account what is proper for places, circumstances, and persons, so that we may not indiscreetly convict them of sin. It is possible for a wise man to eat the most delicious food without any sin of sensuality or gluttony, while a fool is ravenous for the meanest food with a raging hunger that is most unseemly. Any sane man would rather eat fish as the Lord did, than eat lentils as did Esau,⁴ Abraham's grandson, or barley the way oxen do. The fact that they are fed upon coarser food does not indicate that most animals are more self-restrained than we. For, in all cases of this kind, it is not the quality of the things we use, but our motive in using them and our way of striving for them, that causes our actions to be either commendable or reprehensible.

(20) Upright men of former times represented and foretold the kingdom of heaven under the guise of an earthly kingdom. Since it was in order to provide sufficiently numerous descendants, the practice of one man having several wives at the same time⁵ was unobjectionable. But the same reason did not make it virtuous for one woman to have several husbands. A woman is not more fruitful for that reason, but, on the contrary, it is gross shamelessness to strive for either profit or children by prostitution. In regard to practices like these, Holy Scripture does not condemn anything the holy men of those ages did that was uninfluenced

---

3 Osee 1.2.
4 Luke 24.43; Gen. 25.34.
5 Gen. 16.3.

by lust, even though they did things which could only be done in our times through lust. And anything of such a kind that is there related is understood not only in its historical and literal application, but also in its figurative and prophetic implication, and must always be interpreted toward that purpose of charity, whether it pertains to God, our neighbor, or both. It was a disgrace among the ancient Romans to wear tunics that reached to the ankles and had long sleeves; now it is unseemly for those of noble birth, when they wear tunics, not to have that kind. Just so we must notice in using other things, too, that we must keep aloof from lust; for, not only does it wickedly abuse the custom of those among whom we live, but often, even exceeding limits of custom, exposes in a very shameful upheaval its own foulness, which was hidden within the cover of established morality.

Chapter 13

(21) Further, whatever is in harmony with the usage of those with whom we must spend this life, because it is either necessary or our duty to do so, must be applied by pious and noble men to utility and kindness, either literally, as is our obligation, or figuratively, as is permitted to the prophets.

Chapter 14

(22) When men, ignorant of any other manner of living, happen to read about these deeds, unless they are deterred by an authority, they consider them sins. They cannot understand that their own entire mode of living, in connection with marriage, banqueting, dress, and the other necessities and refinements of human life, seems sinful to people of other nations and other times. Aroused by this diversity of

innumerable customs, some souls, drowsy so to speak, who were neither settled in the sound sleep of folly nor able to waken fully to the light of wisdom, have thought that justice did not exist of itself, but that each nation regarded as right that which was its own custom. Since this or that custom is different for every nation, while justice must remain immutable, it becomes evident that there is no justice anywhere. They have not understood (not to multiply instances) that the maxim,[1] 'Do not do to another what you do not wish to have done to you,' cannot be varied in any way by any national diversity of customs. When this rule is applied to the love of God, all vices die; when it is applied to the love of our neighbor, all crimes vanish. No one wants to despoil his own house. Therefore, he should not dishonor the house of God, namely, himself. Further, no one is willing to be injured by another; then, neither should he himself harm anyone.

Chapter 15

(23) When the tyranny of lust has been brought low, charity rules with its eminently righteous laws of the love of God for His own sake, and the love of one's self and one's neighbor for the sake of God. In figurative expressions, therefore, a rule like this is to be heeded; to reflect with careful consideration for a long time upon what is being read until the interpretation is drawn over to the sway of charity. If it now has this meaning literally, it is not to be regarded as a figurative expression.

---

1 Acts 15.20,29 (*lect. var.*); Tob. 4.16.

Chapter 16

(24) If the passage is didactic, either condemning vice, or crime, or prescribing utility or kindness, it is not figurative. But, if it appears to prescribe vice or crime, or to condemn utility or kindness, it is figurative. The Lord said:[1] 'Unless you eat the flesh of the Son of Man, and drink His blood, you shall not have life in you.' This seems to prescribe a crime or a vice; therefore, it is a figure of speech directing that we are to participate in the Lord's passion and treasure up in grateful and salutary remembrance the fact that His flesh was crucified and wounded for us. Scripture says:[2] 'If thy enemy is hungry, give him food; if he is thirsty, give him drink.' This undoubtedly prescribes a kindness, but the part that follows—'For by so doing thou wilt heap coals of fire upon his head,'—you might suppose was commanding a crime of malevolence. So, do not doubt that it is a figurative expression. Although it can have a two-fold interpretation, by one intending harm, by the other intending a good, charity should call you away from the former to kindness, so that you may understand that the coals of fire are the burning lamentations of repentance by which that man's pride is healed and he grieves that he has been an enemy of the man who relieves his misery. And so, when the Lord said:[3] 'He who loves his life, shall lose it,' He must not be interpreted as condemning the utility with which everyone ought to preserve his life. He must be interpreted, instead, as saying figuratively: 'Let him lose his life'; that is, let him cut off and lose the bad and irregular use of his life which

---

1 John 6.54.
2 Prov. 25.21,22; Rom. 12.20.
3 John 12.25.

he is now making and by which he is inclined to temporal things and kept from seeking eternal goods. It is written:[4] 'Give to the merciful and uphold not the sinner.' The end of this sentence seems to condemn kindness, for it says: 'uphold not the sinner.' You should understand that 'sinner' is set down figuratively instead of 'sin,' so that it is his sin that you are not to uphold.

Chapter 17

(25) It often happens, further, that someone who is on a higher level of the spiritual life, or thinks he is, considers the things which have been enjoined upon those on lower levels as figurative. For instance, if he has embraced a life of celibacy and made himself a eunuch 'for the kingdom of heaven's sake,'[1] he argues that whatever the Sacred Books teach about loving and governing a wife[2] should not be accepted literally, but figuratively. And if anyone 'has decided to keep his virgin'[3] unmarried, he attempts to interpret as figurative the passage which says:[4] 'Marry thy daughter, and thou shalt do a great work.' Therefore, among the principles for understanding the Scriptures, there will also be this one: that we are to understand that some injunctions are given to everyone in general, but others are given to individuals and certain classes of persons, in order that the medicine may conduce not only to the general state of well-being, but also to the peculiar infirmity of each member.

---

4 Eccli. 12.4.

1 Matt. 19.12.
2 Eph. 5.25. al.
3 1 Cor. 7.37.
4 Eccli. 7.27.

For, what cannot be elevated to a higher level must be attended to in its own condition.

Chapter 18

(26) We must also be careful not to think that what is understood in the Old Testament, because of the circumstances of those times, as neither a vice nor a crime, even though it is interpreted not figuratively but literally, can be applied to these times as a mode of life. No one will do this, unless he is dominated by a lust which seeks protection even in the very Scriptures by which it should be destroyed. The unhappy man does not realize that those things have been set before his mind for this useful purpose, namely, that men of good hope may understand with profit that a practice which they scorn can have a good use, and one which they adopt can lead them to damnation, if charity motivates the use of the first practice, and lust, the use of the second.

(27) Even if it were then possible, because of the circumstances, for anyone to posses many wives chastely, it is now possible for another man to be lustful with only one. I have more regard for a man who makes use of the fruitfulness of many wives for the sake of an ulterior purpose than for a man who indulges in carnal pleasures with only one wife for the sake of that pleasure. In the first case, a benefit in harmony with the circumstances of the times is sought; in the second instance, lust concerned with temporary sensual pleasures is gratified. Those to whom the Apostle 'by way of concession' allowed carnal intercourse with one wife because of their 'lack of self-control'[1] are less advanced on the road to God than those who, although they each

---

1 1 Cor. 7.2.6.

had several wives, looked only toward the begetting of children in this union; just as a wise man looks only to the health of his body in the matter of food and drink. And so, if they had been living at the time of the Lord's coming, when the time had come to gather the stones and not to scatter them,[2] they would at once have made themselves eunuchs for the 'kingdom of heaven's sake.' For, there is no difficulty in denying ourselves something, unless there is lust in enjoying it. In fact, those men knew that, even in the case of married persons themselves, excess and intemperance were abuses. The prayer of Tobias when he was united to his wife testifies this:[3] 'Blessed art thou, O Lord God of our fathers, and blessed be thy Name forever. May the heavens and all thy creation bless thee. Thou madest Adam and gavest him Eve for a helper. And now, Lord, thou knowest that not for fleshly lust do I take my sister to wife, but because of truth itself, that thou mayest have mercy on us, O Lord.'

Chapter 19

(28) There are some, however, who, in unbridled passion either wander about abandoning themselves to numerous impurities or, with only one wife, not only exceed the bounds of moderation in regard to the procreation of children, but, with the utterly shameless license of a sort of slavish freedom, even heap up the uncleannesses of a more bestial intemperance. These men do not believe that it was possible for the men of ancient times to possess many wives with moderation, considering in that intercourse only the obligation of propagating their race which was proper to that time. What they, hampered as they are by the chains of passion, do not

---
2 Eccle. 3.5; John 11.52.
3 Cf. Tob. 8.7-10.

observe with even one wife; they judge cannot be observed at all with many wives.

(29) These men can maintain further that good and saintly men should not be respected and esteemed,[1] because, when they are respected, they are puffed up with pride and are more avid for the most worthless praise the oftener and the more extensively a flattering tongue extols them. They become so light-minded because of this flattery that a little breeze of gossip, whether it is judged as favorable or unfavorable, drives them into whirlpools of vice or flings them against the reefs of crime. Those, then, who so maintain may notice how arduous and troublesome it is not to be allured with the bait of praise or pierced by the stings of insults, but they are not to judge others by themselves.

Chapter 20

They should rather believe that our Apostles were neither conceited when they were esteemed by men nor humiliated when they were scorned. Certainly, neither trial was wanting to those men, for they were honored by the commendation of believers and dishonored by the curses of their persecutors. They made use of all these things, according to circumstances, and were not misled. Just so, those men of ancient times, applying the use of their wives to the circumstances of their times, did not submit to that tyranny of passion to which those who do not believe these things are subject.

(30) For, if any such passion had troubled them, they could in no way have restrained themselves from irreconcilable hatred of their sons, who, they knew, had tempted or seduced their wives and concubines.

---

[1] Eccli. 44.1.

Chapter 21

When King David had endured this affliction from his wicked and treacherous son,[1] he had not only tolerated his uncontrolled passion, but even lamented his death.[2] He was not held ensnared by a carnal jealousy, since it was not the outrages inflicted on him, but rather the sins of his son, that troubled him. For, he had forbidden that his son be killed if he were conquered, in order that opportunity for repentance might be reserved for him after he was vanquished. Since this was impossible, he did not grieve because of his bereavement in the death of his son, but because he realized into what punishments such a wickedly adulterous and murderous soul was precipitated. For, on a former occasion, he was distressed because of the sickness of another son who was guiltless, but was able to be cheerful when he died.[3]

(31) It is particularly evident from the following incident with what moderation and self-control those men possessed their wives. When the same king, prevailed upon by the ardor of his youth and by prosperity in temporal goods, had illicitly seized upon one woman whose husband he had commanded to be killed,[4] he was denounced by the prophet. When he had come to point out to the king his sin, he related a parable about a poor man who had one ewe-lamb.[5] Although this man's neighbor had many, when a guest arrived he offered him as a feast his poor neighbor's only small lamb. David, incensed at the man, ordered him to be killed

---

1 2 Kings 16.22.
2 2 Kings 18.33.
3 2 Kings 12.16ff.
4 2 Kings 11.2ff.
5 2 Kings 12.1ff.

and the lamb to be restored four-fold; the result was that he who had sinned intentionally was condemning himself unintentionally. When this had been made clear to him and the punishment of God had been pronounced against him, he expiated his sin by repentance. However, in this parable only the adultery was represented by the poor neighbor's ewe-lamb. For, in the parable David was not questioned about the murder of the woman's husband, that is, about the killing of the poor man who had the one ewe-lamb, so the sentence of condemnation was pronounced only against the adultery. From this it is evident with what restraint he possessed many wives, since he was compelled to punish himself because he exceeded the bounds of moderation in the case of one woman. But, in this man's case, this unbridled passion was not a lasting disposition, but only a passing one. For this reason that illicit passion was called by the prophet, in his accusation, a guest.[6] He did not say that the man had offered the poor man's ewe-lamb as a feast to his king, but to his guest. On the other hand, in his son Solomon, this lust did not pass on like a guest, but took possession of his kingdom. Holy Scripture has not kept silence about him, but has condemned him as a lover of women.[7] The beginning of his reign glowed with his desire of wisdom; when he had obtained it through spiritual love, he lost it through carnal love.[8]

Chapter 22

(32) Although all or nearly all of the deeds which are recorded in the Old Testament must be regarded, there-

---

[6] 2 Kings 12.4 (ancient version).
[7] 3 Kings 11.1.
[8] 2 Par. 1.7ff.

fore, not only in their literal sense, but figuratively as well, the reader should interpret as a symbol even those acts which he has taken literally if those who have done them are praised, even though their actions differ from the custom of the good men who have kept the divine commands since the coming of our Lord. However, he should not carry that same action over to his own conduct, for there are many deeds which were performed in accordance with duty at that time which can be performed now only through lust.

Chapter 23

(33) On the other hand, when he reads of any sins of noble men, even though he can observe and verify in them some figures of future events, he may still apply the proper meaning of the action to this end, namely, that he will by no means venture to boast about his own virtuous deeds, nor, because of his own uprightness, look down upon others as if they were sinners,[1] when he sees in such noble men the storms of passions that must be shunned and the shipwrecks that must be lamented. The sins of those men have been written down for a reason, and that is that the following passage of the Apostle might be formidable everywhere:[2] 'Therefore let him who thinks he stands take heed lest he fall.' There is practically no page of the Holy Books which does not cry out that 'God resists the proud, but gives grace to the humble.'[3]

Chapter 24

(34) We must discover, first of all, whether the expression

---
[1] Luke 18.9.
[2] 1 Cor. 10.12.
[3] James 4.6; 1 Peter 5.6; Prov. 3.34.

which we are trying to understand is literal or figurative. When we have made certain that it is figurative, it is easy, by employing the rules concerning things which I explained in the first book, to reflect upon it under all its aspects until we reach the idea of truth, particularly when practice, invigorated by the observance of piety, is added to it. We can discover whether an expression is literal or figurative by considering the principles mentioned above.

Chapter 25

When the expression is seen to be figurative, the words of which it is composed will be discovered to be derived either from similar things or from those that are related by some affinity.

(35) But, since things appear similar to each other in many ways, we should not imagine there is any precept that we must believe that, because a thing has a certain analogical meaning in one place, it always has this meaning. For example, the Lord represented leaven in a condemnatory fashion when He said:[1] 'Beware of the leaven of the Pharisees'; and as an object of praise when He said:[2] 'The kingdom of heaven is like a woman who hid leaven in three measures of flour, until all of it was leavened.'

(36) The rule for this diversity, therefore, has two forms. Anything that is a sign of one thing and then another is such that it signifies either things that are contrary or else things that are only different. They indicate contraries, for instance, when the same thing is expressed by way of analogy at one

---

[1] Matt. 16. 6-11.
[2] Matt. 13.33. This sentence marks the point to which the author arrived in composing the first stage of this work; see Introduction p. 4.

time in a good sense, and at another in a bad sense, like the leaven mentioned above. Another such instance is this: A lion signifies Christ in this passage:[3] 'The lion of the tribe of Juda has prevailed'; but it signifies the devil in this other:[4] 'Your adversary the devil, as a roaring lion, goes about seeking someone to devour.' The serpent is depicted in a good sense:[5] 'Be wise as serpents'; but, also in a bad sense:[6] 'The serpent seduced Eve by his guile.' Bread is represented with a good meaning:[7] 'I am the living bread that has come down from heaven'; and with a bad one:[8] 'Eat with pleasure the hidden bread.' There are very many other examples like these. Those which I have mentioned are by no means uncertain in their meaning, for only clear passages ought to be mentioned by way of example. Yet, there are some passages where there is uncertainty with respect to the meaning in which they ought to be understood; for example: 'In the hand of the Lord there is a cup of strong wine full of mixture.' It is doubtful whether this signifies the wrath of God, but not to the extreme penalty, that is, to 'the dregs'; or whether it signifies the grace of the Scriptures passing from the Jews to the Gentiles, because 'He hath poured it out from this to that,' although certain practices continue among the Jews which they understand carnally, because 'the dregs thereof are not emptied.'[9] And we have an instance where the same thing is not expressed in a contrary, but only in a different, sense: Water signifies people,[10] as we read in the Apocalypse;

---

3 Apoc. 5.5.
4 1 Pet. 5.8.
5 Matt. 10:16.
6 2 Cor. 11.3.
7 John 6.51.
8 Cf. Prov. 9.17.
9 Ps. 74.8,9; cf. Aug. *Enarr. in Ps.* 74.11.12.
10 Apoc. 17.15; 19.6.

it also signifies the Holy Ghost, as in this example:[11] 'From within Him there shall flow rivers of living water.' Thus, water is understood to signify one thing in one place and another in another place, according to the passages in which it is mentioned.

(37) Similarly, other things are not single in their meaning, but each of them signifies not only two but sometimes even many different things, according to its relation to the thought of the passage where it is found.

Chapter 26

Moreover, we must learn from passages in which they are expressed more plainly how we are to interpret them in obscure passages. The best way for us to have a clear understanding of this passage addressed to God:[1] 'Take hold of arms and shield and rise up to help me,' is to read from that other passage:[2] 'O Lord, Thou hast crowned us, as with a shield of Thy good will.' Yet, we are not to understand that, wherever we read about a shield placed for some defense, we should interpret it only as the good will of God, for there is this passage:[3] 'The shield of faith, with which you may be able to quench all the fiery darts of the most wicked one.' Again, for the same reason, we should not attribute faith to the shield alone, in speaking of spiritual armor like this, since in another passage the breastplate of faith is mentioned. 'Let us put on the breastplate of faith and charity,'[4] says the Apostle.

---
11 John 7. 38.

1 Ps. 34.2.
2 Ps. 5.13.
3 Eph. 6.16.
4 1 Thess. 5.8.

Chapter 27

(38) Besides, not only one but perhaps two or more interpretations are understood from the same words of Scripture. And so, even if the meaning of the writer is unknown, there is no danger, provided that it is possible to show from other passages of the Scriptures that any one of them is in accord with truth. A man who thoroughly examines the Holy Scriptures in an endeavor to find the purpose of the author (through whom the Holy Ghost brought Holy Scripture into being), whether he attains this goal or whether he elicits from the words another meaning which is not opposed to the true faith, is free from blame, if he has proof from some other passage of the Holy Scriptures. In fact, the author perhaps saw that very meaning, too, in the same words which we are anxious to interpret. And, certainly, the Spirit of God who produced these words through him also foresaw that this very meaning would occur to the reader or listener; further, He took care that it should occur to him because it also is based upon truth. For, what could God have provided more generously and more abundantly in the Holy Scriptures than that the same words might be understood in several ways, which other supporting testimonies no less divine endorse?

Chapter 28

(39) When such a meaning is elicited that its uncertainty cannot be explained by the unerring testimonies of the Holy Scriptures, however, it remains for us to explain it by the proof of reason, even if the man whose words we are seeking to understand were perhaps unaware of that meaning. This, however, is a dangerous practice. It is much safer to walk by means of the Holy Scriptures. When we are trying

to search out those passages that are obscured by figurative words, we may either start out from a passage which is not subject to dispute, or, if it is disputed, we may settle the question by employing the testimonies that have been discovered everywhere in the same Scripture.

Chapter 29

(40) Furthermore, learned men should know that our authors have used all the modes of expression which grammarians call by their Greek name, 'tropes,' and they have employed them in greater numbers and more eloquently than those who do not know these writers, and have learned the figures in other works, can suppose or believe. Yet, those who know these tropes recognize them in the Holy Scriptures, and the knowledge of them is a considerable aid in understanding the Scriptures. But, it is not proper for me at this point to teach them to the inexperienced, lest I should appear to be teaching grammar. To be sure, I suggest that they be learned apart from this work, although I have already given this advice above in the second book, when I discussed the necessary knowledge of languages. The letters from which grammar derives its name—the Greeks call letters *grammata*—are certainly the signs of sounds that relate to the articulate voice with which we speak. In the Holy Books there are seen not only examples of these tropes, just as of all figures, but even the names of some of them; for example, 'allegory,' 'enigma,' and 'parable.' And yet, almost all of these tropes which are said to be learned in the liberal arts are also discovered in the speech of those who have not studied under any grammarians, but are satisfied with the manner of speech which ordinary people use. For, who does not say: 'So may you flourish'? This trope

is called a 'metaphor.' Who does not speak of a fishpond, even when it contains no fish and was not made for fish, but still it derives its name from fish?[1] This trope is called 'catachresis.'

(41) It would be tedious to describe the others in this fashion. The speech of the common people employs even those which are more unusual because they mean the opposite of what they say; examples are those called 'irony' and 'antiphrasis.' Irony shows by the inflection of the voice what it intends us to understand, as when we say to a man who is behaving badly, 'You are doing well.' Antiphrasis, on the other hand, is not made to signify contrary meanings by an inflection of voice, but uses its own words, whose origin is from the contrary, as when a grove is called *lucus* because it has very little light;[2] or when we say 'Yes,' even though, on the contrary, it would be 'No,' as when we are seeking what is not in a place and we receive the answer: 'There is plenty'; or, by adding words, we cause what we say to be understood in the contrary sense, as 'Beware of him, because he is a good man.' What unlearned man does not use such expressions, and still is utterly unaware of the nature or the names of these tropes? A knowledge of them is necessary in explaining the obscurities of the Scriptures, because, when the meaning is unreasonable if understood in the literal signification of the words, we must, of course, try to find out whether it has been expressed in some figure or other which we do not know. And so, many passages which were obscure have been interpreted.

---

1 The word *piscina* (literally, 'fishpond') could designate, for example, a swimming pool.
2 This punning etymology of *lucus* is made clear in the Latin of the last six words: *quod minime luceat*.

Chapter 30

(42) A certain Tyconius,[1] although he was a Donatist, has written most convincingly against the Donatists, and appears in this matter to have had a very illogical mind, since he was unwilling to leave them altogether. He has written what he has called the *Book of Rules*, because in it he has outlined seven rules by which, as if they were keys, the obscurities of the Holy Scriptures may be unlocked. The first of these is about the Lord and His Body; the second, about the two divisions of the Lord's Body; the third, about the promises and the law; the fourth, about species and genus; the fifth, about times; the sixth, about recapitulation; and the seventh, about the Devil and his body. Indeed, when these rules have been carefully examined, as they are explained by him, they help greatly in penetrating the hidden meanings of the Sacred Scriptures. It is not possible, however, to learn by these rules all the things which have been written in such a way that they are not easy to understand; we must employ several other methods, also. These he has been so far from including in this group of seven that he himself explains many obscurities and applies to them none of these rules of his, because there was no need of them. For nothing covered by them occurs there or is brought into question. For example, when he inquires how we are to interpret, in the Apocalypse of St. John, the seven angels[2] of the churches to

---

1 The moderate Donatist Tyconius (died *ca.* 390) was an older contemporary of St. Augustine. Besides his important hermeneutical manual, the *Book of Rules* (PL 18 15ff; critical edition of F. C. Burkitt Cambridge 1894), his works include a lost commentary on the Apocalypse, largely restorable from later quotations. Both works date from *ca.* 380.

2 Apoc. 1.20ff.

whom John is commanded to write, he reasons in various ways and reaches the conclusion that we are to understand that the angels themselves are the churches. In this very lengthy consideration he applies none of his rules, and, certainly, the matter investigated there is very obscure. Enough has been said by way of example. It would be too tedious and too difficult to assemble all the obscure passages in the canonical Scriptures that do not demand any of these seven rules.

(43) Yet Tyconius, when he was recommending these as rules, assigned as much importance to them as if, by knowing them fully and applying them, we would be capable of understanding all the things which we have discovered expressed figuratively in the law, that is, in the Holy Books. He began this book with these words: 'In preference to all the subjects which recommend themselves to me, I considered it necessary to write a little book of rules and, in a certain sense, to fashion keys and windows for the hidden places of the law. For there are certain mystical rules which gain access to the secret recesses of the whole law and make visible those treasures of truth which are invisible to many. If the theory of these rules is received as I have imparted it, without jealousy, every closed place will be opened, and everything obscure will be made clear, so that anyone traversing the boundless forest of prophecy will be prevented from going astray, if he is guided by these rules as by pathways of light.' If he had said: 'For there are certain mystical rules which give access to some of the secret recesses of the law'; or even: 'which give access to the great secret recesses of the law,' instead of saying as he did: 'the secret recesses of the whole law'; and, if he had not said: 'every closed place will be opened,' but, instead: 'many closed places will be

opened,' he would have spoken the truth, without giving more importance than the facts required to such an elaborate and beneficial work as his, and would not have guided his reader and judge into a false hope. I thought that I ought to say this in order that the book may be read by students (because it is a very important aid toward understanding the Scriptures), yet without hoping for more from it than it possesses. To be sure, we must read it prudently, not only because of certain human mistakes he has made in it, but especially because of the things he has said as a Donatist heretic. I shall now explain briefly what those seven rules teach or suggest.

Chapter 31

(44) The first rule is 'About the Lord and His Body.' In this rule we know that the title of head and body, that is, of Christ and the Church, is sometimes made known to us as of one person (for the Apostle did not tell the faithful without a purpose: 'then you are the offspring of Abraham,'[1] since there is but one offspring of Abraham, 'who is Christ.'[2] We are not to be at a loss when there is a change from head to body or from body to head; yet the subject is not changed from one and the same person. In the following a single person is speaking:[3] 'He hath placed a crown upon me as upon a bridegroom, and He hath adorned me as a bride with an ornament.' Yet, we must surely interpret which of these refers to the head and which to the body, that is, which to Christ and which to the Church.

---

1 Gal. 3.29.
2 Gal 3.16.
3 Isa. 61.10 (Tycon.).

Chapter 32

(45) The second rule is 'About the Two Divisions of the Lord's Body.' However, it should not have been designated this way, because what will not be with Him forever is not in reality the Body of the Lord. Tyconius should have said: 'About the True and the Mixed Body of Our Lord'; or: the 'true and the pretended'; or something else, because hypocrites should not be said to be with Him even now, not to mention in eternity, even though they seem to be in His Church. For this reason, that rule could have been entitled in such a way as to read: 'About the Mixed Church.' The rule demands a watchful reader, when Scripture, although it is at this moment speaking to or about other persons, seems as if it were speaking to or about those very persons to whom or about whom it was just now speaking, just as if both of them were one body because of their temporary mingling and participation in the Sacraments. There is a passage in the Canticle of Canticles to which this observation applies: 'I am black but beautiful as the tents of Cedar, as the curtains of Solomon.'[1] The spouse did not say: 'I *was* black as the tents of Cedar, and I *am* beautiful as the curtain of Solomon'; she said she *is* both, because of the temporal union of the good and the bad fish within one net.[2] The tents of Cedar refer to Ismael, who will not be heir 'with the son of the free woman.'[3] And so, when God proclaimed concerning the good part:[4] 'I will lead the blind into the way which they know not; and the paths which they know not they will tread.

---

1 Cant. 1.4. (Tycon.).
2 Matt. 13.47f.
3 Gen. 21.10; Gal. 4.30.
4 Isa. 42.16 (Tycon.).

And I will make darkness light before them and crooked things straight: these words I will carry out and I will not forsake them,' He immediately says about the other part (which was mixed with evil): 'They are turned back.' Others are meant by these words, yet, since they are now united in one body, He speaks as though referring to the very ones of whom He was speaking just before. They will not always be in one body. Indeed, one of them is that servant mentioned in the Gospel, whose master, when he comes, 'will cut him asunder and make him share the lot of the hypocrites.'[5]

Chapter 33

(46) The third rule is 'About the Promises and the Law.' It can otherwise be called 'On the Spirit and the Letter,' the title I used when I wrote a book dealing with this subject. It can also be called 'About Grace and the Law.' In my opinion, this is an important question in itself, rather than a rule which should be used in solving questions. Because they did not understand this question, the Pelagians either established their heresy, or at least strengthened it. Tyconius did good work in his discussion of this subject, but his treatment is incomplete. For, in reference to faith and works he said that works were given to us by God because of our faith which merited them, but that faith itself is so inherent in us that it is not a gift from God. He did not pay attention to the Apostle, who said:[1] 'Peace be to the brethren, and love and faith, from God, the Father, and the Lord Jesus Christ.' He had not become acquainted with this heresy which has originated in our times, and which has given us a great deal of trouble in

---

5 Matt. 24.48ff.

---

1 Eph. 6.23.

defending against it the grace of God, which is through our Lord Jesus Christ. According to the Apostle:[2] 'There must be factions so that those who are approved may be made manifest among you.' This heresy has made us much more vigilant and painstaking in observing in the Holy Scriptures what was overlooked by Tyconius, who, since he had no enemy, was less observant and less troubled about the fact that even faith itself is the gift of Him who 'has apportioned to each one the measure of faith.'[3] In accordance with this thought the Philippians were taught: 'For you have been given the favor on Christ's behalf, not only to believe in Him, but also to suffer for Him.'[4] Accordingly, who can doubt that both of these graces are the gift of God, if with faith and understanding he here learns that both have been given? There are many other evidences, too, which make this clear. I am not discussing this matter now, yet I have discussed it very often in one place or another.

Chapter 34

(47) The fourth rule of Tyconius is 'About Species and Genus.' So he designates it, intending that *species* be understood as the part, and *genus* as the whole, of which what he terms *species* is a part; for example, each individual city is a part of the community of nations. He calls the city the *species,* and all the nations he terms the *genus.* In this discussion we do not have to make use of that exactness of distinction between these two which is insisted upon by the logicians, who discuss very profoundly the difference between a part and a species. The same reasoning applies when we

---

2 1 Cor. 11.19.
3 Rom. 12.3.
4 Phil. 1.29.

find in the Sacred Scriptures anything of this kind that concerns, not a single city, but a single province, tribe, or territory. For example, it is not only about Jerusalem or some city of the Gentiles, either Tyre, Babylon, or any one at all, that things are said in the Holy Scriptures which go beyond the boundary of that city and are more applicable to all the nations. Something may be said also about Judea, Egypt, Assyria, or some other nation in which there are very many cities (although the nation is still not the whole world, but only part of it), which goes beyond the boundary of that nation and is more applicable to the whole world, of which it is a part; or, as Tyconius puts it, to the *genus* of which it is a *species*. These words have come even to the attention of the common people, with the result that even the uneducated understand the particular and general regulations enunciated in any imperial edict. This also happens in regard to men; thus, the things which are recorded of Solomon[1] transcend his limitations, but become clear when they are applied instead to Christ or His Church, of which Solomon is a part.

(48) We do not always go beyond the species. We often say things of such a nature that they are manifestly consistent with it as well as with something else, or perhaps apply only to it. When Scripture, however, although it has been speaking uninterruptedly of species, changes from species to genus, the attention of the reader should be so directed as not to see in the species what he can find better and more accurately in the genus. Certainly, what the Prophet Ezechiel said is easily understood: 'The house of Israel dwelt in the land and defiled it by their own way and with their idols and with their sins. Their way was before my face like the unclean-

---
[1] Cf. Tycon., *Lib. reg.* 4, ed. Burkitt pp. 37ff.

ness of a menstruous woman. And I poured out my wrath upon them, and I scattered them among the nations and dispersed them through the countries. I have judged them according to their ways and according to their sins.'[2] It is easy, I repeat, to understand this of that house of Israel of which the Apostle says:[3] 'Behold Israel according to the flesh,' because the carnal-minded people of Israel did and suffered all these things. The other passages which follow are also understood as referring to the same people. But, when the Prophet begins to say: 'And I will sanctify my great and holy Name, which was profaned among the nations, which you have profaned in the midst of them: and the Gentiles will know that I am the Lord,' the reader ought to be observant of the way in which he passes over the species and applies himself to the genus. For he goes on to say:[4] 'When I shall be sanctified in you before their eyes. And I will take you from among the Gentiles and will gather you together out of all countries and will bring you into your own land. And I will sprinkle clean water upon you, and you shall be cleansed from all your idols, and I will cleanse you. And I will give you a new heart and put a new spirit within you: and I will take away the stony heart out of your flesh, and will give you a heart of flesh. And I will put My spirit in the midst of you; and I will cause you to walk in my commandments and to keep my judgments and to do them. And you shall dwell in the land which I gave to your fathers, and you shall be my people, and I shall be your God, and I will cleanse you from all your uncleannesses.' We know that this was a prophecy of the New

---

2 Ezech. 36.17-19 (Tycon.).
3 1 Cor. 10.18.
4 Ezech. 36.23-29 (Tycon.).

Testament to which pertain not only the remains of that one nation of which the Apostle writes in another place:[5] 'Though the number of the children of Israel is as the sands of the sea, the remnant shall be saved,' but also the other nations which were promised to their fathers, who are likewise our fathers. No one who contemplates it has any doubt that the 'bath of regeneration,'[6] which we now see given to all nations, is here promised. And the Apostle says, when he is praising the grace of the New Testament and its eminence compared with the Old:[7] 'You are our letter, . . . written, not with ink, but with the spirit of the living God; not on tablets of stone, but in the fleshy tablets of the heart.' He looks back and sees that this has been derived from the passage in which the Prophet says:[8] 'And I will give you a new heart and put a new spirit within you: and I will take away the stony heart out of your flesh, and will give you a heart of flesh.' The Prophet intended that the 'heart of flesh' (which caused the Apostle to say: 'the fleshy tablets of the heart') be distinguished from the 'stony heart' by a sentient life, and by a sentient life he meant an intelligent life. So the spiritual Israel is composed, not of one nation, but of all which were promised to our fathers in their offspring 'who is Christ.'[9]

(49) Therefore, this spiritual Israel is distinguished from that carnal Israel which consisted of one nation by newness of grace and not by noble origin, by disposition of heart and not by nationality. However, the Prophet's profound inspira-

---
5 Rom. 9.27 (Isa. 10.22).
6 Titus 3.5.
7 2 Cor. 3.2f.
8 Ezech. 36.26.
9 Gal. 3.16.

tion, while he is speaking of or to the carnal Israel, passes over to without warning the spiritual Israel. And, although he is now speaking of or to the spiritual Israel, he still seems to be referring to the other; not because he grudges us an understanding of the Scriptures as if he were our enemy, but because he disciplines our understanding as our physician. We should not take 'carnally' as relating to the carnal Israel, but spiritually as relating to the spiritual Israel, that passage of the Prophet: 'And I will bring you into your own land'; and what he says a little later, as if repeating the same thing: 'And you shall dwell in the land which I gave to your fathers.' Indeed, the Church, without spot or wrinkle,[10] gathered from all nations and destined to rule forever with Christ, is herself the land of the blessed, 'the land of the living.'[11] We should understand that it was given to our fathers when it was promised to them by the fixed and unchangeable Will of God; what our fathers believed was to be given in its own time was already granted, because of the steadfastness of the promise and intention. Just so, the Apostle, in writing to Timothy of that grace which is granted to the saints, says:[12] 'Not according to our works, but according to his own purpose and the grace which was granted to us in Jesus Christ before this world existed, but is now manifested by the coming of our Savior.' He speaks of the grace as given when those to whom it was to be given were not yet in existence, because, in the disposition and predestination of God, that which was to be given in its own time had already been accomplished, and he says that it is now manifested. It is quite possible that these words may be under-

---

10 Eph. 5.27.
11 Ps. 26.13.
12 2 Tim. 1. 9f.

stood of the land of the world to come, when there will be a 'new heaven and a new earth,'[13] in which the wicked will not be able to live. The meek are rightly told that the land is theirs[14] (because no part of it will belong to the wicked), for it was really given when the promise that it was to be given was made.

Chapter 35

(50) A fifth rule was proposed by Tyconius, which he entitles 'About Times.' With this rule, intervals of time which are obscure in the Holy Scriptures may frequently be elucidated or surmised. Moreover, he remarks that this rule is observed in two ways, either by the figure called 'synecdoche' or by 'legitimate numbers.' By the figure of synecdoche he wants us to discern the whole from a part or a part from the whole. For example, one Evangelist says 'after eight days,' and another, 'after six days,' in speaking of the occasion when on the mountain in the presence of only three disciples the Lord's 'face shone as the sun, and His garments became white as snow.'[1] What was said about the number of days could not be true for both, unless the one who said 'after eight days' is interpreted as having counted as two whole days the last part of the day on which Christ foretold what would happen and the first part of the day on which He showed the consummation of the prophecy; while the Evangelist who said 'after six days' counted only the whole and completed days between. This mode of expression, which puts the part for the whole, also explains that disputed point about the Resurrection of Christ. For, unless the last part

---
13 Apoc. 21.1.
14 Matt. 5.4.

---
1 Matt. 17.1; Mark 9.2; Luke 9.28; cf. Aug. *De cons. Ev.* 2.56.113.

of the day on which He suffered is augmented by the preceding night and considered as a whole day—and, unless the night in the last part of which He rose is augmented by the dawn of the Lord's Day and counted as a whole day—we cannot account for the three days and three nights during which He foretold He would be 'in the heart of the earth.'[2]

(51) Now, he terms as 'legitimate numbers' those which Holy Scripture especially favors, such as seven, ten, twelve, or any others which those who are careful in reading learn readily. Now, numbers of this kind frequently are placed for time as a whole; for example, 'Seven times a day I will praise thee'[3] is only another way of saying 'His praise shall be always in my mouth.'[4] They have just the same value when they are multiplied by ten, as seventy and seven hundred. (This is the reason why the seventy years mentioned in Jeremias[5] can be interpreted spiritually as the whole time during which the Church is among strangers.) Or they can be multiplied by themselves, as ten multiplied by ten equals one hundred, and twelve multiplied by twelve equals one hundred and forty-four. This last number signifies in the Apocalypse[6] the entire multitude of saints. It is clear from this that it is not questions of time alone that are to be explained by these numbers, but that their meanings can be applied rather extensively and can touch upon many matters. For that number in the Apocalypse relates not to times, but to men.

---

2 Matt. 12.40.
3 Ps. 118.164 (Tycon.).
4 Ps. 33.2.
5 Jer. 25.11.
6 Apoc. 7.4.

Chapter 36

(52) Tyconius calls his sixth rule the 'Recapitulation,' found by diligent research in the obscurity of the Scriptures. Some things are related in such a way that they seem to be following the order of time or occurring in chronological succession, when actually the narrative, without mentioning it, refers to previous events which had been left unmentioned. Unless we come to this understanding from this rule, we shall fall into error. For example, we find in Genesis:[1] 'And the Lord God had planted a paradise of pleasure [in Eden toward the east]: wherein He placed man whom He had formed. And God brought forth of the ground all manner of trees fair to behold and pleasant to eat of.' This last mentioned event would seem to have occurred after God had made man and placed Him in Paradise, although, after both of these facts have been mentioned briefly (that is, that God planted a paradise and there 'placed man whom He had formed'), the narrative turns back by means of recapitulation and relates what had been previously omitted, namely, how Paradise had been planted and that 'God brought forth of the ground all manner of trees fair to behold and pleasant to eat of.' Then the following passage is added:[2] 'the tree of life also in the midst of Paradise, and the tree of knowledge of good and evil.' Then is mentioned the river by which Paradise is watered and which is 'divided into four heads' of four streams, all of which relates to the arrangement of Paradise. When the writer had finished this, he repeated the statement he had already made, of what in reality followed the events just related, saying:[3] 'And the Lord

---
1 Gen. 2.8f.
2 Gen. 2.9.
3 Gen. 2.15.

God took man whom He had made and put him in Paradise' and so forth. For man, as the order of the narrative itself now indicates, was placed there after these things had been done; those things not having been done after man had been created, as what was first said could be understood to mean if the recapitulation, by which we are referred to what had been omitted, were not carefully understood.

(53) In the same book, too, when the generations of the sons of Noah are recalled to our minds, we read:[4] 'These are the children of Cham in their tribes according to their tongues, in their lands and nations.' Also, in enumerating the sons of Sem, it is said:[5] 'These are the children of Sem in their tribes according to their tongues, in their lands and nations.' And this is added in reference to all of them:[6] 'These are the tribes of the sons of Noah, according to their generations and according to their nations. From these were the islands of the nations scattered over the earth after the flood. And the whole earth was one tongue and there was one speech for all.' And so, because this sentence was added: 'And the earth was one tongue and there was one speech for all' (that is, one language for them all), it could be inferred that at that time, when men had been scattered according to the islands of the nations over the earth, there was one language common to all of them. Without a doubt, this contradicts the words used above, 'according to their tribes and tongues.' For, each single tribe which had formed individual nations would not be said to have had its own tongue, when there was a common one for all. So it is by way of recapitulation that there is added: 'And the earth

---

4 Gen. 10.20.
5 Gen. 10.31.
6 Gen. 10.32; 11.1.

was one tongue and there was one speech for all'; the narrative, without mentioning it, goes back to tell how it came about that the one language common to all men was broken up into many tongues. And immediately we are told about the building of the tower,[7] when this punishment for their pride was inflicted upon them by the divine Judgment. After this event they were scattered over the earth according to their languages.

(54) Such recapitulation may become even more obscure, as when the Lord says in the Gospel:[8] 'On the day that Lot went out from Sodom, it rained fire from heaven and destroyed them all. The day on which the Son of Man is revealed will be like this day. In that hour let him who is on the housetop and his goods in the house, not go down to take them away; and likewise let him who is in the field not turn back. Let him remember Lot's wife.' Is it after the Lord has been revealed that we are to observe these commands that no one is to look back, that is, seek after the past life which he has renounced? Should we not rather observe them at this time, so that, when the Lord has been revealed, we may each find a recompense for the commands we have kept and the prohibitions we have obeyed. But, because it is written 'in that hour,' it might be thought that those commandments are to be kept when the Lord has been revealed, unless the reader's mind is intent on understanding the recapitulation with the aid of another passage of Scripture. This, spoken even at the time of the Apostles themselves, declares:[9] 'Children, it is the last hour.' Therefore, the very time at which the Gospel is preached, until the time when

---

[7] Gen. 11.4ff.
[8] Luke 7.29-32 (Tycon.).
[9] 1 John 2.18.

the Lord will be revealed, is the hour in which we must observe these commandments, because the Lord's revelation itself pertains to that same hour which will be ended by the Day of Judgment.

Chapter 37

(55) The seventh and last rule of Tyconius is 'About the Devil and His Body.' He himself is the head of the wicked, who are, in a certain sense, his body and who are to go with him into the punishment of eternal fire;[1] just as Christ is the head[2] of the Church, which is His Body and will be with Him in His Kingdom and everlasting glory. In the first rule which he calls 'About Our Lord and His Body,' when Scripture speaks of one and the same Person, we must be alert to understand what pertains to the head and what to the body. Just so, in this last rule, what is said about the Devil can be observed in his body rather than in him. This body consists not only of those who are very plainly 'outside,'[3] but even of those who, although they belong to him, are still mingled with the Church for the time being, until they depart individually from this life or until the chaff is separated from the wheat by the final winnowing-fan.[4] This was written in Isaias:[5] 'How is he fallen from heaven, Lucifer, who did rise in the morning'; and the other passages, which, under the figure of the King of Babylon, were spoken in the same context about the same person or to the same person, and are certainly to be understood of the Devil. Yet, the statement in the passage:[6] 'He is crushed

---
1 Matt. 25.41.
2 Eph. 1.22.
3 1 Cor. 5.12.
4 Matt. 3.12; Luke 3.17.
5 Isa. 14.12 (Tycon.).
6 *Idem.*

upon the earth who sends to all nations' does not entirely apply to the head. Although the Devil sends his angels to all nations, yet it is his body and not himself that is crushed upon the earth, except that he himself is in his body which is crushed like 'dust which the wind driveth from the face of the earth.'[7]

(56) Now, all these rules, except the one which is called 'About the Promises and the Law,' cause one thing to be understood from another, which is characteristic of the figurative mode of expression. This subject, in my opinion, is too extensive to be understood completely by anyone. Wherever we say one thing, intending another to be understood, we have a figurative expression, even though the name of that trope is not discovered in a text book of rhetoric. When this occurs in a customary place, the intellect perceive it without any trouble, but, when it occurs in an unusual place, we must exert ourselves to understand it, either more or less, according to the greater or less gifts of God in the matter of human talents or the helps that are given. Accordingly, in literal words, which I discussed above, things are to be understood as they are said, but in figurative words, which cause figurative expressions, one thing is to be understood from another, and I have dealt with these matters as far as seemed sufficient. Students of these revered writings should be advised not only to learn the kinds of expressions in the Holy Scriptures, to notice carefully how they are customarily expressed there, and to remember them, but also to pray that they may understand them, and this is chiefly and especially necessary. Indeed, in these books which they are studying earnestly, they read that 'the Lord giveth

---

[7] Ps. 1.4.

wisdom; and out of his mouth cometh prudence and knowledge.'[8] It is from Him that they have received that zeal for study, if it is endowed with piety. But these things are enough to say about signs, so far as words are concerned. It remains for me to discuss in the following book whatever the Lord vouchsafes to me about the methods of making known our thoughts.

---

8 Prov. 2.6.

BOOK FOUR

Chapter 1

ACCORDING TO the plan adopted at the outset, I divided this work of mine, which is entitled *Christian Instruction,* into two parts. After the introduction, in which I replied to those who would have censured it, I said: 'The entire treatment of the Scriptures is based upon two factors: the method of discovering what we are to understand and the method of teaching what has been understood. I shall discuss first the method of discovery and then the method of teaching.'[1] Therefore, since the method of ascertaining the meaning has been discussed at length in the first three books, with the help of the Lord I shall confine what I have to say about the method of teaching to one book, if possible, thus completing this entire work in four books.

(2) And so, at the outset, in this preamble I am restraining the hope of such readers as, perhaps, believe that I intend to present the rhetorical rules which I learned and taught in the secular schools. I admonish them not to expect these from me, not because they have no utility, but because, should they have any, they must be learned somewhere else, if, perhaps, some good man has leisure to learn them; however, they should neither in this work nor in any other be demanded of me.

---

1 *De doctr. chr.* 1.1.1.

Chapter 2

(3) Since persuasion both to truths and falsehoods is urged by means of the art of rhetoric, who would venture to say that truth, in the person of its defenders, ought to stand its ground, unarmed, against falsehood, so that those who are trying to convince us of falsehoods should know how to induce their listeners to be favorably inclined, attentive, and docile, by means of their preface, while the defenders of truth do not know how to do this? Should the former proclaim their falsehoods briefly, explicitly, and plausibly,[1] while the latter tell the truth in such a way that it is tedious to listen to, difficult to understand, and, finally, disagreeable to believe? Should the former attack truth and defend falsehood with specious arguments, and the latter be unable either to vindicate truth or disprove falsehood? Should the former, influencing and urging the minds of their listeners to error by their eloquence, terrify, sadden, gladden, and passionately encourage them, while the latter, indifferent and cold in behalf of truth, sleep on? Who is so foolish as to claim this? The power of eloquence—so very effective in convincing us of either wrong or right—lies open to all.[2] Why, then, do not the good zealously procure it that it may serve truth, if the wicked, in order to gain unjustifiable and groundless cases, apply it to the advantages of injustice and error?

Chapter 3

(4) The skillful use of language rich in vocabulary and rhetorical ornament is guided by the rules and principles of eloquence and oratory. Those who can learn quickly should

---
1 Cf. *Auct. ad Her.* 1.9.14.
2 Cf. *De doctr. chr.* 2.36.54; Cic. *De orat.* 1.32.145; *De invent.* 1.5.7.

master those rules apart from these writings of mine, at a proper and fitting age, when a suitable time has been set apart for this purpose. For even the masters of Roman eloquence themselves did not hesitate to say that, unless a person could master this art quickly, he could never master it at all.[1] Why question the truth of this statement? Even if these principles could finally be learned sometime by those who are rather slow of apprehension, I do not regard them as being so important that I would be willing to have men devote their adult or even their advanced years to learning them. It is sufficient for them to claim the attention of young men,[2] and not even of all those whom we wish trained for the service of the Church, but only of those who have not yet become engrossed in a more pressing interest, which undoubtedly should be preferred to this study. Eloquence grows upon those who read and listen eagerly and intelligently to the eloquent more easily than upon those who strive merely to imitate the rules for eloquence.[3] Even outside the Canon, which is established for our benefit on the rock of authority, there is no lack of ecclesiastical writings. By reading these, a talented man in the course of his reflections is imbued with the eloquence with which they are expressed, even though he does not strive for this, but is intent only upon the subjects there described. This is especially true if he joins to his reading a practice in writing, dictating, and finally even in expressing what he thinks,[4] according to the rule of piety and faith. However, if such natural ability is lacking, those principles of rhetoric are either not understood, or if, after being inculcated wth great pains, they are understood to some small

---

1 Cf. Cic. *De orat.* 3.36.146.
2 Cf. Cic. *De orat.* 3.31.125; Quint. *Inst. or.* 1.1.2.
3 Cf. Cic. *De orat.* 1.32.146; 1.34.156.
4 Cf. Cic. *De orat.* 2.23.96; 1.33.150.

degree, they are of no benefit. Even those who have learned these rules and speak fluently and elegantly cannot all reflect upon them when they are speaking, in order to express themselves according to those rules, if they are not speaking about the rules themselves. On the contrary, it is my opinion that there are hardly any of them who could do both things: speak well and, in order to do this, reflect upon the rules of rhetoric while they are speaking. For, we must be careful that what we ought to say does not escape our minds while we are intent upon saying it according to theory. Yet, in the speeches and utterances of eloquent men, the rules of eloquence are found to have been fulfilled, although those men did not think of them in order to speak well or while they were speaking, whether they had learned them or whether they had not even come in contact with them.[5] In fact, they observe them because they are eloquent; they do not employ them in order to be eloquent.

(5) Therefore, since the infant learns to talk only by learning the expressions of those who can talk, why can they not become eloquent without being taught rules of oratory, but simply by reading and listening to the eloquence of orators and imitating them as much as possible?[6] Do we not find this happening in actual cases? I know of many men who are more eloquent without the rules of rhetoric than many who have learned them, but I know of no one who has become eloquent without reading and listening to the speeches and discourses of eloquent speakers. Children would not need the art of grammar from which they learn to speak correctly, if they were permitted to grow up and live among men who spoke correctly. In fact, without knowing any of the names

---
5 Cf. Cic. *De orat.* 1.20.91; 1.19.87.
6 Cf. Cic. *De orat.* 2.22.90.

of errors, they would hear whatever was incorrect in the discourse of any speaker and, in accordance with their own correct usage, would criticize and avoid it, just as city people, even those who are illiterate, criticize country people.

Chapter 4

(6) Therefore, it is an obligation of the commentator and teacher of the Sacred Scriptures, the defender of the true faith and the conqueror of error, both to teach right and to correct wrong. Accordingly, this work of speaking obliges him to win over opponents, to arouse the negligent, and to inform the ignorant of what is hapening now and of what they should look for.[1] But, when he has found his listeners favorably inclined, attentive, and docile, or has himself caused them to be so, he must proceed with the other points as the case requires. If those who listen to him are in need of instruction, the subject under discussion must be made clear by exposition, on condition, however, that there is need of it. However, to settle doubtful points, he must reason them out through the use of proofs. On the other hand, if his listeners need to be roused, rather than instructed, that they may not be careless in observing what they already know and may give their consent to the things which they admit are true, there is need for greater powers of oratory. In that case, entreaty and reproof, exhortation and rebuke, and all other means designed to arouse hearts, are indispensable.

(7) In fact, very few men, when they employ eloquence, fail to observe all these things I have mentioned.[2]

---

[1] Cf. Cic. *De orat.* 2.28.121; 2.77.310; 2.27.15; *Brut.* 49.185; *De opt. gen,* 1.3;5.16.

[2] For a definition of Cicero's ideal orator, cf. *De orat.* 1.15.64; *Orat.* 2.7-9; *De orat.* 1.8.31; 2.8.34; 1.46.202.

Chapter 5

Since some use these principles bluntly, dully, and with poor taste, and others employ them intelligently, gracefully, and forcibly, this work about which I am speaking should be undertaken by a man who can argue and speak with wisdom, even though he cannot speak eloquently. It is his wisdom which benefits his hearers; although he himself is less useful than he would be if he were an eloquent speaker also. But the one to guard against is the man whose eloquence is no more than an abundant flow of empty words.[1] His listener is more easily charmed by him in matters that are unprofitable to hear about and, all too frequently such eloquence is mistaken for truth. Moreover, this opinion did not escape the notice of those who believed that the art of rhetoric should be taught. They acknowledged that 'wisdom without eloquence is of small benefit to states, but eloquence without wisdom is frequently very prejudicial, and never beneficial.'[2] Those who have propounded the rules of eloquence have been compelled by the force of truth to admit this in the very books in which they treat of eloquence, unaware as they were of the true, that is, of the heavenly wisdom which has come down from the 'Father of Lights.'[3] How much more, consequently, ought we, who are the children and ministers of this wisdom, to be influenced by no other view? Furthermore, a man speaks more or less wisely in proportion as he has made more or less progress in the Holy Scriptures. I do not mean in the extensive reading and memorizing of them, but in a thorough understanding and careful search-

---
[1] Cf. Cic. *De orat.* 1.12.50; 1.12.53; 1.6.20; 1.18.83; 1.20.92; 3.35.142; *Orat.* 19.65.
[2] Cf. Cic. *De invent.* 1.1.1.
[3] James 1.17.

ing into their meanings. Some men there are who read them, but pay no attention to them; they read in order to remember, but they are indifferent about understanding. Undoubtedly, we must greatly prefer to these men those who have less grasp of the words, but see with the eyes of their heart the soul of Scripture. But, better than either of these is the man, who, when he wishes, both cites Scripture and understands it as he should.

(8) Therefore, it is particularly essential for the man who should say with wisdom even what he cannot say eloquently to remember the words of the Scriptures. For, the poorer he sees himself to be in his own speech, the more he should enrich himself with that of the Scriptures, so that he may prove from them what he says in his own words and, although inferior in his own words, he may rise in distinction, as it were, by the testimony of the great. His proofs give pleasure where his manner of speaking does not. Besides, if anyone is desirous of speaking not only wisely, but also eloquently, since he will be of much more use if he can do both, he ought to be advised to read and hear eloquent men, and to imitate them through practice,[4] rather than to devote himself to the teachers of the art of rhetoric.[5] Those whom he reads and listens to, of course, are to be such as have been justly recommended as having spoken or as now speaking not only with eloquence but also with wisdom. Those who speak eloquently are listened to with delight; those who speak wisely are listened to with profit. For this reason Scripture does not say: 'The multitude of the eloquent,' but 'the multitude of the wise is the welfare of the whole world.'[6]

---

4 Cf. Cic. *De orat.* 2.20.85.
5 Cf. Cic. *De orat.* 1.19.87; 1.20.91.
6 Wisd. 6.26.

Just as we must often take bitter things that are conducive to health, so we must always avoid a sweetness that is harmful. What is better than a wholesome sweetness or a sweet wholesomeness? The more sweetness is desired, the more easily is the wholesomeness beneficial. Accordingly, there are ecclesiastical writers who have handled Holy Scripture not only with wisdom, but also with eloquence. For the reading of these there is not sufficient time for students and those at leisure to be able to exhaust them.

Chapter 6

(9) At this point, perhaps, someone may ask whether our authors, whose divinely inspired writings have formed the Canon with an authority that is very beneficial for us, are only wise, or whether they should be designated as eloquent also. Certainly, for myself and for those who agree with me in what I maintain, this question is very readily answered. For, when I understand them, it seems to me that not only could no one be wiser, but also that no one could be more eloquent than they are. And I venture to maintain that all who understand correctly what those writers are saying understand at the same time that they should not have said it any other way. A certain kind of eloquence is more fitting for youth, and another is more becoming for old age; so much so that we should not call it eloquence if it is not appropriate for the person of the speaker.[1] There is a kind of eloquence, then, which is becoming for men eminently worthy of the highest authority and manifestly inspired by God. Biblical writers have spoken with this kind of eloquence; no other kind becomes them, nor is that kind suitable

---
1 Cf. Cic. *Orat.* 21.71.

for other writers. It is appropriate for them, and the more humble it seems to be, the higher it rises above others, not because of its conceit, but because of its solidity. On the other hand, when I do not understand them, to be sure, their eloquence is less evident to me, yet I do not doubt that it is of the same quality as it is when I do understand. Further, the obscurity of the sacred and saving utterances had to be a component of that kind of eloquence whose purpose was to benefit our intellects, not only through their discovery of truth, but also through their own application.

(10) Still, if there were time, I could point out to those who set their own language ahead of that of our writers (not because of its greatness but because of its extravagance)[2] that all the qualities and oratorical ornaments they boast about are found in the sacred writings[3] of those whom divine Providence has provided to instruct us and lead us from this wicked world to the blessed one. It is not what these men have in common with pagan orators and poets that gives me more pleasure in that eloquence than I can say. I feel greater admiration and surprise because they have used our eloquence in a way which is all their own, so that it is neither lacking nor ostentatious in them. It was not right for them either to condemn eloquence nor to make a display of it. The former would have happened if they had avoided it, and the latter could have been believed of them, if they had made their eloquence easily recognizable. And, in those places where it happens to be recognized by the learned, such matters are being discussed that the words by which they are expressed seem not to have been sought after by the speaker, but to have been associated naturally with those

---

2 Cf. *De doctr. chr.* 2.31.48.
3 Cf. *Conf.* 3.5.9.

very matters, as if you were to understand wisdom as going out of her home,[4] that is, the heart of the wise man, 'and eloquence like an inseparable servant following her even though unbidden.[5]

Chapter 7

(11) Who would not see what the Apostle was trying to say and how wisely he spoke, when he said:[1] 'We exult in tribulations, knowing that tribulation works out endurance, and endurance, tried virtue, and tried virtue, hope. And hope does not disappoint, because the charity of God is poured forth in our hearts by the Holy Spirit who has been given to us'? Here, if anyone unlearnedly learned (if I may use the expression) were to argue that the Apostle had followed the rules of the art of rhetoric, would he not be laughed at by both learned and unlearned Christians? Nevertheless, we recognize in this passage the figure which is called *climax* in Greek, and *gradatio* in Latin,[2] by some, since they do not wish to call it *scala* ['ladder'], when words or thoughts are joined together, one proceeding from another. Here, for example, we see 'endurance' proceeding from 'tribulation,' 'tried virtue' from 'endurance,' and 'hope' from 'tried virtue.' Here, too, we perceive another ornament of style. After certain statements completed in a single tone of expression, which our writers call *membra*[3] and *caesa*[4] ['clauses' and 'phrases'], while the Greeks call them *cola* and *commata*,

---

4 Prov. 9.1.
5 Cf. Cic. *Orat.* 21.70.

---

1 Rom. 5.3-5.
2 Cf. *Auct. ad Her.* 4.25.34; Quint., *Inst. or.* 9.3.55.
3 Cf. *Auct. ad Her.* 4.19.26; Quint., *Inst. or.* 9.4.123.
4 Cf. Cic. *Orat.* 62.211; Quint. *Inst. or.* 9.4.22; Aquila, *Rhet.* 18.

there follows a rounded sentence[5] or period which the Greeks call *periodos*, whose *membra* are held suspended by the voice of the speaker until it is completed by the last one.[6] The first *membrum* of those preceding the period is: 'since tribulation works out endurance'; the second is: 'and endurance, tried virtue'; and the third is: 'and tried virtue, hope.' Then follows the period itself, which is completed in three *membra*. The first of these is: 'And hope does not disappoint'; the second is: 'because the charity of God is poured forth in our hearts'; and the third is: 'by the Holy Spirit who has been given to us.' These things and others like them are taught in the art of rhetoric.[7] Therefore, just as I do not maintain that the Apostle followed the rules of rhetoric, so I do not deny that eloquence followed his wisdom.

(12) Writing in his second Epistle to the Corinthians, he contradicts certain false apostles among the Jews who were disparaging him. Since he is forced to speak of himself, as if attributing this folly to himself, how wisely and how eloquently he speaks! He is the companion of wisdom and the leader of eloquence. The former he follows; for the latter, he leads the way, not spurning it, however, when it chooses to follow him. He says:[8] 'I repeat, let no one think me foolish. But if so, then regard me as such, that I also may boast a little. What I am saying in this confidence of boasting, I am not speaking according to the Lord, but, as it were, in foolishness. Since many boast according to the flesh, I too will boast. For you gladly put up with fools, because you are wise yourselves! For you suffer it if a man enslaves you, if a

---

5 Cf. Cic. *Orat.* 61.204; Quint. *Inst. or.* 9.4.124; Mart. Cap. 5. 527.
6 Cf. Cic. *Brut.* 8.34.
7 Cf. *Auct. ad Her.* 4; Cic. *De orat.* 3; Quint. *Inst. or.* 9.
8 2 Cor. 11.16-30.

man devours you, if a man takes from you, if a man is arrogant, if a man slaps your face! I speak to my own shame, as though we had been weak. But wherein any man is bold—I am speaking foolishly—I also am bold. Are they Hebrews? So am I! Are they Israelites? So am I! Are they offspring of Abraham? So am I! Are they ministers of Christ? I—to speak as a fool—am more: in many more labors, in prisons more frequently, in lashes above measure, often exposed to death. From the Jews five times I received forty lashes less one. Thrice I was scourged, once I was stoned, thrice I suffered shipwreck, a night and a day I was adrift on the sea; in journeyings often, in perils from floods, in perils from robbers, in perils from my own nation, in perils from the Gentiles, in perils in the city, in perils in the wilderness, in perils in the sea, in perils from false brethren; in labor and hardships, in many sleepless nights, in hunger and thirst, in fastings often, in cold and nakedness. Besides those outer things, there is my daily pressing anxiety, the care of all the churches! Who is weak, and I am not weak? Who is made to stumble, and I am not inflamed? If I must boast, I will boast of the things that concern my weakness.' Attentive souls can see how much wisdom is in these words. Even one who is deep in sleep can observe also with what a noble flow of eloquence they rush on.

(13) Further, anyone who has learned about them observes that, inserted with a most suitable variety,[9] those *caesa,* called *cómmata* by the Greeks, and the *membra* and periods of which I spoke a little while ago, created the whole figure and expression, so to speak, of a style which charms and arouses even the unlearned. From the place where I began to introduce this passage there are periods. The first is the

---

9 Cf. Cic. *De orat.* 1.32.144; *Orat.* 29.103.

smallest, that is, it has two *membra* (periods cannot have less than two *membra,* although they may have more).¹⁰ The first, then, is: 'I repeat, let no one think me foolish.' The second follows with three *membra*: 'But if so, then regard me as such, that I also may boast a little.' The third, which comes next, has four *membra*: 'What I am saying, in this confidence of boasting, I am not speaking according to the Lord, but as it were in foolishness.' The fourth has two: 'Since many boast according to the flesh, I too will boast.' The fifth has two: 'For you gladly put up with fools, because you are wise yourselves!' The sixth also has two: 'For you suffer it if a man enslaves you.' Three *caesa* follow: 'If a man devours you, if a man takes from you, if a man is arrogant.' Then come three *membra*: 'If a man slaps your face! I speak to my own shame, as though we had been weak.' A period of three *membra* follows: 'But wherein any man is bold—I am speaking foolishly—I also am bold.' From this point on, after several *caesa* have been proposed as questions, so separate *caesa* are given back in answer;¹¹ three answers to three questions: 'Are they Hebrews? So am I! Are they Israelites? So am I! Are they offspring of Abraham? So am I!' Although the fourth *caesum* has been expressed with the same interrogation, he does not reply with the balance of another *caesum,* but of a *membrum*: 'Are they ministers of Christ? I—to speak as a fool—am more.' Then, after the form of interrogation has been properly set aside, the four following *caesa* are poured forth: 'in many more labors, in prisons more frequently, in lashes above measure, often exposed to death.' A short period is then inserted, because by the elevation of our voice we must

---
10 Cf. *Auct. ad Her.* 4.19.26; Cic. *Orat.* 66.221-222; Quint. *Inst. or.* 9.4.125; Aug. *Mus.* 4.17.36.
11 Cf. Cic. *Orat.* 40.137; *De orat.* 3.54.207.

distinguish 'From the Jews five times,' making it one *membrum* to which is joined the other: 'I received forty lashes less one.' Then he returns to *caesa* and uses three: 'Thrice I was scourged, once I was stoned, thrice I suffered shipwreck.' A *membrum* follows: 'a night and a day I was adrift on the sea.' Then fourteen *caesa* flow forth with appropriate vigor: 'in journeyings often, in perils from floods, in perils from robbers, in perils from my own nation, in perils from the Gentiles, in perils in the city, in perils in the wilderness, in perils in the sea, in perils from false brethren; in labor and hardships, in many sleepless nights, in hunger and thirst, in fastings often, in cold and nakedness.' After these he inserts a period of three *membra*: 'Besides those outer things, there is my daily pressing anxiety, the care of all the churches!' And to this we join two *membra* as a question: 'Who is weak? and I am not weak? Who is made to stumble, and I am not inflamed?' Finally, this whole passage, as if panting for breath, is completed by a period of two *membra*: 'If I must boast, I will boast of the things that concern my weakness.' After this outburst, because he rests, as it were, and makes his hearer rest by inserting a little narrative, it is impossible to describe adequately what beauty and what charm he produces. For, he continues by saying: 'The God and Father of our Lord Jesus, who is blessed forevermore, knows that I do not lie.'[12] And then he tells briefly how he has been exposed to danger and how he escaped.

(14) It would be tedious to recount other examples or to indicate these in other passages of the Holy Scriptures. What if I had tried to point out also the figures of speech which are taught in the art of rhetoric and are present in those passages at least which I have quoted from the Apostle's

---
12 2 Cor. 11.31.ff

eloquence? Is it not true that thoughtful men would more readily have believed that I am going to excess rather than that any students would have felt that I was meeting their needs? When all these principles are taught by masters, they are considered of great value, are purchased at a high price, and are sold with considerable display. I myself have a dread of being tainted by that ostentation while I am discussing these matters in this way. However, I must give an answer to the ill-informed men who believe that our authors should be despised not because they do not possess, but because they do not make a display of, the eloquence which those others value too highly.

(15) Someone might think that I have selected the Apostle Paul as if he were our one eloquent speaker. For when he said: 'Even though rude in speech, but not in knowledge,'[13] it seems as if he spoke by way of concession to his detractors, not as if he were recognizing it as true by acknowledging it. On the other hand, if he had said: 'Indeed rude in speech, but not in knowledge,' nothing else could possibly be understood. He did not hesitate to declare his knowledge openly, because without it he would not have been able to be the 'teacher of the Gentiles.'[14] Surely, if we quote any utterance of his as a model of eloquence, we certainly quote from those Epistles which even his detractors, who were anxious that his spoken word be considered of no consequence, had to acknowledge were 'weighty and telling.'[15] Consequently, I see that I must say something about the eloquence of the Prophets, where many points are kept hidden through a figurative manner of speaking. The more

---

13 Cf. 2 Cor. 11.6.
14 1 Tim. 2.7.
15 2 Cor. 10.10.

these seem to be concealed by figurative words, the more delightful they become when they have been explained. At this point I should quote something of such a nature that I shall not be compelled to explain what has been said, but only to praise the manner in which it was said. In preference to all others I shall select this from the book of the Prophet who says that he was a shepherd or herdsman, and was withdrawn from that occupation by divine Providence and sent to prophesy to the people of God.[16] Nor shall my example be according to the Septuagint translators, who, translating also under the guidance of the Holy Ghost, seem to have altered some passages so that the attention of the reader might be the more encouraged to investigate thoroughly the spiritual meaning (for this reason, several passages of theirs are even more obscure because they are more figurative). I shall use, instead, these passages as they have been translated from Hebrew to the Latin language by the priest Jerome, a skilled interpreter of both languages.[17]

(16) When, then, he was reproving the wicked, the proud, the voluptuous, and those who were very careless about fraternal charity, this peasant, or this one-time peasant turned prophet, exclaimed:[18] 'Woe to you that are wealthy in Sion, and to you that have confidence in the mountain of Samaria: ye great men, heads of the people, that go in with state into the house of Israel. Pass ye over to Chalane, and see, and go from thence into Emath the great: and go down into Geth of the Philistines, and to all the best kingdoms of these: if their border be larger than your border. You that are separated unto the evil day: and that approach to the throne of iniquity: You that sleep upon beds of ivory,

---
16 Amos 7.14f.
17 Aug. *Epist.* 71.4.6; *De civ. Dei* 18.43.
18 Amos 6.1-6.

and are wanton on your couches; that eat the lamb out of the flock, and the calves out of the midst of the herd: You that sing to the sound of the psaltery: they have thought themselves to have instruments of music like David: that drink wine in bowls, and anoint themselves with the best ointment: and they were not concerned for the affliction of Jospeh.' Would those men who, as if they themselves were learned and eloquent, despise our prophets as illiterate and unskilled in speaking—would they have wished to express themselves otherwise, if they had been obliged to say something like this to such people—those of them, at least, who would not have wanted to act like madmen?

(17) What more could discriminating listeners desire from this eloquence? At first, with what a roar the invective itself is hurled as against senses steeped in sleep, in order to arouse them! 'Woe to you that are wealthy in Sion, and to you that have confidence in the mountain of Samaria: ye great men, heads of the people, that go in with state into the house of Israel.' In order to show that they are ungrateful for the gifts of God, who has given them the spacious expanses of their kingdom, in that they put their trust in the mountain of Samaria, where idols are worshipped, the prophet then says: 'Pass ye over to Chalane, and see, and go from thence into Emath the great: and go down into Geth of the Philistines, and to all the best kingdoms of these: if their border be larger than your border.' Even at the same time that he says these words, his discourse is adorned, as if by lights, with the names of such places as Sion, Samaria, Chalane, Emath the great, and Geth of the Philistines. Then, the words used in these places are very appropriately varied: 'You are wealthy,' 'you have confidence,' 'pass ye over,' 'go,' and 'go down.'

(18) Next he announces that a future captivity under a hostile king is approaching when he adds: 'You that are separated unto the evil day: and that approach to the throne of iniquity.' Then the evils of luxury are brought to mind: 'You that sleep upon beds of ivory, and are wanton on your couches; that eat the lambs out of the flock, and the calves out of the midst of the herd.' Those six *membra* formed three periods of two *membra* each. He does not say: 'You that are separated unto the evil day, that approach to the throne of iniquity, that sleep upon beds of ivory, that are wanton on your couches, that eat the lambs out of the flock, and the calves out of the midst of the herd.' If he had expressed it this way, so that each of the six *membra* began with the same pronoun repeated each time and so that each one was ended by the tone of the voice, it would certainly have been beautiful. But it has become more beautiful because the *membra* were joined in pairs to the same pronoun, and these developed three sentences: one, a prediction of the captivity: 'You that are separated unto the evil day: and that approach to the throne of iniquity'; the second pertaining to lust: 'You that sleep upon beds of ivory, and are wanton on your couches'; and the third concerning gluttony: 'that eat the lamb out of the flock, and the calves out of the midst of the herd.' The result is that it is left to the inclination of the speaker whether he will finish each one separately and make six *membra,* or whether he will raise his voice at the first, third, and fifth, and, by linking the second to the first, the fourth to the third, and the sixth to the fifth, very properly create three periods of two *membra* each; one to tell of impending disaster, the other to denounce impurity, and the third to censure intemperance.

(19) Next, he rebukes their immoderate pleasure in the

sense of hearing. When he had said: 'You that sing to the sound of the psaltery' (since music can be used with wisdom by those who are wise), he checks the vehemence of his invective with admirable beauty of style, speaking now not to them, but about them. To impress upon us that we should discriminate between the music of the wise man and the music of the voluptuous man, he does not say: 'You that sing to the sound of the psaltery and think you have instruments of music like David'; but, when he had said to the licentious what they should hear: 'You that sing to the sound of psaltery,' he pointed out their ignorance to others, adding: 'They have thought themselves to have instruments of music like David: that drink wine in bowls, and anoint themselves with the best ointment.' These three are pronounced more correctly if the voice is kept raised for the first two *membra* and the period is completed with the third.

(20) The following is now added to all the former passages: 'And they were not concerned for the affliction of Joseph.' Whether it is pronounced continuously to form one *membrum,* or it is more appropriate to keep the voice raised for 'And they were not concerned,' and, after this separation, say 'for the affliction of Joseph' to form a period of two *membra*—in any case, he did not say: 'they were not concerned for the affliction of their brother,' but with wondrous beauty used the word 'Joseph' instead of 'brother.' In this way every brother is signified by the proper name of the man whose renown among his brothers is celebrated both for the wrongs which he suffered and for the benefits which he paid in return.[19] In fact, I do not know whether that figure by which Joseph is taken to mean every possible brother is taught by that art of rhetoric which I have learned

---
19 Gen. 37ff.

and taught. But, it is pointless to tell anyone who does not realize it himself how beautiful it is and how it influences those who read with understanding.

(21) Indeed, many points which apply to the rules of eloquence can be discovered in this very passage which I have used as an example. A sincere reader is not so much instructed when he carefully analyzes it as he is set on fire when he recites it with glowing feeling. For, not by human effort were these words devised; they have been poured forth from the Mind of God both wisely and eloquently, so that wisdom was not bent upon eloquence, nor did eloquence separate itself from wisdom. As some very eloquent and intelligent men could observe and maintain, if those principles which are learned in the art of oratory could not be respected, observed, and brought to these teachings, unless they were first discovered in the natural ability of orators,[20] is it any wonder that they are discovered in those men sent by Him who creates natural abilities? Therefore, let us admit that our canonical writers and teachers were not only wise, but truly eloquent, with such an eloquence as was appropriate for persons of this kind.

Chapter 8

(22) Although we take several examples of expression from their writings which are understood without difficulty, we should by no means imagine that we should imitate them entirely. They have uttered some passages with a beneficial and salutary obscurity, to exercise and, in a sense, to polish the minds of their readers, to break down aversions and spur on the zeal of those who are anxious to learn, as well

---

[20] Cf. Cic. *De orat.* 1.32.146; Quint. *Inst. or.* 2.17.9; Aug. *De doctr. chr*, 2.36.54.

as to conceal the meaning from the minds of the wicked, either that they may be converted to righteousness or excluded from its secrets. In fact, they spoke in such a way that their followers who understood and interpreted them correctly found another mark of favor in the Church of God, unequal to theirs, to be sure, but still closely approaching it. Their interpreters, then, should not speak with a similar authority, as if they are proposing themselves for interpretation, but in all their words their first and greatest endeavor should be to make themselves understood as much as possible by clearness of style.[1] In this way either the person who does not understand is very stupid, or the reason why what we say is not understood, or is understood rather slowly, lies not in our manner of speaking, but in the difficulty and subtlety of the matters which we are trying to explain and make clear.

Chapter 9

(23) There are some passages which are not understood in their proper force or are understood with difficulty, no matter how great, how comprehensive, or how clear the eloquence with which they are handled by the speaker. These should be spoken to a public audience only rarely, if there is some urgent reason, or never at all.[1] However, some books are written in such a way that, when understood, they bind the reader to themselves, as it were, but, when not understood, they are annoying to those who do not care to read them. In familiar conversations with any person, we must not neglect this duty of bringing the truths which we have now perceived, although they are very hard to understand, to the

---

[1] Cf. Quint. *Inst. or.* 8.2.1.

---

[1] Cf. Quint. *Inst. or.* 8.2.18.

knowledge of others.² We should do this, no matter how much labor of reasoning is entailed, provided that our listener or partner in conversation has a desire to learn and does not lack the comprehension which can grasp the truth in whatever way it is made known. As for the teacher, he is not to be anxious about how much eloquence he employs in teaching, but about how clear he is.³

Chapter 10

(24) Sometimes, an assiduous striving after this clearness disregards the more elegant expressions and is not concerned about what sounds well, but only about what reveals and makes known satisfactorily what one is endeavoring to express. For this reason, a certain author, discussing this type of speaking, says that there is a kind of careful negligence in it.¹ This takes away ornaments, but does not produce vulgarities of speech. However, good teachers have, or ought to have, such great care in teaching that, where a word cannot be pure Latin without being obscure or ambiguous, they should use it according to the idiomatic usage, if it avoids ambiguity and obscurity. They should employ it not as it is used by the learned, but rather as the unlearned usually express it.² Our translators were not reluctant to say: *non congregabo conventicula eorum de sanguinibus* ['I will not gather together their meetings for blood offerings'],³ since they felt that it aided the thought to use here in the plural

---
2 Cf. Aug. *Contr. Cresc.* 1.15.19.
3 Cic. *De orat.* 3.10.37-39; Quint. *Inst. or.* 8.2.22.

1 Cic. *Orat.* 23.77ff.
2 Cf. *Auct. ad Her.* 4.12.7; Cic. *Orat.* 23.79; *De orat.* 3.11.10; Quint. *Inst. or.* 8.2.24; 1.5.5.
3 Ps. 15.4.

this noun [*sanguinibus*] which is used only in the singular in the Latin language. Why, then, should a teacher of religion, speaking to ignorant people, be reluctant to say *ossum* instead of *os*,[4] if he fears that *os* might be understood not as the singular of *ossa* [bones], but as the singular of *ora* [mouths], African ears not distinguishing between the long and short sound of vowels?[5] What benefit is a purity of speech[6] which the understanding of the hearer does not follow,[7] since there is no reason at all for speaking, if those for whose enlightenment we are speaking do not understand what we are saying?[8] Therefore, the teacher will avoid all expressions which do not instruct.[9] If he can employ other correct and intelligible words instead of them, he will do better to choose them. If he cannot do this, either because they do not exist or because they do not occur to him at the time, he will even use words that are less correct,[10] provided that the subject itself is taught and learned correctly.[11]

(25) Certainly, in order that we may be understood, this point must be insisted upon, not only in familiar conversations whether with one person or with several, but even much more when a sermon is being delivered before throngs of people.[12] In familar conversations each one has the opportunity to ask questions, but, when all are silent to hear one person and are looking at him attentively,[13] it is neither

---

4 Cf. Quint. *Inst. or.* 1.5.10; Cic. *De orat.* 3.14.52.
5 Cf. Aug. *De ord.* 2.17.45.
6 Cf. Aug. *De catchs rud.* 9.13; *Conf.* 1.18.29; *Contr. adv. Leg.* 1.24.52.
7 Cf. Cic. *De orat.* 3.13.48ff.
8 Cf. Cic. *De orat.* 3.14.52.
9 Cf. *Auct. ad Her.* 4.12.17; Cic. *Orat.* 24.80.
10 Cf. Quint. *Inst. or.* 1.5.71.
11 Cf. Aug. *De catech. rud.* 9.13.
12 Cf. Aug. *De catech. rud.* 15.23.
13 *Idem.*

customary nor fitting for anyone to ask a question about what he does not understand. The speaker should be especially watchful, therefore, to assist those who are silent.[14] For, a crowd that is eager to learn usually indicates by its movement whether it understands, and, until it shows this, he must keep going over what he is discussing with a manifold diversity of expression.[15] Those who are delivering what they have previously prepared and memorized word for word cannot do this. However, as soon as the speaker makes himself understood, he should either end his discussion or pass over to other matters. For, just as a speaker is pleasing when he makes clear things that should be learned, so he is irksome when he keeps emphasizing facts that are already known,[16] at least to those whose whole expectation was depending upon the explanation of the obscurity of those passages which are being discussed. In order to give pleasure, even things that are known are discussed[17] when attention is centered not on the things themselves, but on the manner in which they are handled. Yet, if even this manner is already known, but still pleases its hearers, it makes almost no difference whether the man who is talking is a speaker or a reader. Things that have been attractively written are usually not only read with pleasure by those who are learning about them for the first time, but are even reread with pleasure by those who know them very well already and from whose memory forgetfulness has not yet effaced them. At any rate, both of these classes listen to them willingly. Further, a person is taught whatever he has forgotten when he is reminded of it. I am not speaking now about the manner of pleasing; I am

---

14 Cf. Quint. *Inst. or.* 8.2.23.
15 Cf. Quint. *Inst. or.* 8.2.24; Aug. *De catech. rud.* 13.18.
16 Cf. Aug. *De catech. rud.* 13.18; *Enarr.* 2.1.12 *in Ps.* 32; *Serm.* 348.4.
17 Cf. Cic. *De orat.* 3.30.121; 3.31.125.

speaking about the way in which those who are anxious to learn should be taught. And the best way is the one that causes the listener to hear the truth and to understand what he hears. When the discussion has attained this end, no further effort has to be spent on the matter itself as if it required further explanation, but perhaps we may have to take pains about praising it so that it may become firmly implanted in the heart. If this seems the right thing to do, it should be done so discreetly that it does not lead to tedium.

Chapter 11

(26) This eloquence in teaching consists, certainly, not in having our speaking cause a person to like what was distasteful or to do what he was reluctant to do, but in causing what was obscure to become clear.[1] Yet, if this is accomplished without elegance, its benefit certainly reaches a few very zealous students[2] who are anxious to know what they should learn, although it is being expressed improperly and crudely. When they have obtained this, they feast upon truth itself with delight; it is an outstanding quality of noble minds to love the truth in words and not the words themselves. Of what use is a golden key, if it is unable to open what we desire? Or what objection is there to a wooden one, if it can? We are asking only that what is closed be opened. But, since eating and learning have some similarity to each other, even the very food without which we cannot live must be seasoned[3] to satisfy the tastes of the majority.

Chapter 12

(27) Accordingly, a certain orator has said, and said

---
1 Cf. Cic. *De orat.* 1.53.229; 2.27.115.
2 Cf. Cic. *De orat.* 3.11.41; *Auct. ad Her.* 4.11.16.
3 Cf. Cic. *Orat.* 6.21.

truly, that an eloquent man should speak in such a way that he 'teaches, pleases, and persuades.' Then he added: 'To teach is a necessity, to please is a satisfaction, and to persuade is a triumph.'[1] Of these three, the one mentioned first, that is, the necessity of teaching, depends upon what we say; the other two depend upon the manner in which we say it.[2] Therefore, a man who speaks with the intention of teaching should not think that he has said what he intended to the person he is trying to instruct, so long as he is not understood. Although he has said what he himself understands, he thus is not to be regarded as having yet spoken to the man who has not understood him. However, if he has been understood, he has spoken, no matter how he expressed himself.[3] But, if he is also trying to please or persuade the person to whom he is speaking, he will not succeed by speaking in any way whatsoever, for the manner in which he speaks is important in order that he may produce this effect.[4] Just as the listener must be pleased in order that he may be kept listening, so he must be persuaded in order that he may be influenced to act. And, just as he is pleased if you speak attractively, so he is moved if he finds pleasure in what you promise, dreads what you threaten, hates what you condemn, embraces what you praise, grieves over what you emphasize as deplorable, rejoices when you say something he should rejoice at, pities those whom in your discourses you set before his eyes as objects of pity, avoids those whom you by awakening fear point out should be avoided. Whatever

---

[1] Cf. Cic. Orat. 21.69; De orat. 2.27.115; 2.28.121; 2.77.310; Brut. 49.185; De opt. gen. 1.3; 5.16.
[2] Cf. Aug. Contr. Cresc. 1.13.16; De dial. 7; Cic. De orat. 2.77.310; Brut. 23.89.
[3] Cf. Aug. Contr. Cresc. 1.13.16.
[4] Idem.

else can be accomplished through grand eloquence to influence the hearts of one's listeners, they must be persuaded not that they may know what should be done, but to do what they already know they should do.

(28) However, if they do not yet know this, they must certainly be taught before they are persuaded. And perhaps, when they have learned these very things, they will be influenced to such an extent that there will be no necessity for persuading them by greater powers of eloquence. Yet, when this is necessary, it should be done. And there is a necessity when, although persons know what should be done, they do not do it. Therefore, 'teaching is a necessity.' Men can either do or refrain from doing what they know about. But, who would say that they ought to do what they do not know about? Therefore, persuasion is not a necessity, because there is not always a need of it, provided that the listener agrees with the one who is teaching or even pleasing him. But, 'to persuade is a triumph,' because it is possible for a man to be taught and pleased, and still not agree. Besides, what good are those first two, if this third effect is wanting? Neither is there any necessity here for pleasing, since, when truths are pointed out in speaking (and this is the duty of teaching), this is not done by means of eloquence, nor is it intended that either the subject or the eloquence should give pleasure; the truths made clear give pleasure of themselves because they are true. Consequently, even falsehoods frequently give pleasure when they are detected and refuted. They are not pleasing because they are falsehoods, but, because it is a truth that they are falsehoods, the very mode of expression which demonstrates that this is true is pleasing.

Chapter 13

(29) To the art of pleasing those whose pampered tastes truth does not satisfy, if it is presented in any way other than an agreeable one, no small place has been assigned in eloquence.[1] Yet, when this art has been added, it does not satisfy the obstinate, who have benefited neither from having understood, nor from having been pleased by, the teacher's style. What use are these two to a man who both acknowledges the truth and praises the eloquence, but does not yield his consent, although it is only for this consent that the speaker gives careful attention to the matters which he is discussing when he is urging something?[2] If the things being taught are of such a nature that belief in them and knowledge of them is sufficient, yielding consent to them is nothing else than acknowledging that they are true. But, when what is being taught must be carried out, and when the teaching occurs for that very reason, we are uselessly persuaded of the truth of what is said and uselessly pleased by the very manner in which it is said, if we do not learn it in such a way that we practice it. Therefore, the Christian orator, when he is urging something that must be put into practice, must not only teach in order to instruct, and please in order to hold attention, but must also persuade in order that he may be victorious. Indeed, it now remains for that man to be persuaded to consent through sublime eloquence, since this was not effected in him by a demonstration of truth that gained his own admission and was accompanied, moreover, by attractiveness of style.

Chapter 14

(30) Men have devoted so much attention to this matter

1 Cf. Cic. *Orat.* 6.20; 25.83; *De orat.* 3.25.97.
2 Cf. Cic. *De invent.* 1.5.6; *De orat.* 1.61.260; 1.31.138; 1.49.213.

of attractiveness that numerous very wicked and shameful things, which we should not only not commit, but should even avoid and loathe, are now cloaked in a pleasant style. The eloquent works of wicked and dishonorable men are read not for instruction, but merely for pleasure.[1] May God avert from His Church what the Prophet Jeremias relates about the synagogue of the Jews, when he says:[2] 'Dread and horrible things have been done upon the land. The prophets prophesied wickedness, and the priests clapped their hands: and My people loved such things: and what will you do in the future?' O eloquence, so much the more terrifying because it is plain, and so much the more forceful because it is genuine! O truly 'an ax that breaketh the rocks in pieces'![3] God Himself has said through this same prophet that His word, spoken through the holy Prophets, is like this ax. Hence, may it never happen that our priests applaud those who speak wickedness or that the people of God love such things. May it never happen, I repeat, that such great madness be ours! What shall we do in the future? Let what we say be less intelligible, less pleasing, less persuasive, but still by all means, let it be said; and let truths, not falsehoods, be listened to with pleasure. But this, of course, would be impossible, unless they were expressed attractively.

(31) In the case of a 'strong people,' such as God has spoken about:[4] 'I will praise Thee in a strong people,' there is no pleasure in that attractiveness of style, which certainly does not teach falsehoods, but ornaments trifling and perish-

---

[1] Cf. Aug. *Contr. Cresc.* 1.2.3; 1.1.2; *Conf.* 1.18,28; Cic. *De orat.* 1.11.47.
[2] Jer. 5.30f. (ancient version).
[3] Jer. 23.29 (ancient version).
[4] Ps. 34.18.

able truths with a frothy showiness of style such as would not be a fitting or dignified adornment for noble and enduring truths. There is something like this in a letter of the blessed Cyprian, which I believe either happened accidentally or was done designedly, that succeeding ages might perceive how the soundness of Christian teaching has restrained his style from that redundancy and restricted it to a more dignified and more moderate eloquence, such as in his later writings is safely admired and anxiously sought after, but imitated only with very great difficulty. He says, for example, in a certain place:[5] 'Let us seek this abode. The neighboring solitudes offer a place of retirement where, while the wandering tendrils of the vines creep through the trellis-supports with overhanging interlacings, the leafy covering has formed a colonnade of vines.' This is expressed with a wonderful fluency and luxuriance of style, but, because of its immoderate profuseness, it is displeasing to the serious reader. Those who like this style think that those who do not use it, but express themselves with greater restraint, cannot speak in that style, not realizing that they avoid it deliberately. This holy man shows both that he can speak in that way, because he has done so here, and that he does not prefer to do so, since he never does so afterward.

Chapter 15

(32) And so, an orator, in speaking of justice, sanctity, and virtue (for he should not preach on other topics), tries as far as possible, when he is speaking of these matters, to make his words understandable, pleasing, and persuasive. And he should not doubt that he can do this, if it is possible and as far as it is possible, more through the piety of his

---

5 Cypr. *Ad Donat.* 1.

prayers than through the power of his oratory. Thus, in praying for himself and for those whom he is about to address, he should be a suppliant before he is a speaker. As the hour when he is to speak is at hand, before he uses his tongue in preaching, he should raise his parched soul to God, that he may utter only that with which he has become imbued and manifest what has inspired him. For, in regard to every subject to be discussed according to faith and love, although there are many things to be said and many ways in which they may be said by those who know about them, who knows what is either fitting for us to say or proper to be heard through us for the present, except Him who sees 'the hearts of all'?[1] Who can make us say what we should and say it in the way we should, except Him in whose 'hand are both we and our words'?[2] Therefore, anyone who is anxious to know and teach should, indeed, learn all the things that must be taught and acquire a skill in speaking becoming to an ecclesiastic. Yet, at the time of his discourse, he should consider what the Lord says as more suitable for a well-disposed mind:[3] 'Do not be anxious how or what you are to speak; for what you are to speak will be given to you in that hour. For it is not you who are speaking, but the Spirit of your Father who speaks through you.' Therefore, if the Holy Ghost speaks in those who are delivered to their persecutors for the sake of Christ, why will he not speak in those who are transmitting Christ to their disciples?

Chapter 16

(33) Further, anyone who says that men do not have

---

1 Acts 1.24.
2 Wisd. 7.16.
3 Matt. 10.19f; cf Cic. *De orat.* 1.26.119; 1.26.121.

to be given rules about what or how they should teach, if it is the Holy Ghost that forms teachers, can maintain that we do not have to pray, either, because our Lord says:[1] 'Your Father knows what you need, before you ask Him.' Or he can maintain that the Apostle Paul should not have given rules to Timothy and Titus about the matter and manner of their instruction of others. A man who has been assigned the position of teacher in the Church should keep before his eyes these three Epistles of the Apostle. Do we not read in the first Epistle to Timothy:[2] 'Announce and teach these things'? What these things are I explained above. Is not the following admonition also found there:[3] 'Do not rebuke an elderly man, but exhort him as you would a father'? In the second Epistle did not the Apostle say to Timothy:[4] 'Hold to the form of sound teaching which thou hast heard from me'? In the same place does he not also say:[5] 'Use all care to present thyself to God as a man approved, a worker that cannot be ashamed, rightly handling the word of truth'? There is also found this passage:[6] 'Preach the word, be urgent in season, out of season: reprove, entreat, rebuke with all patience and teaching.' And likewise, does he not say to Titus that a bishop ought to be holding fast in accordance with the teaching 'of the faithful word, that he may be powerful in sound doctrine and able to confute opponents'?[7] He also says in the same Epistle:[8] 'But do thou speak what befits the sound doctrine: that elderly men be reserved,'

---

1 Matt. 6.8.
2 Cf. 1 Tim. 4.11.
3 1 Tim. 5.1.
4 2 Tim. 1.13.
5 2 Tim. 2.15.
6 2 Tim. 4.2.
7 Cf. Titus 1.9.
8 Titus 2.1.

and so on. There is also this passage: 'Thus speak, and exhort, and rebuke with all authority. Let no one despise thee.'⁹ 'Admonish them to be subject to princes and authorities,'¹⁰ and so on. Consequently, what are we to think? Does the Apostle contradict himself, declaring that teachers are formed by the operation of the Holy Ghost, while he himself gives them directions about what and how they are to teach? Or are we to understand that, although the Holy Ghost gives Himself abundantly, the functions of men in instructing even the teachers themselves must not remain unused, and yet, 'neither he who plants is anything, nor he who waters, but God who gives the growth.'¹¹ For this reason, although the preachers themselves are holy men and although the holy angels themselves are active, no one correctly learns the things which concern our life with God, unless God makes him docile to Himself, to whom this passage in the Psalms is addressed:¹² 'Teach me to do Thy will, for Thou art my God.' And so the Apostle, speaking as a teacher to a pupil, says the same thing to Timothy himself:¹³ 'But do thou continue in the things that thou hast learned and that have been entrusted to thee, knowing of whom thou hast learned them.' Bodily medicines which men apply to men are a help only to those for whom God ordains health, since He can cure even without them. Although they are powerless without Him, still they are applied, and if this is done obligingly, it is numbered among the works of mercy or kindness. In the same way, the benefits of teaching applied by a human being are a help

---

9 Titus 2.15.
10 Titus 3.1.
11 1 Cor. 3.7.
12 Ps. 142.10.
13 2 Tim. 3.14.

to the soul when this benefit is ordained by God who could have transmitted the Gospel to man even 'not from men nor by man.'[14]

Chapter 17

(34) Consequently, a man who is endeavoring through speech to convince of what is good rejects none of these three aims, namely, to teach, to please, and to persuade, but should also pray and strive, as I said previously, that his words may be intelligible, pleasing, and persuasive. When he does this properly and suitably, he can justly be called eloquent,[1] even though he does not obtain the agreement of his listener. To these three aims, that is, teaching, pleasing, and persuading, the author of Roman eloquence himself seems to have intended to relate the three styles when he maintained in the same way:[2] 'He will be eloquent, then, who can speak about trivial subjects in a subdued style, ordinary subjects in a moderate style, and noble subjects in a grand style.' It is as if he were adding the three ends mentioned above, developing one and the same thought in this way: He will be eloquent, then, who, in order to teach, can speak about trivial subjects in a subdued style; in order to please, can discuss ordinary subjects in a moderate style; and in order to persuade, can treat of noble subjects in a grand style.

Chapter 18

(35) That author could have exemplified in legal cases[1] those three styles as they have been defined by him;

---
14 Gal. 1.1.

---
1 Cf. Cic. *Orat.* 35.123; *De orat.* 1.61.260; 1.32.144.
2 Cf. Cic. *Orat.* 29.101; 21.69; *De orat.* 3.45.177; 3.52.199; 3.55.212; *Auct. ad Her.* 4.8.11.

---
1 Cf. Cic. *Orat.* 29.102.

but he could not have done so in ecclesiastical questions, which depend upon a mode of expression of the kind which I intend to describe. In legal questions, matters are considered trivial when the case involves financial matters; they are considered important when they concern human welfare or life. But, where neither of these cases is involved, and he is not striving to have the hearer act or pronounce a decision, but merely to please him, the subject matter is midway between the two, as it were, and for this reason is called middling, that is, moderate.[2] For *modus* ['measure'] gives us the word 'moderate,' and we are not speaking correctly when we misuse 'moderate' for 'small.' However, in our questions, we should refer everything, especially what we say to the people from the pulpit, not to man's temporal, but to his eternal, welfare; since we must also warn there against eternal damnation, everything we say is important. So true is this that whatever the Christian teacher says about financial matters, either in regard to gain or loss, or whether the amount be large or small, should not seem unimportant. For justice is not unimportant, and we should certainly protect it even in regard to small amounts of money, because the Lord says:[3] 'He who is faithful in a very little thing is faithful also in much.' Therefore, what is a very little thing is a little thing, but to be faithful in a very little thing is a great thing. Just as the nature of a circle (namely, that all lines drawn from a point in the center to the circumference are equal) is the same in a large disk as it is in a little coin, so, where unimportant matters are transacted with justice, the dignity of justice is not lessened.

---

[2] *Auct. ad Her.* 4.8.11; Cic. *De orat.* 3.52.199; 3.55.212; *Orat* 26.91; Quint. *Inst. or.* 12.10.58.
[3] Luke 16.10.

(36) Finally, when the Apostle was speaking about worldly trials (and what did these concern if not financial matters?) he said:[4] 'Dare any of you, having a matter against another, bring your case to be judged before the unjust and not before the saints? Do you not know that the saints will judge the world? And if the world will be judged by you, are you unworthy to judge the smallest matters? Do you not know that we shall judge angels? How much more worldly things! If, therefore, you have cases about worldly matters to be judged, appoint those who are rated as nothing in the Church to judge. To shame you I say it. Can it be that there is not one wise man among you competent to settle a case in his brother's matter? But brother goes to law with brother and that before unbelievers. Nay, to begin with, it is altogether a defect in you that you have lawsuits one with another. Why not rather suffer wrong? Why not rather be defrauded? But you yourselves do wrong and defraud, and that to your brethren. Or do you not know that the unjust will not possess the kingdom of God?' Why is it that the Apostle is so angry that he reproves, censures, rebukes, and threatens in this way? Why is it that he gives evidence of the state of his feelings by such numerous and harsh alterations of his voice? Why is it, finally, that he speaks in such a grand style about very unimportant matters? Did worldly affairs deserve so much attention from him? Far from it! He does this for the sake of justice, and charity, and godliness,[5] which no reasonable mind doubts are noble subjects even in regard to the most trifling matters.

(37) Of course, if I were advising men how to plead worldly cases, either for themselves or for their friends, be-

---
4 1 Cor. 6.1-9.
5 1 Tim 6.11.

fore ecclesiastical judges, I would properly urge them to plead them in a subdued manner, as if they were trifling matters. But, since I am discussing the eloquence of the man whom we wish to be a teacher of those things which deliver us from eternal evils and lead us to eternal blessings,[6] these matters are important wherever they are mentioned, whether in public or in private, to one person or to several, to friends or to enemies, in uninterrupted discourse or in familiar conversation, in treatises or in books, in long letters or in short. Unless, perhaps, since a 'cup of cold water' is a very little and very cheap thing, we are to regard as also very little and very cheap the Lord's promise that he who gives a cup of cold water to his disciple 'shall not lose his reward.'[7] Or, perhaps, when a teacher delivers a sermon in church upon this text, he should think that he is saying something unimportant and for that reason should not say it in the moderate or grand style, but in the subdued style. When we happened to speak about this subject in public and God inspired us so that we did not speak inappropriately,[8] did not a kind of flame blaze up, as if from that cold water,[9] which kindled even the cold hearts of men to accomplish the works of mercy for the hope of a heavenly reward?

Chapter 19

(38) Although our teacher should be one who speaks of noble subjects, he should not always express them in the grand style, but use the subdued style when he is teaching, and the moderate style when he is condemning or praising.

---

6 Matt. 6.13.
7 Matt. 10.42.
8 St. Augustine may have here in mind *Sermo* 39 (Migne PL 39.211) or *Enarr. in Ps.* 102 (PL 37.1326).
9 2 Mac. 1.32.

Yet, when something should be done and we are addressing those who should do it, but are unwilling, then important things must be expressed in the grand style as the one suitable for the persuasion of their wills.[1] Sometimes we handle the same important theme in a subdued manner when we are teaching, in a moderate manner when we are praising it, and in a grand manner when we are persuading a mind alienated from truth to be converted to it. For, what is greater than God Himself? Is that a reason why we should not learn about Him? Or should one who is teaching the Unity of the Trinity handle it only in the subdued style of speaking, in order that a subject so hard to distinguish may be understood as far as possible? Are ornaments of style to be sought here instead of proofs? Is the listener to be persuaded to do something, instead of being instructed that he may learn? Besides, when we are praising God either for Himself or for His works, what beauty of noble and brilliant eloquence[2] reveals itself to the man who can praise, as far as is possible, Him whom no one praises fittingly, but whom everyone praises in some way! If He is not worshipped, or if idols, whether they are demons or any creature at all, are worshipped with Him or even in preference to Him, we certainly should proclaim in the grand style how great this evil is and how men should be turned away from it.

Chapter 20

(39) To speak more definitely, there is an example of subdued style[1] in the Apostle Paul when he says:[2] 'Tell me,

---

1 Cf. Cic. *Orat.* 21. 70; 35.123.
2 Cf. Cic. *Orat.* 27.96.

1 Cf. Quint. *Inst. or.* 12.10.59; *Auct. ad Her.* 4.10.14; Cic. *Orat.* 23.76; 24.79; 28.99.
2 Gal. 4.21-26.

you who desire to be under the Law, have you not heard the Law? For it is written that Abraham had two sons, the one by a slave-girl and the other by a free woman. And the son of the slave-girl was born according to the flesh, but the son of the free woman in virtue of the promise. This is said by way of allegory. For these are the two convenants: one indeed from Mount Sinai, bringing forth children unto bondage, which is Agar. For Sinai is a mountain in Arabia, which corresponds to the present Jerusalem, and is in slavery with her children. But that Jerusalem which is above is free, which is our mother,' and so on. And likewise where he reasons,[3] saying: 'Brethren (I speak after the manner of men); yet even a man's will, once it has been ratified, no one annuls or alters. The promises were made to Abraham and to his offspring. He does not say, "And to his offsprings," as of many; but as of one, "And to thy offspring," who is Christ. Now I mean this: The Law which was made four hundred and thirty years later does not annul the convenant which was ratified by God, so as to make the promise void. For if the right to inherit be from the Law, it is no longer a promise. But God gave it to Abraham by promise.'[4] Because it could occur to the mind of his listener to ask: 'Why, then, was the Law given, if there is no inheritance from it?' he cast this up to himself and said as if he were inquiring: 'What then was the Law?' Then, he answered: 'It was enacted on account of transgressions, being delivered by angels through a mediator, until the offspring should come to whom the promise was made. Now there is no intermediary where there is only one; but God is one.' And here an objection occurred which he proposed to himself: 'Is the Law then contrary to the promises of God?' And he answered: 'By

---
3 Cf. Cic. *Orat.* 5.20; Quint. *Inst. or.* 12.10.59.
4 Gal. 3.15-18.

no means!' and, giving his reason, said: 'For if a law had been given that could give life, justice would truly be from the Law. But the Scripture shut up all things under sin, that by the faith of Jesus Christ the promise might be given to those who believe,'[5] and so on. And similar examples could be cited.[6] Therefore, it is the business of teaching not only to explain obscurities and settle the difficult points of questions, but also, while this is being done, to meet other questions which might possibly occur, so that they may not make void or disprove what we are saying. Care must be taken, however, that the answer to these difficulties occurs at the same time as the question, so that we may not stir up what we are unable to remove. Further, it happens that, when other questions arising from one question and others again arising from these are investigated and answered, the effort of reasoning is drawn out to such a length that, unless the disputant has a very powerful and vigorous memory, he cannot return to the original question.[8] However, it is very beneficial to refute whatever objection can be made, if it occurs to the mind, so that it may not present itself at a place where there will not be anyone to answer it, or that it may not occur to someone who is indeed present, but who keeps silent about it and would go away uncorrected.

(40) However, in the words of the Apostle which follow, the style is moderate:[9] 'Do not rebuke an elderly man, but exhort him as you would a father, and young men as brothers, elderly women as mothers, younger women as

---

5 Gal. 3.19-22.
6 Literally, 'and whatever is of this kind.'
7 Cf. Cic. *Orat.* 29.102; 33.116; 35.122.
8 Cf. Cic. *De orat.* 2.88.359.
9 *Auct. ad Her.* 4.9.13; Cic. *Orat.* 6.21; 26.91ff.; 27.96; Quint *Inst. or.* 12.10.58-60.

sisters';[10] as it is in these words: 'I exhort you, therefore, brethren, by the mercy of God, to present your bodies as a sacrifice, living, holy, pleasing to God.'[11] Almost the entire passage in which this exhortation occurs employs the moderate style of eloquence. There is more beauty in those portions where, as if in payment of a just debt, things that belong together proceed fittingly from one another;[12] for example: 'But we have gifts differing according to the grace that has been given us, such as prophecy to be used according to the proportion of faith; or ministry, in ministering; or he who teaches, in teaching; or he who exhorts, in exhorting; he who gives, in simplicity; he who presides, with carefulness; he who shows mercy, with cheerfulness. Let love be without pretence. Hate what is evil, hold to what is good. Love one another with fraternal charity, anticipating one another with honor. Be not slothful in zeal; be fervent in spirit serving the Lord, rejoicing in hope. Be patient in tribulation, persevering in prayer. Share the needs of the saints, practising hospitality. Bless those who persecute you; bless and do not curse. Rejoice with those who rejoice; weep with those who weep. Be of one mind towards one another.' And how beautifully all these outpourings[13] are brought to a close in a period of two *membra*: 'Do not set your mind on high things but condescend to the lowly!'[14] And a little farther on he says: 'Persevering unto this very end, render to all men whatever is their due; tribute to whom tribute is due; taxes to whom taxes are due; fear to whom fear is due; honor to whom honor is due.' After these have been poured

---

10 1 Tim. 5.1f.
11 Rom. 12.1.
12 Cf. Cic. *Orat.* 12.38; 49.163.
13 Cf. Quint. *Inst. or.* 12.10.60; Cic. *Orat.* 6.21; 27.96.
14 Rom. 12.6-16.

forth as *membra,* they are also concluded in a period formed from two *membra*: 'Owe no man anything except to love one another.'¹⁵ And a little later he says: 'The night is far advanced; the day is at hand. Let us therefore lay aside the works of darkness, and put on the armor of light. Let us walk becomingly as in the day, not in revelry and drunkenness, not in debauchery and wantonness, not in strife and jealousy. But put on the Lord Jesus Christ, and as for the flesh, take no thought for its lusts.'¹⁶ But if someone were to express the last phrase this way: *et carnis providentiam ne in concupiscentiis feceritis* (instead of *et carnis providentiam ne feceritis in concupiscentiis*), unquestionably he would delight the ear with a more rhythmical ending,¹⁷ but the stricter translator has preferred to keep even the order of the words. How this would sound in the Greek language in which the Apostle spoke, those whose skill in that language is adequate for such questions would know.¹⁸ However, it seems to me that what has been translated for us in the same word order does not run on melodiously even in that language.

(41) Indeed, we must admit that our writers lack this adornment of style which is produced by rhythmical endings. Whether this was done by the translators or whether, as I consider more likely, the authors themselves intentionally shunned such ostentation,¹⁹ I do not venture to assert, since I confess I do not know. However, I do know that if someone skilled in this rhythm should arrange the sentence endings of those writers according to the law of harmony, which is very easily accomplished by changing certain words which

---

15 Rom. 13.6-8.
16 Rom. 13.12-14.
17 Cf. Cic. *Orat.* 49.163; 55.183; 20.67; Quint. *Inst. or.* 9.4.61.
18 Cf. Aug. *Conf.* 1.14.23; *De Trin.* 3.1.1.
19 Cf. Cic. *Orat.* 12.39; 69.230ff.

have the same meanings or by changing the order of those he finds there, he would see that these divinely inspired men lacked none of those qualities which he learned to regard as important in the schools of the grammarians and rhetoricians. Furthermore, he will find many examples of great beauty of style,[20] which are elegant in our language, to be sure, but are especially so in the original, although we discover none of these in the writings of which they are so proud. We must be careful, however, not to detract from the authority of inspired and serious thoughts while we are adding rhythm.[21] Our prophets were so far from lacking that musical training in which this harmony of prose is learned in its entirety, that Jerome, a very learned man, mentions even the meters of some of them, at least in the Hebrew language.[22] In order to preserve the integrity of this language in regard to words, he did not transfer these meters from the original language. I, however (to offer my own opinion, which is naturally better known to me than to others and than the opinion of others is to me), while I do not neglect these rhythmical endings in my own speech within the limits of moderation, still I am more pleased that among our own writers I find them used very seldom.

(42) Now, the grand style of eloquence differs from this moderate style principally in the fact that it is not so much embellished with fine expressions as it is forceful because of the passionate feelings of the heart.[23] It adopts nearly all those ornaments of style,[24] but it does not search for them if it does not have them at hand. In fact it is

---

20 Cf. *De doctr. chr.* 3.37.56; 3.29.40.
21 Cf. Cic. *Orat.* 58.197.
22 Jerome *Prolog. super Job.*
23 Cf. Cic. *Orat.* 37.128; 28.97; 5.20; Quint. *Inst. or.* 12.10.61.
24 Cf. *Auct. ad Her.* 4.8.11; Cic. *Orat.* 39.134.

driven on by its own ardor and, if it chances upon any beauty of style, carries it off and claims it, not through a concern for beauty,[25] but because of the force of the subject matter. It is sufficient for the purpose that appropriate words conform to the ardent affection of the heart; they need not be chosen by carefulness of speech. For, if a brave man, eagerly bent upon battle, is armed with a golden and jewel-studded sword, he certainly achieves whatever he does with these weapons, not because they are costly, but because they are weapons. Yet, he is the same man and is very powerful even when 'anger provides a weapon for him as he cast about for one.'[26] The Apostle is endeavoring to persuade us, for the sake of the preaching of the Gospel, to endure patiently all the misfortunes of this life with the consoling help to the gifts of God. It is a noble subject delivered in the grand style, and it does not lack the ornaments of eloquence.[27] 'Behold,' he says, 'now is the acceptable time; behold, now is the day of salvation! Giving no offense to anyone, that our ministry may not be blamed. On the contrary, conducting ourselves in all circumstances as God's ministers, in much patience; in tribulations, in hardships, in distresses; in stripes, in imprisonments, in tumults; in labors, in sleepless nights, in fastings; in innocence, in knowledge, in long-suffering; in kindness, in the Holy Spirit, in unaffected love; in the word of truth, in the power of God; with the armor of justice on the right hand and on the left; in honor and dishonor, in evil report and good report; as deceivers and yet truthful, as unknown and yet we are well known, as dying and behold, we live, as chastised but not killed, as sorrowful yet always rejoicing,

---

25 Cf. Cic. *Orat.* 35.123ff.
26 Verg. *Aen.* 7.507.
27 Cf. Cic. *Orat.* 39.136; 40.137.

as poor yet enriching many, as having nothing yet possessing all things.' See him still aflame: 'We are frank with you, O Corinthians; our heart is wide open to you'[28] and the rest which is too long to quote.

(43) In the same way, he urges the Romans to overcome the persecutions of this world by charity with a sure hope in the help of God. He pleads in the grand style, and also with polish,[29] as he says: 'We know that for those who love God all things work together unto good, for those who, according to his purpose, have been called. For those whom he has foreknown he has also predestined to become conformed to the image of his Son, that he should be the firstborn among many brethren. And those whom he has predestined, them he has also called; and those whom he has called, them he has also justified, and those whom he has justified, them he has also glorified. What then shall we say to these things? If God is for us, who is against us? He who has not spared even his own Son but has delivered him for us all, how can he fail to grant us also all things with him? Who shall make accusations against the elect of God? Is it God who justifies?[30] Who shall condemn? Is it Christ Jesus who died; yes, and rose again, he who is at the right hand of God, who also intercedes for us? Who shall separate us from the love of Christ? Shall tribulation, or distress, or persecution, or hunger, or nakedness, or danger, or the sword? Even as it is written, "For Thy sake we are put to death all the day long. We are regarded as sheep for the slaughter." But in all these things we overcome because of him who

---

28 2 Cor. 6.2-11.
29 Cf. Cic. *Orat.* 39.135; 40.137.
30 See above, 3.3.6. for a rhetorical discussion of this and the two following sentences. The translation of the Confraternity of Christian Doctrine does not follow St. Augustine's punctuation.

has loved us. For I am sure that neither death, nor life, nor angels, nor principalities, nor things present, nor things to come, nor powers, nor height, nor depth, nor any other creature will be able to separate us from the love of God, which is in Christ Jesus our Lord.'[31]

(44) Although the whole Epistle to the Galatians was written in the subdued style of eloquence, except in the concluding passages where the eloquence is moderate, he inserts one passage of such passionate feeling that, although it lacks any ornaments of style such as are found in those I have cited as examples, it could only be expressed in the grand style. He says: You are observing days and months and years and seasons. I fear for you, lest perhaps I have labored among you in vain. Become like me, because I also have become like you, brethren, I beseech you! You have done me no wrong. And you know that on account of a physical infirmity I preached the gospel to you formerly; and though I was a trial to you in my flesh, you did not reject or despise me; but you received me as an angel of God, even as Christ Jesus. Where then is your self-congratulation? For I bear you witness that, if possible, you would have plucked out your very eyes and given them to me. Have I then become your enemy, because I tell you the truth? They court you from no good motive; but they would estrange you, that you may court them. But court the good from a good motive always, and not only when I am present with you, my dear children, with whom I am in labor again, until Christ is formed in you! But I wish I could be with you now, and change my tone, because I do not know what to make of you.'[32] In this pas-

---
31 Rom. 8.28-39.
32 Gal. 4.10-20.

sage have antithetical words balanced each other, have any words been joined to one another in a climax, or did *caesa, membra,* or periods ring in our ears? Nevertheless, not on that account is there any diminution in the stirring emotion with which we feel it vibrate.

Chapter 21

(45) Although these words of the Apostle are so intelligible, they are also profound. They are so written and commended to posterity that they demand not only a reader or a listener, but even an interpreter, if anyone not satisfied with the outer shell would search into their depths. Therefore, let us consider the styles of eloquence in those who, through their reading of the writers of Scripture, have made progress toward the knowledge of divine and salutary truths and have presented this knowledge to the Church. The blessed Cyprian uses the subdued style of speaking in that book where he discusses the Sacrament of the chalice. In fact, in that book he answers the question about whether the chalice of the Lord should contain water only, or water mixed with wine. I should quote something from this work as an example. After the introduction of his letter, then, as he is beginning to answer the proposed question, he says: 'Now you know that we have been admonished to preserve the Lord's instruction in offering the chalice and do nothing different from what the Lord did first for us. Consequently, the chalice which is offered in commemoration of Him is to be offered mixed with wine. For since Christ says: "I am the true vine,"[1] the Blood of Christ is certainly not water, but wine; and His Blood, by which we have been redeemed and vivified, cannot be seen in the chalice when

---

[1] John 15.1.

the chalice is empty of the wine which signifies Christ's Blood, which is foretold by the revelation and testimony of all the Scriptures. We find in Genesis in regard to this Sacrament that Noah has prefigured it and presented a type of the Lord's Passion: he drank wine, became intoxicated, was uncovered in his tent, and lay naked with limbs exposed, and the nakedness of the father was pointed out by his second son, but covered by his eldest and youngest sons.[2] It is not necessary to describe the other circumstances, since it is sufficient to understand this one fact, that Noah, signifying a type of the Truth to come, drank, not water, but wine, and thus represented an image of the Lord's Passion. We see the Sacrament of the Lord prefigured also in the priest Melchisedech, according to what the Holy Scripture testifies and declares: "But Melchisedech the king of Salem, brought forth bread and wine. For he was the priest of the most high God and he blessed Abraham."[3] Furthermore, in the Psalms the Holy Ghost declares that Melchisedech signifies a type of Christ, when in the person of the Father speaking to the Son, He says: "Before the day star I begot Thee. Thou art a priest forever according to the order of Melchisedech."[4] These words and the following ones of this letter[5] preserve the subdued style of speaking, as it is easy for readers to discover.

(46) Saint Ambrose, too, although he is discussing the noble subject of the Holy Ghost, in order to prove that He is equal to the Father and the Son, uses the subdued style of speaking. The subject he has taken for discussion does

---

2 Gen. 9.21-23.
3 Cf. Gen. 14.18-19.
4 Ps. 109.3-4.
5 Cypr. *Epist. ad Caecil.* 63.2-4.

not demand elegance of expression or a feeling of emotion to move hearts, but the evidences of truth. In the prologue of this work, then, he says among other things: 'When Gedeon was disturbed because of the divine announcement by which he had heard that, although thousands of people were wasting away, the Lord in the person of one man would free His people from their enemies, he offered the kid of goats and according to the direction of the angel placed its flesh and unleavened bread upon a rock and poured the broth over them; as soon as the angel of God touched them with the tip of the rod which he was carrying, fire arose from the rock and consumed the sacrifice which was being offered.[6] It seems evident from this sign that the rock was a symbol of the Body of Christ, because it is written: "For they drank from the rock which followed them, but the rock was Christ."[7] Certainly, this referred, not to His Divinity, but to His Flesh, which has flooded the hearts of His thirsty people with the everlasting stream of His Blood. Therefore, it was then made evident in a mystery that the Lord Jesus, crucified in His Flesh, would efface the sins of the whole world, and not only the transgressions of their deeds but also the lusts of their hearts. For the flesh of the kid refers to sinfulness of deed; the broth, to the allurements of passions, as it is written: "For the people strove for the worst lust and said: 'Who will feed us with flesh?' "[8] Therefore, this incident, where the angel extended his rod and touched the rock from which fire came forth, shows that the Flesh of Our Lord, animated by the Spirit of God, would consume all the sins of humanity. For this reason, the Lord says: "I have come to cast fire upon the

---

6 Judges 6.11-21.
7 1 Cor. 10.4.
8 Num. 11.4,

earth" '⁹—and so on where he devotes himself chiefly to teaching and proving his subject.¹⁰

(47) In the moderate style, there is the famous encomium of virginity from Cyprian: 'I am now speaking to virgins, whose loftier renown is likewise our greater concern. They are the flower of the fruit of the Church, the beauty and adornment of spiritual grace, a joyful nature of praise and honor, a spotless and uncorrupted work, an image of God reflecting the sanctity of the Lord, the more illustrious part of the flock of Christ. The glorious fruitfulness of our Mother the Church takes pleasure in them and flourishes abundantly in them; and the more illustrious virginity increases her ranks, the more the joy of our Mother increases.' And in another place at the end of the letter, he says: ' "As we have borne the likeness of the earthy, let us bear also the likeness of the heavenly."¹¹ This image virginity bears, and so do integrity, sanctity, and truth; those mindful of the teaching of God bear it; so do those who hold to justice with conscientiousness, who are steadfast in faith, humble in fear, brave in enduring everything, meek in bearing injustices, willing to show mercy, of one mind and one heart in fraternal peace. Each of these things you should observe, love, and fulfill, O good virgins, who, free for God and Christ, lead the way by reason of your nobler and better lot to the Lord to whom you have vowed yourselves. You who are advanced in years, be instructors for the younger ones; you who are younger, be a help to the older ones and an incentive to your equals. Animate yourselves by mutual encouragement. Provoke one another to glory by emulous

---

9 Luke 12.49.
10 Ambros. *De Spir. sancto* 1, Prolog. 2f.
11 1 Cor. 15.49.

examples of virtue. Endure bravely, proceed spiritually, attain your object successfully. Only remember us then, when your virginity begins to be honored.'[12]

(48) In a style moderate yet ornate, Ambrose also describes to virgins who have made religious profession, as if by way of example, what they are to copy in their conduct, when he says: 'She was a virgin not only in body but also in mind, since she did not defile her pure heart by any contact with deceit; humble of heart, dignified in language, discreet in mind, rather moderate in speaking and quite attentive to study. Placing her confidence, not in the uncertainty of riches, but in the prayer of the poor man, attentive to her work, modest in speech, accustomed to seek as the judge of her conscience, not man, but God, hurting no one wishing well to all, yielding to her elders, not envious of her equals, avoiding boastfulness, following reason, loving virtue. When did she wound her parents even by a glance? When did she disagree with her relatives? When did she shrink from the humble? When did she laugh at the weak? When did she shun the needy? She was accustomed to visit only those gatherings of men at which mercy would not blush and which modesty would not disregard. There was no arrogance in her glance, no boldness in her words, no immodesty in her actions. Her bearing was not sensual, her gait was not too free, nor her voice querulous, so that her very physical appearance was an image of her mind and a portrayal of modesty. Certainly, a good home should be recognized at its very entrance, and assert at the first step within that there is no darkness hiding inside, as if the light of a lamp placed within were lighting up the exterior. Why, then, do I describe her temperance in regard to food, her

---

12 Cypr. *De hab. virg.* 3.23.

excess in the matter of kindnesses, the one excessive beyond nature, the other almost neglecting nature itself? In the one there were no periods of intermission; in the other, days were doubled in fasting; and when the desire of refreshment had arisen, the food offered was often of a kind that would prevent death, not furnish pleasure'[13]—and so on. But I have presented these words as an example of the moderate style, not because he is encouraging those who had not yet vowed virginity to do so, but because he is discussing what sort of people those who have already consecrated themselves should be. For, in order that the mind may undertake such an important resolution, it must certainly be roused and inflamed by the grand style of speaking. On the other hand, the martyr Cyprian wrote about the dress of virgins, not about embracing the life of virginity. However, that bishop rouses them even to this with noble eloquence.

(49) I shall now quote examples of the grand style from a subject which both of these men have discussed. Both have assailed those women who color, or rather discolor, their faces with paint. Cyprian, in treating of this subject, says among other things: 'If some artist had depicted in a painting the features, form, and bodily appearance of a man in colors that rival nature's and another, as if he were more skilled, were to apply his hand to the manifestly finished likeness to improve what has already been fashioned and painted, the affront to the first artist would be considered grave and his indignation would be regarded as righteous. Do you think that you can manifest such shamelessly rash insolence, an indignity to God the Artist, with impunity? Even if you may not be unchaste about men or defiled by

---
[13] Ambros. *De virg.* 2.1.7-8.

rouges intended to be alluring, yet, by corrupting and profaning the things of God, you are known as worse than an adulteress. The fact that you think that you are adorned and embellished thereby is an attack upon the work of God; it is a falsification of truth. The word of the Apostle is a warning: "Purge out the old leaven, that you may be a new dough, as you really are without leaven. For Christ, our passover, has been sacrificed. Therefore let us keep festival, not with the old leaven, nor with the leaven of malice and wickedness, but with the unleavened bread of sincerity and truth."[14] Do sincerity and truth survive when the things that are sincere are contaminated and those that are true are changed into falsehood by the adulterations of coloring and the artifices of cosmetics? Your Lord says: "Thou canst not make one hair white or black,"[15] and you are trying to be stronger so that you may refute the word of your Lord. With brazen effort and sacrilegious contempt you dye hair; with an ominous foreboding of the future you already begin to have hair of the color of flames.'[16] All that follows would be too long to include.

(50) Ambrose, on the other hand, in speaking against such women, said: 'Temptations to sin proceed from this that, inasmuch as they dread being unattractive to men, they paint their faces with affected coloring, and from defilement of their faces they reflect upon defilement of their chastity. What great foolishness this is, to change the likeness of nature and search for a picture of it, and, in dreading their husband's disapproval, to reveal their own! The woman who is anxious to alter what has been designed by nature

---

14 1 Cor. 5.7-8.
15 Matt. 5.36.
16 Cypr. *De hab. virg.* 15f.

is the first to pronounce sentence on herself. So, while she is striving to please another, she is first unattractive to herself. What more equitable judge of your ugliness do we need, woman, than you yourself, since you are afraid to be seen? If you are beautiful, why do you conceal yourself? If you are ugly, why do you pretend that you are beautiful, since you will not possess the esteem of your own conscience nor the recompense of deluding a stranger? If he loves another woman, you wish to be attractive to another man. And you are angry if he loves another woman, but he is taught to commit adultery through you. You are the evil teacher of your own wrong. Even one who has suffered from the pander's art shrinks from playing the part of a pander, and, although she is an abandoned woman, still she sins not against another, but against herself. Crimes of adultery are almost more endurable. For, there chastity is defiled; here, nature is violated.'[17] It is sufficiently clear, I think, that women are earnestly urged by this eloquence, not to defile their faces with cosmetics, but to practice modesty and fear. Thus we notice that the style of speaking is neither subdued nor moderate, but certainly grand. And in these two, whom of all writers I chose to quote, and in other ecclesiastical writers who speak the truth and speak it well, that is, intelligently, artistically, and passionately as the subject requires, these three styles can be discovered throughout their numerous writings and discourses. By constant reading and listening, combined with practice, they will become fixed in the mind of students.

Chapter 22

(51) No one should think that it is contrary to our

---

17 Ambros. *De virg.* 1.6.28.

teaching to blend these styles. On the contrary, delivery should certainly be varied with every kind of style, insofar as this can be accomplished gracefully.[1] When a speech is long drawn out in one style, it does not hold the listener; when a change is made from one style to another, the speech proceeds more effectively, even though it continues longer. Yet, in the speech of eloquent men, each style has its own diversities[2] which do no not permit the feelings of the listeners to grow cool or decrease in ardor.[3] However, the unrelieved subdued style can be more easily tolerated for a longer time than the unvaried grand style.[4] Indeed, the more agitation of soul that must be incited to cause our listener to agree with us, the less time he can be maintained in that emotion when it has been sufficiently aroused.[5] For this reason we must be careful, while we are trying to arouse to a higher pitch what is already high, that it does not fall from the emotional height to which it had been carried.[6] But, after inserting subjects which we must deliver in the more subdued style, we return effectively to those which must be delivered in the grand style, so that the vehemence of our speech ebbs and flows like the waves of the sea. Consequently, if the grand style of eloquence must be maintained for a rather long time, it should be varied by introducing the other styles. Yet, the composition as a whole is assigned to that division of style which predominates.[8]

---

1 Cf. *Auct. ad Her.* 4.11.16; Cic. *Orat.* 29.103; Quint. *Inst. or.* 12.10.71.
2 Cf. Quint. *Inst. or.* 12.10.67.
3 Cf. *De doctr. chr.* 2.36.54.
4 Cf. Cic. *Orat.* 28.98.
5 Cf. Cic. *Orat.* 28.99.
6 Cf. Cic. *Orat.* 28.98.
7 Cf. Aug. *Contr. Cresc.* 1.16.20.
8 Cf. Aug. (?) *De dial.* 7.

Chapter 23

(52) Now, it is important what style is to be joined with another style, or should be employed in certain essential places.[1] For, even in the grand style it is proper that the introduction always, or almost always, be moderate.[2] It is in the power of the speaker to use the subdued style even for some things which could be delivered in the grand style, so that the thoughts which are expressed in the grand style may become more majestic through a comparison with the others, and may be made, as it were, to appear more brilliant because of their shadows. But, in whatever style any knotty questions must be answered, there is a need for keenness of intellect which the subdued style especially appropriates for itself.[3] Therefore, this style must be employed even in the other two styles, when such questions occur in them. Similarly, we must employ and insert the moderate style, no matter with what other style it occurs, to praise or condemn anything where there is no question of anyone's condemnation or acquittal, or his agreement to any course of action. So, in the grand style, and also in the subdued, the other two find their proper places.[4] However, the moderate style, not always, to be sure, but sometimes, needs the subdued style if, as I said, a knotty question occurs which must be solved, or when things that could be adorned are left unadorned and are expressed in the subdued style, that they may grant a more prominent place to certain extravagances[5] (as it were) of

---

1 Cf. Quint. *Inst. or.* 12.10.69; Cic. *Orat.* 35.122.
2 Cf. Cic. *Orat.* 36.124.
3 Cf. Cic. *Orat.* 36.124ff.
4 Cf. Cic. *Orat.* 36.125.
5 Cf. Cic. *Orat.* 6.21.

ornament. The moderate style does not require the grand style; it is employed to please minds, not to persuade them.

Chapter 24

(53) However, if a speaker is applauded repeatedly and eagerly, we should not for that reason believe that he is speaking in the grand style. It is the keenness of intellect in the subdued style and the ornaments of the moderate style which also have this effect. The grand style usually restrains voices by its own weight, yet it elicits tears. Indeed, at Caesarea in Mauritania when I was dissuading the people from civil war, or worse than civil war—which they called *Caterva*[1] (for not only fellow-citizens, but even relatives, brothers, yes, parents and children, divided into two factions, and, according to custom, fought one another with stones for several successive days at a certain time of the year and each one killed whomever he could)—I pleaded in the grand style as powerfully as I could that I might extirpate and banish by my speech such a barbarous and deep-rooted evil from their hearts and customs. However, it was not when I heard them applauding, but when I saw them weeping, that I realized I had accomplished anything. By their applause they signified that they were instructed and pleased, but by their tears they showed they were persuaded. When I saw these, I believed, before they demonstrated it by fact, that the frightful custom handed down from their fathers and grandfathers, and from their far-off ancestors, which was besieging their hearts like an enemy, or rather was in possession of them, had been completely conquered. As soon as my speech was finished, I

---

[1] 'Mob rule' suggests the meaning of this word in the present context; on this passage, see Introduction, p. 5.

directed their hearts and lips to thank God. And, behold! for nearly eight years or more, by the grace of Christ, nothing like that has been attempted there. There are numerous other experiences, also, from which I have learned the effects that the grand style of a wise speaker can produce in men. It is not their acclamation, but rather their groans, and sometimes even their tears, and ultimately a transformation of life.

(54) Many have been transformed even by the subdued style of eloquence, but with the result that they learned what they did not know, or believed what formerly seemed incredible to them; not with the result that they did what they knew should be done but were unwilling to do. For, the grand style must be employed to prevail upon insensibility of this kind. When praises and reproaches are delivered eloquently, even though they are in the moderate style, they have such an effect on some people that they are not only charmed by the eloquence of the eulogies and denunciations, but they themselves also strive to live in a praiseworthy manner and avoid living in a manner deserving of blame. But is it true that all who are charmed are transformed, just as all who are persuaded in the grand style act accordingly, and as all who are instructed in the subdued style learn or believe that what they do not know is true?

Chapter 25

(55) Consequently, we conclude that the purpose which those two styles endeavor to accomplish is one that is particularly indispensable for those who are trying to speak wisely and eloquently. The object of the moderate style, however, is to give pleasure by its very eloquence. It must

not be exercised for its own sake, but in order that, because of the pleasantness of the style, agreement may be given a little more readily or may adhere more persistently to the matters which are being beneficially and nobly discussed. This is presuming, of course, that instructive or persuasive eloquence is not needed, because the listeners are both informed and sympathetic. Since it is the universal responsibility of eloquence in any of the three styles to speak properly in order to persuade, and, since the end at which you are aiming is to persuade by your eloquence, the eloquent man certainly speaks properly to persuade in any of these three styles. But, unless he persuades, he does not reach the goal of his eloquence.[1] Now, in the subdued style, he persuades us that what he says is true. In the grand style, he persuades us to do what we know should be done but are not doing. In the moderate style, he persuades us that he is speaking beautifully and elegantly. What use have we for this end? Let those seek this end who are honored for their eloquence and who make a display in eulogies and utterances of such a nature that the listener does not have to be instructed or persuaded to do something, but needs only to be charmed. Let us refer this end to another purpose: that we strive for the same result that we wish to effect when we speak in the grand style, that is that good morals may be loved or evil ones avoided. If men are not so hostile to this action that they appear to need urging to it by the grand style of speaking, or, if they are already practicing it, our purpose is that they may do so more zealously and persevere in it steadfastly. So it happens that we use even the adornment of the moderate style, not ostentatiously, but discreetly, not satisfied with merely pleas-

---

[1] Cf. Cic. *De invent.* 1.5.6; *De orat.* 1.61.260; 1.31.138; 1.49.213.

ing the listener, but laboring rather for this end, that by reason of his being pleased he may be helped even to the good of which we are anxious to persuade him.

Chapter 26

(56) Consequently, those three ends for which, as I explained previously, a man who is anxious to speak wisely and also eloquently should strive, namely, that he may be listened to with understanding, pleasure, and persuasion, here may have need of further clarification. They are not to be understood as if each is to be attributed to one of the three styles of eloquence in such a way that being understood pertains to the subdued style, giving pleasure, to the moderate style, and being heard with persuasion, to the grand style. Rather, they are to be applied in such a way that the speaker always keeps in mind and uses these three as much as possible, even when he is concerned with each one of them separately. We do not wish even what we say in the subdued style to be boring, and, therefore, we are anxious not only to be listened to with understanding, but also with pleasure. Besides, why do we urge what we are teaching by means of divinely inspired proofs, except that we may be listened to with compliance, that is, that our hearers may believe with the assistance of Him to whom it was said: 'Thy testimonies are become exceedingly credible.'[1] If someone narrates a story to those who are learning, even in the subdued style, what does he desire except to be believed? And who would care to listen to him unless he could hold his listener with some attractiveness of style? Who is unaware of the fact that he cannot be heard with pleasure or persuasion if he is not understood? The subdued style has its own proper

---
1 Ps. 92.5.

functions. It answers very difficult questions and proves them with an unexpected explanation. It elicits and displays very acute opinions from sources from which nothing was expected.[2] It clearly proves the error of its opponent and teaches that what seems to be irrefutable is false, especially when it is attended by a certain unsought, but somehow natural, beauty and by unostentatious, but almost essential, rhythmical sentence endings, drawn from the subject itself. Yet, very often it occasions such thunderous applause that it is recognized with difficulty as the subdued style. It advances unadorned and unarmed and enters the contest, as it were, stripped bare, and yet that fact does not prevent it from shattering its opponent by its vigor and strength, and with its very strong arms from breaking down and destroying the falsehood that resists it. Why are those who speak in this way applauded repeatedly and enthusiastically, except that when truth has been proved, defended, and invincibly maintained in such a manner, it affords pleasure? Therefore, in this subdued style our teacher and speaker should strive to make his words not only understandable, but also pleasing and persuasive.

(57) Eloquence of the moderate style, too, in the case of the ecclesiastical orator is not left unornamented, nor is it adorned unbecomingly. Neither does it seek only to please, which is the only thing it professes to do in the case of other orators. Rather, in the subjects which it praises or condemns, it naturally desires to be heard with a persuasion that will lead its hearers to seek or more firmly hold to the objects of its praise, and avoid or reject the objects of its condemnation. However, if it is not heard with understand-

---

2 Cf. Cic. *Orat.* 24.79.

ing, it cannot be pleasing. Accordingly, even in this style where attractiveness holds pre-eminence, we must strive for these three ends, namely, that those who are listening may understand, be pleased, and be persuaded.

(58) Now, when it is necessary to influence and persuade the listener by means of the grand style (this is necessary when he acknowledges the truth and attractiveness of what has been said, but is still unwilling to act upon it), without doubt you must speak in this grand style. Who is persuaded if he is unaware of what is being said, or who is prevailed upon to listen if he is not pleased? Therefore, even in this style, when a stubborn heart is to be persuaded to obedience by the grand style of eloquence, unless the speaker is listened to with understanding and pleasure, his words cannot be persuasive.

Chapter 27

(59) However, in causing his words to be persuasive, the life of a speaker has greater influence than any sublimity of eloquence, no matter how great it may be.[1] A man who speaks wisely and eloquently, but leads a wicked life, does indeed teach many who are desirous of learning,[2] yet, as it is written, he is 'unprofitable to his own soul.'[3] Hence the Apostle also says:[4] 'whether in pretense or in truth, Christ is being proclaimed.' However, Christ is 'Truth'[5] and truth can still be preached even though not with truth, that is, that what is virtuous and true may be preached from a

---

1 Cf. Cic. *De orat.* 2.43.182; 2.20.85; 3.14.5; Quint. *Inst. or.* 12.1.1.
2 Cf. Quint. *Inst. or.* 12.1.2-3.
3 Eccli. 37.21.
4 Phil. 1.18.
5 John 14.6.

vicious and deceitful heart. So, Jesus Christ is truly preached by those who 'seek their own interests, not those of Jesus Christ.'[6] However, good Christians do not obey any man at all, but the Lord Himself who said:[7] 'The things they command do; but do not do the things they do; for they talk but do nothing.' For that reason, even those who do not lead useful lives are heard with profit. They are diligent about seeking their own ends, but, naturally, they do not dare to teach their own doctrines from the pulpit of ecclesiastical authority, which sound teaching has established. For this reason the Lord Himself, before He said what I have related about such men, declared:[8] 'They have sat on the chair of Moses.' That chair, then, which was not theirs but Moses,' compelled them to speak what was good, even though they were not doing good. They accomplished their own purposes in their own lives, but the chair which belonged to another did not permit them to teach their own doctrines.

(60) And so, they benefit many by preaching what they do not practise, but they would benefit far greater numbers by practising what they preach. For, there are many who seek a defense of their own evil lives in their directors and teachers, replying in their hearts, or even with their lips (if they give vent to this extent), and saying:[9] 'Why do you not practise yourself what you are preaching to me?' The result is that they do not listen with submission to a man who does not listen to himself. They despise the word of God which is being preached to them,[10] and at the

---

6 Phil. 2.21.
7 Matt. 23.3.
8 Matt. 23.2.
9 Cf. Quint. *Inst. or.* 12.1.29.
10 Cf. Quint. *Inst. or.* 12.1.32.

same time they despise the preacher himself. In fact, when the Apostle, writing to Timothy, had said: 'Let no man despise thy youth,' and added how he was to avoid being despised, he said: 'but be thou an example to the faithful in speech, in conduct, in charity, in faith, in chastity.'[11]

Chapter 28

(61) A teacher like this, in order to make his words persuasive, expresses himself without shame, not only in the subdued and moderate style, but even in the grand style, because he lives uprightly. He chooses a good life in such a way that he does not disregard a good reputation, but as far as possible, takes forethought for what is 'honorable in the sight of God and men,'[1] by fearing God and taking care of men. Even in his very speech he should choose to please by his subjects rather than by his words, and not believe that a thing is better expressed unless it is expressed more truthfully. The teacher should not be a slave to words, but the words should be subject to the teacher. This is what the Apostle says:[2] 'Not with the wisdom of words, lest the cross of Christ be made void.' What he says to Timothy has this meaning, too: 'Do not dispute with words, for that is useless, leading to the ruin of the listeners.'[3] This was not said so that we would not say anything in defense of truth when our enemies are attacking it. Where shall we place what he said when he was explaining, among other things, what kind of a man a bishop should be:[4] 'That he

---

11 1 Tim. 4.12.

---

1 2 Cor. 8.21.
2 1 Cor. 1.17.
3 2 Tim. 2.14.
4 Titus 1.9.

may be able in sound doctrine also to confute opponents'? Disputing with words is not being solicitous how error may be overcome by truth, but how your eloquence may be preferred to another's.[5] A man who does not dispute with words, whether he speaks in the subdued, the moderate, or the grand style, strives by means of his words to make truth clear, pleasing, and persuasive. Even charity itself, which is the end and 'fulfillment of the Law,'[6] cannot be right in any way, if the things which are loved are not true but false. Moreover, just as one whose body is handsome, but whose mind is deranged, is more to be pitied than if his body also were misshapen, so those who say eloquently things that are false are more to be pitied than if they said such things inelegantly. Therefore, in what does speaking, not only eloquently, but also wisely, consist except in employing adequate words in the subdued style, brilliant ones in the moderate style, and forceful ones in the grand style, yet always on a subject which deserves to be heard?[7] Whoever cannot do both should speak wisely what he does not say eloquently, rather than speak eloquently what he says foolishly.

Chapter 29

However, if he cannot even do this, let him live in such a way that he will not only prepare a reward for himself but will also furnish an example to others. And let his beauty of life be, as it were, a powerful sermon.

(62) Of course, there are some who can preach well, but they are unable to think of anything to preach. If they take what has been written eloquently and wisely by

---

5 Cf. Cic. *Orat.* 19.65.
6 Cf. 1 Tim. 1.5; Rom. 13.10.
7 Cf. Cic. *Orat.* 21.70.73; Quint. *Inst. or.* 12.10.79-80.

others, memorize it, and deliver it to the people, they are not acting dishonestly as long as they cling to their part. In this way, and it is certainly beneficial, there arise many preachers of the truth, but not many teachers, provided that they all speak the same words of the one true Teacher,[1] and there are 'no dissensions' among them.[2] They are not to be frightened by that utterance of the Prophet Jeremias, through whom God reproves those 'who steal His words everyone from his neighbor.'[3] Those who steal take what belongs to another. The word of God is not another's for those who obey it; on the contrary, he delivers another's words who, although he speaks well, lives badly. For, whatever he says that is good seems to be devised by his own genius, but it is really foreign to his character. And so, God said that those men are stealing His words who are anxious to appear good by speaking the words of God, although they are wicked in putting their own doctrines into practice. And, in fact, if you consider the matter carefully, they themselves are not saying the good words which they proclaim. For, how can they proclaim by their words what they reject by their deeds? Indeed, it is no idle remark that the Apostle has made about such persons:[4] 'They profess to know God, but by their works they disown Him.' In a certain way they are speaking, but again in another way they are not speaking, since each of the two statements is true because Truth has uttered it. In speaking about such men, He said: 'The things they command, do; but do not do the things they do'; that is, do whatever you hear from their lips; do not do what you see in their

---

1 Matt. 23.8.
2 1 Cor. 1.10.
3 Jer. 23.30.
4 Titus 1.16.

actions. 'For they talk,' He said, 'but do nothing.'⁵ Therefore, although they do nothing, they still talk. In another place, reproving such men, He said:⁶ 'You hypocrites, how, can you speak good things, when you are evil?' Accordingly, even what they say, when they speak good things, they do not say of themselves, because they are certainly rejecting in desire and deed what they are saying. Consequently, it can happen that an eloquent but evil man may himself write a sermon through which truth is to be preached by another man who is good but not eloquent. When this happens, the wicked man surrenders from himself what belongs to another, while the good man receives from another what is his own. On the other hand, when good Christians bestow this service upon good Christians, both say what is their own, because God is theirs and His are the words they speak. They make their own even those things which they could not compose themselves when they live properly in accordance with those words.

Chapter 30

(63) Whether he is just about to speak before the people or before some smaller group, or whether he is going to compose something to be spoken before the people or read by those who are willing and able to do so, he should pray that God will put a good sermon into his mouth. For, if Queen Esther, who was about to speak before the king in behalf of the temporal well-being of her nation, prayed that God would put 'a well-ordered speech'¹ in her

---

5 Matt. 23.3.
6 Matt. 12.34.

---

1 Esth. 14.13.

mouth, how much more should he pray to obtain such a gift who is laboring 'in the word and in teaching'[2] for the eternal well-being of men? Those who are going to preach what they have obtained from others, even before they receive it, should pray for those from whom they are obtaining it, that they may be granted what they wish to receive themselves. And, when they have received it, they should pray that they may preach it profitably and that those to whom they preach may accept it. They should give thanks for a favorable outcome of their speech to Him from whom they are aware they have received it, that 'he who takes pride, may take pride'[3] in Him in whose 'hand are both we and our words.'[4]

Chapter 31

(64) This book has turned out to be longer than I desired and intended. But it is not tedious for a reader or listener who finds it agreeable. However, anyone who finds it tedious, but wishes to learn about it, should read it in parts. On the contrary, a person who is reluctant to learn about it should not complain about its length. However, I thank God that, with whatever small ability I possess, I have discussed in these four books not the kind of man I am, because I have many failings, but the kind of man he should be who strives to labor in sound teaching, that is, in Christian teaching, not only for himself, but also for others.

---

2 1 Tim. 5.17.
3 1 Cor. 1.31.
4 Wisd. 7.16.

ADMONITION AND GRACE

(De correptione et gratia)

Translated

by

JOHN COURTNEY MURRAY, S.J., S.T.D.
Woodstock College

IMPRIMI POTEST:
F. A. McQuade, S.J., Praep. Prov.

Neo Eboraci
die 30 Junii 1946

INTRODUCTION

T. AUGUSTINE'S immediate purpose in writing *Admonition and Grace* was to effect a final settlement of a dispute that had risen among the monks in the famous monastery in Hadrumetum, a sea-coast town in the African province of Byzacene. The dispute arose when the monk Felix brought back to his monastery a copy of St. Augustine's second Letter to Sixtus,[1] a Roman priest, later Pope. Felix had come across the Letter when he and his companion Florus were on a visit to the monastery in Uzale, of which St. Evodius, the bishop, was superior. In this Letter, St. Augustine argued at length, against the Pelagians, that faith is a gift of God, that in crowning our merits God does but crown His own gifts, and that predestination is gratuitous.

This doctrine shocked a small group among the monks of Hadrumetum, who were apparently infected with Pelagian tendencies. They thought that St. Augustine had so exalted the power and need of grace as to deny free will and the principle of merit. However, the majority of the Hadrumetan monks were in accord with St. Augustine. In the midst of the ensuing argument, Florus arrived home and found himself blamed for the dissension. He put the whole matter before Valentine, the superior. After other measures for settling the dispute had failed, Valentine sent the recalcitrant monks off to Hippo, to have St. Augustine's doctrine at first hand. The

---
1 *Epist.* 194; PL 33 874-91.

two who arrived, Cresconius and a certain Felix, were later joined by the Felix who had brought to Hadrumetum the Letter to Sixtus which had started the trouble.

On perceiving more fully the import of the dispute and the difficulties of the Hadrumetan monks, St. Augustine wrote, among other things, the book, *Grace and Free Will*, in which he again developed the theme of the necessity of grace, and emphasized that the freedom of the will must be so defended as not to deny the necessity of grace. This book had a great effect in Hadrumetum; the controversy apparently subsided. St. Augustine heard the fact from Florus, who, at St. Augustine's own request had been sent by Valentine to Hippo, with a report on the situation. It seems, however, that St. Augustine also heard from Florus that the matter of monastic admonitions, or rebukes administered by the superior, had been among the topics of argument. From St. Augustine's doctrine on the necessity of grace someone had apparently drawn the extreme conclusion that admonitions should be abolished; erring monks were simply to be prayed for, not rebuked. It was to refute this position, as well as to do away with the last remnants of doctrinal discord at Hadrumetum, that St. Augustine wrote the work which he entitled *Admonition and Grace*. It was written, it would seem, in the year 427.

The opening chapters dispose of the difficulties against the efficacy of grace and vindicate the place of admonitions in monastic discipline. However, the bulk of the work is devoted to the doctrine of perseverance—the gratuity of the gift, and its relation to predestination. From this discussion St. Augustine is led on to describe the difference between the divine aid given to Adam and that now given to the predestined. The conclusion is a further commendation of the practice of admonitions, together with a brief discussion of the meaning of God's salvific will.

St. Augustine himself regarded the book, *Admonition and Grace*, as his fullest and best exposition of the doctrine of perseverance.[2] The work was of decisive importance in the Pelagian controversy; and Prosper of Aquitaine testifies to the value it had in refuting by anticipation the errors taught by those who were later known as Semipelagians.[3] During the great controversies on grace at the time of the Baian and Jansenist heresies, probably no other work of St. Augustine was more diligently scanned. Cardinal Noris called it 'the key which opens the way to the whole doctrine of St. Augustine of divine grace and free will.'[4]

No modern critical text of the work is available; it has not yet been issued in the Vienna *Corpus Scriptorum Ecclesiasticorum Latinorum*. The text here used is that of the *Maurini*, as exhibited, with a few suggested emendations, by C. Boyer, S.J., in *Textus et Documenta*, Series Theologica, 2, Divi Augustini *De Correptione et Gratia* (Romae 1932). The same text is found in Migne. PL 44.

---

2 *De dono perseverantiae* 21.55; PL 45 1027.
3 *Epist.* 225 (among the Letters of St. Augustine) 2; PL 33 1002-3.
4 *Historiae Pelagianae* 1.23; *Opera Omnia* 1 206 (Venice 1769).

SELECT BIBLIOGRAPHY

Bourke, V., *Augustine's Quest of Wisdom* (St. Louis 1945).
Merlin, N., *Saint Augustin et les dogmes du péché originel et de la grace* (Paris 1931).
Janssen, K., *Die Entstehung der Gnadenlehre des hl. Augustinus* (Rostock 1936).
Guzzo, A., *Agostino e il sistema della grazia* (Torino 1930).
Boyer, C. S.J., "Le système de S. Augustin sur la grace d'après le De correptione et gratia," *Recherches de Science Religieuse* 20 (1931) 481-505.
Rahner, K., S.J., "Augustinus und der Semipelagianismus," *Zeitschrift für katholische Theologie* 62 (1938) 171-96.

CONTENTS

PART ONE

Chapter	Page
1 The Necessity of Grace	245
2 The Necessity of Human Cooperation with Grace	247
3 The Usefulness of Admonitions	249
4 Objection: Can Admonition be Deserved?	250
5 Answer: Human Responsibility for Sin	250
6 (No. 9) The Ultimate Cause of Sin	253

PART TWO
Grace, Admonition, and Perseverance

Section 1
The Gift of Perseverance

6 (No. 10) The Gratuity of the Gift of Perseverance	255
7 The Justice of Damnation and the Effects of Predestination	258
8 The Mystery of the Judgment of God	264
9 The Problems of the Just Who Do Not Persevere	268

Section 2
The Gift of Perseverance and the Grace of Adam

10 The Grace of the Angels and the Grace of Adam	276
11 The Grace of Adam and our Grace	280
12 Two Kinds of Divine Assistance and of Human Freedom	285
13 The Mercy and Justice of God	293

PART THREE

Conclusion

Chapter	Page
14 Admonition Made Salutary Through Grace	297
15 Zeal in Admonishing	301
16 The Need of Prayer	304

ADMONITION AND GRACE

Chapter 1

DEAR BROTHER Valentine, my fellow servant of God: I have read the letter you kindly sent me, in answer to my own, by brother Florus and those who with him visited me; and I thanked God for the knowledge it brought me of your peace in the Lord, your agreement with me in the truth, and the fervor of your charity. What the enemy planned for the subversion of some among you has had the opposite effect, by the mercy of God who turns the wiles of the enemy to the advantage of His servants. None of you has been damaged, but some have come to a better understanding.

Consequently, it is not necessary to go over the whole matter, which has been sufficiently covered in the book we sent you.[1] Your reply indicates that the book was well received; nevertheless, do not by any means suppose that one reading of it could make its contents sufficiently known to you. If you would derive the most fruit from it, determine to become entirely familiar with it by repeated reading, so that you may know very clearly the important questions that are answered therein not by a human, but by a heavenly, authority, from which we must not depart, if we wish to reach the goal of our striving.

(2) The Lord Himself not only shows us the evil we

---

[1] The book was *De gratia et libero arbitrio;* on the circumstances of its writing, cf. the Introduction p. 240.

are to avoid and the good we are to do (which is all that the letter of the law can do),² but also helps us to avoid evil and to do good³—things that are impossible without the spirit of grace. If grace is lacking, the law is there simply to make culprits and to slay; for this reason, the Apostle said: 'The letter killeth, the spirit giveth life.'⁴ He, therefore, who uses the law according to the law learns from it good and evil, and, trusting not in his own strength, has recourse to grace, which enables him to avoid evil and to do good. But when has a man recourse to grace, except when the steps of a man are directed by the Lord and he delighteth in His way?⁵ Therefore, even the desire for the help of grace is itself the beginning of grace; about it he said: 'And I said: Now have I begun; this is a change due to the right hand of the Most High.'⁶

It must, therefore, be admitted that we have a will free to do both evil and good; but, in doing evil, one is free of justice and the slave of sin; on the other hand, in the matter of good no one is free unless he be freed by Him who said: 'If the Son makes you free, you will be free indeed.'⁷ Not,

---

2 Pelagius asserted that the only 'grace' man needed was that of being shown the good he was to do and the evil he was to avoid. This was adequately done by the law and teaching of the Gospel; with their external aid man's natural possibilities were sufficient unto salvation.
3 Ps. 36.27.
4 2 Cor. 3.6.
5 Ps. 36.23.
6 Ps. 76.11.
7 John 8.36. Here and in similar contexts throughout the work St. Augustine is speaking of good works that have value for eternal life —what a later theology calls 'salutary action,' or 'supernatural acts.' He does not deny that by the native powers of his own free will man can do certain naturally good acts (e.g., love of parents, loyalty to country, chivalry and self-sacrifice in war, devotion to a life of learning, zeal for the common good in a democracy, sympathy for the poor, desire to rectify injustices in the social order, etc.). However, if done without grace these acts have no supernatural value.

however, as if one no longer needed the help of his liberator, once he has been freed from the domination of sin; rather, hearing from Him: 'Without me you can do nothing,'[8] one must oneself say: 'Be thou my helper, forsake me not.'[9] I am happy to have found this faith in our brother Florus; it is indubitably the true, prophetic, apostolic, and Catholic faith. Wherefore, they are rather to be corrected who did not understand him; indeed, I gather that they have already been corrected, by the favor of God.

Chapter 2

(3) This is the right understanding of the grace of God through Jesus Christ our Lord, by which alone men are freed from evil, and without which they do no good whatsoever, either in thought, or in will and love, or in action; not only do men know by its showing what they are to do, but by its power they do with love what they know is to be done.[10] In fact, this inspiration of a good will and deed was what the Apostle was begging for those to whom he said: 'But we pray God that you may do no evil at all, not wishing ourselves to appear approved, but that you may do what is good.'[11] Who could hear this, and not be awakened, and admit that the avoidance of evil and the performance of good are given us by the Lord God? Notice that the Apostle does not say: 'We admonish, we teach, we exhort, we chide'; rather, he says: 'We pray God that you may do no evil at all, but that you may do what is good.' Never-

---
8 John 15.5.
9 Ps. 26.9.
10 'with love': that is, with a will that is 'good' in virtue of a supernatural goodness imparted to it by grace. St. Augustine has other phrases for the same idea: *recte* (rightly), *sicut oportet ad salutem* (in the way required for salvation), etc.
11 2 Cor. 13.7.

theless, he used to talk to them, and he did all the things I have just mentioned: he admonished, he taught, he exhorted, he chided. But he knew that there was no value in all these things, which he did in public by way of planting and watering, unless He who in secret makes things grow were to hear and answer his prayers. As the same Doctor of the Gentiles said: 'Neither he who plants is anything, nor he who waters, but God who gives the growth.'[12]

(4) Accordingly, let no one deceive himself saying: 'Why are we preached to, and given commands, in order to have us avoid evil and do good, if it is not we ourselves who do these things, but God who effects in us the will and the deed?' Let them rather grasp the fact that, if they are the sons of God, they are acted on by the Spirit of God,[13] in order that they may do what ought to be done, and, when they have done it, give thanks to Him by whom they did it; for they are acted on, in order that they may act,[14] not in order that they may have nothing to do. And to this end it is shown them what they ought to do, in order that, when they do it as it ought to be done—that is, with love and delight in justice—they may rejoice in the experience of the sweetness which the Lord gave, that their earth might bring forth its fruit.[15] On the other hand, when they fail to act, either by doing nothing at all, or by not acting out of charity, let them pray to receive what they do not yet have. For what will they have, except what they shall re-

---
12 1 Cor. 3.7.
13 Rom. 8.14.
14 By this formula, and others equivalent to it, St. Augustine preserves the right harmony between the action of grace and that of free will. Our salutary acts are indeed graces, but they remain free acts. He says elsewhere: 'We do the works, but God works in us the doing of the works' (*De dono perseverantiae* 13. 33; PL 45 1013).
15 Ps. 84.13.

ceive? And what have they, except what they have received?[16]

Chapter 3

(5) Again, we hear this said: 'Let our superiors prescribe for us what we are to do, and let them pray for us that we may do it; but let them not admonish or censure us, if we fail to do it.' On the contrary, let all these things be done, since the Apostles, the teachers of the churches, did them all: they prescribed what was to be done, and they admonished if things were not done; and they prayed that everything might be done. The Apostle prescribes when he says: 'Let all that you do be done with charity.'[17] He admonishes when he says: 'Nay, to begin with, it is altogether a defect in you that you have lawsuits with one another. Why not rather suffer wrong? Why not rather be defrauded? But you yourselves do wrong and defraud, and that to your brothers. Or do you not know that the unjust will not possess the kingdom of God?'[18] And we can also hear him praying: 'And may the Lord make you to increase and abound in charity towards one another and towards all men.'[19] He prescribes that charity be practiced; he admonishes because charity is not practiced; he prays that charity may abound. Here is the point: in the superior's precepts learn what you ought to have; in his admonitions learn that it is by your own fault that you have it not;[20]

---

16 1 Cor. 4.7; St. Augustine himself says that it was this verse that early moved him to recognize the primacy of grace in the Christian life; in fact he ascribes his insight to a kind of divine revelation. Actually, however, modern exegesis would not sustain St. Augustine in every point of his interpretation of the verse.
17 1 Cor. 16.14.
18 1 Cor. 6-9.
19 1 Thess. 3.12.
20 St. Augustine clearly excludes all fatalism; the sinner is a sinner, and he is justly admonished, because he sins through his own fault.

in his prayers learn whence you may receive what you wish to have.

Chapter 4

(6) 'How,' it is said, 'am I at fault in not having what I have not received from God? It is His gift, and if He does not give it, there is absolutely no one else from whom it may be had.' Permit me, my brothers, briefly to make a case for the truth of heavenly and divine grace—not against you, whose hearts are right with God, but against those who savor the things of earth, or against purely human modes of thought. These are the words of those who do not wish to be admonished for their evil works by the preachers of this grace: 'Prescribe for me what I am to do; and if I do it, give thanks for me to God, whose gift it was that I did it. But if I do it not, I am not, therefore, to be admonished; but God is to be prayed to, that He may give what He has not given, namely, that faithful love of God and neighbor by which His precepts are obeyed. Pray for me, therefore, that I may receive this charity, and by it do what it commands, from the heart and with a good will. I should indeed be rightly admonished, if by my own fault I did not have charity; that is, if I were able to give it to myself or lay hold of it, and failed to do so; or if, when God was giving it, I were to have refused His gift. But, since the will itself is prepared by the Lord, why do you admonish me, when you see me unwilling to do His commands? Why do you not rather ask Him to effect in me the will to do them?'

Chapter 5

(7) Here is our reply. Whenever you fail to follow the

known commands of God and are unwilling to be admonished, you are for this very reason to be admonished, that you are unwilling to be admonished. For you are unwilling to have your faults pointed out to you; you are unwilling to have them lashed, and to experience a salutary pain, that would make you seek a physician. You are unwilling to have yourself shown to yourself, that you may see your own deformity, and seek one to reform you, and beg Him not to leave you in your ugliness of soul. It is your own fault that you are bad;[21] and it is a worse fault to be unwilling to be admonished because you are bad. Do you suppose that sin is to be praised? Or that it is matter of indifference, in such wise that it is to be neither praised nor blamed? Or that the fear, the shame, the distress of one who has been admonished are of no value? Or that the value of their wholesome stimulus is other than this, that it makes us pray to Him who is good, and transforms the bad, who are admonished, into the good, who may be praised?

One who is unwilling to be admonished (and who says, instead: 'Pray for me') is for this reason to be admonished, that he may himself act. As a matter of fact, the distress of self-displeasure, experienced under the sting of an admonition, stirs him to a love of more prayer, with the result that, by the mercy of God, he is helped by an increase of charity, and ceases to do what is matter for shame and sorrow, and does what is worthy of praise and reward. This is the wholesome value of an admonition, administered more or less severely according to the diversity of sins; it is wholesome when the heavenly physician looks upon its administration. For it is of no avail unless it makes one sorrow for one's sins; and whose gift is this, save His who looked

---

[21] Here again St. Augustine insists on man's own responsibility for his evil actions.

upon Peter in his act of denial and made him weep?[22] Hence, after saying that those who have wrong views are to be gently admonished, the Apostle immediately adds: 'It may be that God will give them repentance to know the truth, and they will recover themselves from the snare of the devil.'[23]

(8) Why do those who are unwilling to be admonished say: 'Just give me commands, and pray for me, that I may do what you command'? In their wrongheadedness, why do they not rather reject both these things, and say: 'I want you neither to give me commands nor to pray for me'? Does it appear that any man prayed for Peter, that God might give him repentance whereby he wept for his denial of the Lord? Did any man instruct Paul in the divine precepts that belong to Christian faith? On hearing him preaching the Gospel and saying: 'For I give you to understand, brethren, that the gospel which was preached by me is not of man. For I did not receive it from man, nor was I taught it; but I received it by a revelation of Jesus Christ,'[24] someone might have made answer to him thus: 'Why this irksome insistence with us, that we should receive from you, and be taught by you, that which you yourself "did not receive from man, and were not taught"? He who gave it to you is powerful also to give it to us, just as to you.' But if they do not dare to speak thus, and rather permit the Gospel to be preached to them by a man (even though it could otherwise be given to man than through men), let them also admit that they ought to be admonished by their superiors, by whom the grace of Christ is preached,

---

22 Luke 22.61-62.
23 2 Tim. 2.25-26.
24 Gal. 1.11-12.

notwithstanding the undeniable fact that God could admonish anyone He wished, even when no man admonished him, and could bring him to the salutary pangs of repentance by the secret and mighty power of His medicine.

And, just as we are not to cease from prayer for those whom we wish to correct, in spite of the fact that the Lord looked on Peter and made him weep for his sin even when no man was praying for him; so also admonitions are not to be foregone, although God can bring back into line whomsoever He wishes, even when no man admonishes them. Moreover, a man actually profits by admonition when God takes pity on him and helps him; for God enables anyone whom He wishes to profit, even without admonition. But why the call to reformation should come to one in this way, and to another in that way, and to still others in other ways, diverse and innumerable, far be it from us to say. Here the potter, not the clay, is judge.[25]

Chapter 6

(9) 'The Apostle,' they object, 'says: "For who singles thee out? Or what hast thou that thou hast not received?"[26] Why, therefore, are we admonished, censured, reprimanded, accused? What are we to do, in case we have not received?' Those who speak thus wish to regard themselves as blameless in their disobedience to God, for the supposed reason that obedience is His gift, necessarily present in those in whom charity is present, and charity is undoubtedly from God,[27] and is given by the Father to His sons. 'We have not received this charity,' they say, 'and why therefore are we admonished, as if we could give it to ourselves, and

---
25 Cf. Rom. 9.20 ff.
26 1 Cor. 4.7.
27 1 John 4.7.

were deliberately unwilling to do so?' They fail to consider that, if they are not yet regenerated, there is a prime reason why they should be displeased with themselves when they are taxed with their disobedience to God—the fact that God made man good at the beginning of the human creation, and there is no iniquity with God.[28] For this reason the initial perversity, whereby God is not obeyed, is from man, because he fell by his own bad will from the goodness in which God originally constituted him, and became perverse.

But are we to suppose that that perversity is not to be admonished in man, because it is not peculiar to him who is admonished, but common to all? On the contrary, that which belongs to all is to be admonished in each. Not for that reason is it not each one's own, because no one is immune from it. Original sin is indeed said to be the sin of another, because each one of us derives it from his parents; but not without reason is it said to be our own, because, as the Apostle says, in that one man all sinned. Therefore, let this source of damnation be admonished, that from the smart of the admonition may spring the will to be reborn; or, if he who is admonished be a son of the promise, that God may effect the will within him by His secret inspiration, as the admonition makes its sound and its stimulus felt from without. Or, if he be already reborn, and, after having been justified, fall back of his own will into an evil life,[29] certainly he cannot say: 'I have not received,'

---

28 St. Augustine has already made it clear that the immediate reason why a man is evil lies in his own free will; he is to be admonished for his faults because he freely committed them. St. Augustine now goes on to speak of the ultimate ('prime') reason for man's proneness to evil. It is not to be found in God, but again in man—in the sin of the first man, which has passed to all his posterity.

29 Man's fall from grace is clearly represented as due to his own free choice; this is to be held in mind, lest St. Augustine be misunderstood when, in what follows, he deals with perseverance as a gift.

since he has lost the grace of God once received, by his own will, which is free to do evil. If, smitten by an admonition, such a man conceives a salutary contrition, and goes back to a good, or better life, assuredly he most evidently illustrates the value of admonitions. At any rate, whether the admonitions given by men are from charity or not, it is only God who can make them beneficial to the one admonished.

(10) Can he who is unwilling to be admonished still say: 'What evil have I done, since I have not received?' when it is clear that he has received, and has lost by his own fault what he received? He will rejoin: 'When you charge me with having fallen by my own will from a good life into an evil one, I can by all means still say: "What have I done, since I have not received? For I received faith which works through love; but I did not receive perseverance to the end therein. Surely, no one would dare to say that perseverance is not a gift of God, and that such an immense favor so lies within our power that the Apostle would be wrong in saying to one who had it: 'What hast thou that thou hast not received?'[30] since he has it without having received it"?'

In reply to this, we cannot deny that perseverance in good unto the end is a great gift of God, not to be had except from Him of whom it is written: 'Every good gift and every perfect gift is from above, coming down from the Father of lights.'[31] Nevertheless, this is no reason for omitting the admonition of one who has not persevered; for it might be that God would give him repentance, and he would escape from the snare of the devil.[32] As I have

---

30 1 Cor. 4.7.
31 James 1.17.
32 2 Tim. 2.25.

mentioned before, the Apostle added this thought to his words on the value of admonition: 'Gently admonishing those who resist, for it may be that God will give them repentance.'[33]

Certainly, if we were to say that this praiseworthy and blessed perseverance so lies within the power of man that he does not have it from God, we would render meaningless what the Lord said to Peter: 'I have prayed for thee, that thy faith may not fail.'[34] What else did He beg for Peter but perseverance to the end? And surely, if a man could have it from man, there would be no need of asking it of God. Again, when the Apostle says: 'But we pray God that you may do no evil at all,'[35] he is undoubtedly asking God for their perseverance. Does not he do evil who deserts the good, and, not persevering in good, turns toward the evil from which he ought to turn away?[36] Moreover, the Apostle says in another place: 'I give thanks to my God in all my remembrance of you, always in all my prayers making supplications for you all with joy, because of your association with me in spreading the gospel of Christ from the first until now. I am convinced of this, that he who has begun a good work in you will bring it to perfection until the day of Christ Jesus.'[37] What else is he promising them from the divine mercy but perseverance in good unto the end?

He likewise says: 'Epaphras, who is one of you, sends you greetings—a servant of Christ Jesus, who is ever solicitous for you in his prayers, that you may stand perfect and

33 *Loc. cit.*
34 Luke 22.32.
35 2 Cor. 13.7.
36 The text here is faulty; the best correction supplies *non* before *perseverans in bono*.
37 Phil. 1.3.

completely in accord with all the will of God.'³⁸ What does the phrase 'that you may stand' mean, except that you may persevere? (For instance, it was said of the devil: 'He stood not in the truth';³⁹ he was in it, but he stood not in it.) The Colossians were indeed at the time standing in the faith; and obviously, when we pray that he who is standing may stand, we are praying simply for his perseverance. Similarly, when the Apostle Jude says: 'Now to him who is able to preserve you without sin and to set you before the presence of his glory, without blemish, in gladness,'⁴⁰ does he not most evidently show perseverance in good until the end to be a gift of God? For what else but perseverance in good does God give, when He preserves from sin, that He may set those who are without blemish before the presence of His glory, in gladness?

We see the same idea in the text of the Acts: 'On hearing this the Gentiles were delighted, and glorified the word of the Lord, and all who were destined for eternal life believed.'⁴¹ Could anyone be destined for eternal life save by the gift of perseverance, seeing that 'he who perseveres to the end shall be saved'?⁴² What is this salvation but eternal salvation? Again, when in the Lord's Prayer we say to God the Father: 'Hallowed be Thy name,'⁴³ what else do we mean than that His name should be hallowed in us? And, since this has already been done by the bath of regeneration, why do the faithful daily put it in their prayers, except that they may persevere in what has been done in them? This is the way the blessed Cyprian understood the matter in his

---
38 Col. 4.12.
39 John 8.44.
40 Jude 24.
41 Acts 13.48.
42 Matt. 10.22.
43 Matt. 6.9.

explanation of the petition: 'We pray,' he says, ' "hallowed be thy name," not that we wish God to be sanctified by our prayers, but we wish that God's name should be sanctified in us. Surely, God Himself is not sanctified; it is He who sanctifies. But, since He said, "Be ye therefore holy, because I am holy,"[44] our prayer and petition is that we who were sanctified in baptism may persevere in what we have begun to be.' The thought of the glorious martyr is that in these words the Christian faithful daily pray for perseverance in what they have begun to be. Unquestionably whoever begs of the Lord perseverance in good, confesses that this perseverance is His gift.

Chapter 7

(11) In view of all this, we admonish, and we rightly admonish those who once were leading good lives but did not persevere in them. Of their own will they went from good to bad, and hence they are deserving of admonition; and if admonition does them no good, and they persevere unto death in their abandoned life, they merit the loss of God forever. Nor will it be any excuse for them, as now they say: 'Why are we admonished?' so then to say: 'Why are we lost, seeing that we did not receive perseverance, whereby we might not go back from good to evil, but remain in the good?' By no means will they rescue themselves from their just condemnation by this excuse. Truth itself has said that no one is freed from the sentence incurred by Adam save through faith in Jesus Christ; even those will not free themselves from this sentence who are able to say that they did not hear the gospel of Christ, and that faith depends on hearing.[45] How much less, then, will those free them-

---
44 Levit. 19.2.
45 Rom. 10.17.

selves who pretend to say, 'We did not receive perseverance.' It is a more reasonable excuse to say: 'We did not hear,' than to say: 'We did not receive perseverance'; for it may be said that a man could, if he wished,[46] persevere in that which he has heard and held; but it may by no means be said that a man could, if he wished, believe in that which he has not heard.

(12) Consequently, those who have not heard the Gospel; and those who, having heard it, and having been once changed for the better, did not receive perseverance; and those who, having heard the Gospel, were unwilling to come to Christ (that is, to believe in Him), as he said Himself: 'No one cometh to me unless it be given to him by my Father';[47] and those who could not even believe because they were infants, needing to be absolved from original sin by the bath of regeneration, but dying without having received it—all these do not stand apart from that mass which, we know, was sentenced to the loss of God; all of them, by reason of one, fall under condemnation. And they are singled out not by their own merits, but by the grace of the Mediator; that is, they are justified in the blood of the second Adam as by a free favor. Hence, when we hear: 'For who singled thee out? Or what hast thou that thou hast not received? And if thou hast received it, why dost thou boast as if thou hadst not received it?'[48] we ought to understand that no one can be singled out of that lost mass for which Adam was responsible,[49] except one

---

46 The immediate reason why the just man does not persevere is again said to lie in his own free will.
47 John 6.65.
48 1 Cor. 4.7.
49 'Massa perditionis,' or elsewhere, 'massa luti,' and massa peccati'; the word 'massa' is taken from the Vulgate text of Rom. 9.21, where it translates the Greek *phurama* (that which is mixed or kneaded, dough). In using the expresssion of Adam's descendants, St. Augustine simply states the doctrine of original sin.

who has this gift; and he who has it, has it by the grace of the Savior. Moreover, this testimony of the Apostle is so important that the blessed Cyprian, writing to Quirinus, treated it under the title, 'There is to be no boasting in anything, since nothing is ours.'

(13) As for those who by the bounty of divine grace are singled out of that original body of the lost,[50] there is no doubt that the opportunity to hear the Gospel is arranged for them; and, when they hear, they believe, and persevere unto the end in the faith which worketh by charity;[51] and, if ever they go off the track, they are chastised by admonitions; and some of them, even though they are not admonished by men, return to the path they had abandoned; and some, too, having received grace at various ages, are withdrawn from the dangers of this life by a swift death. All these things are done in them by Him who made them vessels of mercy, and who also chose them in His Son before the foundation of the world by a gracious choice. 'And if out of grace, then not in virtue of works; otherwise grace is no longer grace.'[52] For they are not so called, as not to be chosen; for which reason it is said, 'Many are called, but few are chosen.'[53] But, since they are called according to God's purpose, they are surely chosen by the choice which we have termed gracious; it is not made in view of their preceding merits, because their every merit is a grace.

---

50 In what follows (nn. 13-16) St. Augustine describes the effects of predestination in the elect. It is clear that he is speaking of predestination in the totality of its effects—therefore, of predestination both to grace and to glory.
51 Gal. 5.6.
52 Rom. 11.6.
53 Matt. 20.16.

(14) Of such as these the Apostle says: 'Now we know that for those who love God all things work together unto good, for those who, according to his purpose, are saints through his call. For those whom he has foreknown he has also predestined to become conformed to the image of his Son, that he should be the firstborn among many brethren. And those whom he has predestined, them he has also called; and those whom he has called, them he has also justified, and those whom he has justified, them he has also glorified.'[54] Of their number no one perishes, because they are all chosen; and they are chosen because they are called according to the purpose—not their own purpose, but that of God. Of this it is elsewhere said: '. . . in order that the purpose of God might stand according to [his] choice, not depending on deeds, but on him who called, it was said to her: "The elder shall serve the younger" ';[55] and again: 'Not according to our works, but according to his own purpose and grace.'[56] When, therefore, we hear the text: 'Those whom he has predestined, them he has also called,' we must understand that they were called according to God's purpose.

The Apostle began by saying: 'All things work together unto good, for those who, according to his purpose, are saints through his call'; and then he goes on to say: 'Those whom he has foreknown he has also predestined to become conformed to the image of his Son, that he should be the firstborn among many brethren.'[57] And to all this he adds: 'Those whom he predestined, them he has also called.' Consequently, he wants to be understood as speaking of those who are called according to God's purpose; lest it

---

54 Rom. 8.28-30.
55 Rom. 9.11-13.
56 2 Tim.1.9.
57 Rom. 8.28 ff.

be thought that there were among them some who are called, but not chosen, as in the text: 'Many are called, but few are chosen.'[58] All those who are chosen are undoubtedly called; but not all who are called are for that reason chosen. As I have repeatedly said, those are chosen who are called according to God's purpose, and they are also predestined and foreknown. If anyone of these perishes, God has falsely sworn; but no one of them does perish, because God does not swear falsely. If anyone of these perishes, God has been overcome by the fault of man; but no one of them does perish, because God is not overcome by anything.

Moreover, they are chosen to reign with Christ, not as Judas was chosen for the work suited to him. Judas was chosen by Him who knows how to make good use even of evil men, in order that through Judas' damnable deed He might bring to completion the deed of reverence which He had come to perform. Therefore, in the text: 'Have I not chosen you, the twelve? Yet one of you is a devil,' we must understand that the one was chosen in judgment, the rest in mercy; the others were chosen to possess His kingdom, the one was chosen to shed His blood.[59]

(15) Rightly these words are spoken to the kingdom of the elect: 'If God is for us, who is against us? He who has not spared his own Son but has delivered him for us all, how can He fail to grant us also all things with him? Who shall make accusation against the elect of God? It is God who justifies! Who shall condemn? It is Christ Jesus

---

58 Matt. 20.16.
59 It must not be supposed, from this example or in any other context, that the election of the just to glory and the despatch of the damned to their punishment happen in the same way. The former happens by the direct will and action of God; the latter, under His foreknowledge and permission.

who died, yes, and rose again, he who is at the right hand of God, who also intercedes for us!'[60] And those who have received the gift of this steadfast perseverance may go on and say: 'Who shall separate us from the love of Christ? Shall tribulation, or distress, or persecution, or hunger, or nakedness, or danger, or the sword? Even as it is written: "For thy sake we are put to death all the day long. We are regarded as sheep for the slaughter."[61] But in all these things we overcome because of him who has loved us. For I am sure that neither death, nor life, nor angels, nor principalities, nor things present, nor things to come, nor powers, nor height, nor depth, nor any other creature will be able to separate us from the love of God, which is in Christ Jesus our Lord.'[62]

(16) It is the elect who are meant in the letter to Timothy, where, after mention of the attempts of Hymenaeus and Philetus to undermine the faith, the text goes on: 'But the sure foundation of God stands firm, bearing this seal: "The Lord knows who are his." '[63] The faith of these latter, which works through charity, either does not ever fail, or, if it fail in some, the loss is repaired before death, the sin that intervened is blotted out, and perseverance to the end is granted. On the other hand, those who are not to persevere to the end, those who are to fall from Christian faith and conduct, in such wise that the end of this life will find them thus fallen—these men are certainly not to be counted in the number of the elect, not even at the time during which they are living in goodness and piety. For they are not singled out of the mass of the lost by the

---

60 Rom. 8.31 ff.
61 Ps. 43.22.
62 Rom. 8.35 ff.
63 2 Tim. 2.18-19.

foreknowledge and predestination of God; consequently, they are not called according to God's purpose, and, for this reason, not chosen. They are called in the company of those of whom it was said: 'Many are called'; but not in the company of those of whom it was said: 'but few are chosen.'[64] Nevertheless, who would deny that they were chosen at the time when they believed, were baptized, and lived according to God? Clearly, they are spoken of as chosen by such as do not know what the future holds for them, not by Him who knows that they have not the perseverance which brings the elect to blessed life, and who knows, too, that they are standing indeed, but in such wise that, as He foresees, they are going to fall.

Chapter 8

(17) At this point, if I am asked why God does not give perseverance to those to whom He once gave the love whereby they lived a Christian life, I answer that I do not know. Not with arrogance, but in the recognition of my condition, I heed the Apostle's words: 'O man, who art thou to reply to God?'[65] 'O the depth of the riches of the wisdom and of the knowledge of God! How incomprehensible are his judgments, and how unsearchable his ways!'[66] Insofar as He has deigned to manifest His judgments to us, let us give thanks; insofar as He has hidden them, let us not murmur against His will, but let us believe that this, too, is most salutary for us.

But you—the enemy of His grace, who put the question—what do you say? I suppose you will not deny that you

---

64 Matt. 20.16.
65 Rom. 9.20.
66 Rom. 11.33.

are a Christian, but will boast of being a Catholic. If, therefore, you admit that perseverance in good to the end is a gift of God, I dare say you are as ignorant as I am of why one receives this gift and another does not; neither of us can penetrate the inscrutable judgments of God in this regard. Or if you say that it depends on the free will of man (which you defend, not in its harmony with the grace of God, but against His grace), whether one perseveres or does not persevere in good, and that it is no gift of God if one perseveres, but the work of the human will, how shall you get around the words: 'I have prayed for you, Peter, that your faith may not fail'?[67] You will hardly dare to say that, even after the prayer of Christ that Peter's faith should not fail, it might have failed, if Peter had wished it to fail—that is, if he had been unwilling to have it persevere to the end. This would mean that Peter would will something else than what Christ prayed that he should will. Obviously, Peter's faith would collapse, if his will to believe were to fail; and it would stand firm, if that will stood firm. But, since 'the will is prepared by the Lord,'[68] the prayer of Christ for him could not be in vain. When, therefore, Christ prayed that Peter's faith might not fail, what else did He pray for, except that Peter might have an entirely free, strong, unconquerable, and persevering will to believe? This is the way in which the freedom of the will is defended in harmony with the grace of God, and not against it.[69] The fact is that the human will does not achieve grace through freedom, but rather freedom

---
67 Luke 22.32.
68 Prov. 8.35 according to the LXX.
69 Implicit here is St. Augustine's constant principle for the solution of the question of the harmony between free will and the grace which is called 'efficacious': the will accepts this grace freely, because His grace creates the will to its own free acceptance.

through grace, and through grace, too, joyous consistency, and invincible strength to persevere.

(18) It is indeed an amazing thing, an extremely amazing thing, that God does not give perseverance to some of His own children, whom He regenerated in Christ, and to whom He gave faith, hope, and love; whereas to His estranged children He grants pardon for many sins, and by the gift of His grace makes them His own children. Who is not amazed at this? Who is not quite overcome with wonder at this? Yet there is another no less amazing thing, which is nevertheless true, and so evident that not even the enemies of the grace of God can find the means of denying it. I mean the fact that God excludes from his kingdom some of the children of His friends, the faithful, reborn and virtuous, who die without baptism while still infants (although surely He in whose power all things lie, could, if He wished, procure for them the grace of baptism), and at the same time He admits to His kingdom their parents. I mean, too, the fact that God brings it about that some of the children of His enemies come into the hands of Christians, and by the laver of baptism are admitted to His kingdom, from which their parents are excluded. Yet of their own personal wills, these latter children have merited no good, and the former no evil. Assuredly, since the judgments of God in these matters are just, they cannot be criticized; and since they are deep, their reasons cannot be reached. So is it with His judgments in the matter of perseverance, which we are now discussing. Confronted with them, let us exclaim: 'O the depth of the riches of the wisdom and of the knowledge of God! How incomprehensible are his judgments, and how unsearchable his ways!'[70]

[70] Rom. 11.33.

(19) And let us not be astonished that we cannot search His unsearchable ways. I shall not pause to consider innumerable things that are given to one, and not given to another, without respect to the merits of free will, by the Lord God, who has no human preferences.[71] Such, for instance, are native aptitudes, strength, health, good looks, extraordinary talents, powers of mind in various fields; such also are things that are extrinsic to man, as, for instance, wealth, nobility, honors, and that sort of thing, whose possession depends on the power of God. Moreover, I shall not delay over the baptism of infants (which, as our adversaries must admit, certainly belongs to the kingdom of God, even if the above-mentioned things do not), nor consider why it is given to one and not to another, when to give or not to give it is equally in the power of God, and without that sacrament no one enters the kingdom of God. I shall, I say, pass over all these things, to look at the case of those whom we are discussing—those who have not perseverance in good, but who die after going from good to bad, as their good will ran out.

Let our adversaries give an answer, if they can, to the question, why God did not snatch them from the perils of this life while they were still living virtuously and piously, and keep wickedness from changing their understanding and guile from deceiving their soul?[72] Was it that He lacked the power, or that He did not know the evils that were coming? Surely, it would be wicked and mad to suggest either alternative. Why, then, did He not rescue them? Let them give an answer who mock us when in these matters we exclaim: 'How incomprehensible are his

---

71 Rom. 2.11.
72 Wisd. 4.11.

judgments, and how unsearchable his ways!'[73] The fact is that God gives this gift to those to whom He wishes to give it; or else Scripture lies when it says of the supposedly premature death of the just man: 'He was caught away lest wickedness should change his understanding or guile deceive his soul.'[74] Why, then, is this immense favor given to some and not to others by God, with whom there is no injustice nor human preferences,[75] and in whose power it lies to determine the length of each man's life, which has been called a warfare here on earth?[76] Consequently, just as they are forced to admit that it is the gift of God if a man ends his days before he changes from good to evil (and they are ignorant of the reason why the gift is given to some and not to others), so also let them admit with us that perseverance in good is a gift of God, according to the Scriptures, many of whose testimonies I have already cited. And let them, without complaining to God, condescend to be ignorant with us of why this gift is given to some and not to others.

Chapter 9

(20) For our part, we are not disturbed by the fact that God does not give perseverance to some of His children. (This, of course, cannot be the case with those who have been predestined and called according to the purpose, and who are truly children of the promise.) While they are living piously, they are indeed said to be children of God;

---

[73] Rom.11.33.
[74] Wisd. 4.11; note that in this passage there is implied the doctrine, later developed, of God's knowledge of the so-called 'futuribles,' that is, of events in the human order that would take place under certain conditions.
[75] Rom. 9.14; 2.11.
[76] Job. 7.1.

but, since they are going to live sinfully and die in their sin, the foreknowledge of God does not call them children of God. There are children of God who are not yet such to us, but are such to God; of these John the Evangelist says: 'Jesus was to die for the nation, and not only for the nation, but that he might gather into one the scattered children of God.'[77] They were, of course, going to become children of God by faith, through the preaching of the Gospel; nevertheless, before this happened, they already were children of God, inscribed as such with indelible permanence in the remembrance of their Father. On the other hand, there are those who are called children of God by us on account of the grace they have received for a time, but who are not such to God; of these John says: 'They have gone forth from us, but they were not of us. For if they had been of us, they would surely have continued with us.'[78] He does not say: They have gone forth from us, and because they did not continue with us, they are no longer of us. Rather, he says: 'They have gone forth from us, but they were not of us'; that is, even when they seemed to be among us, they were not of us. And, as if someone had asked him to establish the point, he adds: 'For if they had been of us, they would surely have continued with us.' It is the voice of the children of God; John speaks, set in a high place among the children of God.

When, therefore, the children of God say of those who have not perseverance: 'They went forth from us, but they were not of us,' and add: 'For if they had been of us, they would have continued with us,' what else do they imply but that the ones in question were not children, even when they made the profession, and had the name of

---
[77] John 11.51-52.
[78] 1 John 2.19.

children? It was not that they counterfeited justice, but that they did not continue in it. He does not, for instance, say: If they had been of us, they would indeed have held with us to true, and not counterfeit, justice. On the contrary, he says: If they had been of us, they would have continued with us. Unquestionably, he wished them to continue in good. Accordingly, they were in good,[79] but, since they did not continue in it (that is, did not persevere to the end), they were not, he says, of us, even when they were with us. That is, they were not of the number of sons, even when they were in the faith of sons, since those who are truly sons are foreknown and predestined to be in the image of His Son, and are called according to the purpose, so as to be chosen.[80] In a word, the son of the promise does not perish, but the son of perdition.[81]

(21) Such men, therefore, were of the multitude of the called, but not of the small group of the chosen. It was not that God failed to give perseverance to His predestined children; they would have had it, if they had been in the number of His children. And what would they have had that they had not received, according to the true mind of the Apostle?[82] In that case, they would have been children given to the Son Christ, as He Himself said to the Father: 'That I should lose nothing of what thou hast given me, but that I should raise it up on the last day.'[83] It is to be understood, therefore, that those are given to Christ who

---

79 These men, therefore, truly possessed the grace of God, even though they were not predestined. This, of course, is quite different from the doctrine of Calvin, who would not grant that any save the predestined ever actually possessed grace.
80 Rom. 8.29,28.
81 John 17.12.
82 1 Cor. 4.7.
83 John 6.39-40.

are destined for eternal life. They are the predestined, called according to the purpose, of whom not one perishes. For this reason, none of them ends his days after having been changed from good to bad, because each is so destined, and hence given to Christ, as not to perish but to have eternal life. Again, among those whom we call His enemies, or the infant children of His enemies, all those whom He is going to regenerate, in such wise that they will end their days in the faith which works by charity—all these, even before the event, are His children in predestination, and they have been given to Christ His Son, so that they may not perish but have eternal life.

(22) We have, finally, the words of the Savior Himself: 'If you abide in my word, you shall truly be my disciples.'[84] Are we to put in their company Judas, who did not remain in His word? Or are we to put in their company those whom the Evangelist mentions, after recounting the Lord's command that men eat His Body and drink His Blood: 'These things he said when teaching in the synagogue at Capharnaum. Many of his disciples, therefore, when they heard this, said: "This is a hard saying. Who can listen to it?" But Jesus, knowing in himself that his disciples were murmuring at this, said to them: "Does this scandalize you? What then if you should see the Son of Man ascending where he was before? It is the spirit that gives life; the flesh profits nothing. The words that I have spoken to you are spirit and life. But there are some among you who do not believe." For Jesus knew from the beginning who they were who did not believe, and who it was who should betray him. And he said: "This is why I have said to you: No one can come to me unless he is enabled to do so by

---

84 John 8.31.

my Father." From this time many of his disciples turned back and no longer went about with him.'[85] Were not these people called disciples in the Gospel? Nevertheless, they were not true disciples, because they did not abide in His word; according to what He said Himself: 'If you abide in my word, you shall truly be my disciples.'

Since, therefore, they did not have perseverance, they were not truly children of God, just as they were not truly disciples of Christ, even when they seemed to be such, and were called such. Hence we call the regenerate whom we see living good lives both chosen and disciples of Christ and children of God; for so they are to be called. But they truly are what they are called, only if they abide in that [grace] on account of which they are so called. On the other hand, if they have not perseverance (that is, if they do not abide on that [grace] in which they have begun to be), they are not truly called what they are only in name, not in reality; for they are not such to Him to whom it is known what they are going to become—that is, good men turned evil.

(23) This is why the Apostle adds: 'For those who are called according to the purpose,'[86] after he has said: 'We know that for those who love God all things work together unto good'; he knew that some love God, but do not abide in that love until the end. However, those who are called according to the purpose abide in their love of God until the end; and, if some swerve from it for a time, they come back, and carry on to the end the good they began. Moreover, by way of showing what is meant by being called according to the purpose, the Apostle adds the words I

---

85 John 6.60 ff.
86 Rom. 8.28.

have already cited: 'For those whom he has foreknown he has also predestined to become conformed to the image of His Son, that he should be the firstborn among many brethren. And those whom he has predestined, them he has also called (namely, according to the purpose); and those whom he has called, them he has also justified; and those whom he has justified, them he has also glorified.'[87] All these things have already been accomplished—the foreknowledge, the predestination, the call, the justification; because all have been already foreknown and predestined, and many have been already called and justified.

Not yet, however, has the final thing come to pass: 'them he has also glorified.' (The 'glory' here is to be understood as that of which St. Paul says: 'When Christ, your life, shall appear, then you too will appear with him in glory.'[88]) It is also true that two other things—the call and the justification—have not yet come to pass in all the men in question; for up until the end of time many are to be called and justified. Still, the Apostle uses the past tense even of things still in the future, as if God had already done the things which from eternity He has arranged to do. So, too, Isaias says of God: 'He has done the things that are to be.'[89] All those, therefore, who in God's disposing providence are foreknown, predestined, called, justified, and glorified—even though they are not yet, I shall not say reborn, but even born—are already children of God, and can by no means perish. These are they who truly come to Christ; for they come as He Himself said: 'All that the Father gives to me shall come to me, and him who comes to me I will not cast out.' And a little

---
87 John 8.29-30.
88 Col. 3.4.
89 Isa. 45.11 according to the LXX.

later: 'This is the will of my Father who sent me, that I should lose nothing of what he has given me.'[90] By Him, therefore, perseverance in good unto the end is also given; and it is not given save to those who are not to perish, because those who do not persevere will perish.

(24) For such as love Him in this way, God makes all things work together unto good—absolutely all things, even to this extent, that if some of them swerve and stray from the path, He makes their very wanderings contribute to their good, because they come back wiser and more humble. They learn that their rejoicing on the right path ought to be with trembling, and that they should not arrogantly rely on their own strength to remain on the right path, nor say in their abundance: 'We shall not be moved forever.'[91] It was said to them: 'Serve God with fear, and rejoice in him with trembling, lest God be angry, and you perish from the right way.'[92] Notice that he does not say, 'lest you fail to come to the right way,' but, 'lest you perish from the right way.' His point is to warn those who are walking in the right way to serve God in fear, that is, 'be not high-minded, but fear.'[93] This means that they are not to be proud, but humble, as he elsewhere says: 'Do not set your mind on high things, but condescend to the lowly.'[94] Let them rejoice in God, but with trembling, boasting of nothing, since nothing is ours; so that he who boasts should boast in the Lord; lest they perish from the right way, in which they have begun to walk, through taking to themselves the credit for walking therein.

---

90 John 6.37,40.
91 Ps. 29.7.
92 Ps. 2.11-12.
93 Rom. 11.20.
94 Rom. 12.16.

This is the advice of the Apostle, where he says: 'With fear and trembling work out your salvation.'[95] And he shows the reason for the fear and trembling: 'For it is God who of his good pleasure works in you both the will and the performance.'[96] That man did not have this fear and trembling who said in his abundance: 'I shall not be moved forever.'[97] However, because, he was a son of the promise, not of perdition, he experienced what he was worth when God left him for a time: 'Lord, in thy favor thou didst give strength for my adornment: [then] thou didst hide thy face, and I was troubled.'[98] Now you see him wiser and therefore more humble, holding to the path, understanding and acknowledging that it was God who in His favor had given him strength for his adornment; whereas he has taken to himself the credit, and, trusting in himself in the midst of the abundance which God had given him, and not trusting in Him who had given the abundance, he had said: 'I shall not be moved forever.' Then he came to grief, in order that he might find himself and learn, in lowly wisdom, in whom to put hope, not only of eternal life, but also of pious conduct and perseverance in this life.

These words might have been spoken by the Apostle Peter. As a matter of fact, he did say in his abundance: 'I will lay down my life for thee,'[99] hastily attributing to himself what was later to be given him by the Lord. However, the Lord turned His face from him, and he came to grief, with the result that he thrice denied the Lord, fearing lest he should have to die for Him. Then the Lord turned His face to him once again, and he washed out his sin with

---
95 Phil. 2.12.
96 Phil. 2.13.
97 Ps. 29.7.
99 John 13.37.

tears. That is the meaning of the words: 'The Lord looked upon Peter':[100] He turned once more to him the face that for a time He had turned away. Peter, therefore, had come to grief; but he learned not to trust in himself, and this itself benefited him, by the power of Him who makes all things work together unto good for those who love Him; for Peter had been called according to the purpose, so that no one could snatch him from the hand of Christ, to whom he had been given.

(25) Consequently, let no one say that he who wanders from the way is not to be admonished, but that prayers are simply to be said for his return and perseverance. No man of prudence and faith should so speak. If the wanderer has been called according to the purpose, God certainly makes his admonishing work with Him unto good. And, since he who does the admonishing cannot know whether the culprit has been thus called, let him do what he knows ought to be done: he knows that the man is to be admonished, and that God will show either mercy or judgment. He will show mercy, if the man who is admonished has been singled out by the bounty of grace from the mass of perdition, and is not among the vessels of wrath which have been fashioned for ruin, but among the vessels of mercy which God has prepared for glory.[101] But He will show judgment, if His man is damned with the vessels of wrath, not predestined with the vessels of mercy.

Chapter 10

(26) At this point, another by no means unimportant question comes up; with the help of the Lord, in whose hand

---
100 Luke 22.61.
101 Rom. 9.22-23.

are both ourselves and our words, it must be attacked and solved. In regard to the gift of God which is perseverance in good unto the end, the question is put to us, what are we to think of the first man, who surely was created just, without any defect. I cannot, for instance, say: If he did not have perseverance, how was he without defect, since he lacked a very necessary gift of God? This latter question is easily answered by saying that he did not have perseverance, because he did not persevere in the good in virtue of which he was without defect. The fact is that at a certain time a defect appeared in him; and, if so, before this happened he was without defect. It is one thing not to have any defect; but another thing not to continue in that goodness wherein there was no defect. We do not say that he was never without defect, but that he did not continue without defect; and thereby we clearly show that he once was without defect, and that his guilt lies in not having continued in that state of goodness.

But there is another question that needs more painstaking discussion. How shall we answer those who say: If he had perseverance in that rectitude in which he was created without defect, he undoubtedly persevered in it. And if he persevered, he obviously did not sin, nor abandon his original rectitude. But the facts proclaim that he did sin, and was a traitor to the good. Consequently, he did not have perseverance in the good; and, if he did not have it, he did not receive it. How could he have received perseverance, and still not have persevered? Furthermore, if he did not have it for the reason that he did not receive it, how did he sin in not persevering, when he did not receive perseverance? It is no answer to say that he did not receive it because he was not singled out from the mass of perdition by the bounty of grace; for the fact is that, before his sin, he was not in the mass of perdition made up of humankind. It was from him that man has his origin in sin.[102]

(27) Wherefore let us freely confess—what is certainly our faith—that God, the Lord of all things, who created all things exceedingly good, and who foresaw that evil was to arise out of good, and who knew that it was more fitting to His omnipotent goodness to bring good out of evil than to permit no evil—let us confess, I say, that God so disposed the life of angels and men as first to show forth in it the power of their free will, and then the power of His grace and the judgment of His justice. In the sequel, some of the angels, whose chief is called the devil, by their free will became fugitives from the Lord God. But, fugitives as they were from His goodness, by which they had been blessed, they could not flee His judgment, by which they were made most miserable. On the other hand, the rest of the angels by their free will stood firm in the truth, and merited the certain knowledge that they would never fall. For if we can ascertain from the Scriptures that none of the good angels will ever fall, by how much the more must they themselves have known this through some higher revelation? As a matter of fact, to us there has been promised an endlessly blessed life, and equality with the angels; and this promise assures us that we shall never fall from that blesssed life, once we have reached it after the judgment. But if the angels have not the like certainty about themselves, we are not equal to them but more blessed than they; yet it was equality with them that Truth has promised to us.[103] Consequently, it is certain that they know by vision

---

[102] St. Augustine has taught that perseverance is given to the predestined purely as a gift of mercy, and that it is quite in accord with divine justice that it should not be given to all the just. He had, therefore, to answer the question: Why was it not given to Adam?
[103] Matt. 22.30.

what we know by faith, namely, that ruin will never befall any of the holy angels.

The devil and his angels were indeed blessed before they fell, and they did not know that they would fall into misery. However, if they had stood in the truth by their free will, there was one thing yet to be added to their blessedness, at the time when they would receive the fullness of the highest beatitude as the reward of their love constancy; namely by the great abundance of the love of God given by the Holy Spirit, they would receive power never thereafter to fall, and they would know most certainly that such was their case. They did not have this fullness of beatitude; but, since they did not know of their future misery, they enjoyed a beatitude of a lesser degree indeed, but still without defect. Clearly, if they had known of their future fall and its eternal punishment, they could not have been blessed; for the fear of this great evil would even then have constrained them to be miserable.

(28) In the same fashion, God made man with free will; and, though man was ignorant of his future fall, he was nevertheless happy, because he knew that it was in his power not to die and not to be wretched. If, then, man had freely and deliberately willed to abide in this right and sinless state, by the merit of this abiding and without any experience of death or unhappiness he would have received the fullness of beatitude wherewith the holy angels are blessed—I mean the impossibility of ever falling, and certain knowledge of this fact. Obviously, man could not have been happy even in paradise—in fact, he would not have been in paradise, where misery is out of place— if the foreknowledge of his fall were to make him miserable through the fear of so great an evil. However, because man of his own free will abandoned God, he experienced the just judgment of God, with the result

that he was damned together with all his progeny, who were all contained in him and who all sinned with him. Those of his progeny who are freed by the grace of God are freed from a damnation under sentence of which they lie; wherefore, even if no one of them were to be freed, nobody could justly criticize the just judgment of God. The fact that a few are saved (they are indeed few in comparison to those who are lost, though their number itself is large) is the work of grace— a free work, for which many thanks are to be rendered[104]—in order that no one may take pride in his own merits, but every mouth be stopped, and that he who takes pride take pride in the Lord.[105]

Chapter 11

(29) What is the conclusion? That Adam did not have the grace of God? On the contrary, he had a great grace, but one different from ours. He had good gifts, which he had received from the goodness of his Creator (he had not garnered them by his own merits), and in their midst he experienced no evil. But the saints in this life, who are the subjects of this grace of liberation, are in the midst of evils, out of which they cry to God: 'Deliver us from evil.' Adam in the midst of his gifts did not need the death of Christ; but the blood of the Lamb absolves the saints from a guilt which is both hereditary and their own. Adam had no need of that help for which the saints beg when they say:[106] 'I see another

---

104 Rom. 3.19.
105 1 Cor. 1.31.
106 The 'help' here is that which is nowadays called 'medicinal' or 'healing' grace, as distinct in concept from 'elevating' grace; the former is a remedy for the moral weakness of human nature; the latter regards the absolute impotence of human nature in the face of supernatural action.

law in my members, warring against the law of my mind, and making me prisoner to the law of sin that is in my members. Unhappy man that I am! Who will deliver me from the body of this death? The grace of God through Jesus Christ our Lord.'[107] In the saints, the flesh is at war with the spirit and the spirit with the flesh. Struggling in this conflict, and in danger, they ask that the power to fight and conquer be given to them through the grace of Christ. Adam, however, was not tempted and troubled by any such conflict between the two selves in him; and in that place of blessedness he enjoyed interior peace with himself.

(30) The result is that the saints in this present life need a grace, not richer indeed, but more powerful. And what more powerful grace is there than the only-begotten Son of God, equal to, and co-eternal with, the Father; who was made man for them, and crucified by sinful men, He in whom there was neither original nor personal sin? Although He rose on the third day, never to die again, He first bore death for mortal man; to those who were dead He gave life, in order that, redeemed by His Blood and possessed of this secure guaranty, they might say: 'If God is for us, who is against us? He who has not spared even his own Son but has delivered him for us all, how can he fail to grant us also all things with him?'[108] God therefore took our nature—that is, the rational soul and the flesh of the man Christ—in a manner uniquely wonderful and wonderfully unique; in such wise that, through no preceding merits of His own justice, He was the Son of God at the first instant that He began to be man—He and the Word which had no beginning were one person.

Obviously, there is no one so blindly ignorant of this matter

---

107 Rom. 7.23-25.
108 Rom. 8.31-32.

of faith, as to dare say that, born as He was a son of man through the Holy Spirit and the Virgin Mary, He merited to be the Son of God by His own free will, by leading a good life and doing good works without sin.'[109] Against such an opinion there stands the Gospel text: 'The Word was made flesh.' Where did this happen, but in the virginal womb in which the man Christ had his beginning? Likewise, when the Virgin asked how that which the angel announced to her was to be done, the angel answered: 'The Holy Spirit shall come upon thee and the power of the Most High shall overshadow thee; and therefore the Holy One to be born of thee shall be called the Son of God.'[110] 'Therefore,' he says—not meaning, because of works (for one not yet born has done none), but because 'the Holy Spirit shall come upon thee and the power of the Most High shall overshadow thee, therefore the one to be born of thee shall be called the Son of God.' That birth, which had no human meriting, joined man to God, flesh to the Word, in the unity of one person. Good works followed upon that birth; no good works merited it. Obviously, it was not to be feared that human nature, mysteriously taken up by the Word of God into the unity of His Person, would freely and deliberately sin; for the very assumption was such that the nature of man thus assumed by God would admit within itself no movement of an evil will. Through this Mediator, whom God so assumed as not to let Him ever be evil, but always good (and not made good out of evil)—through Him God shows that it is He who makes those whom He has redeemed by His Blood to be forever after good, though once they were evil.

---

109 There is a suggestion here of the easy passage, made even in St. Augustine's time, from Pelagianism to Nestorianism; the two errors are akin. The Council of Ephesus, which condemned Nestorius, also added a condemnation of Pelagius.

110 Luke 1.35.

(31) The grace which the first man had was not one whereby he would never will to be evil. But his grace was such that, if he willed to abide in it, he never would be evil; and such, too, that without it he could not be good, even with all his freedom. But he could, nevertheless, freely abandon it. God, you see, did not wish Adam to be without His grace, which He left under the power of Adam's free will; for the power of free choice is sufficient in the matter of evil, but of little avail in that of good, unless it is aided by omnipotent Goodness. And if Adam had not freely and deliberately abandoned the aid which he had, he would have always been good; but he did abandon it, and was abandoned.

His aid was such that he could abandon it, when he willed; or, if he willed, he could hold on to it; but it was not such as to make him will. This was the first grace, that was given to the first Adam; but more powerful than it is the grace in the second Adam. The effect of the first grace was that a man might have justice, if he willed; the second grace, therefore, is more powerful, because it effects the will itself, a strong will, a burning charity, so that by a contrary will the spirit overcomes the conflicting will of the flesh. Not that the first grace whereby the power of free will was displayed, was a small grace; for its help was such that without this aid man would not continue in good; but he could, if he willed, abandon this aid. However, the second grace is so much the greater in this, that it is not enough for it to repair man's lost liberty, nor again enough that without it man could neither lay hold of good nor abide in good even though he willed; actually, by it man is also brought to will.

(32) God, then, in the beginning had given man a good will; He had made him in it, for He had made him right. He had given him an aid, without which he could not continue in it, if he willed; but the will itself to continue was left

to man's free choice. He could therefore continue, if he willed, because the aid was not lacking by which he could, and without which he could not, perseveringly hold on to the good that he willed. The fact that he did not will to continue was certainly his own fault; as it would have been his own merit, if he had willed to continue. This latter was the case with the holy angels; while others fell through their own free choice, they stood firm through the same free choice and merited the due reward of their standing firm—that fullness of beatitude in which they knew most certainly that they would always be blessed. On the other hand, if this aid had been lacking to the angels or to man, when they were first created, they would not have fallen by their own fault, since their nature was not such that they could continue, if they willed, without divine aid; as a matter of fact, the aid, without which they could not continue, would have been lacking.

At present, however, it is a punishment of sin on those to whom this aid is lacking; and to those to whom it is given, it is given by way of grace, not by way of merit. And to those to whom God pleases to give it, through Jesus Christ our Lord, it is given in so much the greater measure, that we have not only that without which we could not continue, even if we willed, but also something of such a kind that we do will. Actually, the effect of this grace of God in us is that, in recovering and holding on to good, we not only are able to do what we will, but we also will to do what we are able to do. This was not the case with the first man; he had one of these things, not the other. You see, he did not need grace in order to recover good, because he had not yet lost it. But for perseverance in it he did need the aid of a grace, without which he was powerless to persevere. He had received the power to persevere, if he willed, but he had not the will to use his power of perseverance; for, had he had that will, he would have persevered. He could have persevered, if he had willed to; and the fact that he did not will goes back to his free choice, which at the time was free in the sense that he could will either good or evil. However, what will be more free than the free will, when it shall have no power to serve sin? This was to have been for man, as it was for the holy angels, the reward of merit. As things are, however, now that our merit is all lost through sin, those who are freed receive as the gift of grace that which was to have been the reward of merit.

Chapter 12

(33) We must have a careful and attentive look at the difference between these two sets of things: to be able not to sin, and not to be able to sin; to be able not to die, and not to be able to die; to be able not to forsake good, and not to be able to forsake good. The first man was able not to sin, he was able not to die, he was able not to forsake good. Are we to say that he was not able to sin, having this kind of free will? Or that he was not able to die, seeing that it was said to him: 'If you sin, you shall die'? Or that he was not able to forsake good, when he did forsake it by sin, and for that reason died? As I say, the first freedom of the will was in being able not to sin;[111] the final freedom will be much greater—in not being able to sin. The first immortality was in being able not to die; the final immortality will be much greater—in not being able to die. The first power of perseverance was in being able not to forsake good; the final power will be the blessedness of perseverance—in not being

---

111 The word 'liberty' (*libertas*) in St. Augustine is used to designate the will's power to adhere to good of the supernatural order; it is a supernatural endowment. The will's power of free choice, of evil as well as good, is connoted in the simple term 'will' (*voluntas*), or at times in the term 'free will' (*liberum arbitrium*).

able to forsake good. Because these latter gifts are better and more desirable, the former gifts are not therefore of no account or of small account.

(34) In the same fashion, the aids themselves are to be distinguished. One is an aid without which something is not done; the other, by which something is done.[112] For instance, we cannot live without food; but even when one has food, it does not make him live, if he wishes to die. Food, therefore, is an aid without which there is no living, not an aid by which one is made to live. On the other hand, take beatitude; when it is given to a man who did not have it, immediately he becomes blessed. It is, therefore, an aid not only without which that does not come to pass for which it is given, but also by which it does come to pass. You see, then, how this is an aid both by which something is done, and without which it is not done; first, because a man immediately becomes blessed, if beatitude is given to him, and secondly, he never becomes blessed, if it is not given to him. On the other hand, food does not inevitably make a man live, and still he cannot live without it.

To the first man, then, who was created just and who received the power not to sin, the power not to die, and the power not to forsake good, there was given an aid to perseverance, not by which he would be made to persevere, but without which he could not of his own free will persevere. At the present time, however, this sort of aid is not given to the saints predestined by grace for the kingdom of God; but an aid is given of such a kind that perseverance itself is given them. The result is that not only are they unable to persevere

---

112 The two 'helps' which are here described are specifically helps for perseverance; they do not so much regard individual acts as permanence in the Christian life. The distinction between *adjutorium quo* and *adjutorium sine quo non* is not equivalent to the distinction between efficacious and sufficient grace.

without this gift, but also by reason of this gift they cannot fail to persevere. As you remember, the Lord not only said: 'Without me you can do nothing';[113] He also added: 'You have not chosen me, but I have chosen you, and have appointed you that you should go forth and bear fruit, and that your fruit should remain.' By these words He indicated that He had given them not only justice, but perseverance in it. For when Christ appointed them that they should go forth and bring forth fruit, and that their fruit should remain, who would make bold to say that it will not remain? Or that perhaps it will not remain? 'For the gifts and the call of God are without repentance,'[114] meaning the call of those who are called according to the purpose. Consequently, with Christ interceding for them, that their faith may not fail, it will most certainly not fail ever. It will, then, persevere unto the end, and the end of this life will find it abiding in them.

(35) The fact is that a greater liberty is necessary against many severe temptations, which were not found in paradise —a liberty fortified and made steady by the gift of perseverance, that it may overcome this world with all its loves and fears and errors. The martyrdom of the saints has taught us this. As it turned out, Adam, with the use of his free will, affrighted by nothing, and actually in the face of God's fear-inspiring command, did not stand firm in his great happiness, in his ability not to sin. But the martyrs, in the face of the world's terrors and even its furious rages against their steadfastness, stood firm in faith. Adam saw the actual gifts that he was to give up; the martyrs did not see the future gifts that they were to receive. How did this come about, except by God's gift? From Him they obtained mercy, that they might be faithful; from Him they received the Spirit, not of

---
113 John 15.5.
114 Rom. 11.29.

fear, in which they would yield to their persecutors, but of strength and love and self-control,[115] in which they overcame all threats, all blandishments, all tortures. To the sinless Adam there was given at his very creation a free will, and he made it the slave of sin; but the will of the martyrs, though it had been the slave of sin, was freed by Him who said: 'If the Son makes you free, you will be free indeed.'[116]

And such a measure of freedom do they receive by this grace, that, although they struggle all their lives against unruly sinful desires (and some faults come upon them unawares, for which they daily pray: 'Forgive us our trespasses'),[117] they do not, for all that, serve the sin which is unto death, of which John the Apostle speaks: 'There is a sin unto death, and I do not mean that anyone should ask as to that.'[118] It is not said what this sin is, and there can be different views about it; for my part, I say that it consists in forsaking the faith, which works through charity, even unto death. To this sin they are not slaves—not that they are at their first creation, like Adam, free; but that they have been, by the grace of God through the second Adam, freed; and, thus set free, they have a free power of choice, by which they serve God, and are not prisoners of the devil. Having been set free from sin, they have become the slaves of justice,[119] in which they will stand firm right up to the end, seeing that God is giving them perseverance—God who foreknew, and predestined, and called them according to the purpose, who justified and glorified them. He has already done even the future things which He has

---
115 2 Tim. 1.7.
116 John 8.36.
117 Matt. 6.12; against the Pelagians, St. Augustine maintains that the just (with the exception of the Blessed Virgin) cannot live entirely without venial sins.
118 1 John 5.16.
119 Rom. 6.18.

promised in their regard; in His promise 'Abraham believed, and it was credited to him as justice .... He gave glory to God, being fully aware that (as it is written) whatever God has promised he is able to perform.'[120]

(36) You see, then, that God makes men good, that they may do good. Not because He foresaw that men would be good of themselves did He promise them as [descendants] to Abraham; in that case, He would be promising, not something of His own, but of theirs. This was not the faith of Abraham; rather, 'he did not waver in unbelief, but was strengthened in faith, giving glory to God, being fully aware that whatever God has promised he is able to perform.'[121] It is not said that He is able to promise what He has foreseen; or that He is able to make manifest what He has foretold; or that He is able to foresee what He has promised; but, 'what he has promised he is able to perform.' He, therefore, who makes men good, makes them persevere in good. And those who fall and perish were not in the number of the predestined. Hence, although the Apostle was speaking to all the regenerate when he said: 'Who art thou to judge another's servant? To his own lord he stands or falls,'[122] he turns immediately to the predestined, to say: 'But he will stand'; and, lest they take credit to themselves for this, he adds: 'For God is able to make him stand.' Accordingly, it is God who gives perseverance; God who is able to make those stand most perseveringly firm who are standing firm, and to set upright again those who have fallen; for 'God raiseth up those who are bowed down.'[123]

(37) In view of the fact that the first man did not receive this gift of God (that is, perseverance in good), but persever-

---
120 Rom. 4.3,20.
121 Rom. 4.20-21.
122 Rom. 14.4.
123 Ps. 145.8.

ance or non-perseverance was left to his power of choice, he had such energies of will—a will that was made without sin and met no resistance from any interior conflict—that the power of perseverance might fittingly be entrusted to it, considering its goodness and the ease with which it could live well. God, it is true, foresaw the evil that man would do (foreseeing it, of course, He did not force man to it), but at the same time He knew the good that He would Himself make come out of it. As things are now, after the loss of that great liberty in consequence of sin, a weakness remains that must be aided by still greater gifts. It has pleased God completely to extinguish the pride of human presumption, 'lest any flesh should pride itself before him.'[124] In what respect may flesh not pride itself before Him, save in respect of its merits? It could indeed have had merits, but it lost them; and it lost them by the very thing through which it might have had them—its free will.

Consequently, for those who need to be freed there remains only the grace of Him who frees. So it is that no flesh may pride itself before Him. The wicked cannot pride themselves, for they have no reason for pride; nor can the just pride themselves, since they have from Him their reason for pride; in fact, they have only Him for their pride, to whom they say: 'Thou art my pride, and the one who lifts up my head.'[125] You see, then, that all men are meant in the text: 'Lest any flesh should pride itself before him';[126] and the just are meant in the text: 'He who takes pride, let him take pride in the Lord.' This is evidently the mind of the Apostle, who, after he had said: 'Lest any flesh should pride itself before him,' immediately, lest the saints should think that they

---

124 1 Cor. 1.29.
125 Ps. 3.4.
126 1 Cor. 1.29.

were left without reason for pride, goes on to say: 'From him you are in Christ Jesus, who has become for us God-given wisdom, and justice, and sanctification, and redemption; so, that, as it is written, "Let him who takes pride, take pride in the Lord."[127] Hence it is that in this place of afflictions, where the life of man on earth is a warfare,[128] 'strength is made perfect in weakness.'[129] And why this kind of strength? In order that he who takes pride, may take pride in the Lord.[130]

(38) Clearly, then, even in the matter of perseverance in good, God did not want His saints to take pride in their own strength, but in Him; for He not only gives them an aid of the kind given to the first man, without which they are not able to persevere, if they will; but He also effects in them the will itself. The result is that, since there is no perseverance without the power and the will to persevere, both the possibility and the will to persevere are given them by the bounty of divine grace. Their will is so roused by the Holy Spirit that they are able to persevere, because they will to do so; and they will to do so, because God effects this will.[131] If in the weakness of this life (in which, however, strength is to be perfected, that pride may be curbed), their will were to be left to itself, to keep faithful, if it wished, to that aid of God without which they could not persevere, and if God did not effect in them the will itself, their will would, in its weakness, be overcome amid life's many and severe temptations. They would not be able to persevere, because they would fail in their weakness and not will [to persevere]; or at least, by

---

127 1 Cor. 1.30-31.
128 Job 7.1.
129 2 Cor. 12.9.
130 2 Cor.10.17.
131 Here again is St. Augustine's familiar idea that the will is freed by grace, in order to be fully a free will.

reason of the will's weakness they would not so will as to be able to persevere.[132]

Consequently, an aid was given to the weakness of the human will, with the result that it is unwaveringly and invincibly influenced by divine grace,[133] and consequently, whatever its weakness, it does not fail, and is not overcome by any difficulty. This is how it happens that the weak and feeble human will perseveres through the power of God in the little good it has; whereas the strong and healthy will of the first man did not persevere in the larger good it had, for all that it had the power of free will. The lack was not of that aid of God without which Adam could not persevere, if he willed, but of that by which God would effect in him the will. The fact is that He permitted and allowed the strong one to do what he willed; but for the weak he reserved this, that by His gift they should invincibly will what is good, and invincibly refuse to forsake it. Let us, then, understand the words of Christ: 'I have prayed for thee, that thy faith may

---

132 This statement affords the clarifying principle in this difficult subject. St. Augustine conceives the human will as situated in the midst of all the temptations of this life, which are the consequence of man's fallen nature, and of the interior division between spirit and flesh. What man wills to do is *de facto* to persevere in good. But in his present situation man cannot do what he wills to do (persevere in good), because he cannot at every moment in the series of life's actions will to do it; such is his mutability in the face of continuous temptation. At any given moment, when he begins to cease to will his own perseverance, he *could* will to persevere; hence his fall from grace is free. Here is where the grace of perseverance enters; it makes him so will to remain faithful as to be able to do what he wills—that is, always and at every moment to will to be faithful.

133 When it is said that the will is 'invincibly (*insuperabiliter*) influenced' by grace, it is not meant that grace 'overcomes' the will by destroying its freedom. The idea is that the will, assisted by the gift of perseverance, has an unwavering, invincible power in the face of temptation. This sense is declared in what follows: '. . . and is not overcome by any difficulty.'

not fail,'¹³⁴ as spoken to him who was built upon a rock. So it is that the man of God who takes pride is to take pride in the Lord, not only because he has obtained mercy, with the result that he has faith, but also because his faith does not fail.

Chapter 13

(39) I have said all this about those who have been predestined to the kingdom of God, whose number is so fixed that not one can be added to it, or taken from it. I have not been speaking of those who, although He had declared and spoken, have become too numerous to count.¹³⁵ These can be said to have been called, but not chosen, because they were not called according to His purpose. The fact that the number of the elect is fixed, not to be increased or diminished, is suggested even by John the Baptist, where he says: 'Bring forth therefore fruit befitting repentance, and do not think to say to yourselves, "We have Abraham for our father"; for I say to you that God is able out of these stones to raise up children to Abraham.'¹³⁶ The words show that those who do not bring forth fruit are to be cut off, in such a way, however, that the number [of children] promised to Abraham will not fall short. However, it is more openly declared in the Apocalypse: 'Hold fast what thou hast, that no one receive thy crown';¹³⁷ for if another is not to receive a crown, unless someone first lose it, the number is fixed.

(40) There is another point. Even as spoken to the saints who are to persevere, these words seem to imply some uncertainty about their perseverance. The saints ought indeed

---

134 Luke 22.32.
135 Ps. 39.6.
136 Matt. 3.8-9.
137 Apoc. 3.11.

so to understand these words; for it behooves them not to be highminded, but to fear.[138] So long as this mortal life endures, no one of the faithful may presume that he is in the number of the predestined. That fact is necessarily hidden here on earth, where pride is so carefully to be guarded against; even the great Apostle was buffeted by an angel of Satan, lest he be puffed up.[139] Hence our Lord said to the Apostles: 'If you abide in me';[140] although, when He spoke, He knew that they would indeed abide. And He said by the Prophet: 'If ye be willing and obedient,'[141] although He knew those in whom He would effect the will.[142] And there are many other texts to the same purpose.

On account of the value of secrecy in this matter—to keep anyone from being puffed up, and to keep all in fear, even those who are running well, so long as it is not known who are to reach the goal—on this account, I say, it must be supposed that some of the sons of perdition, although they have not received the gift of perseverance to the end, do begin to live in the faith which works through charity, and so for a time live well and faithfully, and afterwards fall, and are not taken from this life before this happens to them. If this were never the case, men would have that salutary fear by which pride is crushed only so long as they had not arrived at the grace of Christ; and thereafter they would be quite assured that they would never fall away from Him. But this would not be beneficial in this place of temptation, where our weakness is such that security can generate pride. In the end, we shall have this security; but only then will men have it, as the

---
[138] Rom. 11.20.
[139] 2 Cor. 12.7.
[140] John 15.7.
[141] Isa. 1.19.
[142] Phil. 2.13.

angels now have it, when there can no longer be any pride. I say, then, that the number of the saints predestined by the grace of God to the kingdom of God, to whom perseverance unto the end is likewise given, will be filled up to completeness, and in its full completeness will be kept blessed without end. The mercy of their Savior will cleave to them all, alike when they are converted, and when they are in the strife, and when they are crowned.

(41) You see, even in that last event the mercy of God is necessary for them, as Holy Scripture testifies, where the saint speaks to his soul of the Lord God, 'who crowneth thee with mercy and compassion.'[143] Likewise, the Apostle James says: 'For judgment is without mercy to him who has not shown mercy';[144] here he makes clear that even at the judgment, at which the just are crowned and the wicked condemned, some are judged with mercy and others without mercy. For the same reason the mother of the Maccabees said to her son: 'that I may have thee back in that mercy with thy brethren.'[145] As it is written: 'For when the just king shall be seated on his throne, there will be no evil before him to oppose him; Who shall boast that his heart is chaste, or who shall boast that he is clean from sin?'[146] Consequently, at that moment also the mercy of God will be needed; by it he will be made blessed, to whom the Lord has not imputed iniquity.[147] But this very mercy will then be granted by a just judgment, according to the merits of good works. For when it is said: 'Judgment is without mercy to him who has not shown mercy,' it is made clear that judg-

---

143 Ps. 102.4.
144 James 2.13.
145 2 Macc. 7.29.
146 Prov. 20.8-9 according to the LXX.
147 Ps. 31.2.

ment is passed with mercy on those in whom are found the good works of mercy; and, consequently, that mercy itself is granted in return for the merits of good works.

Such is not the case now; for now, without any antecedent good works, and even with many antecedent evil works, on the part of man, God's mercy is beforehand with him,[148] to free him from evils—those which he has done, and those which he would have done except that the grace of God kept him from going wrong, and those, too, which he would have suffered in eternity, except that he was rescued from the power of darkness, and carried over into the kingdom of the Son of God's love.[149]

Notwithstanding all this, eternal life itself, which is certainly bestowed as something due to good works, is called by the Apostle a grace of God.[150] And consequently, since a grace is not bestowed in view of works but as a free favor, we must without any hesitation confesss that eternal life is called a grace because it is bestowed in view of merits which grace has given to men. This is the true sense of what we read in the Gospel: 'Grace for grace';[151] that is, for the merits which grace bestowed.

(42) On the other hand, those who do not belong to the number of the predestined, who are brought along to the kingdom of God, whether before the use of free will, or by the use of free will (a will, I mean, free because it has been freed by grace)—these, I say, who do not belong to that certain and blessed number, are most justly judged according

---

148 Grace has a preventive power, to shield us from temptations which would be the occasion of falling. St. Augustine makes much of what is called the external providence of God.
149 Col. 1.13.
150 Rom. 6.23.
151 John 1.16.

to their merits. Either they lie fallen under the sin which they incurred at the first moment of their generation, and die with this hereditary guilt not forgiven them by regeneration; or again, they have added other sins to it by their own free will—a will, I mean, that is free, but not freed (free of justice but the slave of sin), by which they are thrown into the midst of various criminal passions, some of them more wicked, others less wicked, but all of them wicked, and due for degrees of punishment according to their degree of wickedness; or, finally, they receive the grace of God, but are in it only for a time, and do not persevere—they forsake it, and are forsaken; by a just and secret judgment of God, they are given over to their free will, not having received the gift of perseverance.[152]

Chapter 14

(43) Let, therefore, men allow themselves to be admonished when they sin. And let them not use admonitions as an argument against grace, nor grace as an argument against admonitions. A just punishment is due to sin, and part of it is a just admonition, which is used as a medicine, even if the recovery of him who is sick is uncertain. The intention is that, if he who is admonished belongs to the number of the predestined, the admonition may be to him a health-giving remedy; or, if he does not belong to their number, a suffering inflicted as punishment. The admonition is to be administered out of charity, in uncertainty as to its effect,

---

[152] Even in the absence of the gift of perseverance, a man may have many individual graces, not only sufficient but efficacious; actually, those who persevere only for a time (*temporales sunt*) could not do this without efficacious graces. And when they do fall, they do so in spite of having sufficient grace to stand; for no one is abandoned by God till he himself abandons God. Like Adam (n.31), they abandon God and are abandoned.

which is not known; and prayers are to be said for him to whom it is administered, that he may be healed. Actually, when men come, or come back, to the way of justice as the result of an admonition, who is it that effects salvation in their hearts, but God? No matter who plants or waters, no matter who labors in the fields or forests, it is God who makes things grow; and when He wills to save a man, no human will resists Him. To say 'yes' or 'no' is indeed in the power of the man who says it, but in such a way that he may not thwart the will of God nor overcome His power.

(44) Let me add here that the text, 'God wills all men to be saved'[153] (given the fact that not all are saved), can be understood in many ways. I have mentioned some of them in other works of mine; but here I mention one.[154] This text, 'God wills all men to be saved,' may be understood of all the predestined, because every type of man is among them. In the same sense it was said to the Pharisees, 'You pay tithes on every herb,'[155] meaning simply 'every herb that you have'; for they surely did not pay tithes on every herb in the whole world. This manner of speech is found, too, in the text: 'even as I myself in all things please all men.'[156] Surely, Paul, who said this, did not please his many persecutors; but he did please every kind of man which the Church of Christ was

---

153 1 Tim. 2.4.
154 St. Augustine therefore grants that the text is susceptible of other interpretations than those put forward in his writings. He himself more commonly understood St. Paul to be speaking of an *absolute* will of God; and for this reason he sought various ways of interpreting the text so as to reconcile it with the fact that all men are not saved. His main difficulty came from the case of infants dying without baptism. However, at least once he understood the text as implying a conditioned will of God, whose fulfillment would depend on man's response to grace (cf. *De spiritu et littera* 33. 58).
155 Luke 11.42.
156 1 Cor. 10.33.

gathering—those already within the Church, and those, too, who were to be brought in.

(45) Accordingly, there is no doubt that human wills cannot resist the will of God, 'who hath done whatsoever he pleased in heaven and on earth,'[157] and who has even 'done the things that are to come.'[158] Nor can the human will prevent Him from doing what He wills, seeing that even with the wills of men He does what He wills, when He wills to do it. Take, for instance, the case of Saul. When God willed to give the kingdom to Saul, was it in the power of the Israelites to subject themselves to him, or not to subject themselves? In a sense, yes; but not in such a way that they were able to resist God Himself. As a matter of fact, God carried the matter through by means of the wills of men themselves, having, as He undoubtedly does, the almighty power to bend human hearts whithersoever He pleases. So it is written: 'And Samuel sent away all the people, everyone to his own house. Saul also departed to his own house in Gabaa; and there went with him a part of the army, whose hearts God had touched. But the children of Belial said: Shall this fellow be able to save us? And they despised him, and brought him no presents.'[159] Surely, no one will say that any one of those whose hearts God had touched, that they should go with Saul, failed to go with him, or that any of the children of Belial, whose hearts God had not so touched, did go with him.

There is the like case of David, whom God with happier outcome set up over the kingdom. We read of him: 'And David went on growing and increasing, and the Lord of hosts was with him.'[160] Then, shortly thereafter, it is said:

---
157 Ps. 134.6.
158 Isa. 45.11 according to the LXX.
159 1 Kings 10.25-27.
160 1 Par. 11.9.

'But the spirit came upon Amasai, the chief among thirty, and he said: We are thine, O David, and for thee, O son of Isai; peace, peace be to thee, and peace to thy helpers; for thy God helpeth thee.'[161] Could Amasai have opposed the will of God, instead of doing His will, since God, through His spirit, with which Amasai was clothed, wrought in his heart that he should so will, and speak, and act? In like fashion, a little later on, Scripture says: 'And all these men of war, well appointed to fight, came with a perfect heart to Hebron, to make David king over all Israel.'[162] Obviously, it was of their own will that these men made David king; the fact is clear and undeniable. Nevertheless, it was God, who effects in the hearts of men whatsoever He wills, who wrought this will in them. This is why Scripture first says: 'And David went on growing and increasing, and the Lord of hosts was with him.' The Lord God, therefore, who was with David, brought these men to make him king. And how did he bring them to this? Surely, it was not by binding them with any material chains. Rather, He worked within them; He seized their hearts; He drew them on by means of their own wills,[163] which He had Himself created within them. When, therefore, God wills to set up kings on earth, He holds the wills of men more in His own power than they are in the power of men themselves. And if this is so, it is surely He, and no other, who makes admonitions salutary, and effects amendment in the heart of him who is admonished, with the result that he is established in the heavenly kingdom.

---

161 1 Par. 12.18.
162 1 Par. 12.38.
163 Hence the 'drawing' (*tractio*), or 'delight' (*delectatio*), of which St. Augustine so often speaks, and which account in his mind for the victory of grace, include the use of the free human will.

Chapter 15

(46) Let, therefore, the subject brethren be admonished by their superiors, out of charity, with greater or less severity according to the different fault. In fact, even the punishment called 'condemnation,' inflicted by episcopal judgment, which is the Church's severest penalty, can, if God so wills, result in a most salutary admonition, and be of benefit. Actually, we do not know what will happen in days to come; otherwise we should have to despair of someone before the end of this life, or contradict God, by denying that He may graciously turn and grant penitence, and, having accepted the sacrifice of a troubled spirit and a contrite heart,[164] absolve a man from the guilt of the 'condemnation' (however just it was), and Himself not condemn the one who was 'condemned.'

Nevertheless, lest dangerous contagions should spread any farther, it is a matter of pastoral necessity to separate the ailing sheep from the healthy; perhaps He, to whom nothing is impossible, will heal the ailing by virtue of the very separation. Not knowing who does, and who does not, belong to the number of the predestined, we ought to be so stirred by the spirit of charity as to will that all men be saved. We do this, in effect, when, as we come across various people, and the opportunity presents itself, we strive to bring them to this, that, justified by faith, they should have peace with God.[165] It was this peace which the Apostle preached when he said: 'On behalf, therefore, of Christ we are acting as ambassadors, God, as it were, appealing through us. We exhort you, for Christ's sake, be reconciled to God.'[166] What is reconciliation to God but peace with Him? Of this peace our Lord Himself

---
164 Ps. 50.19.
165 Rom. 5.1.
166 2 Cor. 5.20.

spoke to His disciples: 'Whatever house you enter, first say, "Peace to this house!" And if a son of peace be there, your peace will rest on him; but, if not, it will return to you.'[167] When they of whom it was foretold: 'How beautiful upon the mountains are the feet of him that bringeth good tidings, and that preacheth peace,'[168] announce this gospel of peace, then each one begins to be a son of peace when he obeys and believes this gospel, and, justified by faith, begins to have peace with God.

However, according to the predestination of God he already was a son of peace. For it is not said: He upon whom your peace shall have rested, he will become a son of peace; but: 'If a son of peace be there, your peace will rest on him.' Already, therefore, before this peace was announced to him, a son of peace was there; and he was known and foreseen to be such, not by the Evangelist but by God. It is our part, however, since we do not know who is a son of peace, to leave no one out, to set no one aside, but to will that all those be saved, to whom we preach this peace. Nor are we to fear lest we lose our peace, if he to whom we preach it is not a son of peace, and we are ignorant of the fact. Our peace will return to us; that is, our preaching will profit us, not him; but if the peace we preach rests upon him, it will profit both us and him.

(47) God, therefore, commands us, in our ignorance of those who are to be saved, to will that all those to whom we preach this peace should be saved; and He pours out this charity in our hearts by the Holy Spirit who is given to us.[169] Consequently, the text, 'God wills all men to be saved,'[170] can

---
167 Luke 10.5-6.
168 Isa. 52.7.
169 Rom. 5.5.
170 1 Tim. 2.4.

be understood in this way, that He makes us will [their salvation]; as in the text: 'God has sent the Spirit of his Son into our hearts, crying, "Abba, Father, " '[171] the meaning is: 'making us cry.' As a matter of fact, in another place it is said of the same Spirit: 'We have received our adoption as sons, by virtue of which we cry, "Abba, Father." '[172] It is we who cry, but He is said to cry who makes us cry. If, therefore, Scripture says that the Spirit cries when He makes us cry, God is likewise rightly said to will, when He makes us will.

Since, then, in our admonitions we are to have no other purpose than that of keeping men at peace with God, or bringing back to this peace those who have strayed, let us without despairing go on doing what we do. If he whom we admonish is a son of peace, our peace will rest on him; if not, it will return to us.

(48) Granted that the sure foundation of God stands firm, even while the faith of some is undermined (for the Lord knows who are his),[173] let us not for that reason be backward or remiss in admonishing those who ought to be admonished. For it was not said in vain that 'evil companionships corrupt good morals,'[174] nor that 'through thy "knowledge" the weak one will perish, the brother for whom Christ died.'[175] Let us not argue against these precepts, and the salutary fear they inspire, saying: 'Let evil companionships corrupt good morals, and let the weak one perish—what is that to us? The sure

---

171 Gal. 4.6.
172 Rom. 8.15.
173 2 Tim. 2.19.
174 1 Cor. 15.33.
175 1 Cor. 8.11. The universality of God's saving will is most strikingly seen, as a fact, in the universality of Christ's redeeming death; on this latter doctrine St. Augustine is insistent.

foundation of God stands firm, and "no one perishes but he who is a son of perdition."[176]

Chapter 16

This is idle talk. And we may by no means believe ourselves secure in the midst of such negligence. It is indeed true that no one perishes but he who is a son of perdition; but God has said through the Prophet Ezechiel: 'The same wicked man shall die in his iniquity, but I will require his blood at thy hand.'[177]

(49) Wherefore, so far as we are concerned, since we cannot distinguish the predestined from those who are not predestined, and for this reason must will that all should be saved, we must administer to all the strong medicine of admonition, lest any should perish, or cause the ruin of others. On His part, God will make our admonitions useful to those whom He has foreknown and predestined to become conformed to the image of His Son.[178] And if at times we do not give an admonition out of fear lest someone thereby perish, shall we not also give admonitions out of fear lest someone thereby perish all the more? Surely, we have not a greater heart of charity than the blessed Apostle, who said: 'Reprove the irregular, comfort the fainthearted, support the weak, be patient towards all men; see that no one renders evil for evil to any man.'[179] The meaning is that evil is actually rendered for evil when one who ought to be admonished is not admonished, but [his fault] is passed over by an evil piece of dissembling. The Apostle also says: 'When they sin, rebuke them in the

---
176 Cf. John 17.12.
177 Ezech. 3.18.
178 Rom. 8.29.
179 1 Thess. 5.14-15.

presence of all, that the rest also may have fear.'[180] He is speaking, of course, of public faults, and is not contradicting the word of the Lord, who said: 'But if thy brother sin against thee, go and show him his fault, between thee and him alone.'[181] At that, the Lord Himself brought severity in admonition to such a point that He could say: 'If he refuse to hear even the Church, let him be to thee as the heathen and the publican.'[182] Yet who has a greater love for the weak than He, who was Himself made weak for the sake of all, and for the sake of all was in His weakness crucified?

The conclusion is that grace does not forbid admonitions, nor do admonitions deny grace. Consequently, [the works of] justice are to be made a matter of precept, at the same time that the grace of God is implored, in faithful prayer, in order that by it the precept may be fulfilled.[183] And both precept and prayer are so to be employed that just admonitions are not left out of account. Finally, all these things are to be done with charity; for charity never causes sin, and covers a multitude of sins.[184]

---

180 1 Tim. 5.20.
181 Matt. 18.15.
182 Matt. 18.17.
183 St. Augustine lays great stress on prayer for grace; the most famous text is: 'Da quod jubes, et jube quod vis' (*Confess.* 10.29.40; cf. *ibid.* 37.60.).
184 1 Peter 4.8.

THE CHRISTIAN COMBAT

(De agone Christiano)

Translated

by

ROBERT P. RUSSELL, O.S.A. Ph.D.
Villanova College

NIHIL OBSTAT:

    THOMAS F. ROLAND, O.S.A.
        CENSOR DEPUTATUS

    VERY REV. MORTIMER A. SULLIVAN, O.S.A.
        PRIOR PROVINCIALIS

March 12, 1946

INTRODUCTION

THE SHORT work entitled *The Christian Combat* was written at Hippo during the first years of St. Augustine's episcopate. In the *Retractations,* a critical, but incomplete, review of his writings, Augustine assigns this book to the third place among the works composed after he had become bishop. The earliest composition of this period, *Various Question to Simplicianus,* is a series of queries addressed by Bishop Simplicianus of Milan to Augustine, together with the latter's replies. Since Simplicianus is referred to in the *Retractations* as Ambrose's successor in the See of Milan,[1] it is evident that the subsequent work, *The Christian Combat*, must have been composed some time after April 4, 397, the date of St. Ambrose's death.

The opinion which assigns the composition of this work to the year 396 is based largely upon a reference to the Donatist sect in Chapter 29. There Augustine points ironically to the internal schisms within the sect itself, yet he fails to make any mention of the two Donatist bishops, Pretextatus and Felicianus, who had been restored to full communion even after their formal condemnation by the Donatist council of Bagua.

Since this event, which took place about the beginning of 397, would have given added force to Augustine's remarks, it is argued that, had the incident already occurred, he

---
1 Cf. 2.1.

would have made good use of it, hence, the conclusion that Augustine may have written the work, *The Christian Combat,* during the preceding year. Obviously, however, any such argument *ex silentio* is seriously weakened by the more positive and formal evidence furnished by the *Retractations* in favor of the year 397.

The designation of the Christian life as a 'combat' is familiar in early Christian literature, inspired in large part by the language of St. Paul's Second Epistle to Timothy.[2] Augustine found it necessary to add the term 'Christian,' in order to distinguish the true soldiers of Christ from the self-styled 'agonistici'[3] of the Donatist sect. Referred to as Circumcellions by the Catholics, these fanatics indulged in the cruellest excesses to propagate their schism.

Augustine's purpose in composing the present work is summed up in these few words from the *Retractations*: 'The book on the Christian combat, containing a rule of faith and precepts for right living, was written in a plain style for the brethren who were not proficient in the Latin language.'[4]

Among the 'brethren' unskilled in the Latin tongue were to be found not only many of the Roman population, but also, and more especially, those inhabitants of North Africa who, while acquainted with the official language of Rome, still retained their ancient Punic tongue.[5] Augustine himself testifies to the actual survival of this language in his day and occasionally makes use of its expressions and proverbs in the instruction of his flock.

---

2 Cf. 4.7.
3 Cf. St. Augustine, *Enarrationes in Psalmos* 132.6.
4 Cf. 2.3.
5 Cf. "Sehr wahrscheinlich ist den ersten Lesern das Punische geläufiger gewesen als das Lateinische." (O. Bardenhewer, Geschichte der Altkirchlichen Literatur, Vol. 4.491 (Freiburg 1924).

The opuscule, *The Christian Combat,* cannot be fairly compared with the more profound and erudite works of the African Doctor. Its very simplicity, however, reveals the wonderful versatility of Augustine's genius, which can soar the lofty heights of speculation and yet impart its richness to the unlearned with equal ease and assurance. Further, the concise presentation of basic doctrines of faith and the complementary treatment of opposed heresies give the work a literary and historical value which has not escaped the attention of modern scholarship.[6]

The present translation has been made from the critical text of J. Zycha, in the *Corpus Scriptorum Ecclesiasticorum Latinorum* 41 (Vienna 1900). So far as St. Augustine's text permitted, the rendering of Biblical quotations has been taken, for the Old Testament, from the Challoner revision of the Douay Bible, for the New, from the version published in this country in 1941 under the patronage of the Episcopal Committee of the Confraternity of Christian Doctrine.

---

6 Cf. A. D'Alès, "De agone Christiano," ' *Gregorianum* 11 (1930) 131-45.

SELECT BIBLIOGRAPHY

Texts:

    J. P. Migne, *Patrologia Latina* 40. 289-309 (Paris 1841).

    J. Zycha, *Corpus Scriptorum Ecclesiasticorum Latinorum* 41 (*Vienna* 1900).

Secondary Works:

    O. Bardenhewer, *Geschichte der Altkirchlichen Literatur* Vol. 4 (Freiburg 1924).
    L. Billiot, *De Verbo Incarnato* (Rome 1927).
    A. D'Alès, *De agone Christiano, Gregorianum* 11 (Rome 1930).

CONTENTS

Chapter	Page
1 The crown promised only to those who with Christ's aid defeat the Devil	315
2 How the Devil is defeated—Invisible powers are defeated when we conquer our internal desires	316
3 How the demons are in the heavens and are lords of darkness	317
4 The Manichaean error concerning the rebellion of the tribe of darkness against God	318
5 The meaning of 'spiritual forces of evil in the heavens'	320
6 Bodily discipline necessary for victory over the world and the Devil	321
7 Subjection of the body through submission to God, whom every man, willy nilly, serves	322
8 All things governed by divine Providence	324
9 Exhortation to taste the sweetness of the Lord	325
10 The Son of God made man on our account—Free will	326
11 The suitability of man's freedom having been won through the Incarnation	327
12 The Christian faith everywhere powerful and victorious	330
13 Right faith and good action—Only a mind free of vice is capable of truth—The doctrine of the Trinity	331
14 No hearing should be given to those who deny the Three Persons	332
15 Nor to those who say there are three Gods	333
16 Nor to those who deny the equality and eternity of the Persons	333

Chapter	Page
17 Nor to those who deny the divinity of Christ	334
18 Nor to those who deny to Christ a true human body	335
19 Nor to those who deny to Him a human mind	336
20 Nor to those who do not distinguish between the wisdom of the God-Man and that of men called wise	336
21 Nor to those who affirm that the Word assumed only a human body	338
22 Nor to those who deny that Christ's body was formed from a woman and liken it to the dove-body in which the Holy Spirit is represented	338
23 Nor to those who affirm that the Son of God was a creature, since He suffered	340
24 Nor to those who deny that the resurrected body of Christ was of the same sort as that which was buried	341
25 Nor to those who deny that the body of Christ ascended into heaven	342
26 Nor to those who deny that Christ sits at the right hand of the Father	342
27 Nor to those who deny the future judgment	343
28 Nor to those who affirm that the Spirit promised in the Gospel came in Paul or Montanus or some other man	345
29 Nor to the Donatists who deny that the Church is spread throughout the whole earth	346
30 Nor to the Luciferians who do not practice rebaptism, yet cut themselves off from the Church	348
31 Nor to the Cathari who deny the power of the Church to forgive all sins and forbid widows to remarry	350
32 Nor to those who deny the resurrection of the body	351
33 As children we must be nourished upon the simplicity of Faith—The virtue of charity—Only a clean heart can comprehend truth	352

THE CHRISTIAN COMBAT

Chapter 1

THE CROWN of victory is promised only to those who engage in the struggle. Moreover, in the divine Scriptures we repeatedly read that we are to receive a crown if we emerge victorious. To obviate a lengthy enumeration of these passages, we mention St. Paul's unmistakable testimony:[1] 'I have completed the work, I have finished the course, I have kept the faith; now there remains for me a crown of justice.

We ought to know, then, who that very adversary is, at whose defeat we are going to receive a crown. It is he whom our Lord first overcame, so that, by abiding in Him, we, too, might be victorious. In fact, the power and wisdom of God, and the Word of God—God's only Son, through whom all things have been made—remains alone unchangeable, superior to every creature. And, since even sinless creatures are subject to Him, how much more so are sinful creatures? Seeing, therefore, that all the good angels are subject to Him, how much more so are all the wicked angels, whose chief is the Devil? But, since the Devil had deceived our nature, God's only-begotten Son deigned to take upon Himself our human nature, so that the Devil might thereby be vanquished and that, having always been subject to Him, he might be made subject to us also.

---

1 2 Tim. 4.7,8.

He is referring to the Devil where He says:[2] 'The prince of this world has been cast out.' Not that he has been cast out of the world, as certain heretics suppose, but that he has been cast out of the souls of men who holds fast to the word of God and are not lovers of the world, of which he is the prince. The Devil rules over lovers of temporal goods belonging to this visible world, not because he is lord of this world, but because he is ruler of those covetous desires by which we long for all that passes away. Consequently, those who neglect God, who is eternal, and love what is fleeting and changing, are made subject to Him. 'For covetousness is the root of all evil, and some in their eagerness to get rich have strayed from the faith and have involved themselves in many troubles.'[3]

By this covetousness the Devil rules within man and takes possession of his heart. Such are all the lovers of this world. But the Devil is cast out when we renounce this world with all our heart. The Devil, who is prince of this world, is thus renounced when we renounce his corruption, his pomp, and his angels. Therefore, when the Lord Himself was already invested with His victorious human nature, He said:[4] 'Know that I have overcome the world.'

Chapter 2

(2) Many people, however, ask this question: 'How can we overcome the Devil, since we do not see him?' The answer is that we have a Master who has deigned to show us how invisible foes are conquered, for the Apostle said of Him:[1] 'Freeing Himself of His body, He made an example of the

---
2 John 12.31.
3 1 Tim. 6.10.
4 John 16.33.

---
1 Col. 2.15.

principalities and powers, confidently triumphing over them within Himself.' Consequently, when invisible and sinful desires are overcome, we then overcome the unseen power of our enemy. Hence, by overcoming within ourselves the inordinate love for things temporal, we are necessarily, within ourselves, overcoming him also who rules within man by these sinful desires. For, at the time when it was said to the Devil: 'Thou shalt eat earth,' it was said to the sinner: 'Thou art earth, and into earth shalt thou go.'[2]

What is here implied is that the sinner has been handed over as food for the Devil. And so, if we would not be eaten by the Serpent, we should not become earth. Just as the food our body assimilates becomes a part of us, so by a bad life of wickedness, pride, and ungodliness do we become ourselves one with the Devil. That is to say, we become like the Devil and, just as our body is subject to us, so we are made subject to him. This is the meaning of the expression 'to be eaten by the serpent.' Hence, all who fear the fire prepared for the Devil and his angels should take means to overcome the Devil within themselves. For we win an interior victory over the adversaries who assail us from without by conquering the evil desires by which those adversaries hold sway over us. And those whom they find like themselves they drag along with them unto punishment.

Chapter 3

(3) In this connection the Apostle also declares that he carries on an internal struggle against powers from without. For, he says:[1] 'Our wrestling is not against flesh and blood but

---
[2] Gen. 3.14,19.

[1] Eph. 6.12.

against the princes and powers of this world, rulers of this darkness, against the spiritual forces of wickedness in the heavens.' This air of ours, in which winds, clouds, storms, and hurricanes occur, is also called the 'heavens,' as the Scripture testifies in many places: 'And the Lord thundered from the heavens';[2] again: 'the birds of the heavens';[3] and again: 'the creatures that fly in the heavens';[4] for it is apparent that birds fly through the air. And it is also customary for us to refer to the 'air' as the 'heavens.' When we inquire if the weather be clear or cloudy, we sometimes ask: 'What's the air like?'; at other times: 'What are the heavens like?' I have made mention of this fact, lest anyone imagine that the evil spirits have their abode where God has assigned the sun, the moon, and the stars.

The reason why the Apostle calls these evil demons spiritual powers is that in the Scriptures the bad angels are also called spirits. But he styles them 'rulers of this darkness,' because he designates as 'darkness' the sinful men over whom these spirits rule. Therefore, the Apostle testifies in another place:[5] 'For you were once darkness, but now you are light in the Lord.' For, from being sinners, they had been made just. Let us not imagine, then, that the Devil dwells with his angels in the uppermost heavens, from which we believe him to have fallen.

Chapter 4

(4) The Manichaeans have erred in this fashion, alleging that before the creation of the world there existed a tribe of darkness which rebelled against God, These unhappy people

---

2 Ps. 17.14.
3 Ps. 8.9.
4 Matt. 6.26.
5 Eph. 5.8.

fancy that in this conflict Almighty God could only help Himself by dispatching a portion of His substance against that tribe. The chiefs of this tribe, so they relate, devoured the portion belonging to God and were so affected by this commingling that it was possible to form the world from them. They maintain that God thus issued victorious by subjecting His members to considerable distress, anguish and misfortune. They say that these members were commingled with the murky entrails of those chiefs, in order to restrain and check their fury. They do not see that their sect is sacrilegious even to the point of believing that Almighty God waged war with the darkness, not by a creature of His making, but by His own nature—a detestable thing to believe. And not only that, but they further add that the vanquished were rendered more perfect for having their fury restrained, while God's nature, the victorious side, emerged in a most pitiful state. They assert that, as a result of this commingling, the divine nature was deprived of understanding and happiness, being involved in serious error and misfortunes.

If these heretics were to say that this nature will eventually be wholly purified, they would still be uttering a grave blasphemy against Almighty God, believing as they do that a portion of His nature has been tossed about for so long a time in error and punishment, though innocent of any sin. Now, these wretched people are bold enough to affirm that the divine portion cannot be wholly purified, and that the uncleanable part serves as a bond by which the grave of wickedness can be bound and sealed. Consequently, the ill-fated part of God remains forever in that place, and, though sinless, it is forever fastened to the prison of darkness. The Manichaeans say these things to ensnare simple souls. But who is so simple as not to see that the doctrines they profess are sacrilegious, namely: that Almighty God was compelled of necessity to yield a good and sinless portion of His substance to be overwhelmed by such great torments and defiled by such great foulness; that He could not liberate all His substance; that He would consign what He could not liberate to endless servitude.

What man is there who will not abominate these doctrines? Who can fail to see that they are blasphemous and ought not even be mentioned? But when these heretics are laying snares for men, they do not mention these points at first. If they did, they would be laughed to scorn and everyone would run away from them. Instead, they select chapters of Scripture which simple people do not grasp. By means of these they ensnare uninstructed souls, raising the question: 'Where does evil come from?' This is exactly what they do in that chapter where the Apostle has written:[1] 'Rulers of this darkness and the spiritual forces of wickedness in the heavens.' These deceivers seek out a man unskilled in the sacred Scriptures and ask him: 'From whence are the rulers of darkness?' Consequently, when he is unable to give an answer, he is won over by them through curiosity, since every untaught soul is curious. But, one who has learned the Catholic faith well, and is fortified by a good life and solid piety, will still know how to answer them, even though he is unacquainted with their heresy. Nor can he be taken in who already knows what pertains to the Christian faith, which, being spread over the world, is called Catholic, and, under the Lord's guidance, is made secure against all the ungodly and sinners, secure even against her own careless children.

Chapter 5

(5) Accordingly, since the Apostle Paul has indicated that our struggle is against the rulers of darkness and the spiritual

forces of wickedness in the heavens, as we were saying, we must believe that our strife is against the Devil and his angels, who rejoice over our afflictions. And we have shown that even the air surrounding the earth is called 'heaven.' For, in another place the Apostle himself refers to the Devil as the 'prince of the power of the air above us.'[1] However, that passage where the Apostle mentions 'the spiritual forces of wickedness in the heavens' is also susceptible of another meaning, namely, that he was not speaking of wicked angels dwelling in the heavens, but of us, concerning whom he says in another place: 'Our citizenship is in the heavens.'[2] Having our abode, then, among heavenly things, that is, walking in the spiritual commandments of God, we should war against the spiritual forces of wickedness seeking to draw us away from our abode. This matter of how we can war victoriously against unseen enemies must be investigated further, therefore, so that the unwise may not fancy that we are striving against the air.

Chapter 6

(6) Accordingly, the Apostle says himself by way of instruction:[1] 'I so fight as not beating the air; but I chastise my body and bring it into subjection, lest perhaps after preaching to others, I myself should be found rejected.' Similarly:[2] 'Be imitators of me as I am of Christ.' From this we are to understand that the Apostle himself had won an interior victory over the powers of this world, such as he had spoken of concerning the Lord, whom he professes to imitate. Therefore, we also should imitate him, as he exhorts us, and, if we would overcome the world, we should chastise our body and bring it

---
1 Eph. 2.2.
2 Phil. 3.20.

---
1 1 Cor. 9.26,27.
2 1 Cor. 11.1.

into subjection. For it is by sinful pleasures, by vanity, and baneful curiosity that the world can obtain the mastery over us. That is to say, these things of the world, by their deadly delight, enslave the lovers of things transitory, and compel them to serve the Devil and his angels. But if we have renounced all these things, we should bring our body into subjection.

Chapter 7

(7) Lest anyone pose the very question of how we are to bring our body into subjection, I reply that it is easy to understand and to do, provided we are already living in subjection to God by a good will and unfeigned charity; for every creature, willingly or unwillingly, has been made subject to its one God and Lord. This is a reminder to serve our Lord God with an undivided will. The just man serves Him in a spirit of freedom, but the unjust man serves him like a shackled slave. Yet, all are subject to divine Providence. Some conform with filial obedience and cooperate with Providence in the performance of good, while the rest are cast into chains, like slaves, being dealt with according to their merits. In this manner, Almighty God, Lord of all the universe, who, as it is written, 'hath made all things very good,'[1] has so ordered them that He can accomplish good from both the good and evil. What is done according to justice, is done well. And it is according to justice that the good are happy, and it is according to justice that the wicked suffer punishment. Therefore, God deals aright with both the good and the wicked, for He does all things according to justice. Now, they are good who serve God with an undivided will, but the wicked serve Him out of necessity: no one escapes the laws of the Almighty. To observe

---
1 Gen. 1.31.

what the law commands is one thing; to suffer the penalties it inflicts is something different. Wherefore, the good act according to law, and the wicked suffer according to law.

(8) Nor should we be unsettled by the fact that during this life the just endure many grave and bitter hardships by reason of the body they carry about. No harm can come to those who can already voice the sentiments expressed by that spiritual man, when he exclaimed in rapture:[2] 'We exult in tribulations, knowing that tribulation works out endurance, and endurance tried virtue, and tried virtue hope. And hope does not disappoint, because the charity of God is poured forth in our hearts by the Holy Spirit who has been given to us.' If in this life, where so much affliction is found, the good and just can not only endure patiently when suffering such trials, but can even glory in the love of God, what are we to think of the life promised us, wherein we shall experience no bodily discomfort? For, the bodies of the just will rise again for a different reason than the bodies of the wicked, as it is written:[3] 'We shall all rise again, but we shall not all be changed.' And lest anyone imagine that this change is promised not for the just, but rather for the wicked, thinking it a punishment, the Apostle goes on to say:[4] 'And the dead shall rise incorruptible and we shall be changed.' Accordingly, all those who are evil have been subjected to this ordinance; each one is hurtful to himself, and all are obnoxious to one another. For that after which they reach out can only be loved to their destruction and can be easily taken away from them. And this they take from one another when they persecute one another. And when temporal goods are

---

2 Rom. 5.3-5.
3 1 Cor. 15.51.
4 1 Cor. 15.52.

taken away from them, they are sorely afflicted because of their love of them, while those who take them away are gleeful.

Such delight, however, is blindness and utter misery, for it ensnares the soul all the more and leads it on to worse afflictions. The fish is delighted, too, when, failing to notice the hook, it devours the bait. But, when tne fisherman begins to draw his line, first the fish's inner parts are dislocated; after that it is dragged to its destruction, away from all the pleasure that its joy in the bait had brought it.[5] So it is with all who imagine they are happy with temporal goods. They have swallowed the hook and wander aimlessly about with it. The time will come for them to experience how much anguish they have devoured in their greediness. The wicked can cause no harm to the good, for they do not deprive them of what they love. No one can take from them the object of their love and the source of their happiness. In fact, bodily suffering makes wicked souls miserable, but, borne with fortitude, it purifies souls that are good.

Thus it is that both the wicked man and the bad angel do service for divine Providence, but they are ignorant of the good which God effects through them. On this account, they receive wages not for services rendered, but in accordance with their demerits.

Chapter 8

(9) But these spiritual natures, endowed with intelligence and intent upon doing harm, have been subjected to order under God's law to safeguard others from unjust injury. Similarly, all things are governed according to their proper

---

5 St. Gregory of Nyssa had previously made use of this figure to illustrate how the Devil, lured by the humanity of Christ, had fallen victim to the power of His hidden divinity, which he had been unable to discern. Cf. *Oratio catechetica* 24 (PG 45 66).

what the law commands is one thing; to suffer the penalties it inflicts is something different. Wherefore, the good act according to law, and the wicked suffer according to law.

(8) Nor should we be unsettled by the fact that during this life the just endure many grave and bitter hardships by reason of the body they carry about. No harm can come to those who can already voice the sentiments expressed by that spiritual man, when he exclaimed in rapture:[2] 'We exult in tribulations, knowing that tribulation works out endurance, and endurance tried virtue, and tried virtue hope. And hope does not disappoint, because the charity of God is poured forth in our hearts by the Holy Spirit who has been given to us.' If in this life, where so much affliction is found, the good and just can not only endure patiently when suffering such trials, but can even glory in the love of God, what are we to think of the life promised us, wherein we shall experience no bodily discomfort? For, the bodies of the just will rise again for a different reason than the bodies of the wicked, as it is written:[3] 'We shall all rise again, but we shall not all be changed.' And lest anyone imagine that this change is promised not for the just, but rather for the wicked, thinking it a punishment, the Apostle goes on to say:[4] 'And the dead shall rise incorruptible and we shall be changed.' Accordingly, all those who are evil have been subjected to this ordinance; each one is hurtful to himself, and all are obnoxious to one another. For that after which they reach out can only be loved to their destruction and can be easily taken away from them. And this they take from one another when they persecute one another. And when temporal goods are

---

[2] Rom. 5.3-5.
[3] 1 Cor. 15.51.
[4] 1 Cor. 15.52.

taken away from them, they are sorely afflicted because of their love of them, while those who take them away are gleeful.

Such delight, however, is blindness and utter misery, for it ensnares the soul all the more and leads it on to worse afflictions. The fish is delighted, too, when, failing to notice the hook, it devours the bait. But, when tne fisherman begins to draw his line, first the fish's inner parts are dislocated; after that it is dragged to its destruction, away from all the pleasure that its joy in the bait had brought it.[5] So it is with all who imagine they are happy with temporal goods. They have swallowed the hook and wander aimlessly about with it. The time will come for them to experience how much anguish they have devoured in their greediness. The wicked can cause no harm to the good, for they do not deprive them of what they love. No one can take from them the object of their love and the source of their happiness. In fact, bodily suffering makes wicked souls miserable, but, borne with fortitude, it purifies souls that are good.

Thus it is that both the wicked man and the bad angel do service for divine Providence, but they are ignorant of the good which God effects through them. On this account, they receive wages not for services rendered, but in accordance with their demerits.

Chapter 8

(9) But these spiritual natures, endowed with intelligence and intent upon doing harm, have been subjected to order under God's law to safeguard others from unjust injury. Similarly, all things are governed according to their proper

---

5 St. Gregory of Nyssa had previously made use of this figure to illustrate how the Devil, lured by the humanity of Christ, had fallen victim to the power of His hidden divinity, which he had been unable to discern. Cf. *Oratio catechetica* 24 (PG 45 66).

nature and position, both living and non-living, being subject to the laws of divine Providence. Therefore, the Lord says:[1] 'Are not two sparrows sold for a farthing? And yet not one of them will fall to the ground without your Father's leave.' He said this for the purpose of showing that what men regard as lowly is governed by God's omnipotence. So also are the birds of the air fed by Him and the lilies of the field clothed by Him. It is the voice of Truth that speaks, declaring that even our hairs are numbered. God exercises a direct Providence over holy, rational natures (whether the most exalted and excellent of the angels, or men who serve Him wholeheartedly), but rules everything else by means of these. Accordingly, it was also possible for the Apostle to say in all truth:[2] 'For God has no care for oxen.'

God teaches men in the sacred Scriptures how to deal with their fellow-man, and how they are to serve God Himself. But men themselves know how to handle their sheep; that is, they know how to provide for their well-being from experience, practical skill, and native intelligence, all of which they have received of course from the Creator's bountiful resources. Whoever, therefore, is able to understand how God the Creator rules over all creation by means of holy spirits, His heavenly and earthly ministers—for these holy spirits have also been made by Him and hold the first place in His creation —whoever, I say, is able to understand this, let him understand and enter into the joy of his Lord.

Chapter 9

(10) However, if this objective is unattainable so long as we are in the body and exiled from the Lord, let us at

---
[1] Matt. 10.29.
[2] 1 Cor. 9.9; the Vulgate text is framed as a question.

least taste how sweet the Lord is, for He has given us the Spirit as a pledge, in whom we may experience His sweetness. Let us also thirst for the fountain of life itself, wherein we shall be inebriated and refreshed by a sober excess, like the tree which was planted near the running waters, bringing forth fruit in due season, and whose leaves do not fall to the ground.[1] For, the Holy Spirit says:[2] 'But the children of men shall put their trust under the covert of thy wings. They shall be inebriated with the plenty of thy house; and thou shalt make them drink of the torrent of thy pleasure. For with thee is the fountain of life.' This kind of inebriation does not overthrow reason, but transports it to the regions above, making it forgetful of all things earthly—but only when we are able to say with all our heart: 'As the heart panteth after the fountains of water, so my soul panteth after thee, O God.'[3]

Chapter 10

(11) If, perchance, we are as yet unfit to taste how sweet the Lord is, because of infirmities contracted by the soul's love of the world, then let us believe the testimony of God. For He has willed that the sacred Scriptures should testify concerning His Son who, in the words of the Apostle,[1] 'was born to Him according to the flesh of the offspring of David.' 'All things were made through him,' as it is written in the Gospel, 'and without him was made nothing that has been made.'[2]

He has taken compassion on our weakness—a weakness that comes, not from His work, but from the just merits of our free

---

1 Ps. 1.3.
2 Ps. 35.8-10.
3 Ps. 41.2.

---

1 Rom. 1.3.
2 John 1.3.

will. For God created man incorruptible³ and gave him free choice of the will. Man would not be perfect if he were to obey God's commandments out of necessity, and not by his free will. This is a very simple matter, as far as I can see. But they who have abandoned the Catholic faith do not want to see; yet they wish to be called Christians. Now, if they are one with us in acknowledging that our nature is healed only by right living, let them also acknowledge that it is weakened only by sinfulness.

We must not, therefore, believe that our soul is the same substance as God. If it were, it could not change for the worse, either by some kind of necessity or by its own choice. God is thought to be absolutely unchangeable—but by those who think of the Lord in goodness, in a spirit of Christian humility and seek Him in simplicity of heart,⁴ not by those who because of strife, jealousy, and love of vain glory, like to prate about things of which they are ignorant. Therefore, the Son of God has deigned to assume our weakness. 'And the Word was made flesh and dwelt among us.'⁵ His eternity has not undergone change, but He has revealed to the changing vision of men the changeable nature which He has assumed in the unchangeableness of His majesty.

Chapter 11

(12) Now, they are wanting in wisdom who pose this question: 'Why could not God in His wisdom have found a way to liberate men other than by assuming man's nature,¹ being born of a woman and suffering all those injuries at the

---
3 Cf. Wisd. 2.23.
4 Cf. Wisd. 1.1.
5 John 1.14.

1 In this and similar passages the term *homo* has been advisedly rendered

hands of sinners?' To these we reply: Most assuredly, God could have devised another plan;[2] but, if He had acted otherwise, He would incur your stupid displeasure just the same. For, if He had not come into bodily view of sinners, they would not be able to behold with their unclean minds His eternal Light, which is seen by the eyes of the soul.

But, now that He has deigned to remind us by His visible presence to prepare for things unseen, He is a source of displeasure to the greedy, because He did not have a body made of gold; a source of displeasure to the impure, because He was born of a woman (for the unchaste detest the fact that women conceive and beget children); a source of displeasure to the proud, because He bore insults with perfect patience; a source of displeasure to lovers of ease, because He suffered torments; a source of displeasure to the faint-hearted, because He suffered death. To remove the impression that they are defending their own vices, they say that these points displease them, not as found in man, but as found in the Son of God. They do not understand the meaning of God's eternity that has assumed a human nature; they do not have a grasp of human nature itself, which by a change within itself was restored to original soundness. We may thus learn from the Lord's teaching that the infirmities we have contracted by sinning can be healed by right living.

We have been shown to what a weakened state man has

---

by *human nature,* in order to convey more accurately Augustine's true conception of the subsistence of Christ's human nature in the Divine Personality of the Word.

2 In allowing that God in His Omnipotence could have effected the salvation of man otherwise than according to the present Dispensation, Augustine is in complete agreement with other earlier writers, as well as with the almost unanimous teaching of later theologians, who defend the merely hypothetical necessity of the Incarnation. Cf. St. Thomas, *Summa Theologica,* IIIa q.1 a.2. L. Billiot, *De Verbo Incarnato* (7th ed. Rome 1927) 21-30.

come by his own fault and how he is liberated from that state by divine assistance. The Son of God then assumed a human nature and bore patiently therein all human misery. The healing power of this medicine for men is beyond all comprehension. For, what pride can be cured, if it is not cured by the humility of the Son of God? What avarice can be cured, if it is not cured by the poverty of the Son of God? What anger can be cured, if it is not cured by the patience of the Son of God? What ungodliness can be cured, if it is not cured by the charity of the Son of God? Finally, what want of courage can be cured, if it is not cured by the resurrection of the body?

Let the human race take hope and rediscover its own nature. Let it see what an important place it occupies among the works of God. Men! do not despise yourselves—the Son of God assumed manhood. Women! do not despise yourselves —the Son of God was born of a woman. Yet, do not love things carnal, for in the sight of the Son of God we are neither male nor female. Do not love things temporal; for, if it were right to love them, the human nature assumed by the Son of God would have loved them. Do not be afraid of insults and crosses and death, for, if these were harmful to man, the human nature assumed by the Son of God would not have suffered them.

This entire exhortation, which is now everywhere preached, everywhere reverently received, restoring health to docile souls, would have no place in human affairs, had not those events occurred which are a source of displeasure to the unwise. For example, what can bring a perverse pride to the practice of virtue, if it is ashamed to imitate Him of whom it was said before His birth:[3] 'He shall be called the Son of

---
3 Luke 1.33.

the Most High.' And it is an undeniable fact that He is now called the Son of the Most High throughout all nations. If we have a high opinion of ourselves, let us deign to imitate Him who is called the Son of the Most High. If we have a lowly opinion of ourselves, let us presume to imitate the fishermen and publicans who imitated Him.

O Medicine, making provision for all: deflating what is distended; renewing what is wasting away; cutting away what is superfluous; preserving what is necessary; restoring what has been lost; curing what is corrupted! Who will now raise himself up against the Son of God? Who can despair of his own salvation, for whom the Son of God has willed to become so lowly? Who can believe that happiness is to be found in those things which the Son of God has taught us to despise? What tribulation can overcome him who believes that in the Son of God human nature was preserved intact amid violent persecution? Who can imagine himself shut out from the kingdom of heaven when he knows that publicans and prostitutes have imitated the Son of God? What wickedness can be found in him who makes that Man's deeds and words the object of his contemplation, love, and striving, in whom the Son of God revealed Himself to us as a pattern of life?

Chapter 12

(13) Hence, both men and women and people of every age and worldly rank have already been aroused to the hope of life eternal. Some soar upwards in spirit to things divine, having no concern for temporal goods. Others fall short of the virtues belonging to those who so live, and approve what they do not presume to imitate. But, there are still a few grumblers who are troubled by an unwarranted jealousy. They include: those who, while appearing to be Catholics, seek their own

interests in the Church; heretics who look for glory in the very name of Christ; Jews eager to justify their impious crime; pagans fearful of losing their empty joy in ever curious satisfactions.

The Catholic Church, however, spread over the length and breath of the whole world, has turned back these assaults of former times and has become increasingly stronger—not by resistence, but by patient endurance. Nowadays it scoffs at their clever questions with complete confidence; it is careful to dispose of them by skillful refutations. It is not troubled by the charge of harboring unworthy members, for it is on its guard to distinguish carefully between the harvest season, the threshing season, and the storage season. As for those who vilify her worthy members, it puts them on the right path, if they are going astray; if they are inspired by envy, it reckons them among the thorns and cockle.

Chapter 13

(14) Let us subject our soul to God, therefore, if we want to bring our body into subjection and win the victory over the Devil. It is faith that first makes souls subject to God. Next come the precepts for right living. When these are observed, our hope is made firm, charity is nurtured, and what before was only believed begins to be clearly understood. For, since knowledge and activity render a man happy, error in knowledge must be avoided, just as sin is to be shunned in our actions. Whoever fancies he can have an insight into virtue, while he is yet leading a wicked life, is mistaken. It is wicked to love this world and the things which come into being and pass away. It is wicked to esteem them highly, to covet and labor to acquire them, to rejoice when they are possessed

in abundance, to be fearful lest they be lost, to be made sad when, in fact, they are lost.

This manner of life cannot behold that pure, genuine, and unchangeable Truth; it cannot abide therein, remaining forever unchanged. Hence, before the soul can be purified, we must believe what we are not yet able to understand. For, it has been truly said by the Prophet:[1] 'Unless you believe, you shall not understand.'

(15) The Church's faith is taught in very few words. In it eternal truths are proposed which cannot yet be grasped by the carnal-minded; also deeds of past and future time, which God in His eternal Providence has accomplished and will accomplish for the salvation of men. Therefore, let us believe in the Father, in the Son, and in the Holy Spirit. These truths are everlasting and unchanging, namely, that there is one God, the eternal Trinity, having one nature—God, from whom and through whom and in whom are all things.[2]

Chapter 14[1]

(16) Let us not heed those who say there is only the Father, who has no Son and with whom there is no Holy Spirit; but that the same Father is sometimes called the Son, sometimes called the Holy Spirit. These heretics do not understand the First Principle from whom all things have their existence; or His image, through whom all things have been made; or His Sanctifier, in whom all things are made subject to order.

---

1 Isa. 7.9 (Sept.).
2 Rom. 11.36.

Chapter 15

(17) Let us not heed those who are highly offended and indignant because we do not say there are three Gods to be adored. These heretics fail to understand a nature that is on and the selfsame. Being deceived by sense images, by which they are accustomed to perceive three animals in bodily fashion, or any three bodies at all separated by space, they suppose that we are to conceive of the divine nature in the same manner. Because of their pride, they have gone far astray; and, since they are unwilling to believe, it is impossible for them to learn.

Chapter 16

(18) Let us not heed those who say that only the Father is the true and eternal God, while the Son was not begotten of Him, but was made by Him out of nothing; and that there was a time when the Son did not exist, yet, He occupies the highest place in all the creation. And the Holy Spirit, they say, is inferior to Him in majesty, having been made after the Son. And the substances of these three differ in nature, as gold, silver, and brass. Unaware of what they are saying, these heretics carry over into their disputations the deceitful sense-images of those objects which they are wont to perceive by bodily eyes. Now, it is really a great attainment for the

---

1 Beginning with the present and continuing through the next eighteen chapters, Augustine presents a summary of the main articles of faith by a refutation of opposed heretical doctrines. With few exceptions, the names of the heresiarchs and heresies are not given, in keeping, perhaps, with the avowed simplicity of the work. A more complete, but usually less detailed, catalogues of heresies is to be found in the *De haeresibus ad Quodvultdeum,* composed by Augustine about two years before his death. For a comparison of the two lists of heresies drawn up by Augustine, cf. A. D' Alès, *op. cit.* 141-142.

mind to discern a form of generation which does not take place from some point of time, but is eternal, or to behold Love Itself and Holiness, by which the Begetter and the Begotten are united with one another in an unspeakable Union. Yes, it is a great and difficult achievement for the mind to behold these truths, even though it has reached a state of peaceful tranquillity.

Consequently, those who are too intent upon earthly generation cannot possibly conceive of these matters. And to the darkness of their ignorance they further add smoke, which they are incessantly raising up by their daily wrangling and strife. Having spent their souls upon sense pleasures, they are like dampened pieces of wood in which the fire cannot give forth bright flames, but only smoke. And this indictment can in fact be justly made about all heretics.

Chapter 17

(19) Believing, therefore, in the unchangeable Trinity, let us also believe in the divine plan revealed in time for the salvation of the human race. And let us not heed those who say that Jesus Christ, the Son of God, is nothing more than a man, although He is so holy a man that He is deservedly called the Son of God. The discipline of the Catholic Church has cast out these heretics also, for, deceived by the desire for vain glory, they chose to engage in bitter controversy before understanding the true nature of the power and the wisdom of God, and the meaning of the words: 'in the beginning was the Word, through whom 'all things have been made'; and how 'the Word was made flesh and dwelt among us.'[1]

---
[1] John 1.1,3,14.

Chapter 18

(20) Let us not heed those who say that the Son of God did not assume a real human nature and was not born of a woman, but that He disclosed an unreal flesh and the feigned appearance of a human body to those who saw Him. For these heretics do not see how the nature of God can in any way escape contamination in the work of managing the whole of creation. And yet, these same heretics proclaim publicly that the visible sun spreads its rays over all kinds of bodily foulness and filth, and nevertheless preserves these rays everywhere pure and undefiled. If pure visible objects, therefore, can come into contact with those that are unclean, without being contaminated, why, for a greater reason, could not the invisible and changeless Truth deliver man from all his misery without injury to Himself? For, He has assumed a complete human nature, joining Himself to man's intellectual nature through the soul, and, through the soul, uniting Himself to the body.

Hence, these heretics are sorely perplexed and, being fearful lest the Truth be defiled by human flesh—a sheer impossibility—they allege that the Truth has been guilty of a lie. And, though He has given this command:[1] 'let your speech be, "yes, yes;" "no, no" '; and the Apostle has exclaimed:[2] 'There was not in Him now "Yes" and now "No," but only "Yes" was in Him,' these heretics contend that His whole body was an unreal flesh. If they do not deceive their hearers, they feel they are not imitating Christ.

---

1 Matt. 5.37.
2 2 Cor. 1.19.

Chapter 19

(21) Let us not heed those who truly acknowledge a Trinity in one and the same eternal Substance, but presume to assert that the human nature assumed by the Word for his temporal mission had no human intellect, but only an animal soul and a body. This is the same as saying: He was not a man but He possessed the human members of a body. Animals have both a soul and a body, but do not have reason, which belongs properly to the mind.

But, if we must abhor those who deny He had a human body—the lowliest part of man—I am amazed that these heretics are not ashamed to deny Him what is most excellent in man. It is pitiful for the soul to be overcome by its own body, since it has not been renewed in that Man, whose human body has itself already been elevated to the dignity of a heavenly condition. But far be it from us to give credence to these fanciful tales which a rash blindness of mind and proud talkativeness have fabricated.

Chapter 20

(22) Let us not heed those who say that this Human Nature, born of a virgin, was assumed by the Eternal Wisdom in the same way that this Wisdom makes men wise who are perfect in wisdom. These heretics do not see the peculiar mystery involved in the Human Nature of the Word, and they suppose that It excelled among the other saints only because It was born of a virgin. If they examine this point carefully, they may perhaps come to the belief that His Human Nature merited the virgin-birth, in preference to the other saints, because Its assumption by the Word had a character all its own, different from the other saints. Now, merely to become

wise by the influence of God's wisdom is one thing; to be the very Personification of God's Wisdom is something else.

For, though the Body of the Church is one in nature, anyone can discern what a great difference there is between the Head and the other members. If that Man is the Head of the Church, by whose assumption 'the Word was made flesh and dwelt among us,' the other members are all the saints by whom the Church is made perfect and entire. Now, the soul gives life to and quickens our whole body, but, in the region of the head, the soul perceives sensations of life, sight, sound, smell, taste, and touch, but in the other members, only the sensation of touch. And on this account, in carrying out their functions, all the members are subject to the head. But, the head occupies a higher position in order to take counsel, since, to a certain extent, it plays the role of the soul itself, which takes counsel for the body; for all the senses are to be found in the head.

Similarly, the Man Jesus Christ, the Mediator between God and men, is constituted the Head for the entire multitude of the saints, as for a single body. The wisdom of God, therefore, and His Word, through whom all things were made in the beginning, did not assume this Human Nature in the way in which It has taken unto itself the other saints, but in a manner far more excellent and exalted. Just as it was necessary that this Nature, in which Wisdom was to appear to men, should alone be assumed in this manner, so was it fitting for this Wisdom to manifest Itself outwardly.

Accordingly, the other men, whoever they are, or whoever they may have been or will be, are made wise in one way, but it is different with the one Mediator between God and men, the Man Jesus Christ. He not only enjoys the benefit of Wisdom Itself, by which all men are made wise, but also is the very personification of Wisdom. For it may be properly said of all other wise and religious souls that they possess within them the Word of God, by whom all things were made. It may never be rightly said of any one of them that 'the Word was made flesh and dwelt among us'; because, strictly speaking, this can only be said of our Lord Jesus Christ.

Chapter 21

(23) Let us not heed those who say that only the body of a man was assumed by the Word of God. These heretics so interpret the words 'And the Word was made flesh' as to deny that this Human Nature possessed a soul, or any part of man's nature, with the sole exception of flesh. They are greatly mistaken. Neither do they realize that mention is only made of 'flesh' in this expression, 'the Word was made flesh,' because only the flesh could be seen by men's eyes, for whose sake this assuming of human nature took place.

Now, if it is ridiculous and altogether unbecoming this human nature not to have a human spirit, as we considered above, how much more ridiculous and unbecoming is it for this nature to have neither a spirit, nor a soul, and to have that part which even in animals is of lesser worth and dignity, namely, the body. Let this impious belief, too, be excluded from our faith, and let us believe that a human nature, whole and entire, was assumed by the Word of God.

Chapter 22

(24) Let us not heed those who say that our Lord had a body like that of the dove which John the Baptist beheld coming down from heaven, as a symbol of the Holy Spirit, and resting upon Him. These heretics endeavor to persuade people that the Son of God was not born of a woman by this line of reasoning: If He had to be seen by bodily eyes, He could have

assumed a body, they say, as the Holy Spirit assumed one. That dove, they say, was not born from an egg, yet it could be seen by the eyes of men.

Our first answer to these heretics ought to be this: Where we read that the Holy Spirit appeared to John in the form of a dove, there we also read that Christ was born of a woman. We ought not believe one part of the Gospel and disbelieve another. For, how do you come to believe that the Holy Spirit appeared in the form of a dove, if not because you have read it in the Gospel? Accordingly, I, too, believe that Christ was born of a virgin because I have read it in the Gospel. Now, the reason why the Holy Spirit was not born of a dove, whereas Christ was born of a woman, is this: The Holy Spirit did not come to liberate doves, but to declare unto men innocence and spiritual love, which were outwardly symbolized in the form of a dove. The Lord Jesus Christ, having come to liberate human beings, including both men and women destined for salvation, was not ashamed of the male nature, for He took it upon Himself; or of the female, for He was born of a woman. Besides, there is the profound mystery that, as death had befallen us through a woman, Life should be born to us through a woman. By this defeat, the Devil would be tormented over the thought of both sexes, male and female, because he had taken delight in the defection of them both. The freeing of both sexes would not have been so severe a penalty for the Devil, unless we were also liberated by the agency of both sexes.

And we do not mean to imply that only the Lord Jesus Christ had a true body, but that the Holy Spirit took on an unreal appearance in the eyes of men. We believe that both those bodies were real. As it was impossible for the Son of God to deceive men, so was it unworthy of the Holy Spirit to deceive men. Now, it was not difficult for Almighty God, who formed the whole creation out of nothing, to fashion the real body of a dove without the agency of other doves, just as it was not difficult for Him to form a real body in Mary's womb without human semen. Every created body is subject to the command and will of God, whether it is a question of forming a man within a woman's womb, or a dove within the world itself. But foolish men, wretched as they are, imagine that not even Almighty God could accomplish what they themselves are incapable of doing, or have never seen done in their lifetime.

Chapter 23

(25) Let us not heed those who would constrain us to number the Son of God among creatures because He endured suffering. If he endured suffering, they say, He was subject to change. And if He is subject to change, He is a creature because God's substance is unchangeable. We are one with these heretics in affirming that God's substance is unchangeable and that a created nature is subject to change. But, being a creature is one thing; to assume a created nature is something different. Therefore, God's only-begotten Son, the Power and Wisdom and Word of God, through whom all things were made, assumed a human nature, seeing that He is in no way subject to change. And He has deigned to raise up our fallen nature and to impart a new life to its decrepit condition. Nor has He undergone a change for the worse in that nature because of His suffering; rather, He has changed that nature for the better because of His resurrection.

We must not on this account deny that the Word of the Father was born and suffered for us—He who is the only-begotten Son of God, through whom all things were made. For, we assert that the martyrs also suffered and died for the sake of the kingdom of heaven; yet their souls were not destroyed in this suffering and death. For, the Lord says:[1] 'And do not be afraid of those who kill the body but are unable to do anything to the soul.' Therefore, just as we affirm that the martyrs endured suffering and death in the bodies they carried about, without suffering destruction or death to their souls, so we declare that the Son of God underwent suffering and death in the human nature He bore, without undergoing any change or death in His Divinity.

Chapter 24

(26) Let us not heed those who say that the Lord's risen body was not like the one placed in the tomb. For, if it had not been the same, the Lord could not have said to His disciples after His resurrection:[1] 'Feel and see; for a spirit does not have flesh and bones, as you see I have.' It is sacrilegious to suppose that our Lord has been guilty of any falsehood, since He Himself is Truth. Nor should we be unsettled by the fact that He suddenly appeared to the disciples when, as it is written, the doors were closed. We must not on this account deny that that was a human body because we observe that it is contrary to the nature of such a body to walk upon the waters, and yet, not only did the Lord Himself before His passion walk upon the waters, but He also caused Peter to walk upon them. In this way, then, He was able to do whatever He wished with His body after His resurrection. For, if before His passion He could give it a brilliance like the brightness of the sun, why, too, after His passion could He not instantaneously

---
[1] Matt. 10.28.

---
[1] Luke 24.39.

make it as subtle as He pleased, so it could enter through closed doors?

Chapter 25

(27) Let us not heed those who say that our Lord did not ascend into heaven with His body, alleging in support the words of the Gospel:[1] 'And no one has ascended into heaven except him who has descended from heaven.' They contend that, as His body did not descend from heaven, it could not ascend into heaven. They lack a proper understanding, for the body (as such) did not ascend into heaven. It was the Lord who ascended; the body, however, did not ascend. But, the body was raised up to heaven, being raised up by Him who ascended.

If, by way of illustration, someone descends unclothed from a mountain and, after coming down, clothed himself, and again ascends the mountain being clothed, we are surely right in saying: No one ascended except him who descended. We are not thinking about the clothing he raised up with him; we assert that he who was clothed alone ascended.

Chapter 26

(28) Let us not heed those who deny that the Son sits at the right hand of the Father. Can the Father, they say, have a right and a left side, as bodies have? We do not believe this of the Father, either, for God is not bounded or circumscribed by bodily configuration. But, 'the right hand of the Father' is everlasting happiness, which is promised to the saints, just as His left hand appropriately refers to everlasting unhappiness, which is the lot of the wicked. Thus, the terms 'right'

---

[1] John 3.13.

and 'left' are understood, not of God Himself, but of creatures, as we have indicated. So the body of Christ, which is the Church, will likewise be on that right hand, that is to say, it will possess perfect happiness according to the Apostle's words:[1] 'He has raised us up together and seated us together in heaven.' For, while we are not yet there in body, our hope is already there. For this reason, too, the Lord Himself after His resurrection commanded the disciples whom He found fishing to cast their nets on the right side. When they had done so, they got a catch. And all the fish were large, that is to say, they symbolized the just who have been promised a place on His right side. It is likewise suggestive of the Lord's saying that at judgment He will set the lambs on His right hand, but the goats on His left.

Chapter 27

(29) Let us not heed those who deny there will be a day of judgment, citing in support the words of the Gospel, that he who believes in Christ is not judged, but he who does not believe in Him is already judged.[1] If the believer, they say, will not come to judgment, and the unbeliever is already judged, where are they whom He will judge on the day of judgment?

These heretics fail to grasp how the Scriptures employ past time for future, as in the case mentioned above, where the Apostle says of us: 'He has seated us together in heaven.' This has not yet taken place, but, since it will most certainly happen, it is spoken of as if it had already taken place. We

---
1 Eph. 2.6.

---
1 John 3.18.

find a similar instance where the Lord said to the disciples:[2] 'All things that I have heard from the Father I have made known to you.' And then, shortly after, He declared:[3] 'Many things I have to say to you, but you can not bear them now.' How, then, did He say: 'All things that I have heard from the Father I have made known to you,' except in this way, that what He was certainly going to accomplish through the Holy Spirit, He spoke of us as if He had already accomplished it? Therefore, whenever we hear that he who believes in Christ will not come to judgment, we are to understand that he will not come to damnation. The word 'judgment' is used in place of 'damnation,' as where the Apostle says:[4] 'let not him who does not eat judge him who eats,' that is, let him not think evil of him. And the Lord says:[5] 'Do not judge that you may not be judged.' He does not take from us the power to judge, since the Prophet also declares:[6] 'If you truly love justice, judge right things, ye sons of men.' And the Lord says Himself:[7] 'Judge not according to personal considerations, but give just judgment.' But, in that passage where He forbids judging, He admonishes us not to condemn a person whose purpose is hidden from us, or when we do not know how a person will turn out later on. Accordingly, when He said: 'He shall not come to judgment,' He meant that he will not come to damnation. And in saying: 'But He who does not believe is already judged,' He meant that such a person stands already condemned in the foreknowledge of God, who knows what is in store for non-believers.

---

2 John 15.15.
3 John 16.12.
4 Rom. 14.3.
5 Matt. 7.1.
6 Ps. 57.2.
7 John 7.24.

Chapter 28

(30) Let us not heed those who say that the Holy Spirit, promised to the disciples by the Lord in the Gospel, has come either in the person of the Apostle Paul, or in the persons of Montanus and Priscilla, according to the Cataphrygians; or, as the Manichaeans allege, in the person of a certain Manes or Manichaeus.[1] These heretics are too headstrong to grasp the plain meaning of the Scriptures, or else, having no concern about their salvation, they do not read them at all. For, in reading the Gospel, who can fail to understand what is written following the Lord's resurrection, where He says:[2] 'And I send forth upon you the promise of my Father. But wait here in the city, until you are clothed with power from on high.'

These heretics do not take cognizance of the fact that on the tenth day after the Lord had withdrawn from the sight of the Apostles, on the day of Pentecost, the Holy Spirit came in a very evident manner, according to the Acts of the Apostles; and that, while they were in the city, as He had told them beforehand, they were so filled by the Holy Spirit that they spoke in tongues. Now, the different nations that were there at the time understood the Apostles, each hearing his own language.[3] These heretics, on the other hand, deceive those who are unwilling to learn, and who neglect the Catholic faith, and that very faith of their own which is clearly contained in the Scriptures; and, what is more serious and lament-

---

[1] Augustine informs us that, when Manichaeanism was first introduced into Greece, its followers chose to call their founder Manichaeus rather than Manes, since the latter name bore a curious resemblance to the Greek word *mania*, signifying madness. Cf. *De haeresibus ad Quodvultdeum* 46.
[2] Luke 24.49.
[3] Cf. Acts 2.1-11.

able, while they live carelessly as Catholics, they lend an attentive ear to the heretics.

Chapter 29

(31) Let us not heed those who deny that the holy Church, which alone is Catholic, is spread throughout the world, and who imagine that it wields influence only in Africa, namely, in the Donatist sect. Consequently, they turn a deaf ear to the Prophet's words:[1] 'Thou art my Son, this day have I begotten thee. Ask of me, and I will give thee the Gentiles for thy inheritance, and the utmost parts of the earth for thy possession.'

And there are many other passages, in the books of both the Old and New Testaments, which have been written to make it perfectly evident that the Church has been spread over the world. When we confront them with this objection, they answer that all those prophecies were already fulfilled before the rise of the Donatist sect. Afterwards, so they say, the whole Church became extinct, and the remains of it have been preserved only within the Donatist sect. How haughty and blasphemous is this language of theirs! Their boast would not hold true even if afterwards they had really so lived as to keep peace even among themselves. It does not occur to their minds that the words: 'With what measure you measure, it shall be measured to you,' have already been fulfilled in Donatus himself. For, just as he tried to divide Christ, so is he himself being divided by daily schisms at the hands of his own followers.

And this saying of our Lord also applies here:[2] 'For he who strikes with the sword will die by the sword.' In this passage

---
1 Ps. 2.7,8.
2 Matt. 26.52.

the term 'sword,' used in an unfavorable sense, signifies the quarrelsome tongue by which that unhappy Donatus afflicted the Church at that time, but did not destroy it. The Lord did not say: 'He who *kills* by the sword will die by the sword'; but, He who will *make use* of the sword will die by the sword.'

Donatus, then, has afflicted the Church by the same quarrelsome tongue whereby he is now being cut to pieces himself, that he may be completely destroyed and die. Yet, the Apostle Peter used the sword, not out of pride, but out of love for the Lord, even though it was a human love. And so, when he was admonished, he put away the sword. But this Donatus did not do so, even after he had been defeated. In fact, when he pleaded his cause at Rome with the Bishop Cecilian before the bishops to whom he himself appealed, he was unable to prove any of the charges he had made. And so, he remained in schism to perish by his own sword.

Since his own followers do not hear the Prophets and Gospel where it is very plainly set down that Christ's Church is spread throughout all the nations, they give sufficient indication that they are slaves without freedom and that their right ear has been cut off. Thus they listen to the schismatics who seek not God's glory, but their own. It was because of a mistaken love for the Lord that Peter cut off the ear not of a free man, but of a servant. This circumstance is significant of the fact that those who are wounded by the sword of schism and are slaves to carnal desires have not yet been led to the freedom of the Holy Spirit, so that they no longer place their hope in man. It also signifies that they do not hear what is on the right, namely, the glory of God spread far and wide through the Catholic Church, but listen to the left, to the sinister error of human conceit.

Since the Lord says in the Gospel that the end of the world will come when the Gospel will have been preached throughout all the nations, how do these Donatists contend that all the other nations have defected from the faith and that it is only in the Donatist sect that the Church survives? It is apparent that, since this sect was cut off from unity, some nations have later embraced the faith, and some still exist that have not yet believed, to whom the Gospel does not cease to be preached daily. Who is not astounded to find a person who, while wishing to be called a Christian, is so enraged by wickedness against Christ's glory as to voice this hardihood, that all the people of the nations who are yet coming to the Church of God, and hasten to profess their belief in the Son of God, are doing so in vain, because they are not baptized by a Donatist?

Men would undoubtedly abominate these doctrines and leave the schismatics at once, if they were seeking Christ, if they loved the Church, if they were free men, if they kept their right ear intact.

Chapter 30

(32) Let us not heed those who, although not rebaptizing anyone, have nevertheless cut themselves off from unity. These heretics have preferred to be called Luciferians, rather than Catholics. In understanding that Christian baptism ought not to be repeated, they are doing what is right, for they are aware that the Sacrament of the holy font exists nowhere unless it derives from the Catholic Church. That is the source of the form they now have, receiving it, as it were, from the whole vine before they were cut off and had become the brushwood they now are.[1] It is these of whom the Apostle says:[2] 'Having

---

1 Strikingly parallel is the 'S' strophe of St. Augustine's abecedarian *Psalmus contra partem Donati* (Migne PL. 43.30). There, also, rebaptism is marked for avoidance and the figure of the vine and the brushwood cut therefrom is elaborated. The *Psalmus*, like the *De agone Christiano*, was intended for the unlearned.

2 2 Tim. 3.5.

a form of piety, but disowning its power.' Great, indeed, is the power of piety, manifesting itself in peace and unity, for God is one.

The Luciferians do not possess this power, since they have been cut off from unity. Thus, when any of them come to the Catholic Church, they do not receive again the 'form of piety,' which they have, but receive the 'power of piety,' which they do not have. For, the Apostle teaches very clearly that even the amputated branches can be grafted again in the vine, provided they have not continued in unbelief.[3]

Since the Luciferians understand this point and do not rebaptize, we do not condemn them. But, who can fail to see that, in wishing to be cut off from the root, their conduct is abominable? And they have done this chiefly because of their displeasure over that practice in the Catholic Church which is really the mark of Catholic holiness. For, nowhere should loving kindness prevail more than in the Catholic Church. Like a true Mother, She should neither trample haughtily upon her erring children nor be reluctant to pardon those who have made amends. It is not without reason that, among all the Apostles, it is Peter who represents the Catholic Church. For the keys of the kingdom of heaven were given to this Church when they were given to Peter.[4] And when it was said to him, it was said to all: 'Lovest thou me? Feed my sheep.'[5]

The Catholic Church, therefore, ought willingly to forgive Her children, once they have made amends and have become strong in virtue. We see that pardon was granted to Peter, who represents the Church, and, that, having made amends and become strong in virtue, he reached the glorious goal of

---
3 Cf. Rom. 11.23.
4 Matt. 16.19.
5 Cf. John 21.17.

suffering like our Lord. And all this, when he had faltered upon the waters and had called back the Lord from His suffering by human sentiment; when he had cut off the servant's ear with his sword and had thrice denied the Lord Himself; and when he had afterwards fallen into superstitious dissimulation.

Thus, after the persecution by the Arians, the peace, which the Catholic Church now possesses in the Lord, was restored again by secular rulers. Many bishops who had yielded to Arian perfidy during that persecution wished to return to the Church after their amendment, repudiating what they had either believed or pretended to believe. The Catholic Church received these bishops into Her maternal bosom, as She did Peter after he had wept over his denial, being reminded by the crowing of the cock; or as She received this same Peter after his evil dissimulation, when he was reprimanded by the voice of Paul. These heretics view this Mother's charity in a spirit of pride, and in their wickedness hold it up to censure. And because they have not greeted Peter upon his rising after the cock's crowing, these heretics have deservedly fallen with Lucifer, who rose in the morning.[6]

Chapter 31

(33) Let us not heed those who deny that the Church of God can remit all sins. Failing to recognize in Peter the 'rock,' these unhappy souls have accordingly lost possession of the keys; they are unwilling to believe that the keys of the kingdom of heaven have been given to the Church. These are the people who condemn as adulteresses widows who marry, and who boast that theirs is a purity superior to the teaching of

---

6 Cf. Isa. 14.12.

the Apostles. If they would only acknowledge their own names,[1] they would call themselves 'wordly' [*mundanos*] rather than 'pure' [*mundos*]. For, by their unwillingness to be corrected when they have sinned, they have simply chosen to be condemned with this world [*mundo*].

These heretics do not preserve the spiritual health of those to whom they deny forgiveness of sins. They take away medicine from the infirm, forcing their widows to be consumed by the heat of passion, when they will not permit them to marry. Certainly these heretics are not to be accounted wiser than the Apostle Paul, who preferred that widows should marry, rather than be so consumed by passion.[2]

Chapter 32

(34) Let us not heed those who deny the future resurrection of the body, alleging the words of the Apostle Paul:[1] 'Flesh and blood shall not possess the kingdom of God.' These heretics do not grasp the words of the same Apostle:[2] 'This corruptible body must put on incorruption, and this mortal body must put on immortality.' When this has taken place, the body will no longer be flesh and blood, but a heavenly body.[3] The Lord made this promise in saying:[4] 'Neither will they marry nor take wives, but they will be like the Angels of God.' For, when they will have become like to the Angels, they will no longer live for men, but for God. Flesh and blood,

---

1 *Cathari*; in Greek, 'the pure.'
2 Cf. 1 Cor. 7.9.

---

1 1 Cor. 15.50.
2 1 Cor. 15.53,54.
3 In the *Retractations* (2.3) Augustine insists that this expression, 'heavenly body,' is not to be construed as a denial of the true corporeal nature of the glorified body.
4 Matt. 22.30.

therefore, will be changed, and the body will become heavenly and angelic. 'And the dead indeed shall rise incorruptible, and we shall be changed.'[5] Accordingly, it will be true to say that flesh shall rise again, and, also, that flesh and blood shall not possess the kingdom of God.

Chapter 33

(35) Let us be fed in Christ, nourished by the milk of a simple and unaffected faith. While we are children, let us not long for the food of adults. But, let us grow in Christ by wholesome nourishment, by the acquisition of good habits, and by Christian righteousness, wherein the love of God and neighbor is made perfect and strong. In this way each one of us can win an interior victory over the hostile Devil and his angels, being united with Christ whom we have put on.

Perfect charity harbors neither covetousness nor fear of the world, that is to say, perfect charity is neither covetous to acquire temporal goods nor fearful of losing them. These are the two doors through which the enemy gains entrance and obtains the ascendancy over us. He must be driven out; first by the fear of God, then by love. We ought, then, to long more eagerly for the clear and distinct knowledge of Truth, according as we see ourselves advancing in charity, having hearts made pure by its simplicity, for it is by the eye of the soul that Truth is perceived. 'Blessed,' indeed, 'are the pure of heart,' says Christ, 'for they shall see God.'[1] 'So that, being rooted and grounded in love,' we may be able 'to comprehend with all the saints what is the breadth and length and height and depth,

---
5 1 Cor. 15.52.

---
1 Matt. 5.8.

to know also the surpassing knowledge of the love of Christ, in order that we may be filled unto all the fullness of God.'[2]

And when our struggle with the unseen enemy is over, may we deserve the crown of victory. To those who lovingly desire Christ, His yoke is easy and His burden light.

---

2 Cf. Eph. 3.17-19.

FAITH, HOPE AND CHARITY

(*Enchiridion de fide, spe et caritate*)

Translated

by

BERNARD M. PEEBLES, Ph.D.
The Catholic University of America

INTRODUCTION

THE PRESENT work belongs to the period in which St. Augustine was Bishop of Hippo. In date it cannot be later than the treatise *On the Eight Questions of Dulcitius*, where it is quoted,[1] which belongs to the third decade of the fifth century and may be as early as A.D. 422.[2] On the other hand it cannot have been completed prior to the death of St. Jerome (which occurred on 30 September in either 419 or 420), since it mentions him as already dead.[3] In view of these facts the *Enchiridion* is commonly dated ca. 421.[4]

As is made clear from the text itself,[5] the *Enchiridion* was composed in answer to a group of questions on Christian doctrine communicated in a letter to St. Augustine by a certain Lawrence. The latter is elsewhere called a brother of

---

1 *De octo Dulcitii quaestionibus*, ad quaest. I.10.13 (PL 40 154-156: sects. 67-69 of the *Enchiridion* are quoted), ad quaest. II.4 (PL 40 158: sects. 109, 110 are quoted).
2 See, e. g., Pope, *St. Augustine of Hippo* 381. — For bibliographical particulars of works incompletely referred to in this introduction and in the notes to the translation, see the bibliography.
3 *Ench.* sect. 87 ('Jerome the priest, of holy memory').
4 E.g., by Pope, *op. cit.* 381, 387. Such a dating is favored by the position assigned to the *Enchiridion* in St. Augustine's *Retractationes*.
5 *Ench.* sects. 3, 4. The circumstances under which the book was composed are also set out in the *Retractationes* 2.89 (63) (ed. P. Knöll, CSEL 36 202; PL 32 655): 'I also wrote a book on faith, hope, and charity, having been asked by the addressee of the book for some small work of mine that he might always have at hand, the type called by the Greeks a handbook (*enchiridion*) . . . '

the tribune Dulcitius,⁶ to whom the treatise *On the Eight Questions* above cited was addressed, and Lawrence may have come to North Africa in the company of that official. Nothing in the form in which St. Augustine addresses Lawrence suggests that he was in Holy Orders,⁷ and it is more likely that he was a layman.⁸ Indications of doubtful authenticity derived from the manuscripts of the *Enchiridion* would assign to Lawrence a high station at Rome,⁹ while a remark of the author himself,¹⁰ coupled with the elevated doctrine and good style of the treatise,¹¹ lead to the belief that the addressee of the work was a person of exceptional training in letters.

Lawrence had asked the Bishop of Hippo that his questions should be answered in a small volume (*enchiridion*) which he might always have at hand.¹² St. Augustine, though he was amusingly aware that he had been somewhat lengthy in meeting Lawrence's request¹³ and indeed elsewhere calls the work a 'big book' (*grandis liber*),¹⁴ uses the word *enchiridion* several times in his reply to Lawrence,¹⁵ and it is by this name that the work is most commonly known. However, the words

---

6 *De octo Dulcitii quaestionibus*, ad quaest. I.10. Dulcitius, the addressee of St. Augustine's *Epist.* 204, had been sent to Africa to execute the Imperial orders against the Donatists (*Retract.* 2.85; cf. Pope, *op. cit.* 360).
7 St. Augustine calls Lawrence 'most beloved son' (*Ench.* sect. 1), 'my son' (*Retract.* 2.89[63]), and says that he loved him greatly among the members of Christ's body (*Ench.* sect. 122).
8 So Scheel in the introduction to his edition, p. V; Mitterer in the introduction of his translation, p. 390.
9 See the 'Admonitio' to the Maurist edition (VI 193-194; PL 40 229 f.).
10 *Ench.* sect. 1 (Lawrence's *eruditio*).
11 See F. di Capua, in *Misc. Agost.* II 748 f., on the excellence of the prose rhythm in the *Enchiridion*.
12 *Ench.* sect. 6; cf. *Retract.* quoted above, p. 357 n. 5.
13 *Ench.* sect. 122.
14 *Epistula* 231.7 (ed. A. Goldbacher, CSEL 57 510; PL 33 1026).
15 *Ench.* sect. 4,6 (twice), 122.

'on Faith, Hope, and Charity' are frequently added to the title in view of the fact that St. Augustine organized his treatise as a discussion of these three virtues,[16] being followed in this by St. Thomas Aquinas, whose *Compendium Theologiae* follows the same plan. The title which St. Augustine himself seems to have given to the work was simply *De fide, spe, et caritate*.[17]

Effectively, the *Enchiridion* is a commentary on the Apostles' Creed and the Lord's Prayer.[18] The Creed is taken as the basis of St. Augustine's discussion of faith (sects. 9-113), while the remarks on hope (sects. 114-116) serve as a brief exposition of the Lord's Prayer; the sections dealing with charity (sects. 117-121) are at once an appendage and the crown of the whole work. The *Enchiridion* occupies a place of high distinction among the author's theological writings, since, while confining itself to the essentials of Christian teaching,[19] it is his only systematic treatment of the Church's doctrine as a whole, and, coming late in his career as bishop,

---

16 *Ench.* sect. 3 is the simplest suggestion of his plan. With the language there used, cf. St. Augustine, *De doctrina Christiana* Prol. 6. The last three chapters of this work contain a statement of the inter-relation of the three virtues which merits comparison with *Ench.* sect. 7.

17 See *De octo Dulcitii quaestionibus*, ad quaest. 1.10. (here 'On Faith, Hope, and Charity' is actually called the *title* of the work); *Epist.* 231.7; *Retract*, 2.89 (63). Also the list (*indiculum*) of St. Augustine's writings prepared by his disciple and friend, Possidius, Bishop of Calama, on the basis of a list maintained by St. Augustine himself (*Indiculum* sect. 6 [PL 46 12]; or Dom Wilmart's edition in *Misc. Agost.* II 180, where 'Ad Laurentium de fide, spe et caritate liber unus' is item 30 in section [X³] of the *Indiculum*).

18 Analyses of the *Enchiridion*: Harnack, *History of Dogma* (Engl. transl.) V 222-234; Seeberg, *Text-book of the History of Dogma* (Engl. transl.) I 357-368. Scheel's article in the *Zeitsch. f. Kirchengeschichte* for 1903 appears to be the most ample printed appreciation of the *Enchiridion*. See also article of Rivière cited in bibliography.

19 There is clear evidence in the *Ench.* that the author is omitting certain subjects altogether and abridging the discussion of others: e.g., sects. 5, 6, 20, 34, 38, 40, 58.

shows that fullness of understanding and precision of analysis which his long years of pastoral care and active combat against heresies had produced in him. It is no wonder, then, that the *Enchiridion* has been drawn upon heavily as a synthesis of Augustinian teaching from the days of Peter Lombard[20] (if not before[21]) to our own times.

The present translation is based on the edition of Scheel (1903),[22] representing, along with certain improvements, the last published critical text of the *Enchiridion*, that of Krabinger and Ruhland (1861).[23] In preparing and revising the translation, frequent use has been made of the German translation of Mitterer and especially the very idiomatic English rendering of J. F. Shaw. So far as was possible, the translation of Biblical passages has followed the Challoner revision of the Douay Bible (for the Old Testament), and the revision of the Challoner-Rheims version of the New

---

20 In the *Sententiae* (PL 192) of this influential writer the *Ench.* is the third most-cited work of St. Augustine's (cited more frequently are the much longer *De Trinitate* and *De Genesi ad litteram*); see the article of F. Cavallera in the *Arch. de philosophie* 7.2. Marginal notes in the Maurist edition (not reprinted in PL) give most of the references to the *Sententiae*.

21 The translator has made no attempt to trace the influence of the *Enchiridion* in later writers. The book was not forgotten in the early Middle Ages: Cassiodorus cites it in his commentary on the Psalms (see his *Institutiones*, ed. R. A. B. Mynors [Oxford 1937], Index p. 187), while Alcuin uses it more than once (J. D. A. Ogilvy, *Books Known to Anglo-Latin-Writers from Aldhelm to Alcuin* [Cambridge, Mass. 1936] 16). The abundance of the MSS is further evidence (in their note on *Ench.* ch. 24 sect. 95 the Maurists cite more than 30). (According to E. A. Lowe, in *Misc. Agost.* II 236, the *Ench.* is found in a 6th-century codex of Bamberg [B.IV.21]). Strangely enough, the *Ench.* finds no place among the extensive excerpts from the writings of St. Augustine made by Eugippius (d. after 532); ed. P. Knöll, CSEL 9.

22 Scheel's system of numbering by chapters and sections has been followed.

23 Scheel's departure from his base-text are listed by him on pp. 78-80.

Testament published in this country in 1941 under the patronage of the Episcopal Committee of the Confraternity of Christian Doctrine. Since both of these are renderings of the Vulgate text, it was necessary, when St. Augustine follows an Old Latin version, to adapt the current translation or indeed to translate afresh; the most conspicuous of such cases have been indicated in the notes.[24] Faure's edition shows how readily the *Enchiridion* may be made a vehicle for theological discussion. For twenty odd passages of undoubtedly high theological interest[25] the present translator has referred the reader to Père Portalié's admirable article on St. Augustine in the *Dictionnaire de théologie catholique*.

---

24 Discussion has been avoided. For the most stimulating account of St. Augustine's relations to the text of Holy Scripture, see Dom de Bruyne, in *Misc. Agost.* II 521-606.
25 Those chosen by R. de Journel for his *Enchiridion Patristicum* (*Ench. Patr.*)

SELECT BIBLIOGRAPHY

Editions of the Latin text:

Scheel: *Augustins Enchiridion* hrsg. von O. Scheel (G. Krüger, Sammlung ausgewählter kirchen- und dogmengeschichtlicher Quellenschriften II 4, Tübingen and Leipzig 1903); also, 2nd edit. (1930).

Maurist edition: *Sancti Augustini Hipponensis episcopi opera* VI (Paris 1695) 193-242. Repeated in PL 40 229-290.

Faure: *Enchiridion de fide spe et caritate S. Aurelii Augustini* a Iohanne Baptista Faure theologo Societatis Iesu notis et assertionibus theologicis illustratum (Naples 1847).

Krabinger-Ruhland: Edition of J. G. Krabinger (completed by A. Ruhland) (Tübingen 1861). Not available for consultation.

Translations:

J. F. Shaw: *The Works of Saint Augustine, A New Translation*, edited by the Rev. Marcus Dods, IX (Edinburgh 1892) 173-260. Repeated (with certain changes by Schaff) in *A Select Library of the Nicene and Post-Nicene Fathers of the Christian Church*, edited by Philip Schaff, III (New York 1900) 237-276.

Sigisbert Mitterer, O.S.B.: *Des heiligen Kirchenvaters Aurelius Augustinus ausgewählte Schriften aus dem Lateinischen übersetzt VII* (Bibliothek der Kirchenväter 49, Munich 1925) 397-502.

Chief supplementary works cited:

F. Cavallera, 'Saint Augustin et le livre des Sentences de Pierre Lombard,' *Archives de philosophie* 7.2 (1930: Etudes sur Saint Augustin) 186-199.

CSEL: *Corpus scriptorum ecclesiasticorum latinorum* (Vienna 1866 —).

H. Denzinger, *Enchiridion symbolorum, definitionum et declarationum de rebus fidei et morum* (editio 21-23 Freiburg i. B. 1937).

Ench. Patr.: M. J. Rouët de Journel, S.J., *Enchiridion Patristicum* (Freiburg i. B. 1920).

Adolph Harnack, *History of Dogma*, translated from the 3rd German edition by James Miller, V (London etc. 1898) 222-234.

Misc. Agost.: *Miscellanea Agostiniana*, 2 vols. (Rome 1930, 1931).

PL: J. P. Migne, *Patrologiae cursus completus: Series Latina* (Paris 1844-1864).

Hugh Pope, O.P., *Saint Augustine of Hippo* (London 1937).

E. Portalié, 'Saint Augustin,' in A. Vacant - E. Mangenot - E. Amann, *Dictionnaire de théologie catholique* I.2 (3rd printing, Paris 1923) cols. 2268-2478.

J. Rivière, 'Comment diviser l'Enchiridion de Saint Augustin,' *Bulletin de littérature ecclésiastique* 43 (1942) 99-115. Not available for consultation; cited in *Revue d'histoire ecclésiastique* 41 (1946) 42.

O. Rottmanner, O.S.B., [review of Scheel's edition of the *Enchiridion*], *Theologische Revue* (Münster i. W.) 2 (1903) 478-479.

———, *Geistesfrüchte aus der Klosterzelle* (München 1908).

Otto Scheel, 'Bemerkungen zur Bewertung des Enchiridions Augustins,' *Zeitschrift für Kirchengeschichte* 24 (1903) 401-416.

Reinhold Seeberg, *Text-book of the History of Dogma*, translated by C. E. Hay, I (Philadelphia 1905) 357-368.

CONTENTS

Chapter   *Pages*

1. The author desires for Lawrence the gift of true wisdom.—Man's wisdom is piety.—God to be worshipped by faith, hope, and charity.— Lawrence's questions.—The author's replies 369

2. The Creed and the Lord's Prayer embrace faith, hope, and charity.—General exposition of faith, hope, and charity, and their inter-relation 372

3. Requirements of faith set out.—No need of intricate investigation of the natural world.—It suffices a Christian to believe that all things were created by the supremely good Trinity and are good.—Answer to an heretical opinion concerning the origin of evil.—Why God permits evils to exist.—Evil is only the privation of good 375

4. All creatures are good but, since not supremely good, corruptible.—There is no evil but what is also good.—Good and evil, though contraries, can co-exist in the same thing.—Evils come from good things and are in good things.—Explanation of the parable of trees and fruits 377

5. Whether knowledge of natural causes relates to happiness.—The nature of error.—Not every error harmful.—The author's fortunate error at the crossroads . . 381

6. All lies are sins, but not of equal gravity.—Lying is not to utter the false when ignorant of the true, but to utter as true what the speaker believes false.—Some errors are more ruinous than others, but all are evil . . . 383

7. Not every kind of error is sinful.—Refutation of the Academics, who refuse all agreement in order to avoid error.—Error not always a sin but always an evil.—Every lie a sin 386

Chapter   *Page*

8 The cause of good things is the goodness of God; the cause of evil things is the deficient will of the corruptible good.—Ignorance and concupiscence are other causes of evil.—Penalties imposed on sin.—The penalty of Adam's sin borne by the whole race.—Refutation of a heresy.—Man's condition after Adam's sin 390

9 Upon the fall of the rebellious angels, the others were established in blessedness.—The place of the fallen angels reserved for the remnant of the human race which is saved.—Men saved by grace, not by merits or free will.—Faith, good works, and good will come by the gift of God 393

10 Need of fallen humanity for a reconciliator, Christ.—Christ the Mediator born of Mary through the Incarnation of the Word.—Christ both God and man.—Heresies refuted 398

11 Grace displayed through the raising of the man Christ to the dignity of the Son of God when no merit was present.—Grace likewise displayed in the fact that the birth of Christ was of the Holy Spirit 401

12 Christ born of the Holy Spirit, yet not as of a father; of Mary as mother.—What is born of something is not always to be called the son of that thing.—The manner of Christ's birth of the Holy Spirit manifests the grace of God 403

13 Christ sinless but made sin.—Baptism instituted so that in dying to sin we may have newness of life.—In baptism all die to sin, both infants and adults.—The figurative use of singular for plural, and of plural for singular.—The manifold varities of sin contained in man's first offense.—Probably true that children are involved in the guilt not only of the first pair but of their immediate parents.—Difficulties of defining the point to which the sins of man's other progenitors extend 406

Chapter *Page*

14 Original sin not washed away except through Christ.—Rebirth not effected by the baptism of John.—Why Christ willed to be baptized by John.—Christ takes away not only original sin but all others thereto added.—Since Adam's condemnation, no one freed except through rebirth in Christ.—For both infants and adults, baptism is a similitude of Christ's death and resurrection.—Christ's cross, burial, resurrection, and ascension are images of the Christian life.— The last judgment belongs to actions to be performed at the end of the world.—Judgment of living and dead: two interpretations 410

15 The Creed considers the Holy Spirit and the Church in the proper order.—The Church in Heaven aids that on earth.—The firmness of the Church in Heaven.—The various orders of the angels; uncertainty whether stars are angels.—Difficulty of describing the bodies assumed by angels 416

16 Importance of discerning the wiles by which Satan transforms himself into an angel of light.—The two parts of the Church: angelic and human.—Christ did not die for the angels. Relation between human redemption and the angels.—How in Christ all things are re-established and made at peace.—How the peace of the heavenly kingdom surpasses all understanding . . 419

17 Forgiveness of sins: its place in the Creed.—The life of the saints free of crime, not of sin.—Crimes of whatever kind forgiven in the Church through penance.—Outside the Church no forgiveness of sins.—Forgiveness of sins has reference to the future judgment . . 422

18 Refutation of the belief that all the faithful, no matter how wicked their lives, are to be saved by fire.—Apostle's meaning in the passage about salvation by fire explained.—Possibility of purgatorial fire after this present life 425

Chapter	Page

19 Crimes not redeemed by alms unless life is changed.—Slight sins expiated by the Lord's Prayer.—The many kinds of almsgiving.—The highest type of almsgiving is forgiveness of enemies.—The sins of those who do not forgiven are not forgiven by God 429

20 The wicked and unbelieving not cleansed by almsgiving unless they are changed.—The first alms is to have pity on one's own soul and to live justly.—Wickedness to be forsaken if alms is to avail anything 432

21 Sins which are humanly judged not to be sins.—Apparently trivial sins may be very grave.—Detestable sins may seem through usage trivial 435

22 Two causes of sin: ignorance and weakness; these are insurmountable without divine aid.—Penance the gift to God.—The sin against the Holy Spirit 439

23 The resurrection of the body.—Whether abortive fetuses rise again.—When the fetus begins to live in the womb.—The resurrection of monstrous fetuses.—The renewal of the body, in whatever way it perished.—How superfluous elements of the body return to it.—The resurrected body to show nothing unsightly in form or stature.—The bodies of the saints to rise according to the substance of the flesh but free from every blemish.—In what form the bodies of the damned will rise again.—Who among the damned will receive the mildest punishment 441

24 The benefits of grace to be more fully known by the saints in the eternal life.—God's secret judgments concerning the predestination of man then to be revealed.—God's effectual will.—God does well even in permitting evil to occur.—Whether God's will to save those who wish to be saved is impeded by human will . . 447

25 Although God can convert whomever he wishes, He does not act unjustly when He converts some and does not convert others.—The original chain of condemnation.

Chapter	Page

—As God's mercy is free, His Judgments are just.—The rebellious root of the human race 450

26 Nothing is done without God's will, even that which is done contrary to it.—The good will of God is always fulfilled, equally through the good and the evil wills of men.—God's will is ever undefeated and never evil, whether He takes pity or hardens 454

27 Investigation of the Apostle's saying, 'Who wishes all men to be saved.' 456

28 The will of God with respect to Adam, who He knew would sin.—Men's free will for good or evil to be different in the future life.—Grace necessary for free will as well before the Fall as after it.—Eternal life a free gift as well as a reward.—God's will fulfilled with respect to sinful man.—Our salvation is from God; Christ, had He not been God, could not have freed us 458

29 Condition of the soul between death and the resurrection.—How far and for whom the sacrifice of the altar and almsgiving for the dead are of profit.—The two cities in the afterlife: that of eternal blessedness and that of eternal misery.—The punishment of the damned is eternal.—The death of the wicked is eternal, as is the life of the saints 461

30 All that pertains to hope is contained in the Lord's prayer.—Whoever hopes in himself is accursed.—The seven petitions of the Lord's Prayer as found in St. Matthew.—The five petitions found in St. Luke agree 465

31 Charity (greater than faith and hope) is shed in our hearts by the Holy Spirit.—The four states or ages of man: before the Law, under the Law, under grace, and in peace.—Rebirth abolishes all sin in each of the ages.—Death has no dominion over those who die immediately after baptism 467

32 Charity is the end of all the commandments 470

33 Conclusion 471

FAITH, HOPE AND CHARITY

Chapter 1

CANNOT SAY, most beloved son Lawrence, how greatly I delight in your learning, and how desirous I am that you be wise--not of the number of those of whom it is said:[1] 'Where is the "wise man"? Where is the scribe? Where is the disputant of this world? Has not God turned to foolishness the "wisdom" of this world?' but of those of whom it is written:[2] 'The multitude of the wise is the welfare of the whole world,' and such as the Apostle wishes those to become to whom he says:[3] 'I would have you wise as to what is good, and guileless as to what is evil.'[4]

(2) Now the wisdom of man is piety. This you find in the book of the holy Job, for there is written what wisdom herself has said to mankind:[5] 'Behold piety is wisdom.' But if you ask what manner of piety is meant in this place, you will find a clearer expression in the Greek—*theosébeia,* which is the worship of God. Now, piety is also expressed in Greek by

---

1 1 Cor. 1.20.
2 Wisd. 6.26.
3 Rom. 16.19.
4 The Maurist editors here print an additional sentence, not found by them in the older MSS and ignored by Scheel in his edition: Now just as no one can exist of himself, so also no one can be wise of himself, but only through the illumination of Him of whom it is written 'All wisdom is from God' (Eccli. 1.1).
5 Job 28.28 (Septuagint; for 'piety' the Vulgate reads 'fear of the Lord').

another word, *eusébeia*, by which is meant good worship, although this noun also is applied especially to the worship of God. But, since the passage would define the nature of man's wisdom, the most appropriate word is *theosébeia*, which manifestly conveys the meaning 'worship of God.'

In requesting me to deal with great matters in short compass, do you ask for an answer still more closely packed? Or do you perhaps wish that I explain in a short discourse just how it is that God should be worshipped?

(3) If I here answer you that God should be worshipped by faith, hope, and charity,[6] you would surely say that my brevity had exceeded your wish; and you would then ask that I briefly develop what pertains to these three things—what a man should believe, what he should hope for, what he should love. And when I should have done this, then would you have all those things which you specified in your letter of request to me. If you have a copy with you, it is easy for you to open it and reread it; if you haven't, please recollect it while I remind you of it.

(4) According to your letter, your wish is that I compose a book for you, to serve as what is called a handbook (*enchiridion*), that is, one you may always have at hand. It is to contain answers to certain questions: After what, most of all, should one strive? What, chiefly, given the sundry heresies, should one shun? In what measure does reason come to the help of religion, or what lack of accord is there with reason when faith stands alone? What holds the first and what the final place? What is the sum-total of the whole doctrine? What

---

[6] In the Latin, *caritas*, as in the classic verse, 1 Cor. 13.13. In virtually the same sense St. Augustine uses *dilectio* (found, e.g., in Gal. 5.6) and *amor* (the latter notably four times at the end of sect. 8 below). In the translation 'charity' and 'love' are often used interchangeably.

is the sure and distinctive foundation of the Catholic faith? On all these points about which you ask, you will have true knowledge once you surely know what are the proper objects of our faith, our hope, and our charity, for these are the chief, nay, rather the only, guiding principles of our religion. Whoever speaks against these is either altogether an alien to the name of Christ or a heretic. The defense of reason is to be invoked for things that either originate through the senses of the body or are discovered by the intellect. On the other hand, whatever we have learned not through bodily sense and have not been able to grasp nor will be able to grasp through the mind, these are without any doubt to be believed on the witness of those men who composed that scripture which has justly been called divine, men divinely aided, who, using the eyes, whether of their body or of their spirit, could see these things or even foresee them.

(5) Now the mind, once it has been imbued with the beginning of faith (which works through charity[7]), tends through good living to attain unto sight, whereby the righteous and pure of heart know that ineffable beauty whose full vision is supreme happiness. This is surely what you mean in your question: What holds the first and what the final place? We begin in faith; we achieve by sight. This is the sum-total of the whole doctrine. The sure and distinctive foundation of the Catholic faith is Christ: 'for other foundation no one can lay, but that which has been laid, which is Christ Jesus.'[8] Nor are we to deny that this is the distinctive foundation of the Catholic faith because it may be supposed that this foundation is used by certain heretics in common with us. For, if we diligently consider the things that per-

---
7 Gal. 5.6.
8 1 Cor. 3.11.

tain to Christ, in name Christ will indeed be found among whatever heretics choose to call themselves Christians, but in fact He is not among them. The proof of this would be overlong, for we should have to name all heresies which have existed or do or could have existed under the Christian name, and to show the truth of the proposition in each individual case. Such a disputation would be matter for so many volumes as to appear infinite.

(6) Your request, however, is for an *enchiridion,* a book the hand can hold, not a work which would tax a whole bookcase. To return, then, to the three things by which we said God should be worshipped—faith, hope, and charity. It is easy to state what a man should believe, what he should hope for, what he should love. But how to defend this doctrine against the assaults of those who believe otherwise would require fuller and more laborious instruction. For this, it would not be enough that the hand be filled with an *enchiridion;* rather must a great zeal be kindled in the heart.

Chapter 2

(7) Remember that you have the Creed[1] and the Lord's Prayer. What is there which takes a shorter time to hear or to read, or can more easily be committed to memory? When, in consequence of grave sin, the human race was afflicted with misery and stood in need of the divine mercy, the Prophet, foretelling the time of God's grace, said:[2] 'And it shall come to pass that every one that shall call upon the name of the Lord shall be saved.' Hence prayer. But the Apostle, when, in order to commend this very grace, he had cited the witness

---
1 For St. Augustine's statements on the Creed as an inviolable rule of faith, see Portalié, col. 2340.
2 Joel 2.32.

of the Prophet, immediately added:³ 'How then are they to call upon him in whom they have not believed?' Hence the Creed. In these two you may see those three earlier things exemplified: faith believes, hope and charity pray. But, without faith, the other two cannot exist, and therefore faith also prays. And that is why it has been written: 'How are they to call upon him in whom they have not believed?'

(8) Can anything be hoped for which is not believed? It is true that something which is not hoped for can be believed. Who of the faithful does not believe in the punishment of the wicked? Yet he does not hope for it. Rather, whoever believes himself threatened by such punishment, and shrinks in horror from it, more properly is said to fear than to hope. A certain poet distinguishes these two words when he says:⁴ 'Allow the fearful to hope.' But another poet, although superior, offends propriety in writing:⁵ 'If I have been able to hope for so great a grief.' And some grammatical writers use this case to exemplify improper diction and write:⁶ 'The poet has used "hope" instead of "fear".' Faith, then, may have as its objects both evil things and good, because both good and evil are believed, and the faith that believes them is not bad but good. Moreover, faith may concern the past or the present or the future. For we believe that Christ died: this is past; we believe that He sits at the right hand of the Father: this now is; we believe that He is to come to judge: this is yet to be. Again, faith may deal with one's own circumstances and with another's. For a man may

---
3 Rom. 10.14.
4 Lucan, *Pharsalia* 2.15.
5 Virgil, *Aeneid* 4.419.
6 E.g., the grammarian Servius on this line of the *Aeneid* (ed. Thilo 1 539: ("hope" for "fear" . . . for we *hope* for good things, but *fear* adverse things).

believe that he at some time began to exist and was not eternal, and may hold the same belief of other men and other things. And in what pertains to religion we believe many things not only about other men but about angels as well.

Hope, on the other hand, is concerned with nothing but good things, with those that are yet to be, and which pertain to him who entertains the hope. For these reasons, then, faith must be distinguished from hope not only on the grammatical level but because of a rational difference. The fact that both what we believe and what we hope for are not seen is something common to faith and hope. In the Epistle to the Hebrews, in a passage cited as testimony by renowned defenders of the Catholic rule of faith, faith is said to be[7] 'the evidence of things that are not seen.' However, should someone say that he believes, that is, has reposed his faith upon, not words, not witnesses, not any arguments at all, but only the evidence of things present, he is not in so absurd a position as to be justly liable to the criticism: 'You have seen, therefore you have not believed.' Hence it does not follow that a thing must not be seen if it is to be believed. But we do better, following the teaching of Holy Scripture, to call faith that which has as its object things that are not seen. Concerning hope, also, the Apostle says:[8] 'Hope that is seen is not hope. For how can a man hope for what he sees? But, if we hope for what we do not see, we wait for it with patience.' When, then, we believe that good will come to us, nothing remains but to hope for it.

Now, what is to be said of charity, without which faith is of no avail and hope cannot exist? As the Apostle James says,[9] 'The devils also believe, and tremble'; they neither hope nor love, but rather, believing that what we hope for

---

7 Heb. 11.1
8 Rom. 8.24.
9 James 2.19.

and love will come about, are in terror. Wherefore the Apostle Paul approves and commends faith, which works through charity,[10] and which cannot exist without hope. Wherefore there is no charity without hope, nor hope without charity, and neither without faith.

Chapter 3

(9) When, then, it is asked what a man should believe in regard to religion, there is no need to pry into the nature of things, as was done by those whom the Greeks call *physici*.[1] And we need not have any fear lest a Christian be ignorant of the force and number of the elements, of the motion, order and eclipses of the heavenly bodies, of the shape of the heavens, of the kinds and natures of animals, plants, stones, fountains, rivers, mountains, of the intervals of places and times, of the signs of imminent storms, and a thousand other such things which they either discovered or believe they have discovered.[2] For even they, with such superior genius, burning with zeal, abounding in leisure, investigating some things with the aid of human conjecture, searching into others through the experience of history, even they did not find out all things, and even their vaunted discoveries involve more of opinion than of knowledge. For a Christian it is enough to believe that the cause of created things, whether on earth or in heaven, whether visible or invisible, is nothing other than the goodness of the Creator, who is God, one and

---

10 Gal. 5.6.

1 Natural philosophers.
2 One would have expected: 'or believed they had discovered.' St. Augustine's use of the present tense (*existimant*) suggests that, in addition to the early Greeks, he was thinking also of such *physici* as were his own contemporaries; a subtle and meaningful departure from strict grammatical consistency characteristic of the author.

true, and that there is nothing which either He Himself is not or which does not stem from Him—from Him, the Trinity, the Father, the Son begotten of the Father, and the Holy Spirit proceeding from the same Father, but being the one and the same Spirit of Father and Son.

(10) By this Trinity supremely, equally, and unchangeably good, all things were created; yet these are not supremely, equally, and unchangeably good, but good they are, even taken separately, while together they are very good, because it is of all things that the wonderful beauty of the whole consists.[3]

(11) In this whole even that which is called evil, well-regulated and confined to its own place, serves to give higher commendation to the good, making it, in comparison with the evil, more pleasing and worthy of praise. For not even the Almighty God, who, as even the heathen acknowledge,[4] 'has supreme power over all things,' being Himself supremely good, would ever permit any evil to be in His works, were not His power and goodness such that even out of evil He can do good. Now what is the so-called evil but a privation of the good? In the bodies of animals affliction with diseases and wounds is nothing other than the privation of health. For, when a cure is worked, it does not mean that those evils which were present, that is, the diseases and the wounds, recede thence and are elsewhere; they simply are not. For a wound or a disease is not a substance, but a vice of the

---

3 For the 'very good' cf. Gen. 1.31, Eccli. 39.21. In this section St. Augustine takes a stand against the Manichaean error concerning the origin of evil. It is characteristic of the *Enchiridion* that neither here nor later (sects. 18, 26, 34, 35) are the heresies which St. Augustine opposes mentioned by name (cf. above, sect. 5). The mention of the Donatists in sect. 17 is quite incidental.
4 Virgil, *Aeneid* 10.100.

fleshly substance; the substance, surely something good, is flesh itself, its accidents being the aforementioned evils, that is, privations of that good which is called health. In like manner evils in the soul are privations of natural good. When they are cured, they are not transferred to another place; since they can have no place in the healthy soul, they can be nowhere.

Chapter 4

(12) All natural beings are good, since the Creator of every one of them is supremely good; but because, unlike their Creator, they are not supremely and unchangeably good, their good is capable of diminution and increase. But the diminution of good is an evil, even though, howsoever it be diminished, somewhat of good must necessarily remain, to be the source of its being, if its being is to continue. For, of whatever kind or however small, that good which gives it being cannot be destroyed unless the being itself be destroyed. An uncorrupted being is justly esteemed; yet, if it be also incorruptible, absolutely incapable of corruption, certainly it is all the more worthy of praise. When it is corrupted, then is its corruption an evil, depriving it, as it does, of some sort of good; if it does not deprive it of good, it does no harm, but it does do harm, and therefore removes good. So long as a being is in process of corruption, there is present in it a good of which it is being deprived; and if a part of the being remains which is incapable of corruption, then surely is the being incorruptible, and it is through corruption that it comes to this very great good. But if it does not cease to be corrupted, it does not cease to have that good of which corruption can deprive it. But, if it should be completely and thoroughly consumed, then no good will be present in it, since it will in no wise be a being. For this reason corruption

cannot consume good without consuming its being. Every being, therefore, is good—a great good if it cannot be corrupted; a small one if it can: but only the foolish and ignorant would deny that it is good. And if a being is consumed by corruption, then neither will the corruption remain, no being subsisting there where it can find a place.

(13) Accordingly, that which is called evil does not exist if there is no good. But a good wholly lacking in evil is a perfect good. One in which evil is present is a defective or faulty good; nor can there be any evil where there is no good. From this a strange result emerges. Since every being, insofar as it is a being, is good, when we call a defective being an evil being, we seem to be saying that what is good is evil, and that only what is good can be evil, since every being is good nor could there be an evil thing if the thing itself which is evil were not a being. Nothing, then, can be evil except a good. Although this seems to be an absurd statement, the sequence of our argument forces us to it. Yet we must beware lest we bring on ourselves that utterance of the Prophet, where we read:[1] 'Woe unto them that call evil good and good evil: that put darkness for light, and light for darkness: that put bitter for sweet, and sweet for bitter.' And yet our Lord says:[2] 'The evil man from the evil treasure of his heart brings forth evil things.' But what is an 'evil man' but an evil being, since man is a being? Yet if man is something good (since he is a being), what is an 'evil man' but an evil good? If, however, we distinguish these two things, we find it is not because he is a man that he is an evil nor because he is wicked that he is a good, but a good because he is a man and an evil because he is wicked. Therefore, whoever says: 'To

---

[1] Isa. 5.20.
[2] Matt. 12.35; cf. Luke 6.45.

be a man is an evil' or 'It is a good to be wicked,' he brings upon himself that utterance of the Prophet:[3] 'Woe unto them that call evil good and good evil.' For that man reproaches man, who is a work of God, and praises the vice of man, which is wickedness. Wherefore every being, even if it is defective, insofar as it is a being, is good; insofar as it is defective, is evil.

(14) Accordingly, in the case of these contraries which are called evil and good, there is a failure of the dialectical rule which affirms that in no thing can two contraries exist at the same time. Air, for example, is not at the same time dark and bright; nor is food or drink at the same time sweet and bitter; no body at the same time white in the place where it is black; none at the same time deformed where it is beautiful. And this rule that contraries cannot co-exist in one thing is confirmed in many, indeed in nearly all cases. Yet, although there is no doubt that good and evil are contraries, not only can they exist together, but evil without good and in anything that is not good cannot exist at all; good, however, can exist without evil. For, whereas a man or an angel can be other than wicked, it is only a man or an angel that can be wicked: good because he is a man or because he is an angel, evil because he is wicked. And the co-existence of these two contraries is so conditioned that, were there no good in which it could reside, evil simply could not exist, because corruption would neither have a place of existence nor a source from which to spring, if there were nothing which could be corrupted; and only a good thing can be corrupted, since corruption is nothing other than the destruction of good. Evil things, therefore, arose from good and do not exist except in certain good things, nor was there any other source whence any

---
[3] Isa. 5.20.

evil being could arise. For such source, if it existed, would surely, insofar as it was a being, be good; and, if an incorruptible being, a great good, or, if corruptible, surely nothing other than some sort of good, for it could receive harm from corruption only through the corruption of the good that was in it.

(15) Though we have said that evil arose from good, do not think we have contradicted the Lord's utterance,[4] 'A good tree cannot bear bad fruit.' As Scripture also says,[5] men cannot gather grapes from thorns, because from thorns grapes cannot be born. But from good earth we see born both vines and thorns. And in the same way, just as a bad tree cannot bear good fruit, so an evil will cannot produce good works. But from the being of man, which is good, can arise either a good will or an evil; nor was there any possible original source for an evil will but the nature of angel or man, which is good. This truth is manifested most clearly by the Lord Himself, in the very place in which He was speaking about the tree and its fruit:[6] 'Either make the tree good and its fruit good, or make the tree bad and its fruit bad.' In this He plainly teaches that neither from a good tree may bad fruit spring, nor good fruit from a bad tree, but yet that from the earth itself, to which He was speaking,[7] either kind of tree could grow.

---

4 Matt. 7.18.
5 Cf. Matt. 7.16.
6 Matt. 12.33; not the same context from which the author quoted the earlier Scriptural verse on the tree and its fruit.
7 A striking figure of speech. The author may have had in mind Gen. 3.19, where Adam, representing mankind as a whole, is called, in the Vulgate, 'dust,' but 'earth' (*terra*) according to a text used by St. Augustine, *De agone Christiano* 2.2 (ed. J. Zycha, CSEL 41.103). Also relevant may be Jos. 23.14 and 3 Kings 2.2 (cf. Gen. 6.13 and M. B. Ogle in *Harvard Theological Review* 31 (1938) 41-51), where 'earth' (*terra*)

Chapter 5

(16) In the light of this, when we are pleased by that famous line of Maro's,[1] 'Happy was he who could learn the causes of things,' let us not judge that it pertains to the pursuit of happiness to know the causes of the great movements in the physical world, secrets hidden in the most remote recesses of nature's realm—'whence are earthquakes, through what force swell the lofty seas, bursting their barriers, and then once more returning upon themselves to rest'[2]—and the other things of this kind. Rather it is the causes of good and evil things that we ought to know, so far as knowledge of them is granted to man, in order that we may avoid those errors and tribulations of which this life is so full. For the goal of our tending is that happiness wherein we are tossed by no tribulation nor deceived by any error. If, rather, it were the causes of physical movements that we should know, surely should we know none better than those affecting our own health. But when in our ignorance of these we resort to physicians, is it not clear with what patience we should endure our ignorance of the hidden secrets of the heaven and the earth?

(17) True it is that we should avoid error with all possible diligence, in small matters as well as in great, and that ignorance is the only possible source of error. Still, it does not follow that error is present wherever there is ignorance. He only is in error who thinks he knows what he does not know; he accepts the false for the true, and this is the meaning of

---

stands for the human (or animal) creation. The Pharisees who are addressed (earth), according as they make the tree (their wills) either good or bad, will make the fruit (their works) either good or bad.

---

1 Virgil, *Georgics* 2.490.
2 Virgil, *Georgics* 2.479 f.

error. But it is a matter of much importance in what subject it is that a man is in error. When one and the same subject is in question, knowledge is justly preferred to ignorance, freedom from error to error. But, when several subjects are involved, when one man knows some things which are useful, while another knows others which are less useful or even harmful, who would not, in these latter subjects, prefer the ignorance of the one man to the knowledge of the other? There are, indeed, those things of which ignorance is better than knowledge. Benefit likewise has come to some men through mistaking the road—but in traveling, not in morals. For example, it once befell me to take a wrong turn at a crossroads and thus not to pass by a certain place where, expecting me to come, an armed band of Donatists lay in wait for me. The result was that I reached my destination, but by a long detour. On learning of the plot, I congratulated myself on my mistake and gave thanks to God. Who would not choose to be a traveller who made a mistake like this than the highwayman who made none? And perhaps it is for such reasons, that that best of poets makes a certain wretched lover say:[3] 'When I saw, how was I undone! How was I swept away by an evil error!' For there is an error that is good, one that not only does no harm, but even is of advantage. But let us look more diligently at the truth of the matter. To be in error is nothing other than to think to be true what is false or to think to be false what it true, or to hold the certain as uncertain or the uncertain as certain, whether it be true or false. And this is ugly and unbecoming in the soul in proportion as we perceive it to be fair and seemly when we utter it or assent to it, saying[4] 'Yea yea, nay nay.' This life we live is

---

3 Virgil, *Eclogues* 8.41.
4 Cf. Matt. 5.37.

surely wretched indeed, if only on this account, that sometimes, in order to preserve it, error is necessary. God forbid that such be that life where truth itself is the very life of our soul, where no one deceives and no one is deceived. In this present life, however, men deceive and are deceived, and are more wretched when, through lying, they deceive than when, through believing the lie, they are deceived. Yet to this extent does our rational nature shrink from the false and, so far as possible, shun error, that even those who love to deceive choose not to be deceived. A liar does not think that he is in error, but that he is putting into error the man who believes him. And, indeed, the liar is not in error in that matter which he has cloaked in falsehood, if he does know what the truth is; but in this he is deceived—in thinking that his falsehood does not injure him, when in fact every sin more greatly injures the sinner than the sinned against.

Chapter 6

(18) This discussion gives rise to a very difficult and intricate question: Whether duty ever requires a just man to lie. This question I dealt with in a large book,[1] some answer being then required. Certain men[2] go so far as to contend that it is sometimes a good and pious act to commit perjury and to utter falsehood about matters pertaining to the worship of God and even about the very nature of God. It is my opinion, however, that every lie is a sin, though it makes a great difference with what intention and in what matter the lie is uttered. A man who lies in a desire to help does not sin in

---

[1] According to the Maurists (PL 40 517), *Contra mendacium ad Consentium* is meant; according to Rivière, it is *De mendacio*.

[2] The discussion is advanced against the Priscillianists (see above, p. 376 n. 3.

the same way as does one who lies in a desire to hurt, nor is as much harm done by one who through a lie misdirects a traveller as by him whose lying deception corrupts the course of another's life. And of course anyone who utters the false while thinking it true is not to be adjudged a liar, for he is himself deceived, not consciously a deceiver. Likewise, not falsehood but sometimes rashness is to be imputed to one who through ill-considered judgment holds the false for true. On the other hand, that man is in conscience a liar who utters the true, thinking it false. For, with respect to what pertains to his intention, since he says that which he does not believe, he does not speak the truth, even if what he does say be found true. Nor is a man in any way free from falsehood who with his mouth unwittingly speaks the truth, but with his will, so far as his knowledge goes, lies. Thus, giving heed not to the matter spoken of, but only to the intention of the speaker, the man who through ignorance utters a falsity when he believes it a truth is a better man than one who knowingly intends to lie, but unwittingly utters the truth. In the former case the speaker does not think one thing and say another; in the latter, whatever in itself be the thing actually said, the speaker has one thing hid within his heart, another ready on his tongue,[3] and this evil is the very essence of lying. In considering the truth or falsity of what is actually said, however, it makes a great difference what the matter is in which a man is deceived or lies. Although, in terms of a man's will, being deceived is a lesser evil than lying, still it is far easier to tolerate a lie in matters which have nothing to do with religion than it is to tolerate being deceived in matters the belief or knowledge of which are essential to the worship of God. Examples will illustrate the point. Suppose that one person,

---

[3] Cf. Sallust, *Catil.* 10.

lying, announces that somebody who is dead is alive, while another, being deceived, believes that Christ, after however long a time, will die again. Is it not incomparably better to lie like the former than to be deceived like the latter? And is it not a matter of less grave evil to lead someone into the former error than to be led by someone into the latter?

(19) Deception, therefore, is accompanied in some cases by grave, in some cases by slight evil, in some cases by none at all, and in some, even by a measure of good. It is a great evil for a man to be deceived by not believing that which leads to eternal life or by believing that which leads to eternal death. It is a slight evil for a man to be deceived when, through taking falsehood for truth, he falls into temporal difficulties which, through faithful use of patience, he may indeed turn to good use; as if, for example, someone, believing an evil man good, should suffer some evil from him. But if in this case the deceived should not suffer any evil from the other, no evil befalls the deceived, nor does he come under the Prophet's denunciation:[4] 'Woe unto them that call evil good.' For this text is to be understood to refer not to men, but to those things which make men evil, and the Prophet's accusation is rightly applied to one who calls adultery good. But if someone should call good another whom he believes chaste, not knowing that he is an adulterer, he is deceived not in his understanding of good and evil but through the secrets of human conduct: he is calling good a man whom he believes to possess that which indubitably is good. The adulterer he would call evil, the chaste man good, and he calls good the man in question simply through not knowing that he is an adulterer and not chaste. Further, if through error a man

---

[4] Isa. 5.20.

avoids a calamity—as in the case above mentioned[5] of what befell me on the road—some good actually comes to him through the error. Still, when I speak of a man's being deceived with no evil result or even with good, it is not the error itself that I call no evil or even in some sense a good, but the avoidance of evil or the coming of good occasioned by the error; that is, what comes to pass or else what does not in consequence of the error itself. The error in itself is always an evil, grave in a grave matter or slight in a slight matter. For, is there anyone who, except through error, would deny that it is evil to accept the false for the true, or to reject the true as if it were false, or to hold what is uncertain as certain or what is certain as uncertain? But it is one thing to think a man who is evil to be good (and this is an error), and another not to suffer ulterior evil in consequence of the former evil, supposing the evil man, mistakenly thought good, should do him no injury. Likewise, it is one thing to think that a road, which is not the right one, *is,* and another to derive from this error, which is evil, some good, as, for example, to be delivered from the plotting of wicked men.

Chapter 7

(20) There are errors of a certain sort as to which I am in doubt. When one holds a good opinion of an evil man, not knowing his true nature; or when, instead of the customary perceptions through the bodily senses, things like them occur, perceived in the spirit as if in the body or in the body as if in the spirit (such as happened to the Apostle Peter,[1] when, believing he saw a vision, he was suddenly delivered by

---
5 Sect. 17.

---
1 Acts 12.9.

an angel from the chains of his prison); or when, in respect of bodily sensations themselves, the rough is believed smooth, the bitter sweet, or the ill-smelling fragrant, or when the passing of a vehicle is taken for thunder, or when, of two men very much alike, one is taken for the other (a frequent occurence in the case of twins, styled by our poet[2] 'an error pleasing to parents')—as to these and similar errors, I know not whether they should be called sins or not.

And there is another question, very knotty indeed and a source of great perplexity for the sharp-witted Academics, which I have not undertaken for solution here: Whether the wise man, for fear of falling into error by accepting the false for the true, ought to give his approval to anything—all things, as they affirm, being either hidden or uncertain. This doubt was the source of my writing three books at the very beginning of my conversion,[3] so that I might not be hindered at the very threshold of faith by this opposing doctrine. For, surely, I had to remove the hopelessness of discovering truth, a position apparently strengthened by their arguments. In their thinking, every error is considered a sin, and the one and only way of avoiding it, they contend, is by suspending all agreement. They say that whoever agrees to the uncertain is in error, and, through pointed yet impudent disputation, they contend that there is no certainty in the judgment of man, even when a proposed opinion by chance be true, since the false can indistinguishably liken itself to the true. We hold, however, that 'he who is just lives by faith.'[4] But if you do away with agreement, you do away with faith, since nothing can be believed without agreement. And there are truths, even though they not be evident, which must be believed if

---

[2] Virgil, *Aeneid* 10.392.
[3] *Contra Academicos* (PL 32 905-908; ed. P. Knöll, CSEL 63 1-81).
[4] Rom. 1.17; cf. Hab. 2.4.

we are to come to that happy life which cannot be other than eternal. Now I do not know whether we should dispute with those who not only are ignorant that there is an eternal life before them, but do not even know that they are alive in this one, claiming to be ignorant indeed where ignorance is impossible. It is inadmissible that anyone should not know that he is alive, because, if he is not alive, he cannot even be ignorant of anything, since not only knowledge but also ignorance are attributes only of the living. These men think that, by withholding assent to the proposition that they are alive, they avoid error, when actually, through erring, they prove themselves alive, since only the living can err. Therefore, just as it is not only true but also certain that we are alive, so are many things both true and certain; and God forbid that failure to assent to these things should merit the name of wisdom rather than madness.

(21) When matters are in question such that it makes no difference in gaining the kingdom of God whether they be believed or not, or whether they are true or not, or whether they be believed true or false, to be in error in these things —that is, to mistake one thing for another—should be thought not a sin at all, or, at most, a sin of the least possible consequence. An error of this kind, whatever its scope or character, does not concern the path by which we go to God, the path which is the faith in Christ that 'works through charity.'[5] Nor did that 'error pleasing to parents'[6] in the matter of the twin children involve any deviation from this path, nor the error of the Apostle Peter.[7] In thinking he saw a vision, he so mistook one thing for another as to be unable, until he parted from

---

5 Gal. 5.6.
6 See above, sect. 20.
7 *Ibid.*

the angel who had delivered him, to distinguish the corporeal images among which he thought he was from the true bodies which in fact surrounded him. The case is the same with the Patriarch Jacob,[8] when he mistakenly believed his son had been slain by a wild beast. In the case of these and similar false impressions we are deceived with no offense to the faith which we have in God; we can err without leaving the path which leads us to Him. Yet such errors, even if they are not sins, are to be classed among the evils of this life, which is so far subject to vanity[9] that we accept what is false as if it were true, we reject what is true as if it were false, and we hold what is uncertain as if it were certain. These facts involve no departure from that faith through which we tread the true and certain path to eternal blessedness, but they do contribute to that wretchedness in which we still find ourselves. And, surely, we would never in any way be deceived, whether through the soul's sense or the body's, if we were now enjoying that true and perfect happiness.

(22) But every lie must be called a sin, because man, not only when he himself knows what is true, but also when as man he errs or is deceived, should speak that which is in his heart, whether such be true or whether he believes it so when it is not. Whoever lies speaks with a wish to deceive, contrary to what he thinks in his heart. Speech itself was instituted not to serve for men as a means of mutual deception, but that each might bring his own thoughts to the knowledge of another. Therefore, to use speech for deception, contrary to the purpose of its institution, is a sin. Sometimes we can benefit another by lying, but this gives us no reason for thinking there is any lie which is not a sin. We could likewise help

---

8 Gen. 37.33.
9 Cf. Rom. 8.20.

somebody by stealing, if the poor man to whom the stolen object is given is benefitted, while the rich man, from whom it was taken, feels no loss; yet no one will on that account say that such a theft is not a sin. Or by adultery, if a woman seems certain to die of love unless we consent to her in this, but might, should she live, purify herself by confession; yet no one will deny that such an act of adultery is a sin. But, if we justly value chastity so highly, what is there in truth which so offends us that a wish to help another will not permit our violating the former virtue by adultery, but will not prevent our violating the latter by lying? Men who lie only to prevent harm to another have indeed made substantial progress toward the good, and there is no denying it. But that which in their advance is justly praised or even may receive temporal remuneration is their benevolence and not their deception. It is enough that the latter be pardoned without its being commended, especially among the inheritors of the new covenant, to whom it is said:[10] 'Let your speech be "Yea yea, nay nay"; and whatever is beyond these is of evil.' And it is on account of this evil, which in this mortal life does not cease to creep in, that even the co-heirs of Christ themselves say:[11] 'Forgive us our debts.'

Chapter 8

(23) The foregoing matters have now been treated with the brevity demanded by the present book. The next requirement is to learn what are the causes of good and evil, so much of them, at least, as is required for the path which leads us to the kingdom where there will be life without death, truth without error, happiness without sorrow. To this question we

---
10 Matt. 5.37.
11 Matt. 6.12.

must unhesitatingly reply that the cause of the good things in which we are concerned is none other than the goodness of God, while the cause of evil things is a desertion from the unchangeable good on the part of the will of the changeable good, first in the case of the angels and then in that of man.

(24) This is the first evil experienced by the rational creation, that is, its first privation of good. There then stealthily entered in, unwanted, ignorance of duty and lust after harmful things, slyly joined as companions by error and pain, and when the mind shrinks, upon sensing these two evils to be imminent, there is that which is called fear. Further, the mind, when it obtains its desires, impeded by error from perceiving that they are destructive or empty, is overmastered by an unwholesome delectation or even puffed up by an empty joy. From these sources of vice, rising not out of abundance but out of deficiency, springs all the wretchedness of the rational nature. (25) This nature, however, amidst its evils, could not lose its appetite for happiness.

Now the evils just named are the common heritage of those, be they men or angels, who were condemned for their wickedness by the justice of the Lord. But, through a penalty peculiarly his own, man was punished also by the death of the body. God had indeed threatened man with the suffering of death, if he should sin.[1] Endowing him with free will, but putting him under obedience and pain of death, He placed man in the happiness of paradise (as if giving him a foreshadowing of life

---

[1] Gen. 2.17; 3.19. With this sentence begins the excerpt from the *Enchiridion* which supplies to the Roman Breviary the second nocturn lessons for matins of Septuagesima Sunday. The excerpt runs through the second sentence of sect. 27, where occurs the classic phrase *massa damnata*. For this phrase, as for *massa perditionis* and others of like meaning used by St. Augustine, see A. M. Jacquin, O.P. in *Misc. Agost.* II 862 n. 2.

to come); thence, if he should maintain justice, he should rise to better things.

(26)[2] After his sin, man was driven from paradise into exile. His whole race, corrupted by sin in him as in its root, he involved in the penalty of death and condemnation: whatever offspring might be born from him and his wife (through whom he had sinned and with whom he was condemned), born through carnal lust (a punishment imposed in the likeness of his disobedience), this offspring should inherit the original sin, and by this it would be drawn, through divers errors and sufferings, unto the last, endless punishment, sharing it with the fallen angels, their corruptors and masters and companions in doom. Thus, 'through one man sin entered into the world and through sin death, and thus death has passed into all men because all have sinned.'[3] In this place the Apostle uses 'the world' to mean the whole human race.

(27) Thus, then, matters stood. Lying prostrate and wallowing in wretchedness, the condemned mass of the human race was being thrown from evils to new evils; joined by those of the angels who had sinned, it suffered punishments altogether deserved by its impious rebellion. Whatever the evil freely do through blind and unbridled concupiscence, and whatever they unwillingly suffer in punishments manifest or concealed, pertain to the just wrath of God. Yet the goodness of the Creator does not fail to supply even to the evil angels that provision of life and quickening-power without which they would perish; nor for men, springing though they do from a corrupted and condemned stock, does He fail to form and vivify their seed, justly to dispose their bodily parts, and in all

---

2 The discussion is advanced against the Pelagianists (see above p. 376 n. 3).
3 Rom. 5.12.

changes of season and place to enliven their senses and give provision of food. He judged it better to bring good out of evil than not to permit evil to exist at all. And indeed, if He had willed that with men as with the fallen angels there should be absolutely no change for the better, would it not rightly have come about that man's nature which had deserted God, had misused its power to spurn and transgress the command of its Creator (which it might easily have heeded), which had profaned the image of that Creator that was within it by insolently turning away from His light, and which by an evil use of free will had broken off a wholesome servitude under His laws—should altogether and forever be deserted by the Creator and deservedly suffer eternal punishment? Surely, God would have acted just so if He had not been merciful as well as just and shown forth that mercy of His which is beyond justice, and more plainly so in comparison with the unworthiness of its beneficiaries.

Chapter 9

(28) Now, when some of the angels in their pride and impiety had deserted God and from their habitation in the upper heavens had been cast down into the lowest darkness of this air of ours, the remaining angels abode with God in eternal blessedness and sanctity. For it was not that all the other angels had sprung from one who had fallen and been condemned (whence, as with men, they would have been successively bound by the chains of an original evil and all forced to their due punishment). Rather, when he who became the Devil, along with the companions of his impiety, had been exalted in pride and through that exaltation had, with them, fallen low, all the others remained united to their Lord in dutiful obedience and, unlike the others, received

from Him a sure knowledge which would exempt them from worry concerning their eternal security and freedom from any possible fall. (29) And so it pleased God, creator and moderator of the universe, that, since not all the host of angels had rebelled and so perished, that portion which had perished should remain in perpetual perdition. While the faithful portion should abide with Him, enjoying a happiness surely known to be unending, that other rational creature, which was man, having totally perished through sins and punishments, whether hereditary or incurred through personal guilt, should, by divine agency, be restored and fill out the ranks of the angelic company, which had been diminished through the fall of the Devil. For it had been promised to the saints that upon their resurrection they would be the equals of the angels of God.[1] Thus the heavenly Jerusalem, our mother, city of God,[2] will not be cheated of its full complement of citizens and may even reign over a still more numerous population. We do not know the number of the saints or of those unclean demons into whose place the children of the holy mother called barren[3] on earth shall succeed, to abide without limit of time in that peace from which the rebellious had fallen. The number of these citizens, such as it is now or is to be, is known to the contemplation of that Artificer who 'calls things that are not as though they were'[4] and 'orders things in measure and number and weight.'[5]

(30) But that part of the human race to which God had promised release and the eternal kingdom, could it be restored through the merits of its own works? God forbid. What good

---

1 Cf. Matt. 22.30; Luke 20.36.
2 Cf. Gal. 4.26; Apoc. 21.2.
3 Cf. Isa. 54.1; quoted Gal. 4.27.
4 Rom. 4.17.
5 Wisd. 11.21.

can a condemned man do except as he has been released from his condemnation? Can he by the free decision of his own will? Here again, God forbid. Man misusing his free will destroys both himself and it. A man who kills himself does so, indeed, while he is living; but, in killing himself, no longer lives and cannot restore himself to life. So also, when he has sinned through free will, sin is victorious and his free will is lost; 'for by whatever a man is overcome, of this also he is the slave.'[6] The sentence quoted is from the Apostle Peter. Since it is surely true, what liberty, I ask, can a slave have except when it pleases him to sin. For that service is liberty which freely does the will of the master. Accordingly, he is free to sin who is the servant of sin. Wherefore, no one is free to do right who has not been freed from sin and begins to be the servant of justice. And such is true liberty because he has the joy of right-doing, and at the same time dutiful servitude because he obeys the precept. But, for the man sold into the bondage of sin, where will that freedom of right-doing come from unless he be redeemed by Him who said:[7] 'If the Son makes you free, you will be free indeed'? If this operation has not begun in a man and he is not yet free to do right, how can he glory in free will and in good works, unless he puffs himself up with foolish pride? And this it was that the Apostle spoke against when he said:[8] 'By grace you have been saved through faith.' (31) And lest his hearers should claim that faith itself for themselves, not understanding it to be given of God—as elsewhere the same Apostle says[9] that he has obtained mercy in order to be faithful—in this place also he adds:[10] 'And that not from yourselves, for it is the gift of

---

[6] 2 Peter 2.19.
[7] John 8.36.
[8] Eph. 2.8.
[9] 1 Cor. 7.25.
[10] Eph. 2.8-9.

God; not as the outcome of works, lest anyone may boast.' And, lest it might be thought that good works will fail in those who believe, he adds this also:[11] 'For his workmanship we are, created in Christ Jesus in good works, which God has made ready beforehand that we may walk in them.' We shall be made truly free, then, when God fashions, that is, forms and creates us, not as men—for that He has already done—but to be good men, which He now accomplishes by His grace; that we may be in Christ a new creature,[12] according as it is written:[13] 'Create a *clean* heart in me, O God.' (For God had already created his heart insofar as the physical nature of the human heart is concerned.) (32) Perhaps someone would boast not indeed of his works, but of his free will, as if merit took its beginning from that and the very liberty of good action should be granted to it as a due reward. If so, let him hear yet these words of the same preacher of grace:[14] 'For it is God who of his good pleasure works in you both the will and the performance.' And in another place:[15] 'So, then, there is question not of him who wills nor of him who runs but of God showing mercy.' Now there is no doubt that, if a man has attained the age of reason, he cannot believe, hope, or love unless he wills, nor attain to the prize of God's heavenly call[16] unless he runs voluntarily. How is it true, then, that 'there is question not of him who wills nor of him who runs, but of God showing mercy,'[17] unless because, as it is written,[18] 'the preparation of the will is from the Lord'? Otherwise, if the

---

11 Eph. 2.10.
12 2 Cor. 5.17; cf. Gal. 6.15.
13 Ps. 50.12.
14 Phil. 2.13.
15 Rom. 9.16.
16 Phil. 3.14.
17 Rom. 9.16.
18 Prov. 8.35 (Septuagint).

verse, 'there is question not of him who wills nor of him who runs, but of God showing mercy,' is meant of both things — that is, the will of man and the mercy of God, so that we are to understand the words 'there is question not of him who wills nor of him who runs, but of God showing mercy' as if saying: The will of man alone is not enough, if the mercy of God be not also present—then neither is the mercy of God alone enough, if the will of man be not also present. Accordingly, if we may rightly say 'there is question not of man who wills, but of God showing mercy' (since the will of man alone fails of accomplishment), why then may we not rightly say 'There is question not of God showing mercy, but of man who wills' (since the mercy of God alone fails of accomplishment)? But if no Christian, for fear of openly contradicting the Apostle, will dare say 'There is question not of God showing mercy, but of man who wills,' it follows that the only proper interpretation of the verse, 'There is question not of him who wills nor of him who runs, but of God showing mercy,' is to ascribe all to God, who both makes the good will of man ready to be helped and helps it when it has been made ready. Man's good will precedes many of God's gifts, but not all; and among those which it does not precede it must itself be counted. In Holy Scripture we read both of the following: 'His mercy shall go before me'[19] and 'His mercy will follow me.'[20] It goes before the unwilling that he may be willing; it follows the willing that he may not will in vain.[21] Why are we admonished to pray for our enemies,[22] as for men unwilling to lead a holy life, unless it be that God may work willingness in them?[23]

---

19 Ps. 58.11.
20 Ps. 22.6.
21 For the doctrine contained in the latter part of this section (*Ench. Patr.* no. 1914), see Portalié, cols. 2369, 2385, 2392, 2401, 2406.
22 Cf. Matt. 5.44.
23 Cf. Phil. 2.13.

Likewise, why are we admonished to ask that we may receive,[24] unless it be that what we wish may be brought about by Him who has Himself created the wish? We pray for our enemies, then, so that the mercy of God may go before them as it also goes before us; we pray for ourselves so that His mercy may follow us.

Chapter 10

(33) And so the human race was held fast in a just condemnation, and all men were children of wrath—of that wrath of which it is written:[1] 'All our days are spent; and in Thy wrath we have fainted away. Our years shall be considered as a spider.' Or as Job says,[2] of this same wrath: 'Man, born of a woman, living for a short time, is full of wrath.' And of this wrath the Lord Jesus also speaks:[3] 'He who believes in the Son has everlasting life; he who does not believe in the Son does not have life, but the wrath of God rests upon him.' He does not say it 'will come' but it 'rests' upon him, for every man is born with it. And that is why the Apostle says:[4] 'We were by nature children of wrath even as the rest.' Since men were lying under this wrath because of original sin—sin still more heavy and destructive in proportion as the sins added upon it were great or numerous—there was the need for a mediator, that is, a reconciler, who would placate this wrath by the offering of one sacrifice, of which all the sacrifices under the Law and the prophets were foreshadowings.[5] Where-

---

24 Cf. Matt. 7.7.

1 Ps. 89.9.
2 Job 14.1 (Septuagint)
3 John 3.36.
4 Eph. 2.3.
5 On the doctrine of reconciliation contained in this and the preceding sentence (*Ench. Patr.* no. 1915), see Portalié, col. 2369.

fore, the Apostle says:[6] 'For if, when we were enemies, we were reconciled to God by the death of his Son, much more, having now been reconciled by his blood, shall we be saved through him from the wrath.' Now when God is said to be angry, we do not ascribe to Him any such disturbance of the spirit as we do to an angry man, but, by a transfer of the word from human emotions, His vengeance, which is completely just, receives the name of wrath. So the fact that we through a mediator are reconciled to God and receive the Holy Spirit, so as to become sons from once being enemies—'for whoever are led by the Spirit of God, they are the sons of God,'[7]—this is by the grace of God through Jesus Christ our Lord.

(34)[8] To say about the Mediator as much as would be worthy of Him would occupy too much space, and indeed no man could say these things in a befitting manner. Who could expound in words apt to their subject the single statement,[9] 'The Word was made flesh, and dwelt among us,' so that we might believe in the only Son of God the Father Almighty, born of the Holy Spirit and the Virgin Mary?[10] 'The Word was made flesh': flesh was assumed by Divinity; Divinity was not changed into flesh. Further, we must understand 'flesh' here to mean man, the part signifying the whole, as

---

6 Rom. 5.10,9.
7 Rom. 8.14.
8 Against the Appollinarists (see above, p. 376 n. 3).
9 John 1.14.
10 The expression 'from the Holy Spirit *and* the Virgin Mary' is not uncommon in early texts of the Creeds. Cf. Denziger, nos. 2 (*Psalt. Aethelstani*) and 9; F. J. Badcock, *The history of the Creeds* (2nd ed. London 1938) 11 and 283 (Index, *s.v.* 'Of the Holy Ghost and the Virgin Mary'). Other works of St. Augustine are more fruitful than the *Enchiridion* in reconstructing early texts of the Creeds (Denziger, no. 4), but, among others, Badcock (pp. 107, 229) makes some use of it, as had A. E. Burn, *An introduction to the Creeds* (London 1899) 136 f., 140, 146, 304. See below, p. 403 n. 1.

when it is said:[11] 'For by the works of the law no flesh shall be justified,' that is, 'no man.' It is not right to say that any part was lacking in that human nature He put on, except that it was a human nature altogether free from any bond of sin; not such as is born from the union of the sexes through fleshly concupiscence under the obligation of that sin whose guilt is washed away in regeneration, but such as it was fitting should be born of a virgin, conceived by the mother's faith, not by lust. And if her virginity were marred even in His being born, then He would not have been born of a virgin. And the doctrine that He was born of the Virgin Mary would be false, which God forbid, a doctrine declared by the whole Church, which in imitation of His mother daily brings forth members of His body and remains a virgin. It may please you to read a letter on the virginity of the holy Mary which I wrote to the illustrious Volusianus,[12] whom I here name with honor and affection. (35)[13] Accordingly, Christ Jesus the Son of God is both God and man: God before all ages, man in this age of ours; God because He was the Word of God (for 'the Word was God'[14]), man because in the unity of His person there was joined to the Word a body and a rational soul. Accordingly, insofar as He is God, Himself and the Father are one;[15] insofar as He is man, the Father is greater than He.[16] When He was the only Son of God, not by grace, but by nature, so that He might be also full of grace, He became also the Son of man. He has Himself both natures, and from these two natures is one Christ. 'Though he was in the form of God, he thought

---

11 Rom. 3.20.
12 *Epist.* 137 (PL 33 515-525; ed. A. Goldbacher, CSEL 34 96-125).
13 Against the position later to be held by the Nestorians.
14 John 1.1.
15 Cf. John 10.30.
16 Cf. John 14.28.

it not robbery to be'—what He was by nature—'equal with God, but emptied himself, taking the form of a servant,'[17] neither losing nor diminishing the form of God. Accordingly, He both became less and remained equal, being both in one, as has been said. As the Word, He was one of these; as man, the other: as Word, He is equal with the Father; as man, He is less. One person, He is the Son of God and also the Son of man; one person, He is the Son of man and also the Son of God; not two sons of God, God and man, but one Son of God; God without beginning, man from a beginning, our Lord, Jesus Christ.

Chapter 11

(36) Here we have the grace of God shown forth in a manner altogether sublime and clear. What had the human nature in the man Christ deserved that it should be taken up, in a fashion without parallel, into the unity of the person of the only Son of God? What good will, whose firm and good intention, what good works had gone before to make that man worthy to become one person with God? Had He been a man before and this singular benefit of deserving to be God been bestowed on Him? Surely not. For, from the moment in which He began to be man, He was nothing other than the Son of God, and the only Son of God. As God He was the Word, who, taking on human nature, became flesh and yet was truly God. Just as any man unites in one person a rational soul and a body, so Christ in one person unites the Word and man. How is it that such honor—undeserved surely, since no merit had gone before—came to human nature, unless there be here a clear manifestation, to men of faith and sober reflection, of the power of God's free grace, that

---

17 Phil. 2.6-7.

men may know that they are justified from their sins by the same grace which enabled the man Christ to be free from the possibility of sin. And so the angel saluted His mother, announcing the coming birth with the words, 'Hail, full of grace';[1] and shortly afterwards,[2] 'Thou hast found grace with God.' And she is called full of grace and said to have found grace with God, that she might be the mother of her Lord, yea of the Lord of all things and all men. Speaking of Christ Himself, the Evangelist John, when he had said,[3] 'And the Word was made flesh, and dwelt among us,' added: 'And we saw his glory—glory as of the only-begotten of the Father —full of grace and of truth.' When he says, 'The Word was made flesh,' this is 'full of grace'; when he says 'the glory of the only-begotten of the Father,' this is 'full of truth.' For the Truth Himself, the only-begotten of the Father (not by grace but by nature), by grace took on human nature and so united it to His person that He was at the same time the Son of man.

(37) The same Jesus Christ, the Only-begotten, that is, the only Son of God, our Lord, was born of the Holy Spirit and the Virgin Mary. Now the Holy Spirit is the gift of God, the gift being Himself equal to the giver. Therefore the Holy Spirit also is God, not inferior to the Father or the Son. And the fact that the birth of Christ in His human nature was by the Holy Spirit is surely a further manifestation of grace. For, when the Virgin asked the angel how what he had announced might come about, seeing that she did not know man, the angel answered:[4] 'The Holy Spirit shall come

---

1 Luke 1.28.
2 Luke 1.30.
3 John 1.14.
4 Luke 1.35.

upon thee and the power of the Most High shall overshadow thee; and therefore the Holy One to be born shall be called the Son of God.' And Joseph, when he wished to put her away, suspecting that she was an adulteress, knowing that she was not with child by him, received this answer from the angel:[5] 'Do not be afraid to take to thee Mary thy wife, for that which is begotten in her is of the Holy Spirit,' that is, what you suspect is from another man, is of the Holy Spirit.

Chapter 12

(38) But are we to say that the Holy Spirit is the father of the man Christ, and that as God the Father begot the Word, so the Holy Spirit begot the man, the one Christ deriving from the double substance, being as the Word the Son of God the Father, and in His human nature the Son of the Holy Spirit, because the Holy Spirit as a father begot Christ of His virgin mother? Who will dare to say this? There is no need to show through disputation what other absurdities would follow in consequence, since this proposition is itself so manifestly absurd as to be altogether intolerable to the ears of the faithful. Hence, as we confess,[1] our Lord Jesus Christ, who of God is God, and was born as man of the Holy Spirit and the Virgin Mary, is, by the two substances, the divine and the human, the only Son of God the Father Almighty, from whom the Holy Spirit proceeds. How, then, do we say that Christ was born of the Holy Spirit if the Holy Spirit did not beget Him? Is it that He made Him? Since Jesus Christ is God, 'all things were made through Him,'[2] yet as He is

---

5 Matt. 1.20.

---

1 That is, in the Creed. Some of the phrases which follow may come from an early Creed-text; see above, p. 399 n. 10.
2 John 1.3.

man, He was Himself made, as the Apostle says:³ 'He was made according to the flesh from the seed of David.' But since that created thing which the Virgin conceived and bore, although pertaining only to the person of the Son, was made by the whole Trinity (for the works of the Trinity are not separable), why should the Holy Spirit alone be named with respect to making it? Or is it that, when one of the Three is named in respect of a certain work, the whole Trinity is to be understood to operate? So indeed it is, and it can be shown by examples. But we need no longer dwell on this problem, which essentially is this: How can we say 'born of the Holy Spirit' when He is in no wise the Son of the Holy Spirit? The fact that God made the world does not make it right to say that the world is the son of God, or that it was born of God, but rather that it was made, created, founded, instituted, or whatever form of expression we can properly use. In this case, when we confess that He was born of the Holy Spirit and the Virgin Mary, it is difficult to explain how He is not the Son of the Holy Spirit but is the Son of the Virgin, when He was born both of Him and of her. There is no doubt that He was not born of the Holy Spirit as His Father in the same sense in which He was born of the Virgin as His mother.

(39) It need not be granted, then, that whatever is born of something is consequently to be called the son of that same thing. There is no need of saying that in one sense a son is born of a man, in another a hair, a louse, a stomach-worm, none of these last being a son. We may pass these examples by as detracting from the sublime subject in hand. Yet, surely, those who are born of water and the Holy Spirit[4]

---

3 Rom. 1.3.
4 John 3.5.

would not by anyone rightly be called sons of the water, though they are called sons of God the Father and of Mother Church. Just so, then, there was born of the Holy Spirit the Son of God the Father, not the Son of the Holy Spirit. The foregoing examples of the hair and the other things at least have the value of reminding us that not everything that is born of something is to be called the son of that of which it is born, just as it does not follow that all who are called the sons of anyone are to be said to be born of him, for some sons are adopted. We speak of 'sons of hell,'[5] not as born of hell, but as made ready for it, just as those are 'sons of the kingdom'[6] who are being made ready for it. (40) Since, then, a thing may be born of something, yet in such a way as not to be its son, and, again, since not everyone who is called son is born of him whose son he is said to be, surely the plan by which Christ was born of the Holy Spirit, but not as son, and of the Virgin Mary, yet as son, manifests to us the grace of God. For it was by this grace that a man, without any antecedent merits, in the very inception of his existence, was so united in one person to God the Word that the very same person was Son of God who was Son of man, and the very same person was Son of man who was Son of God. Thus, in the taking on of the human nature, the grace itself somehow became so natural to the man as to admit no possibility of sin. And the reason why it was right that this grace be signified by the Holy Spirit was that He has proper attributes as God which make Him even called the 'gift of God.'[7]—To deal with this subject sufficiently (if indeed such a thing is possible) would be matter for an extended discussion.

---

5 Matt. 23.15.
6 Matt. 8.12; 13.38.
7 John 4.10; Acts 8.20.

Chapter 13

(41) Begotten and conceived, then, without any concupiscent pleasure of the flesh, He therefore inherited no original sin. Joined also by the grace of God to the Word, by nature not by grace the only-begotten Son of the Father, in a wondrous and ineffable unity of person, He Himself could commit no sin. Still, because of the 'likeness of sinful flesh'[1] in which He came, He was Himself actually called sin,[2] since He was to be sacrificed for the washing away of sins. Under the old law, indeed, sacrifices for sins are called sins,[3] while He, of whom those sacrifices were shadows and types, was actually made sin. Accordingly, when the Apostle says:[4] 'We exhort you, for Christ's sake, be reconciled to God,' he immediately adds:[5] 'Him, who knew no sin, he made to be sin for us, so that in him we might become the justice of God.' The Apostle did not say (as is read in certain faulty copies): 'He who knew no sin committed sin for us,' as if Christ Himself sinned for our sakes. What he said is this: 'Him who knew no sin' (that is, Christ) *God,* to whom we are to be reconciled, 'made to be sin for us,' that is, a sacrifice for sins by which we might be reconciled. He, then, is sin, as we are justice, yet not our justice but God's, not in us but in Him, just as He is not His own sin but ours,[6] sin found not in Himself but in us.[7] He, 'by the likeness of sinful flesh' in

---

1 Rom. 8.3.
2 2 Cor. 5.21.
3 E.g., Osee 4.8.
4 2 Cor. 5.20.
5 2 Cor. 5.21.
6 For some of the doctrine of the Incarnation contained in the early part of this section (*Ench. Patr.* no. 1916), see Portalié, cols. 2362, 2369.
7 Punctuating after *constitutum,* where Scheel (28 line 30) has no punctuation.

which He was crucified, showed that, whereas no sin was in Him, still in some sense He died to sin, in dying to the flesh in which was the likeness of sin; and that, while He Himself had never lived the old life of sin, He made His resurrection the symbol of our new life, quickened out of the old life of sin in which we had been destined to die. (42) Such is the meaning of the great sacrament of baptism which is solemnized among us: that those who attain to this grace die to sin, just as we say He died to sin, in that He died to the flesh, that is, to the likeness of sin; and that they live through being reborn at the font (whatever may be the age of the body), just as He lived rising again from the tomb.

(43) Just as no one, from the newborn babe to the old man, is to be barred from baptism, so there is no one who in baptism does not die to sin. While infants die only to original sin, adults die as well to all those sins which through bad living they have added to the sin they inherited upon birth. (44) But even these latter are said to die to sin, though doubtless it is not to one sin that they die but to all the many sins they have committed by thought, word, or deed: for the singular number frequently serves to indicate the plural, as in the line,[8] 'They fill its belly with the armed soldier,' when in fact it took many soldiers to accomplish this. Similarly, in our own Scriptures we read:[9] 'Pray then to the Lord that he may take away from us this serpent.' The speaker, in expressing his meaning, does not say 'serpents,' though the people were suffering from many. And there are countless similar examples. When, however, the original sin is expressed

---

8 Virgil, *Aeneid* 2.20. Servius in his note on this line (editio Harvardiana II 322) calls attention to the use of the singular number for the plural here and gives an example from the *Aeneid* of the converse figure, which is noted just below by St. Augustine.
9 Num. 21.7 (Septuagint).

in the plural number—when we say that infants are baptized 'for the forgiveness of *sins*,' rather than 'for the forgiveness of *sin*,'—this is the converse figure of speech, the use of the plural number for the singular. Thus, in the Gospel we read, after the death of Herod:[10] 'For those are dead who sought the child's life,' not '*he* is dead.' And in Exodus:[11] 'They have made to themselves gods of gold,' when it was one golden calf they had made, saying of it:[12] 'These are thy gods, O Israel, that have brought thee out of the land of Egypt,' here also using plural for singular. (45) Yet in the case of that single sin which through one man entered into the world and passed into all men,[13] wherefore even infants are baptized, many sins may be understood, if the one sin be divided, as it were, into its many component members. For there is pride in it, because man chose to be under his own power rather than under God's; and sacrilege, because he did not believe God; and murder, because he plunged himself into death; and spiritual fornication, because the singleness of the human mind was corrupted by the serpent's persuasion; and theft, because he had misappropriated the forbidden food; and avarice, because he had sought after more than was to have sufficed for him; and whatever other sin a careful search could discover in this one offense.

(46) It is said, with probable correctness, that infants are bound by the sins of their parents, not only by those of the first pair, but also those of their own parents, from whom they were born. The divine judgment, 'I shall visit the sins of the fathers upon their children,'[14] applies to them before they

---
10 Matt. 2.20.
11 Exod. 32.31.
12 Exod. 32.4
13 Cf. Rom. 5.12.
14 Exod. 20.5; Deut. 5.9 (both Septuagint).

enter upon the new covenant through regeneration. That covenant was foretold when it was said, through Ezechiel,[15] that sons would not bear the sins of their fathers, and that it would no longer be a proverb in Israel[16] 'Our fathers have eaten a sour grape, and the teeth of the children are set on edge.'[17] For this is the purpose of rebirth, that a man may be freed from whatever of sin he was born with. Sins which are later committed through evil actions may be healed also through repentance, which in fact after baptism we see done. Accordingly, there is no other reason for the institution of rebirth than that the first birth was sinful; so far so that even one born of lawful wedlock says:[18] 'I was conceived in iniquities: and in sins did my mother nourish me in the womb.' He did not say 'in iniquity' and 'in sin' (though these also he could have said rightly), but preferred to say 'iniquities' and 'sins.' For in that one sin which passed into all men and is so great that thereby human nature was changed and brought to the necessity of death, many sins are found, as I explained above.[19] And there are also the further sins of the immediate parents, which, while unable to change nature, still bind the children under guilt, unless unmerited grace and divine mercy come to their aid. (47) A question is very justly raised about the sins of the other progenitors intervening between Adam and a man's own parents: It may be that anyone who is born is implicated in all their evil deeds and their multiplied original guilt, in such fashion that the later a man is born the worse is his condition. Or it may be that God threatens the

---

15 Cf. Ezech. 18.20.
16 Ezech. 18.2.
17 *Ibid.*
18 Ps. 50.7. The reading 'nourish me in the womb' (instead of 'conceive me') is also found in the 6th or 7th century Verona Psalter MS, Cod. Capit. I (1), *R*, a pure African text of the Psalms.
19 Sect. 45.

descendants unto the third and fourth generation with the sins of their fathers, because He does not extend His anger against the sins of the progenitors farther than the measure of His mercy permits, lest those on whom the grace of rebirth is not conferred should, in their own eternal damnation, be overwhelmed with too great a burden, if forced to bear as original guilt all the sins of the whole line of progenitors from the very beginning of the human race, and to pay the penalties due to those sins. Or it may be that some other solution of this weighty problem could be found if the Holy Scriptures were more diligently searched and compared. Between these three possibilities I am not so bold as to choose.

Chapter 14

(48) Nevertheless, that one sin, so great in view of the happiness of the place and circumstances in which it was committed, that in one man the whole human race in its origin and, so to speak, in its very root was condemned, this sin is not loosened and washed away except through a single mediator between God and men,[1] the man Christ Jesus, who alone could so be born that He had no need of rebirth. (49) Now, they were not reborn who were baptized by the baptism of John (by whom Christ Himself was baptized), but, through the ministry of that precursor, who cried[2] 'Make ready the way for the Lord,' they were being prepared for the one Person, in whom alone they could be reborn. The baptism of Christ is not in water only, as was John's baptism, but also in the Holy Spirit,[3] so that whoever believes in Christ might be reborn by that Spirit in generation from whom Christ

---

[1] Cf. 1 Tim. 2.5.
[2] Cf. Matt. 3.3.
[3] Cf. Mark 1.8; John 3.5.

needed no rebirth. So, those words of the Father which were heard from above at Christ's baptism,[4] 'This day have I begotten thee,' do not refer to that one day of time on which He was baptized, but to the one day of an unchangeable eternity, so as to show that this man is one in person with the Only-begotten. For a day which does not begin from the end of yesterday nor end with the beginning of tomorrow is always today. Christ wished to be baptized in water by John, not that any iniquity in Him might be washed away, but that He might show forth the depth of His humility. Baptism found in Him nothing to wash away, just as death found nothing to punish. In strict justice, then, not through violence of power, was the Devil overwhelmed and conquered. Since he had most wickedly slain Him who was without sin, through that same Person he most justly deserved to lose mastery of those whom he held in the bondage of sin. Both of these things, then, baptism and death, He underwent as part of a fixed dispensation, not through a pitiable necessity, but rather through the mercy of His will, that One might take away the sin of the world,[5] just as one had brought sin into the world,[6] that is, into the whole human race. (50) But with this difference: the first man brought one sin into the world, but this man took away not that one sin alone, but at the same time all which He found added to it. Consequently, the Apostle says:[7] 'Nor is the gift as it was in the case of one man's sin, for the judgment was from one man unto condemnation, but grace is from many offenses unto justification.' That one sin which we bring with us from our beginning, even if it were alone, makes us subject to damnation; but grace brings justifi-

---

4 Ps. 2.7. Cf. Matt. 3.17; Heb. 1.5; 5.5.
5 Cf. John 1.29.
6 Cf. Rom. 5.12.
7 Rom. 5.16.

cation from many offenses to man, who has committed many sins of his very own, besides that one sin which from his beginning he carries with him in common with all men.

(51) Yet a little later comes this verse:[8] 'Therefore as from the offense of the one man the result was unto condemnation to all men, so from the justice of the one the result is unto justification of life to all men.' This clearly shows that no one is born from Adam without being subject to damnation, and that no one is freed from damnation but through rebirth in Christ. (52) Now, when the Apostle had said as much about the penalty brought on by one man and the grace effected through one man as he judged sufficient for that portion of his letter, he then speaks of the holy baptism in the cross of Christ, and shows that baptism in Christ is nothing other than a likeness of the death of Christ,[9] and that the death of Christ crucified is nothing other than a likeness of the forgiveness of sin. Just as in Him there was a true death, so in us there is a true forgiveness of sins; just as in Him there was a true resurrection, so in us there is a true justification. For he says:[10] 'What then shall we say? Shall we continue in sin that grace may abound?' For he had said earlier:[11] 'But where the offense has abounded, grace has abounded yet more.' So he puts to himself the question: Whether for the sake of the consequent abundance of grace there should be a continuance in sin. But he answers:[12] 'By no means!' and adds:[13] 'If we are dead to sin, how shall we still live in

---

8 Rom. 5.18.
9 Cf. Rom. 6.3.
10 Rom. 6.1.
11 Rom. 5.20.
12 Rom. 6.2.
13 *Ibid.*

it?' Then, to show that we are dead to sin, he says:[14] 'Do you not know that all we who have been baptized into Christ Jesus have been baptized into his death?' If, then, this passage shows that we are dead to sin, since we have been baptized into the death of Christ, it follows that even infants who are baptized into Christ die to sin, since they are baptized into His death. For no exception was made to the statement:[15] 'All we who have been baptized into Christ Jesus have been baptized into his death.' And this is said to prove that we are dead to sin. But to what sin do infants die in being reborn, except to that which they brought with them in birth? Consequently, what follows in the letter applies also to them:[16] 'For we were buried with him by means of baptism into death, in order that, just as Christ has arisen from the dead through the glory of the Father, so we also may walk in newness of life. For if we have been united with him in the likeness of his death, we shall be so in the likeness of his resurrection also. For we know that our old self has been crucified with him, in order that the body of sin may be destroyed, that we may no longer be slaves to sin; for he who is dead is acquitted of sin. But if we have died with Christ, we believe that we shall also live together with Christ; for we know that Christ, having risen from the dead, dies now no more. Death shall no longer have dominion over him. For the death that he died, he died to sin once for all, but the life that he lives, he lives unto God. Thus do you consider yourselves also as dead to sin, but alive to God in Christ Jesus.' Now, the Apostle had begun by proving that we should not continue in sin in order that grace might abound,[17] and had

---

14 Rom. 6.3.
15 *Ibid.*
16 Rom. 6.4-11.
17 Rom. 6.1.

said:[18] 'If we are dead to sin, how shall we live in it?' And to show that we are dead to sin, he had added:[19] 'Do you not know that all we who have been baptized into Christ Jesus have been baptized into his death?' Thus he ends the whole passage as he began it. For he has introduced the death of Christ in such a way as to imply that He, too, is dead to sin. To what sin did He die, unless to the flesh in which there was—not sin, but the likeness of sin, and which therefore was called by the name of sin? And so to those baptized into the death of Christ, into which not only adults but also infants are baptized, he says:[20] 'Thus do you consider yourselves also as dead to sin,' that is, as was Christ, 'but alive to God in Christ Jesus.'

(53) What, then, was wrought upon the cross of Christ, in His burial, in His resurrection on the third day, in His ascension into Heaven, in His sitting at the right hand of the Father was so wrought as to serve as a model for the life which the Christian here leads, and in reality, not simply as a mystical showing-forth in words. In reference to His crucifixion, it is written:[21] 'And they who belong to Jesus Christ have crucified their flesh with its passions and desires.' With reference to His burial:[22] 'For we were buried with Christ by means of baptism into death.' With reference to His resurrection:[23] 'In order that, just as Christ has arisen from the dead through the glory of the Father, so also we walk in newness of life.' With reference to His ascension into

---

18 Rom. 6.2.
19 Rom. 6.3.
20 Rom. 6.11.
21 Gal. 5.24.
22 Rom. 6.4.
23 *Ibid.*

Heaven and His sitting at the right hand of the Father:[24] 'If, then, you have risen with Christ, seek the things that are above, where Christ is seated at the right hand of God. Mind the things that are above, not the things that are on earth. For you have died, and your life is hidden with Christ in God.'

(54) But what we confess about Christ's action in the future, when He is to come from Heaven to judge the living and the dead, has no bearing upon the life we now lead here, because it is not part of what He did upon earth, but of those things which are to be done at the end of the world. And it is to this that the Apostle refers, when, after the verse last quoted, he adds:[25] 'When Christ, your life, shall appear, then you too will appear with him in glory.' (55) Now, the doctrine that Christ will judge the living and the dead[26] can be understood in two ways. Either we may understand the living as those here not yet dead and to be found still living in the flesh at His coming, and the dead as those who, before He comes, have gone forth or will have gone forth from the body; or we may understand the living as the just, the dead as the unjust, since the just also are to be judged. Now, the judgment of God is sometimes taken in a bad sense, as in the following:[27] 'But those who have done evil [shall come forth] unto resurrection of judgment'; sometimes, however, in a good sense, as 'Save me, O God, by thy name: and judge me in thy strength.'[28] And naturally so, since it is precisely the judgment of God which divides the good from the evil,[29] so that the good may be segregated

---

24 Col. 3.1-3.
25 Col. 3.4.
26 2 Tim. 4.1.
27 John 5.29.
28 Ps. 53.3.
29 Cf. Matt. 25.33.

at the right, to be delivered from evil and not perish with the evil. And this is why the Psalmist cried:[30] 'Judge me, O God,' and then added, as if in explanation: 'And distinguish my cause from the nation that is not holy.'

Chapter 15

(56) And now, having spoken of Jesus Christ our Lord, only Son of God, with a brevity consistent with a confession of faith, we continue by saying that we also believe in the Holy Spirit, so that the Trinity which is God may be complete. Then we mention the Holy Church. This makes it be understood that the intelligent creation which is the free Jerusalem[1] is to be subordinated in order of speech to the Creator, that is, the Supreme Trinity; for anything that is said of the man Christ has reference to the unity of the person of the Only-begotten. The just order of the Creed demanded that the Church should follow after the Trinity, as a house after its dweller,[2] a temple after the god, a city after its founder. The whole Church is to be understood here, not only that part which is in pilgrimage upon the earth,[3] from the rising of the sun unto the going down of the same[4] praising the name of the Lord and singing a new song[5] after its old captivity, but also that part which is always in Heaven, which ever since its foundation has always remained steadfast to God and has never experienced any evil consequent upon a fall. This part, made up of holy angels,

---

30 Ps. 42.1.

---

1 Cf. Gal. 4.26.
2 Cf. 1 Tim. 3.15.
3 Cf. Heb. 13.14.
4 Ps. 112.3.
5 Apoc. 14.3.

continues in blessedness and gives assistance, as is meet, to that part which is in pilgrimage. The two parts will make one fellowship in eternity, and now are one in the bond of charity, ordained together as a whole for the worship of God. Consequently, neither the whole nor any part of the Church desires that it be worshipped instead of God, nor to be God to anyone who belongs to the temple of God—that temple built out of gods[6] created by the uncreated God. And, accordingly, the Holy Spirit, if a creature and not Creator, would surely be an intelligent creation (for such is creation at its highest). Thus the Holy Spirit would not have a place in the Rule of Faith[7] before the Church, since He Himself would belong to the Church, to that part which is in Heaven. Nor would the Holy Spirit have a temple, but would Himself be a temple. Yet surely He has a temple of whom the Apostle speaks:[8] 'Do you not know that your members are the temple of the Holy Spirit, who is in you, whom you have from God?' Of our bodies, he also says in another place:[9] 'Do you not know that your bodies are members of Christ?' How, then, is He not God, seeing that He has a temple? or less than Christ, whose members He has as a temple? And there is not one temple of the Holy Spirit, another of God, since the same Apostle says:[10] 'Do you not know that you are the temple of God?' and as proof of this adds: 'and that the Spirit of God dwells in you?' It is God, therefore, who dwells in His temple; not only the Holy Spirit, but also the Father and the Son, who also says of His body, through which He was made Head of the Church which is among men ('That in all things He may

---

6 Ps. 81.6; cf. John 10.34.
7 The Creed.
8 1 Cor. 6.19.
9 1 Cor. 6.15.
10 1 Cor. 3.16.

have the first place'[11]) : 'Destroy this temple, and in three days I will raise it up.'[12]

The temple of God, then, that is, of the Supreme Trinity as a whole, is the Holy Church, that is, the Church universal in Heaven and on earth. (57) But of that which is in Heaven, what can I say except that no wicked one is found in it, and that no one has fallen from it (or is to fall) since the time when God 'did not spare the angels when they sinned,' as the Apostle Peter writes,[13] 'but thrusting them into the jail-pits of the darkness of Hell delivered them to be kept for punishment in the judgment.' (58) Now, how that celestial and most blessed company is constituted, how the various ranks differ one from the other, so that, while all the citizens share the general name of *angel* (as we read in the Epistle to the Hebrews:[14] 'Now to which of the angels has he ever said: "Sit at my right hand"?', which shows that all are together called angels), still, there are *archangels* among them; and whether it is these same archangels who are called *hosts,* and the passage[15] 'Praise ye him, all his angels: praise ye him, all his hosts' is to mean 'Praise ye him, all his angels: praise ye him, all his archangels'; and what distinction there is among the four names under which the Apostle seems to embrace the whole celestial company:[16] 'Whether *thrones,* or *dominations,* or *principalities,* or *powers*'—to these questions let those reply who can, if, that is, they can prove their answers true; I acknowledge my own ignorance of these things. I am not even certain on this point, whether the sun and the moon and

---

11 Col. 1.18.
12 John 2.19.
13 2 Peter 2.4 (the text cited shows marked variations from the Vulgate).
14 Heb. 1.13.
15 Ps. 148.2.
16 Col. 1.16.

the other stars belong to this same company, though some believe these to be merely luminous bodies, without either sensation or intelligence. (59) Likewise, who will tell with what bodies angels appear to men, in such fashion as not only to be visible but to be tangible? And again how, not through tangible corporeity but by spiritual power, angels produce certain visions, not to the eyes of the body but to those of the spirit or the mind, or can utter speech, not to the ear from without, but within the soul of man, being themselves placed there, as is written in the book of the Prophets:[17] 'And the angel that spoke in me said to me' (for what the Prophet says is not 'that spoke *to* me,' but '*in* me'); or how they appear also in sleep and speak through dreams (for we read in the Gospel:[18] 'Behold an angel of the Lord appeared to him in a dream, saying'). These methods of communication tend to show that the angels have intangible bodies, and make it a very difficult question how the Patriarchs could wash the feet of angels,[19] and how Jacob could wrestle with an angel in contact so unmistakeable.[20] Asking these questions and answering them with such guesses as we can is not a useless exercise for the mind, if the discussion be kept within bounds and if those who take part avoid the error of thinking they know what they do not know. For what need is there of affirming or denying or making nice distinctions about these and similar matters, when ignorance of them imputes no blame?

Chapter 16

(60) There is greater need of distinction and judgment

---
17 Zach. 1.9.
18 Matt. 1.20.
19 Gen. 18.4; 19.2.
20 Gen. 32.24.

when Satan transforms himself into an angel of light,[1] lest through his deception he seduce us into some harmful act. When he deceives the body's sensations, but does not deflect the mind from that true and right judgment on which living the life of faith depends, there is no danger to religion; or if, feigning to be good, he does or says such things as befit the good angels, although he be believed to be good, no error arises which threatens peril or sickness to the Christian faith. But when by these means he begins to lead to his ends what is not his, then there is need of great vigilance in order to discern his presence and not to follow after him. Yet how few among men are fit to elude all his death-dealing wiles, if God does not direct and protect them? The very difficulty of the matter, however, is useful in this respect, that it prevents men from placing their hope in themselves or in one another, but leads them all to rely on God alone, the course which no pious man doubts is the most expedient.

(61) This part of the Church, then, which consists of the holy angels and hosts of God, will become known to us in its true nature when at the end we are joined to it for the joint possession of eternal blessedness. But that part which, separated from the other, makes its pilgrimage on earth is the better known to us because we belong to it and because it is made up of men and we are men. This part, through the blood of the sinless Mediator, has been redeemed from all sin, and this is the burden of its song:[2] 'If God is for us, who is against us? He who has not spared even his own Son but has delivered him for us all.' Christ did not die for the angels. Yet the redemption of men and their liberation from evil which was wrought through Christ's death was done also

---
[1] Cf. 2 Cor. 11.14.
[2] Rom. 8.31-32.

for the angels, since men's redemption marks a return to grace after the enmity which sins had brought about between men and the holy angels, and in consequence of this redemption the damages done through the fall of the angels are repaired.³

(62) And, of course, the angels, taught by God, in the eternal contemplation of whose truth their happiness consists, know how great an increment from the human race the heavenly city awaits in order to be entire. This is why the Apostle says:⁴ 'To re-establish all things in Christ, both those in the heavens and those on the earth, in him.' The things in the heavens are re-established when the loss occasioned by the fall of the angels is made good from among men; the things on the earth are re-established when those men who are predestined for eternal life are redeemed from their old corruption. And thus by that single sacrifice whose victim is the Mediator, one sacrifice prefigured by the many victims under the Law,⁵ heavenly things are brought into peace with the earthly and the earthly with the heavenly. Wherefore, as the same Apostle says,⁶ 'It has pleased [God the Father] that in him all his fullness should dwell, and that through him there should be reconciled to himself all things, whether on the earth or in the heavens, making peace through the blood on his cross.' (63) That peace, as it is written,⁷ 'surpasses all understanding,' and it cannot be known by us until we come unto the things of Heaven. For how are heavenly things brought into peace unless in respect to ourselves, that is, though

---
3 On the last two sentences of this section (*Ench. Patr.* no. 1917), see Portalié, col. 2370.
4 Eph. 1.10.
5 Cf. Heb. 10.12-14.
6 Col. 1.19; cf. 2.9.
7 Phil. 4.7.

their being in harmony with ourselves? In Heaven there is always peace both for all the intelligent creatures among themselves and between these and their Creator. And this peace, as has been said,[8] 'surpasses all understanding'; but this, of course, means our understanding, not the understanding of those who always see the face of the Father.[9] But we, however great be the human understanding within us, know only in part and we see through a mirror in an obscure manner;[10] but, when we shall be the equals of the angels of God,[11] then we shall see face to face,[12] as they also do, and we shall have as great peace towards them as they have towards us, for we shall love them as much as we are loved by them. And so their peace will be known to us, because our peace will be in kind and extent like theirs, and then it will not surpass our understanding, though the peace of God, which is there shown towards them, without doubt surpasses both our understanding and their own. For any rational creature that is happy derives its happiness from Him; He does not derive His happiness from it. And in this view it is better to interpret 'all' in the passage,[13] 'The peace of God which surpasses all understanding,' as admitting of no exception for the understanding of the holy angels, but only for God's own; for His peace surely does not surpass His own understanding.

Chapter 17

(64) However, the angels are at peace with us even now, whenever our sins are forgiven. Consequently, in the

---

8 *Ibid.*
9 Matt. 18.10.
10 1 Cor. 13.12.
11 Cf. Luke 20.36.
12 1 Cor. 13.12.
13 Phil. 4.7.

order of the Creed, forgiveness of sins finds its place just after the mention of the Holy Church. It is through this that the Church on earth stands; it is through this that what had been lost and was found is not lost.[1] For, with the exception of the gift of baptism, which was ordained against original sin, to remove through rebirth the taint that birth had inherited (though it also removes all actual sins which have been committed, whether in the heart, by the mouth, or in deed); with the exception, then, of this great act of favor (with which man's restoration begins and in which all his guilt, whether original or actual, is removed), the rest of our life, beginning from the first use of reason, howsoever richly that life abounds in justice, constantly requires the forgiveness of sins; for the sons of God, so long as they live under the pain of death, are in conflict with death. And although it has been truthfully said of them:[2] 'Whoever are led by the Spirit of God, they are the sons of God,' yet are they aroused by the Spirit of God and as sons of God advance toward God with this impediment, that they are also led by their own spirit and, under the oppressing weight of a corruptible body,[3] yield as sons of men to certain human motions, drop back to their own level, and therefore sin. Yet there is a difference: for, from the fact that every crime is a sin, it does not follow that every sin is a crime. And so we say that the life of holy men can be found free of crime, even though it has been lived in this mortal frame. Yet, 'if we say,' as writes the Apostle,[4] 'that we have no sin, we deceive ourselves, and the truth is not in us.'[5]

---

[1] Cf. Luke 15.24.
[2] Rom. 8.14.
[3] Cf. Wisd. 9.15.
[4] 1 John 1.8.
[5] On the doctrine of sin contained in this section (*Ench. Patr.* no. 1918), see Portalié, cols. 2384, 2440 f.

(65) Yet we should not despair of God's mercy in the matter of forgiving in the Holy Church even crimes, howsoever great, if we do penance each according to the measure of his sin. But in the doing of penance, when the sin is such as to separate the sinner even from the body of Christ, it is not so much the length of the penance that we should take account of as the sorrow of the penitent.[6] For God does not despise a contrite and humbled heart.[7] But, for the most part, the grief of one man's heart is hidden from another and does not through words or other signs come to the notice of others, although it is manifest to Him to whom it was said:[8] 'My groaning is not hidden from thee.' Therefore, those who have the charge of churches have rightly appointed seasons of penance, that satisfaction may come also to the Church, in which these sins are forgiven; and outside the Church sins are not forgiven. For the Church in her own right has received the pledge of the Holy Spirit, without whom there is no forgiveness of sins whereby those to whom they are forgiven may attain eternal life.

(66) Now, the forgiveness of sins has reference chiefly to the future judgment. For, in this life, there still holds good what is written:[9] 'A heavy yoke is upon the children of Adam from the day of their coming out of their mother's womb until the day of their burial into the mother of all.' Thus we see even infants, after being washed at the fount of rebirth, suffering from the infliction of divers evils, and so we understand that what is effected by the sacraments of

---

[6] On the doctrine of penance contained in the first two sentences of this section (*Ench. Patr.* no. 1919), see Portalié, cols. 2370, 2427-2429.
[7] Cf. Ps. 50.19.
[8] Ps. 37.10.
[9] Eccli. 40.1.

salvation pertains rather to the hope of good things to come than to the retention or gaining of present goods. Many sins, likewise, seem now to be overlooked and visited with no punishments, but the penalties for these are reserved for the time to come; for it is not in vain that that day is called the day of judgment in which the Judge of the living and the dead is to come. On the other hand, sins are punished now which, nevertheless, if they are pardoned, will inflict no harm in the life to come. Accordingly, concerning certain temporal punishments inflicted on sinners in this life, addressing those whose sins are blotted out and not reserved for the final judgment, the Apostle says:[10] 'But if we judged ourselves, we should not be judged by the Lord. But in being judged, we are being chastised by the Lord that we may not be condemned with this world.'

Chapter 18

(67) It is believed by some that those who do not abandon the name of Christ, and have been baptized in the Church and have not been cut off by any schism or heresy, no matter in what wickedness they live, not washing it away by penance nor redeeming it through almsgiving, but persevering in it stubbornly up to the last day of this life, are to be saved by fire (a fire made to endure in proportion to the magnitude of their evil deeds) and not to receive the punishment of eternal fire. But those who believe this and still are Catholics seem to me to be led astray by a kind of human benevolence. For Holy Scripture, when consulted, gives a different answer. I have written a book on this question under the title *On Faith and Works*,[1] in which as far as I was able,

---

10 1 Cor. 11.31-32.

1 *De fide et operibus* (PL 40 197-230; ed. J. Zycha, CSEL 41 33-97).

following the Holy Scriptures and God helping me, I have shown that the faith which saves us is that clearly described by the Apostle Paul when he says:[2] 'For in Christ Jesus neither circumcision is of any avail, nor uncircumcision, but faith which works through charity.' But if it works evil and not good, then without doubt, as the Apostle James says,[3] it is 'dead in itself.' And the same Apostle says again:[4] 'If a man says he has faith, and does not have works, can the faith save him?' And further, if a wicked man on account of faith alone will be saved by fire and if we are to give this interpretation to the words of the Apostle Paul,[5] 'but himself will be saved, yet so as through fire,' then will faith without works avail indeed for salvation, and the words of Paul's fellow Apostle James be proved false. And false too will be another saying of the same Paul himself. 'Do not err,' he says.[6] 'Neither fornicators, nor idolators, nor adulterers, nor the effeminate, nor sodomites, nor thieves, nor the covetous, nor drunkards, nor the evil-tongued, nor the greedy will possess the kingdom of God.' If men persevering in these crimes will yet be saved because of their faith in Christ, how then will they not be in the kingdom of God? (68) But because these most plain and manifest witnesses of the Apostles cannot be false, that obscure saying[7] about those who build upon the foundation which is Christ, not gold, silver, and precious stones, but wood, hay, and straw (for it is these, it is said, who shall be saved as through fire, escaping perdition through the merit of the foundation)—this saying must be understood so as not to be found at variance with the plain

---

2 Gal. 5.6.
3 James 2.17.
4 James 2.14.
5 1 Cor. 3.15.
6 1 Cor. 6.9-10.
7 1 Cor. 3.11 ff.

statements quoted above. Now, wood and hay and straw can reasonably be understood as such desires for worldly things, however lawful these things may be in themselves, as cannot be lost without grief of mind. When this grief burns, if Christ holds the place of foundation in the heart, that is, with nothing preferred to Him, and the man who is experiencing this burning grief chooses rather to lack those things he so loves than to lose Christ, then is he saved by fire. If, however, in the time of temptation he chooses to hold to those temporal and secular things rather than to Christ, he has not Christ as his foundation, because he puts these things in the first place, whereas in a building nothing comes before the foundation. Now, concerning the fire about which the Apostle speaks in this place, it must be understood that both men pass through it, that is, both he who builds upon the foundation gold, silver, and precious stones and he who builds wood, hay, and straw. For the Apostle immediately adds:[8] 'The fire will assay the quality of everyone's work. If his work abides which he has built thereon, he will receive reward; if his work burns, he will lose his reward, but himself will be saved, yet so as through fire.' It is not, then, the work of one of them but that of both that the fire will assay. Now, the fire is the trial of affliction, which is plainly spoken of in another place:[9] 'The furnace trieth the potter's vessels and the trial of affliction just men.' And this fire works in the course of life just as the Apostle says. If it come upon two believers, the one thinking about those things which are of God, how he may please God,[10] that is, building upon Christ the foundation gold, silver, and precious stones, the other thinking about those things which are of the world, how he

---

[8] 1 Cor. 3.13-15.
[9] Eccli. 27.6.
[10] Cf. 1 Cor. 7.32-34.

may please his wife,[11] that is, building upon the same foundation wood, hay, and straw,—the work of the one is not burned, because he did not love those things whose loss brings torment, but the work of the other is burned, since not without sorrow perish those things which are possessed with desire. But since even in the second case proposed he prefers rather to lack these things than to be without Christ, and does not desert Christ through fear of losing such things, though he grieves when he does lose them; still he is saved, yet so as through fire.[12] Grief at the loss of the things he has loved burns him indeed, but it does not subvert nor consume him, strengthened as he is by his firm and incorruptible foundation. (69) That some such thing may happen even after this life is not past belief, and it may be inquired into and either ascertained or left doubtful whether some believers may be saved by a sort of purging fire, more slowly or more swiftly in proportion as they have loved with more or less devotion the goods that perish.[13] But such is not the case of those of whom it is said[14] that they 'will not possess the kingdom of God,' unless after suitable penance their crimes are forgiven them. When I say 'suitable' I mean that they not be unfruitful in almsgiving. On this practice Holy Scripture lays so much stress that our Lord says in advance that it is no other merit but fruitfulness in almsgiving that He will ascribe to those on His right hand, and no other defect but a corresponding unfruitfulness to those on His left, when to the former He will say:[15] 'Come, blessed of my Father, take

---

11 *Ibid.*
12 1 Cor. 3.15.
13 This sentence (*Ench. Patr.* no. 1920) is of capital importance for the doctrine of purgatorial fire; cf. Portalié, col. 2448.
14 1 Cor. 6.10.
15 Cf. Matt. 25.34.

possession of the kingdom,' but to the latter:[16] 'Go ye into the everlasting fire.'

Chapter 19

(70) We must beware, however, lest anyone think that unspeakable crimes, such as those commit who 'will not possess the kingdom of God,'[1] are daily to be perpetrated and daily to be redeemed by almsgiving. Our life must be changed for the better and alms must be used in propitiating God for past sins, not for somehow buying a license to commit these same sins with impunity. For 'He hath given no man license to sin,'[2] even though in His mercy He washes away sins already committed, if a fitting satisfaction is not neglected. (71) Now, our daily sins of a momentary and trivial kind, of which no life is free, find satisfaction in the daily prayer of the faithful. For these can say 'Our Father who art in Heaven,'[3] since to such a Father they have been born again of water and the Spirit.[4] This prayer completely washes away very small sins of daily life.[5] It also washes away those sins which once made the life of the believer very wicked, but which, through penance changed for the better, he has given up, provided that as truly as he says:[6] 'Forgive us our debts' (since there is no lack of debts to be forgiven), so truly does he say:[7] 'As we also forgive our debtors,' that is, if what is said is done, for to forgive a

---

16 Cf. Matt. 25.41.

1 1 Cor. 6.10.
2 Eccli. 15.21.
3 Matt. 6.9.
4 John 3.5.
5 On the doctrine contained in the first three sentences of this section (*Ench. Patr.* no. 1921) that venial sins may be forgiven through the recitation of the Lord's Prayer, see Portalié, cols. 2426 f., 2441.
6 Matt. 6.12.
7 *Ibid.*

man who seeks pardon is itself a giving of alms. (72) And accordingly, our Lord's saying,[8] 'Give alms, and behold all things are clean to you' applies to every useful act of mercy. Therefore, not only does he give alms who gives food to the hungry,[9] drink to the thirsty, clothing to the naked, hospitality to the pilgrim, refuge to the fugitive, visitation to the sick or shut-in, freedom to the captive, lifting-up to the weak, guidance to the blind, consolation to the sorrowful, healing to the unsound of body, a straight course to the wanderer, counsel to him who takes thought, and that which is needful to anyone who needs it, but also he who gives forgiveness to the sinner. And he who corrects by a blow or restrains by any kind of discipline one over whom he has power, and at the same time forgives from the heart or prays that there may be forgiven the sin by which the other has injured or offended him, he also is a giver of alms, not only in that he forgives or prays, but also in that he rebukes and administers corrective punishment, for he shows mercy. Many good deeds are bestowed on unwilling recipients, when not their wish but their advantage is consulted, and they themselves are found to be their own enemies, while their friends are those whom they mistake for enemies; and through error they return evil for good, when a Christian ought not to return evil even for evil.[10]

There are, then, many kinds of alms, by giving of which we aid the forgiveness of our own sins. (73) But of these none is greater than forgiving from the heart[11] the sin that someone has committed against us. It is a comparatively small thing to wish well and even to do well to one who has done you no evil.

---

8 Luke 11.41.
9 Matt. 25.35-36.
10 Rom. 12.17; cf. Matt. 5.44.
11 Cf. Matt. 18.35.

A much finer thing it is and an act of most exalted goodness to love your enemy also and, hearkening to the words of God:[12] 'Love your enemies, do good to those who hate you, and pray for those who persecute you,' always, so far as you are able, to wish and to do good to him who wishes you evil and does that evil if he can. But, since this is a counsel attainable only by the perfect sons of God (although every believer ought to strive after it and by prayer to God and earnest struggling with himself bring his soul to this state of excellence), still this high degree of goodness is not possible for so great a number as we believe are heard when they pray:[13] 'Forgive us our debts, as we also forgive our debtors.' Therefore, without a doubt, the requirements of this agreement are fulfilled if a man who is not yet so far advanced as to love his enemy, still, when asked for forgiveness by one who has sinned against him, forgives him from his heart. For he certainly desires to be forgiven at his own asking, when he prays and says, 'As we also forgive our debtors,' that is, Forgive us our debts when we ask forgiveness, as we also forgive our debtors when they ask forgiveness of us.

(74) Now he who asks forgiveness of the man against whom he has sinned, if it is by his own sin that he is moved to ask, is not to be accounted an enemy in such a sense that it is as difficult to love him now as it was when he was exercising his enmity. And whoever does not from his heart forgive him who asks forgiveness and is repentant of his sin should in no wise suppose that his own sins are forgiven by the Lord, for truth cannot lie. For what reader or hearer of the Gospel can have failed to note who it was who said:[14] 'I am

---

12 Matt. 5.44; Luke 6.27.
13 Matt. 6.12.
14 John 14.6.

the truth'? The same who, when He had taught the prayer, commended this particular petition with these words:[15] 'For if you forgive men their offenses, your heavenly Father will also forgive you your offenses. But if you do not forgive men, neither will your Father forgive you your offenses.' The man whom this thunderous warning does not awaken is not asleep but dead; and yet, so powerful is this voice that it can awaken even the dead.

Chapter 20

(75) Surely those who live in great wickedness and take no pains to correct their life and moral habits, though amid all their crimes and misdeeds they incessantly multiply almsgiving, yet all in vain do they take comfort to themselves from our Lord's saying:[1] 'Give alms; and behold, all things are clean to you.' They do not understand what broad extension this saying has. To understand, let them pay heed to whom it was He spoke. And thus it is written in the Gospel:[2] 'Now after he had spoken, a Pharisee asked him to dine with him. And he went in and reclined at table. But the Pharisee began to ponder and ask himself why he had not washed himself before dinner. But the Lord said to him: "Now you Pharisees clean the outside of the cup and the dish, but within you are full of robbery and wickedness. Foolish ones! Did not he who made the outside make the inside too? Nevertheless, give that which remains as alms; and behold, all things are clean to you." ' Are we to understand this as meaning that to the Pharisees, who have not the faith of Christ, all things are clean if only they give alms as they think they should be given,

---

15 Matt. 6.14-15.

---

1 Luke 11.41.
2 Luke 11.37-41.

even if they have not believed in Him nor been reborn of water and the Spirit? But all are unclean who are not cleansed by the faith of Christ, of which it is written:[3] 'He cleansed their hearts by faith,' and again, in the words of the Apostle,[4] 'but for the unclean and unbelieving nothing is clean; for both their mind and their conscience are polluted.' How, then, could all things be clean for the Pharisees, even though they give alms and yet are not believers? Or how could they be believers, if they had been unwilling to believe in Christ and to be reborn in His grace? And yet what they heard is true:[5] 'Give alms; and behold, all things are clean to you.'

(76) Whoever would give alms in a just manner should begin with himself and give alms first to himself. For alms-giving is a work of mercy, and most truly has it been said:[6] 'Have pity on thy own soul, pleasing God.' The reason why we are born is that we may please God, who is justly displeased by that which we brought with us at birth. Our first alms is that which we give to ourselves. Through the mercy of a pitying God, we seek ourselves out in our wretchedness, we acknowledge as just that judgment of His by which we were made wretched (and of which the Apostle says:[7] 'The judgment was from one man unto condemnation') and we give thanks to His great charity, concerning which the same preacher of grace says:[8] 'But God commends his love towards us, because when as yet we were sinners, Christ died for us.' And thus, making a true judgment concerning our own wretchedness and loving God with that love which He Himself gave to

---
[3] Acts 15.9.
[4] Titus 1.15 (verbal differences from the Vulgate).
[5] Luke 11.41.
[6] Eccli. 30.24.
[7] Rom. 5.16.
[8] Rom. 5.8.

us, we lead a holy and upright life. It is this judgment and love of God which the Pharisees disregarded, though they gave as alms the tithe of all their fruits, even the most insignificant. Thus, they did not give alms beginning from themselves and did not show pity upon themselves in the first instance. This order of love is referred to in the saying:[9] 'Thou shalt love thy neighbor as thyself.' When, then, our Lord had rebuked them for washing themselves on the outside, when inwardly they were full of robbery and wickedness, He admonishes them to make clean the inward parts by that exercise of almsgiving which a man in the first instance owes to himself. 'Nevertheless,' He says,[10] 'give that which remains as alms; and behold, all things are clean to you.' Then, to show forth what He had admonished and what they themselves had not taken care to perform, so that they might not think Him ignorant of their almsgiving, He adds:[11] 'But woe to you Pharisees!'—as if to say: I indeed have admonished you of the need of almsgiving, the kind through which all things will be clean to you—'But woe to you, Pharisees! because you pay tithes on mint and rue and every herb' (for I know these almsgivings of yours; do not imagine that it is of them that I have just now admonished you), 'and disregard justice and the love of God' (by this almsgiving you could be cleansed from all inward defilement, so that your bodies also, which you wash, would be clean.—For this is the meaning of 'all things' here, both inward and outward things, as in another passage:[12] 'Clean the inward parts, and the outward parts also will be clean'). But He wished not to seem to be despising the alms which are made from the fruits of the earth, and so

---

9 Luke 10.27.
10 Luke 11.41.
11 Luke 11.42.
12 Cf. Matt. 23.26.

adds:[13] 'But these things you ought to have done,' that is, justice and the love of God, 'while not leaving the others undone,' that is, almsgiving from the fruits of the earth.

(77) There is no need of such self-deception on the part of those who, through giving, however profusely, alms of their fruits, or of money of whatever kind, believe that they are purchasing the right to persist with impunity in the enormity and wickedness of their misdeeds and vices. Not only do they perform such wickedness, but they so love it as to desire to persist in it forever, provided they can do so with impunity. 'But he that loveth iniquity hateth his own soul';[14] and whoever hates his own soul shows not mercy but cruelty towards it. For in loving it according to the world, he hates it according to God. If, then, he wished to give to it those alms by which all things would be clean to him,[15] he would hate his soul according to the world and love it according to God. Now no one gives alms at all unless he has the means of giving from One who has no need of it; and therefore it has been said:[16] 'His mercy shall go before me.'

Chapter 21

(78) Now what sins are trivial and what are grave it is for divine judgment, not human judgment, to decide. We see that the Apostles themselves have granted indulgence in certain matters. For example, take what the venerable Paul says to married people:[1] 'Do not deprive each other, except perhaps by consent for a time, that you may give yourselves

---

13 Luke 11.42.
14 Ps. 10.6.
15 Cf. Luke 11.41.
16 Ps. 58.11.

---

1 1 Cor. 7.5.

to prayer; and return together again lest Satan tempt you because you lack self-control.' Now, it is possible that it might not have been considered a sin to have intercourse with one's partner in marriage, not for the sake of begetting children, which is the good of marriage, but even for the sake of bodily pleasure, so that to those of weak self-control a means might be given of avoiding the fatal evil of adultery, or fornication, or some other form of impurity shameful even to name, into which lust might drag them through Satan's tempting. It is possible, I say, that this might not have been considered a sin, had not the Apostle added:[2] 'But this I say by way of concession, not by way of commandment.' Who, then, will deny that this is a sin when it is agreed that it was by Apostolic authority that concession was granted to those who do it? Another saying of the Apostle presents a somewhat similar case:[3] 'Dare any of you having a matter against another, bring your case to be judged before the unjust and not before the saints?' And a little later he says:[4] 'If, therefore, you have cases about worldly matters to be judged, appoint those who are rated as nothing in the Church [to judge]. To shame you I say it. Can it be that there is not one wise man among you competent to settle a case in his brother's matter? But brother goes to law with brother and that before unbelievers.' Now, here also it might have been supposed that it was no sin to have a lawsuit against another (the sin consisting only in the wish to have the judgment made outside the Church), unless in what follows the Apostle had added:[5] 'Nay, to begin with, it is altogether a defect in you that you have lawsuits one with

---

[2] 1 Cor. 7.6. For St. Augustine's teaching on marriage, see Portalié, cols. 2430-2432.
[3] 1 Cor. 6.1.
[4] 1 Cor. 6.4-6.
[5] 1 Cor. 6.7.

another.' And lest anyone excuse himself by saying that his matter was just and that he was suffering under a wrong which he wished the verdict of the judges to remove, the Apostle resists these reasons or excuses by saying:[6] 'Why not rather suffer wrong? Why not rather be defrauded?' In so speaking he brings us back to the Lord's saying:[7] 'If anyone would take thy tunic and go to law with thee, let him have thy cloak as well.' And in another place:[8] 'From him who takes away thy goods, ask no return.' Thus the Lord forbids His own from having lawsuits with others about worldly matters, and it is on the basis of this teaching that the Apostle pronounces such action to be a 'defect.' Still, in that he permits such cases between brethren to be decided in the Church, other brethren giving the decision, but sternly forbids such actions outside the Church, it is clear, here also, what indulgence is being granted to the weak by way of concession. It is in view of these and similar sins and others less grave through which we offend in word or thought that the Apostle James acknowledges:[9] 'For in many things we all offend.' We ought, then, daily and constantly to pray to the Lord and say:[10] 'Forgive us our debts,' and avoid being shown to be liars in what follows, 'as we also forgive our debtors.'

(79) There are again, certain sins which might seem very trivial unless in the Scriptures they were shown to be graver than one thinks. For who would think that someone saying to his brother 'Thou fool' is liable to Gehenna, if the Truth did not say so?[11] To the wound our Lord immediately applies

---

6 *Ibid.*
7 Matt. 5.40.
8 Luke 6.30.
9 James 3.2.
10 Matt. 6.12.
11 Matt. 5.22.

the cure, at once adding the precept concerning reconciliation with one's brother:[12] 'Therefore, if thou art offering thy gift at the altar, and there rememberest that thy brother has anything against thee,[13] [leave thy gift before the altar and go first to be reconciled to thy brother, and then come and offer thy gift].' Or who would think how great a sin it is to pay attention to days and months and years and seasons, as do those who will or decline to enter upon undertakings on certain days or in certain months or years, being guided by false teachings of men to regard such times as propitious or unpropitious?[14] And yet we may judge the greatness of the evil from the fear of the Apostle who says to such men:[15] 'I fear for you, lest perhaps I have labored among you in vain.'

(80) And there is also the fact that sins, however grave and terrible, are thought to be slight or not sins at all, when they come to be customary. And this goes so far as to make it seem right not only not to conceal such actions but to proclaim and publish them; and thus, as it is written:[16] 'The sinner is praised in the desires of his soul: and he who worketh iniquity is blessed.' In the divine books such iniquity is called a 'cry.' Thus, in the passage in the prophet Isaias about the evil vineyard we read:[17] 'I looked that he should do judgment, yet he did iniquity and not justice but a cry.' And the same meaning stands behind the passage in Genesis:[18] 'The cry of Sodom and Gomorrha is multiplied,' for in those cities not only were the crimes in question not punished, but were

---

12 Matt. 5.23.
13 The words in brackets have been added to complete the Scriptural quotation, which in St. Augustine ends here.
14 Cf. Gal. 4.9-10.
15 Gal. 4.11.
16 Ps. (10) .3.
17 Isa. 5.7 (Septuagint).
18 Gen. 18.20.

openly committed, as if under law. Similarly, in our own times so many evils, although different ones, have openly come to be customary that we not only do not dare to excommunicate a layman, but do not even dare to degrade a cleric for committing them. Thus it was that some years ago when I was writing an exposition of the Epistle to the Galatians, on that passage where the Apostle says:[19] 'I fear for you, lest perhaps I have labored among you in vain,' I was compelled to exclaim:[20] 'Woe to the sins of men! We shudder at them only when we are unaccustomed to them. As to those that we are accustomed to (and the blood of the Son of God was shed to wash them away), though they be great enough to close the kingdom of heaven firmly against them, yet, by often seeing them, we are forced to tolerate them all and, by often tolerating them, we are forced to practice some of them. And grant, O Lord, that we do not practice all that we are not able to prevent.' But I shall see whether my immoderate grief compelled me here to a certain rashness of speech.[21]

Chapter 22

(81) I shall now say what in other places in my smaller works I have often said. We sin from two causes, either through not yet seeing what we ought to do, or through not doing what we have already seen ought to be done; the first of these evils is ignorance, the second is weakness. We should indeed fight against them, but surely we shall be beaten unless we are divinely aided, not only to see what should be done, but also, by the access of health, to make our delight in justice stronger than

---
19 Gal. 4.11.
20 *Epistolae ad Galatas expositio,* 35 (PL 35 2130).
21 In the *Retractations* (1.23 [24]: PL 32 622; ed. Knöll, CSEL 36 111) St. Augustine is silent as to this doubt.

our delight in those things which, through desire of possessing them or fear of losing them, lead us to sin knowingly and with our eyes open. In such a case we are not only sinners—which we are also when we sin through ignorance—but also transgressors against the Law, since we fail to do what we know should be done or do what we know should not be done. Accordingly, we ought to pray not only for pardon, if we have sinned (wherefore we say:[1] 'Forgive us our debts, as we also forgive our debtors'), but that He guide us not to sin (wherefore we say:[2] 'Lead us not into temptation'). And we are to pray to Him who is addressed in the Psalm:[3] 'The Lord is my light and my salvation,' that His light may take away our ignorance, His salvation our weakness.

(82) Now, even penance itself is often omitted through weakness, when there is adequate cause according to the Church's practice that it be done. For shame is the fear of giving displeasure when the good opinion of men is more attractive than the justice through which a man humbles himself in penance. Therefore, the mercy of God is necessary, not only when penance is being done, but in order that it may be done. Otherwise, the Apostle would not have said of certain persons,[4] 'In case God should give them repentance.' And, before the Evangelist describes Peter as weeping bitterly, he says that the Lord looked upon him.[5] (83) But, whoever believes that sins are not forgiven in the Church, and despises this great gift of divine grace, and ends his last day in this obstinacy of mind, is guilty of that unforgiveable sin against the

---

1 Matt. 6.12.
2 Matt. 6.13.
3 Ps. 26.1.
4 2 Tim. 2.25.
5 Luke 22.61.

Holy Spirit,[6] in whom Christ forgives sins. This difficult topic I have already discussed, as clearly as I was able, in a short book devoted exclusively to the subject.[7]

Chapter 23

(84) Now, concerning the resurrection of the body—by which I mean not the experience of some who have lived again and again died, but resurrection to eternal life, as the body of Christ Himself rose again—I have not discovered how to discuss this matter briefly and do justice to all the questions which are commonly raised about it. This in any case no Christian ought to doubt: that the bodies of all men who have been born and are to be born, and have died and are to die, will rise again.[1]

(85) This doctrine gives rise to our first question, that about abortive fetuses, which have indeed been born in their mothers' wombs, but not so born that they could be born again. If we were to say that they are to rise again, this solution, whatever might be said, could be sustained in the case of those which are fully formed. But who is not rather disposed to think that unformed fetuses perish, like seeds which have not fructified? but who would dare to deny, even if he would not dare to affirm, that the act of resurrection would fill out whatever was lacking to the form? Thus, there would be nothing wanting to the perfection which was to

---

6 Matt. 12.32.

7 Probably *Sermo* 71 (PL 38 445-467); it is to this sermon that an entry, 'De blasphemia spiritus sanctus,' in the *Indiculum* of Possidius (supra, p. 359 n. 17) most likely refers (Wilmart's edition, p. 207: sect. [X6], item 199; cf. *ibid.* 227 and PL 46 21). In annotating the present passage of the *Ench.*, Riviére points out verbal resemblances to *Sermo* 71.

---

1 This sentence (*Ench. Patr.* no. 1922) contains St. Augustine's basic statement on the resurrection of the body; see Portalié, cols. 2449 ff.

come about with time, any more than those blemishes will exist which did come about with time. Nature, then, would not be defrauded of anything fitting and harmonious which the passage of days was to bring nor be disfigured by anything of an opposite kind which passage of days had added, but rather that which was not yet complete would be completed, just as that which had suffered blemish will be renewed.

(86) And accordingly, the following question may be most meticulously probed and disputed among the most learned (though I do not know whether man can answer it), *viz. when* a human being begins to live in the womb; whether there is some form of hidden life before it is apparent in the motions of the living being. It appears to be very rash to deny that those fetuses have ever lived which are cut away limb by limb and ejected from the womb for fear that the mothers too should die, if they were left there dead. Now, from whatever moment a human being begins to live, from that moment it is possible for him to die. And, if he is dead, no matter where death came to him, I can find no reason to deny that he has interest in the resurrection of the dead. (87) Likewise, concerning monsters which are born and live, however quickly they die, neither is resurrection to be denied them, nor is it to be believed that they will rise again as they are, but rather with an amended and perfected body. God forbid that that double-membered man recently born in the East—about whom most trustworthy brethren, who saw him, have reported, and Jerome the priest, of holy memory, left written mention[2] —God forbid, I say, that we should think that at the resurrection there will be one such double man, and not rather two

---

[2] *Epist.* (72) *ad Vitalem presbyterum* 2 (PL 22 674; ed. I. Hilberg, CSEL 55 9): 'Just because in our time, at Lydda, there was born a human being with two heads, four hands, one belly, and two feet, must it be that all men are born so?'

men, as would have been the case had twins been born. And so all other births which, as having some excess or some defect or because of some conspicuous deformity, are called monsters, will be brought again at the resurrection to the true form of human nature, so that one soul will have one body, and no bodies will cohere together, even those that were born in this condition, but each, apart, for himself, will have as his own those members whose sum makes the complete human body.

(88) Now, God does not permit the perishing of the material from which the body of mortals is created. It matters not into what dust or ashes it is dissolved, into what exhalations or vapors it is dispersed, into the substance of what other bodies it is converted (or even into the elements themselves), into the food or the flesh of what animals (man included) it is changed, this material, in a moment of time, returns to that human soul which originally animated it, so that it could become man, live, and grow. (89) This earthly material which, at the departure of the soul, becomes a corpse will not at the resurrection be so restored that those elements which are dispersed and, under various forms and appearances, have become parts of other things must necessarily return to those very same parts of the body where once they were situated, though they do return to the body from which they were dispersed. Otherwise, if the hair receives back that which frequent clipping has removed, and the nails that which repeated paring has taken away, a picture of supreme ugliness presents itself to those who speculate unbecomingly and accordingly deny the resurrection of the body. But consider the case of a statue of some soluble metal: if it had been melted by fire, or been pounded to dust, or reduced to a shapeless mass, and an artificer wished to use all of that metal and none other in restoring it, it would make no difference with respect

to the wholeness of the statue into what part of it a given particle of material was put, provided the statue as restored should again take up all the material of which it had been originally composed. Just so God, an artificer after a wondrous and unspeakable manner, will, with a speed wondrous and unspeakable, restore our body from all that material of which it was once composed, and it will make no difference with respect to its restoration whether hair goes back into hair and nails into nails, or whether the part of these that had perished should be converted into flesh and assigned to some other parts of the body, for the providence of the Artificer will be taking care that nothing unseemly will result.[3]

(90) It is not a necessary consequence of this that there will be differences of stature among individuals entering again upon life, simply because there had been such differences when they were first alive, or that the lean will live again with the same leanness or the fat with the same fatness. But if it is in the Creator's plan that in His workmanship each individual shall preserve his own special features and a recognizable resemblance to his former self (an equality of distribution being attained in respect to other bodily advantages), there may be a modification of the material in a particular case, so that while no loss of the material occurs, God Himself, who could produce what He willed even from nothing, will make good any defect. But if in the bodies of those who rise again there is to be a well-ordered inequality, as there is of the voices which fill out the body of song, this will be realized in each individual through the material of his own body, so as to place a human being among the bands of angels and impose on their senses nothing that is inharmonious. And

---

[3] This analogy of the statue (*Ench. Patr.* no. 1923) is of high importance for St. Augustine's teaching on the resurrection of the body; see Portalié, col. 2449.

surely nothing unseemly will be there, but whatever will be there will be fitting, for if it is not fitting, it will not be. (91) The bodies of the saints, then, will rise free from any blemish or deformity, as they will be free from any corruption, burden, or impediment; their freedom of movement will be as complete as their happiness. It is for this reason that these bodies are called spiritual, since without doubt they are to be bodies and not spirits. For just as now the body is called *animate*[4] and is yet a body and not a soul [*anima*], so then the body will be spiritual, but will be a body and not a spirit. Accordingly, with respect to the corruption which weighs down the soul and the vices through which the flesh lusts against the spirit,[5] there will then be no flesh but a body, for there are bodies which are called heavenly.[6] That is why it is said,[7] 'Flesh and blood will not possess the kingdom of God,' and, as if in explanation of the foregoing:[8] 'Neither shall corruption have any part in incorruption.' What the Apostle first called 'flesh and blood' he afterwards called 'corruption,' and what he first called 'the kingdom of God' he afterwards called 'incorruption.' Yet with respect to the substance, there will be flesh even then; for even after His resurrection the body of Christ is called flesh.[9] Wherefore the Apostle says:[10] 'What is sown a natural body rises a spiritual body.' For then, such will be the harmony between flesh and spirit, while the spirit, with no need of nourishment, will so keep alive the subjugated

---

4 St. Augustine seems to have had in mind 1 Cor. 15.44, quoted later in this section. The word *animale,* commonly rendered in that verse as 'natural,' is here (following Shaw) rendered 'animate' to allow for the double play on words the present sentence contains.
5 Gal. 5.17.
6 1 Cor. 15.40.
7 1 Cor. 15.50.
8 *Ibid.*
9 Luke 24.39.
10 1 Cor. 15.44.

flesh, that there will be no disagreement between the parts of our nature: just as outside ourselves we shall have no enemy to face, so we shall not have ourselves as enemies within.

(92) But those who from the mass of perdition brought into being by one man are not liberated by the one Mediator between God and men,[11] these too shall rise again, each with his own flesh, but in order that they may be punished with the Devil and his angels. Whether these men will rise again with all the bodily blemishes and deformities which their members showed—why need we labor to inquire? When their damnation is sure and eternal, the unsure condition of their bodily form or its beauty should not weary us. Nor need we be moved to ask how their body will be incorruptible if it will be capable of pain, or how it will be corruptible if it will not be capable of death. For there is no true life except one that is lived in happiness, nor any true incorruption except where health is uncorrupted by any pain. But when an unhappy man is not permitted to die, then, if I may so express myself, death itself dies not; and when unceasing pain afflicts but does not destroy, then is corruption itself without an end. It is this that the Holy Scriptures call the 'second death.'[12] (93) Yet neither the first death, wherein the soul is compelled to leave its body, nor the second, wherein it is not permitted to leave the suffering body, would have befallen man, if no one had sinned. And surely the lightest punishment will be for those who added no sin to that which they brought with them originally, while each among those who have committed additional sins will suffer a more endurable damnation in proportion to the slightness of his iniquity.[13]

---

11 1 Tim. 2.5.
12 Apoc. 2.11; 20.6,11.
13 On the doctrine of the last sentence of this section (*Ench. Patr.* no. 1924), see Portalié, cols. 2397, 2450.

Chapter 24

(94) While the reprobate angels and men continue in eternal punishment, the saints will have fuller knowledge of the good conferred on them by grace. Then, through the very facts themselves they will gain a clearer understanding of what is written in the Psalm:[1] 'Mercy and judgment I will sing to thee, O Lord,' for it is only through unmerited mercy that anyone is freed, and only through deserved judgment that anyone is condemned. (95) Then will be clear what now is dark: When one of two children is through His mercy chosen by God for Himself, while the other through His judgment is to be abandoned (the one chosen knowing what would have been his due through judgment, had not mercy come to his aid), why the one rather than the other is chosen, when the condition of the two was the same. Or again, why miracles were not worked in the presence of some men who, had they been worked, would have done penance, while miracles were worked in the presence of those who were not going to believe anyway. For this is the Lord's very clear statement:[2] 'Woe to thee, Corozain! Woe to thee, Bethsaida! For if in Tyre and Sidon had been worked the miracles that have been worked in you, they would have repented long ago in sackcloth and ashes.' And surely there was no injustice in God's not willing that they be saved, though they could have been saved if He had so willed it.[3] Then in the brightest light

---
1 Ps. 100.1.
2 Matt. 11.21.
3 In Latin as follows: *Nec utique deus iniuste noluit salvos fieri, cum possent salvi esse, si* vellet. As regards the last word the MSS are divided: What appear to be the majority read *vellet* ('if God had so willed it'), the others *vellent* ('if they, the men of Tyre and Sidon, had so willed it'). Scheel (*Ench.* p. 77) calls this one of the few cases of variant readings in the whole body of St. Augustine's text where an important dog-

of wisdom will be seen, what now the righteous have by faith, before being able to see it with certain knowledge—how certain and immutable and effectual is the will of God; how many things He is capable of yet does not will, though willing nothing of which He is not capable; and how true is that which is sung in the Psalm:[4] 'But our God is above in heaven: in heaven and on earth he hath done all things whatsoever he would.' And this, of course, is not true, if He ever willed anything and did not do it, or, which is worse, if God's failure to do anything is due to man's will preventing the Almighty from doing what He willed.

Nothing, then, comes about unless God wills it so, either through permitting it to happen or Himself performing it. (96) There is no doubt that God does well even in permitting to happen that which happens ill. For He permits this only through a just judgment, and, surely, everything that is just is good. Therefore, although those things which are evil, insofar as they are evil, are not good, still it is good that not only good things exist but also evil. For, unless it were good that evil things also exist, they would never have been per-

---

matic issue is at stake. Scheel's reading *vellet* has been preferred in the translation; see his edition, pp. 76-78, for his defense. The reading *vellet* had been favored by Faure (p. 180) and, before him, among others, by the Maurist editors · (though *vellent* appears in many copies of the Maurist edition [Rottmanner, *Theol. Rev.* cited below] and hence, it may be supposed, passed into the Migne text [PL]), and by Peter Lombard (*Sent.* 1.43; PL 192 639). For the history of the criticism of this passage, which played no small part in the controversy aroused by the appearance of the Maurist edition, see also the critical note in that edition (6.231: PL 40 275), O. Rottmanner, O.S.B., in *Theologische Revue* (Münster i. W.), 2 (1903) 478-479, the work of Kukula cited by Rottmanner and Scheel, and (not available to this translator) Rottmanner's *Geistesfrüchte aus der Klosterzelle* (München 1908) 99ff.—See Portalié, cols. 2385, 2398 ff. for his discussion of the doctrine of the first part of this section (*Ench. Patr.* no. 1925).

4 Ps. 113.3 bis; 134.6.

mitted to exist by the Omnipotent Good, for whom it is without doubt as easy not to permit to be that which He does not wish as it is to do that which He wishes. Unless we believe this, the very beginning of our confession of faith stands in danger, the part in which we acknowledge our belief in God the Father Almighty. For, unless God can do what He wishes and the effective force of His omnipotent will is not impeded by the will of any creature, there is no ground for truly calling Him omnipotent.

(97) Accordingly, we must enquire in what sense was said of God that which the Apostle has most truly said:[5] 'Who wishes all men to be saved.' For, since not all are saved nor even a majority, it appears that the fact that what God wills to happen does not happen is due to an impediment placed upon the will of God by human will. When it is asked why all are not saved, the customary reply is that they do not want it. This surely cannot be said of infants, who have not yet the power to will or not to will. For, if we could attribute to their will the childish movements they make at baptism, when they resist so far as they can, we could say that they were saved even when they did not want to be. But the Lord has made a clearer statement in the Gospel, upbraiding the unrighteous city:[6] 'How often would I have gathered thy children together, as a hen gathers her young, but thou wouldst not!'—as if the will of God had been overpowered by the will of men and, when the weakest stood in the way through being unwilling, the Most Powerful could not do what He wished. And where is that omnipotence by which 'in heaven and on earth he hath done all things whatsoever he would,'[7] if He willed to gather together the children of

---
[5] 1 Tim. 2.4.
[6] Matt. 23.37.
[7] Ps. 134.6.

Jerusalem and did not do so? Or is it not rather that, while Jerusalem did, indeed, wish that her children not be gathered together by Him, He, in spite of her unwillingness, gathered together those of her children whom He wished? For it is not that some things in heaven and on earth He has willed to do and done and some others He has willed to do and not done, but 'he hath done *all* things whatsoever he would.'

Chapter 25

(98) Who, moreover, will be at once so blasphemous and foolish as to say that God could not have converted to good the evil wills of men, those which He willed, when He willed, and where He willed? But when He does this, He does it through mercy;[1] when He does not do it, it is through judgment that He does not do it. For 'he has mercy on whom he will, and whom he will he hardens.'[2] In saying this, the Apostle commends grace, of which he has just spoken in connection with the twin children in the womb of Rebecca:[3] 'Before they had yet been born, or had done aught of good or evil, in order that the selective purpose of God might stand, depending not on deeds, but on him who calls, it was said to her, "The elder shall serve the younger."' And in reference to this matter, he quoted another prophetic testimony,[4] 'Jacob I have loved, but Esau I have hated.' But perceiving how what he had said could affect those who are unable to penetrate to the depth of this grace, he added:[5] 'What then shall we say? Is there injustice with God? By no means!' For

---
1 On God's freedom of election as set out in these two sentences (*Ench. Patr.* no. 1926), see Portalié, cols. 2385, 2407 f.
2 Rom. 9.18.
3 Rom. 9.11-12.
4 Rom. 9.13; cf. Mal. 1.2-3.
5 Rom. 9.14.

it seems unjust that, in the absence of any merit derived from acts good or bad, God should love the one and hate the other. If in this case the Apostle had wished that future deeds be understood, good on the part of one, evil on the part of the other, both surely within the foreknowledge of God, he would by no means have said[6] 'depending not on deeds,' but would have said 'on future deeds,' and in that way he would have solved the question, or rather, he would have brought it about that there was no question in need of solution. As it is, however, when he had answered[7] 'By no means'—that is, that there should be injustice with God,— then, in order to prove that no injustice on God's part is involved, he added:[8] 'For he says to Moses, "I will have mercy on whom I have mercy, and I will show pity to whom I will show pity." ' For who but a fool thinks God unjust, whether in imposing penal judgment on whoever deserves it or in showing mercy to one who does not deserve it? Finally, he draws his conclusion and says:[9] 'So then, there is question not of him who wills nor of him who runs, but of God showing mercy.' Thus both twins were by nature born children of wrath,[10] through no deeds of their own to be sure, but as bound by the chain of condemnation originating in Adam. But He who said:[11] 'I will have mercy on whom I have mercy' loved Jacob through unmerited mercy, but hated Esau through merited judgment. And, since the judgment was due to both, the former learned from the case of the latter that the fact that he had not, from the same cause, incurred the same punishment gave him no

---

6 Rom. 9.12.
7 Rom. 9.14.
8 Rom. 9.15; Exod. 33.19.
9 Rom. 9.16. See above, sect. 32, for an extended discussion of this verse.
10 Eph. 2.3.
11 **Rom. 9.15.**

reason to boast of any distinctive merits of his own, but rather of the abundance of divine grace; because 'there is question not of him who wills nor of him who runs, but of God showing mercy.'[12] The whole aspect and, if I may so speak, the entire countenance of the Holy Scriptures is seen, in a mystery very deep and salutary, to admonish all who carefully look upon it, 'that he who takes pride should take pride in the Lord.'[13] (99) Now, when the Apostle had commended the mercy of God in saying:[14] 'So then, there is question not of him who wills nor of him who runs, but of God showing mercy,' then, to commend judgment also (for in that mercy is now shown, it is not injustice but judgment; for with God there is no injustice), he added:[15] 'For the scripture says to Pharao, "For this very purpose I have raised thee up, that I may show in thee my power, and that my name may be proclaimed in all the earth." ' Then, when this had been said, he draws a conclusion which applies to both things, that is, to mercy and to judgment:[16] 'Therefore he has mercy on whom he will, and whom he will he hardens.' He has mercy of His great goodness; He hardens from no injustice. Consequently, neither may he who is freed take pride in his own deserts, nor may he who is damned find fault with anything but his own deserts. For it is grace alone that separates the redeemed from the lost, all having been mingled together in one mass of perdition from a common cause leading back to their origin. But if any man were to hear this in such a way as to say:[17] 'Why then does he still find fault? For who resists his will?' (as

---

12 Rom. 9.16.
13 1 Cor. 1.31; cf. Jer. 9.24.
14 Rom. 9.16.
15 Rom. 9.17; cf. Exod. 9.16.
16 Rom. 9.18.
17 Rom. 9.19.

if it seemed that a man should not be blamed for being evil because God 'has mercy on whom he will, and whom he will he hardens'[18]), God forbid that we should be ashamed to make the answer we see the Apostle gave:[19] 'O man, who art thou to reply to God? Does the object moulded say to him who moulded it: Why hast thou made me thus? Or is not the potter master of his clay to make from the same mass one vessel for honorable, another for ignoble use?' Now, some foolish men think that the Apostle had no answer to make in this passage, and through lack of reasonable reply restrained the audacity of his interrogator. But what was said, 'O man, who art thou?, has great weight, and in matters like this recalls man with a brief word to a consideration of his own capacity, and in fact supplies a powerful reason. For if a man does not understand these things, who is he to reply to God? If he does understand them, he finds no better ground for replying. For, if he understands, he sees that the whole human race was condemned in its rebellious head by so just a divine judgment, that if no one were to be freed from it, no one could rightly blame the justice of God. And he sees, too, that those who are freed had to be freed in such a way as to show, from the greater number of those not freed but abandoned in their most just damnation, what the whole mass deserved and to what end the merited judgment of God would have led even those in fact freed, had not the unmerited mercy come to their aid, so that 'every mouth may be stopped'[20] of those who would take pride in their own merits, and that 'he who takes pride may take pride in the Lord.'[21]

---

[18] Rom. 9.18.
[19] Rom. 9.20-21.
[20] Rom. 3.19.
[21] 1 Cor. 1.31.

Chapter 26

(100) These are the 'great works of the Lord, sought out according to all his wills'[1] and so wisely sought out that, when the angelic and human creation sinned (that is, did not what He, but what it willed), He could fulfil His will through that very creature-will by which an act contrary to the Creator's will was done. Supremely good Himself, He made good use also of evils, for the damnation of those whom He had justly predestined to punishment and for the salvation of those whom He had mercifully predestined to grace. In respect to themselves they did what God forbade; in respect to God's omnipotence they were quite unable to effect their purpose. In the very fact that they acted contrary to His will, His will was accomplished. And hence 'great are the works of the Lord: sought out according to all his wills.' For in a strange and ineffable way nothing is done without the will of God, even that which is done contrary to it. Because it would not be done if he did not permit it (and surely His permission is not unwilling, but willing), nor would He who is good permit evil to be done unless in His omnipotence He could turn evil to good.

(101) Now sometimes with a good will a man wishes something which God does not wish, though God's will is also good (evil it can never be) and much more fully and more surely good. For example, a good son wishes his father to live, whom God with a good will wishes to die. And, on the other hand, it can happen that man with a bad will wishes something which God wishes with a good will—for example, if a bad son wishes his father to die and this is also the will of God. To be sure, the good son wishes what God does not

---
1 Ps. 110.2

wish, while the bad son wishes that which God also wishes, yet the piety of the one, even though his wish is contrary to God's, is more in accordance with the good will of God than the impiety of the other, though his wish is the same as God's. There is a great difference between what is proper for a man to will and what is proper for God, and to what end each man applies his wish; on this difference depends the approval or the disapproval of the wish. For God accomplishes some of His purposes, surely good ones, through the evil wills of evil men; for example, it was through malevolent Jews that Christ was slain for us by the good will of the Father—a deed so good that the Apostle Peter, when he would have prevented it, was called Satan by Him who had come in order to be slain.² How good seemed the wishes of the pious faithful who were unwilling that the Apostle Paul should go to Jerusalem,³ for fear that he should suffer there the evils foretold by the prophet Agabus. And yet God, proving the martyr of Christ, willed that he suffer these things for the preaching of the faith of Christ. This good purpose of His God did not accomplish through the good will of the Christians but through the evil of the Jews, and yet they were closer to Him whose wish was contrary to His purpose than were those who were the willing agents of it, for while He and the latter did one and the same thing, He did it through them with a good will, while they did it with an evil will.

(102) But, however strong be the wills of angels or of men, whether of good or bad, whether wishing the same thing that God wishes or something else, the will of the Omnipotent is always undefeated. And this can never be bad,

---
2 Matt. 16.23.
3 Acts 21.12.

because even when it inflicts evils, it is just, and surely, as being just, it is not evil. Almighty God, therefore, whether through pity He has mercy on whom He will or through justice hardens whom He will,[4] never does anything unjustly, never does anything unless He wills it, and does everything that He wills.[5]

Chapter 27

(103) Consequently, when we hear and read in the Sacred Scriptures that God wishes all men to be saved,[1] while we are sure that not all men are saved, still we ought not on that account to restrict the omnipotent will of God, but rather to understand the words, 'Who wishes all men to be saved' as meaning that no man is saved unless He wishes him saved. The meaning would not be that there is no man whose salvation God does not wish, but that no man is saved unless He wills it, and that His will should be sought for in prayer, since, if He wills it, it must be. The subject the Apostle had in mind when he used these words was praying to God. We have a like understanding also of the Gospel verse,[2] 'Who enlightens every man.' It is not that there is no man who is unenlightened, but that no one is enlightened except by Him. Alternatively, the words,[3] 'Who wishes all men to be saved,' do not mean that there is no one whose salvation He does not wish (He who willed not to work miracles among those who, the Apostle says, would have done penance if He had worked them[4]). Rather, they lead us to understand 'all men'

---
4 Rom. 9.18.
5 Ps. 134.6.

---
1 1 Tim. 2.4.
2 John 1.9.
3 1 Tim. 2.4.
4 See above, sect. 95.

as the whole of humankind, in whatever classes it be divided:[5] kings, subjects, nobles, plebeians, the high, the low, the learned, the ignorant, the sound of body, the weak, the quick-minded, the dull, the foolish, the rich, the poor, the middle class, males, females, infants, children, the adolescent, the young, the middle-aged, the old; of every tongue, of every fashion, of all arts, of all professions; in whatever numberless variety of wills and consciences men are constituted; or according to any other principle of distinction among men. For from which of all these classes does God not wish that men throughout all nations should be saved through His Only-begotten Son our Lord—and therefore does save them,—for the Omnipotent cannot will in vain, whatever it be He wills? Now the Apostle had admonished that there be prayer 'for all men,' and especially 'for kings and for those in high position,'[6] whose worldly pride and pomp might be thought to disincline them to the humility of the Christian faith. And then, continuing:[7] 'For this is good in the sight of God our Savior' (that is, to pray even for the mighty), he immediately added, to remove all cause for despair:[8] 'Who wishes all men to be saved and to come to the knowledge of the truth.' God, then, judged it good to vouchsafe to the prayers of the humble the salvation of the mighty, a thing of course which we have long since seen exemplified. Now, we have here a mode of speech which the Lord also used in the Gospel, where He says to the Pharisees:[9] 'You pay tithes on mint and rue and every herb.' For the Pharisees did not pay tithes on what belonged to others nor on all the herbs of all the inhabitants of other lands.

---

5 For the interpretation of 1 Tim. 2.4. contained in the opening of this section (Ench. Patr. no. 1927), see Portalié, cols. 2385, 2407.
6 1 Tim. 2.1,2.
7 1 Tim. 2.3.
8 1 Tim. 2.4.
9 Luke 11.42.

Consequently, just as we may understand 'every herb' as meaning here every kind of herb, so in the former passage we may understand 'all men' as meaning the whole of mankind, or we may understand it in any other way possible. It must only be assured that we be not compelled to believe that the Almighty willed that something be done and it was not done. For if, without any doubt, as the Truth sings of Him,[10] 'in heaven and in earth, whatsoever the Lord pleased he hath done,' surely He has not willed to do anything He has not done.

Chapter 28

(104) Wherefore God would have been willing to maintain even the first man in that state of salvation in which he had been placed and, at a fitting time, after the generation of children, to lead him, without the intervention of death, to a better state, where not only would he have been unable to sin but even to have the wish of sin, if only He had foreseen in him a steadfast wish to persevere without sin, as he was made. But because He foresaw that he would make bad use of his free will, that is, would sin, He arranged His own design so that He would do well concerning man, even when man did evil, and that thus the good will of the Almighty should not be voided by the evil will of man, but might nonetheless be fulfilled.[1] (105) It was fitting that man should be made in the first place with the power to will both good and evil—if good, not without reward;. if evil, not with impunity. In the after-life he will not be able to will evil, and yet he

---

10 Ps. 134.6.

1 On the doctrine of predestination contained in this sentence (*Ench. Patr.* no. 1928), see Portalié, cols. 2390, 2393, 2399, 2404, 2408; Jacquin in *Misc. Agost.* II 860 f.

will not be deprived of his free will. In fact, his will will be much more free, in that it will be in no way subject to sin. For the will is not to be blamed, nor should we say that it was no will or that it was not free, when we so will to be happy that we not only do not will to be wretched, but are quite unable to wish to be. As, then, our soul even now is incapable of desiring unhappiness, so it will then be forever incapable of desiring wickedness. But God's plan was not to be disturbed, whereby He wished to show how good a rational animal is which is capable of not sinning, though one would be better which was incapable of sinning; just as it was a lesser order of immortality (yet immortality nonetheless) in which man was capable of not dying, though that which is to be is of a higher order, in which he will be incapable of dying. (106) That former immortality human nature lost through free will, the latter it is to receive through grace, and was to receive through merit, if it had not sinned, though not even then could there have been any merit without grace. For although sin became possible by free will alone, still free will would not have sufficed for the retention of justice, unless divine assistance had been supplied through a sharing of the immutable good. Although it is in a man's power to die when he wishes—for there is no one who could not kill himself by not eating, to mention no other means,—still, the will is not sufficient for maintaining life, if it be deprived of the help of food or other bodily supports. Just so, man in paradise was capable through his will alone of killing himself through abandoning justice, yet his will would have been insufficient for his continuing the life of justice, unless He who had made him had given him help. But, after man's fall the mercy of God was more abundant, for then the will itself had to be freed from the servitude in which sin, with death, was its master. And the will is brought to freedom not at all through itself, but only through God's grace residing in the faith of Christ; so that, as it is written,[2] 'from God is the preparation of the will,' through which are received those other gifts of God by which we come to the eternal gift.

(107) Accordingly, even eternal life itself, which is surely the reward of good works, is called by the Apostle the grace of God:[3] 'For the wages of sin,' he says, 'is death, but the grace of God is life everlasting, Christ Jesus our Lord.' Now, wages is something paid for military service; it is not a gift. Hence he says: 'The wages of sin is death,' so as to show that death was the recompense of sin, not something imposed undeservedly. But grace is not grace unless it is freely given. It is, then, to be understood that the very merits of man are the gifts of God. And when eternal life is granted in return for these, what else have we but grace given in return for grace?[4] Man, therefore, was so made righteous that he could only persevere in that righteousness by divine aid, yet could depart from it by his own will. Whichever of these courses man chose, God's will would have been done, either actually by man or in any case concerning him. Therefore, since man chose to do his own will rather than God's, God's will concerning him was done. From the same mass of perdition which had its origin in man's lineage God made 'one vessel for honorable, another for ignoble use,'[5] working through mercy in that for honorable use, working through judgment in that for ignoble use, that no one may take pride in man and consequently no one in himself.

(108) For we could not be freed even through the one

---

2 Prov. 8.35 (Septuagint).
3 Rom. 6.23.
4 Cf. John 1.16.
5 Rom. 9.21.

Mediator between God and man, Himself man, Christ Jesus,[6] had not He been also God. Now, when Adam was made, a righteous man, there was no need of a mediator. But when sins had taken the human race far from God, the mediation of Him who alone was born, lived, and was slain without sin was required to reconcile us to God, even to procuring for us the resurrection of the body unto eternal life; and this in order that human pride might be convicted and healed through the humility of God, and that man might be shown how far he had departed from God, when it was through God made flesh that he was being called back. And this was done also in order that an example of obedience in the person of the God-man might be given to man's stubbornness, and with the Only-begotten taking the form of a servant, a form which had no antecedent merit, a source of grace might be opened up, an earnest of the resurrection of the body, which had been promised to the redeemed, might be given in the resurrection of the Redeemer Himself, and the Devil might be overcome through that very nature which he was rejoicing in having deceived, and yet man not be glorified, lest his pride again be born; and for the sake of any other advantages as coming from the great mystery of the Mediator, which those who profit from it may be able to see and tell, or see only, even if it cannot be told.

Chapter 29

(109) Now, in the time intervening between a man's death and the final resurrection, the soul is held in a hidden retreat, enjoying rest or suffering hardship in accordance with what it merited during its life in the body. (110) There is no

---

6 1 Tim. 2.5. For the eloquent summary of the mediatorial work of Christ contained in this section (*Ench. Patr.* no. 1929), see Portalié, col. 2373 f., also 2371 f., 2392 ff.

gainsaying that the souls of the dead find solace from the piety of their friends who are alive, when the sacrifice of the Mediator is offered for the dead or alms are given in the Church. But these means are of profit for those who, when they lived, earned merit whereby such things could be of profit to them. For theirs is a manner of living neither so good that there is no need of these helps after death, nor so bad that they would not be of profit after death. There is, however, a good manner of living which makes the use of these helps unnecessary, and a correspondingly bad manner of living which prohibits their being of any avail once a man has passed from this life.[1] It is here, then, that is won all merit or demerit whereby a man's state after this life can either be improved or worsened. But let no one hope to obtain, when he is dead, merit with God which he earlier neglected to acquire. So, then, the offices used by the Church in commendation of the dead are not contrary to the Apostle's saying which so runs:[2] 'For all of us will stand before the tribunal of Christ, so that each may receive according to what he won through the body, whether good or evil.' For it was while he lived in the body that each person won the merit whereby the helps of which I speak can be of profit. For they are not of profit to all. And why not, unless because of the different kinds of lives which men lead in the body? Accordingly, when sacrifices, whether of the altar or of alms, are offered for all the baptized dead, these are thanksgivings when made for the very good, propitiatory offerings when made for the not very bad, and at least some sort of solace for the living, even if of no help to the dead, when made for the very bad. But

---

[1] For the various eschatological doctrines contained in sect. 109 and the first part of sect. 110 (*Ench. Patr.* no. 1930), see Portalié, cols. 2445, 2448, 2449.
[2] 2 Cor. 5.10.

when they are of profit, their benefit consists either in bringing a full remission of sin or at least in making the condemnation more tolerable.

(111) After the resurrection, however, when the final, general judgment has been made, the boundaries will be laid out of two cities: one of Christ, the other of the Devil, one of the good, the other of the bad; yet both made up of angels and of men. For the one group there will be no will to sin, for the other no power to do so or any possibility of dying. The former will live true and happy lives in eternal life; the latter will continue unhappily in eternal death, with no power to die; the lot of both groups will be without end. But in the one case the abiding blessedness of one man will be more pre-eminent than that of another; in the other case the abiding misery of one man will be more tolerable than that of another.[3] (112) Vainly, then, yielding to human emotions, do some men, and indeed very many, bewail the eternal punishment of the damned and their unvaried, unceasing torments, and do not believe that it shall be so. Without, indeed, going counter to the Divine Scriptures, they yield to their own tendency and soften the hard passages found there, giving a milder turn to statements which they believe more terrible than true. 'God will not forget,' they say, 'to show mercy, nor in his anger shut up his mercies.' So indeed we read in a holy Psalm,[4] but those who are intended there are, without doubt, those who are called 'vessels of mercy,'[5] because they are freed from their misery not through their own merits but through God's mercy. Or, if these interpreters believe that this passage applies to all, there is no need for

---

[3] On the doctrines *de novissimis* set out in sect. 111 (*Ench. Patr.* no. 1931), see Portalić, cols. 2441, 2450, 2452.
[4] Ps. 76.10.
[5] Rom. 9.23.

them therefore to suppose that an end can be put to the punishment of those of whom it is written:[6] 'Thus these will go into everlasting punishment,' lest their manner of thinking lead to the conclusion that at some time will end the happiness of those of whom it is on the other hand said:[7] 'But the just will go into eternal life.' But let them suppose, if this pleases them, that at certain intervals of time the punishments of the damned are somewhat mitigated. For, even so, the wrath of God, that is, the condemnation itself (for this is what is called the wrath of God, not a disturbance of the divine mind[8]), even so the wrath of God abides in them,[9] so that in His wrath (that is, His wrath abiding) He does not shut up His mercies,[10] yet does He not put an end to eternal punishment but rather brings relief or gives respite from its torments.[11] For what the Psalm says[12] is not 'to put an end to his anger' nor 'after his anger,' but 'in his anger.' If this anger stood alone, even in the smallest degree possible, still, to be lost out of the kingdom of God, to be an exile from the city of God, to be a stranger to the life of God, to lack the great abundance of the sweetness of God (which God hides for those who fear Him,[13] but shows forth to those who hope in Him), such would be so great a punishment if of eternal duration that no tortures we know could be compared with it, no matter for how many centuries they were continued.

(113) The perpetual death of the damned, that is, their

---

6 Matt. 25.46.
7 *Ibid.*
8 See above, sect. 33.
9 Cf. John 3.36.
10 Cf. Ps. 76.10.
11 On the doctrines concerning Hell contained in the first part of sect. 112 (*Ench. Patr.* no. 1932), see Portalié, col. 2150 ff.
12 Ps. 76.10.
13 Cf. Ps. 30.20.

alienation from the life of God, will abide without end, and it will be the common punishment of them all, whatever conjectures rising from human emotions men may make about the variety of the punishments and the relief or intermission of their woes. Just so, the eternal life of the saints will abide and be common to them all, no matter how the grades of honor may vary in which they shine, refulgent in harmony.

Chapter 30

(114) Out of that confession of faith which is briefly contained in the Creed and which pondered according to the flesh is the milk of babes, but spiritually considered and studied is the food of the strong, arises the good hope of believers, which holy charity accompanies. But, of all those things which are to be believed by faith, only those pertain to hope which are contained in the Lord's Prayer. For 'cursed be every man that putteth hope in man,' as the Divine Scriptures testify;[1] and, consequently, he who puts hope in himself is also ensnared in the chain of this curse. Therefore, we ought to make petition only from the Lord God, whatever it be that we hope to do well or to obtain as a reward for good works.

(115) Now, in the Evangelist Matthew the Lord's Prayer is seen to contain seven petitions, in three of which eternal goods are asked for, in the remaining four, temporal goods; yet these are necessary for obtaining the eternal goods. For in saying:[2] 'Hallowed be thy name. Thy kingdom come, thy will be done on earth, as it is in heaven' (this last interpreted by some, not incongruently, as meaning 'in body as well as in spirit'), we ask for blessings that are to be retained forever;

---
1 Jer. 17.5.
2 Matt. 6.9-10.

they indeed begin in this life and are increased in us as we progress, but in their perfection, which is to be looked for in another life, they will be owned forevermore. But when we say:[3] 'Give us this day our daily bread. And forgive us our debts, as we also forgive our debtors. And lead us not into temptation, but deliver us from evil,' who does not see that this pertains to the needs of the present life? In that eternal life, where we all hope to be, the making hallowed of His name, His kingdom, and His will in our spirit and body, will be perfected and will abide everlastingly. But daily bread is so called because it is necessary in this life, in whatever amount the soul or the body demands, whether we interpret the word in reference to the spirit, or to the flesh, or in both senses. Also the forgiveness we ask for has reference to this life, in which the sin is committed; likewise with the temptations which allure and drive us to sin; and likewise finally with the evil from which we desire to be delivered. But none of these is to be found in the other life.

(116) But the Evangelist Luke has embraced in the Lord's Prayer not seven petitions but five, and yet, of course, there is no discrepancy, for Luke through his very brevity shows how the seven petitions are to be understood. The name of God is hallowed in spirit; the kingdom of God is to come in the resurrection of the body. Luke, therefore, seeking to show that the third petition[4] is a repetition of the preceding two petitions,[5] makes this better understood by omitting it. The petitions he then adds are three in number:[6] those concerning daily bread, forgiveness of sins, and avoidance

---

[3] Matt. 6. 11-13.
[4] That is, in St. Matthew: 'Thy will be done' (Matt. 6.10).
[5] Matt. 6.9-10; cf. Luke 11.2.
[6] Luke 11.3-4.

of temptation. But, whereas Matthew[7] puts in the last place 'But deliver us from evil,' Luke omits it, so that we may understand that it is embraced in the foregoing petition concerning temptation. And indeed Matthew says *But* deliver,' not 'And deliver,' as if to show that only one petition is in question: Wish not this but that, so that anyone may know that in not being led into temptation he is being delivered from evil.

Chapter 31

(117) Now, as to charity which the Apostle says[1] is greater than the other two graces, faith and hope, the more abundantly it is found in anyone, the better that person is. For when we ask how good a man is, we do not ask what he believes or what he hopes for, but what he loves. He who rightly loves, without doubt, rightly believes and hopes. He who does not love, vainly believes, even if the things he believes are true; he vainly hopes even if the things he hopes for are taught to pertain to true happiness, unless he believes and hopes for this, that he may through prayer attain the gift of love. For, although hope is impossible without love, it may happen that a man not love something that is indispensable to the attainment of his hopes—for instance, if he hopes for eternal life (and who is there who does not love it?) but does not love justice, which is indispensable to the attainment of eternal life. This is the faith of Christ which the Apostle commends, and which works through charity,[2] and if there is anything that it does not embrace in its love, it asks

---

[7] Matt. 6.13.

[1] 1 Cor. 13.13.
[2] Gal. 5.6.

that it may receive it, it seeks that it may find it, it knocks that it may be opened unto it.³ Faith obtains what the Law orders. For, without the gift of God, that is, without the Holy Spirit, through whom charity is poured forth in our hearts, the Law can indeed order, but not help; it can, moreover, make a man a transgressor, since he cannot excuse himself from ignorance. For carnal desire is supreme where there is not the charity of God.⁴

(118) But, when in the deepest shadows of ignorance man lives according to the flesh, with no resistance from reason, this is his first stage. Then, when through the Law knowledge of sin has come to be, though not yet the aid of the divine Spirit, man's desire to live according to the Law is overcome. Man sins with knowledge and, as subjected to sin, serves it ('for by whatever a man is overcome, of this also he is the slave'⁵), knowledge of the Law bringing it about that sin works in man all manner of concupiscence,⁶ with the added guilt of transgression of the Law. Thus is fulfilled what was written:⁷ 'The Law intervened that the offense might abound.' This is man's second stage. But if God has regard to man, so that man believes in God's help toward the accomplishment of His commands, and if man begins to be led by the Spirit of God,⁸ he lusts against the flesh⁹ with the greater strength of charity. Although there still is in man that

---

3 Matt. 7.7.
4 Together with the end of sect. 7 and the beginning of sect. 8 (*Ench. Patr.* no. 1913), this section (*Ench Patr.* no. 1933) gives an admirably simple account of the inter-relation of faith, hope, and charity. For charity and its pre-eminence, see Portalié, col. 2435.
5 2 Peter 2.19.
6 Rom. 7.7.
7 Rom. 5.20.
8 Rom. 8.14.
9 Gal. 5.17.

which strives against him (for his infirmity is not yet healed), still he lives the life of the just by faith,[10] and justly lives insofar as he does not yield to evil concupiscence, pleasure overcoming justice. This is the third stage of a man of good hope. If in this stage a man makes progress through steadfast piety, the final peace remains, and this is fulfilled after this life in the repose of the spirit, and finally in the resurrection of the body. Of these four stages the first is before the Law, the second is under the Law, the third is under grace, the fourth is in full and perfect peace. Thus also was the life of the people of God disposed through intervals of time, in accordance with the pleasure of God, who has 'ordered all things in measure and number and weight.'[11] The first period was before the Law, the second under the Law, which was given to Moses;[12] the next under grace, which was revealed through the first coming of the Mediator.[13] This grace indeed was not lacking even before to those to whom it was to be imparted, although, in conformity with the dispensation of time, it was veiled and hidden. For none of the just men of old was able to find salvation apart from the faith of Christ; and, unless Christ had been known also to them, they could not have served to convey prophecy to us, now openly and now darkly.

(119) Now, in whichever of these four ages (to call them so) the grace of rebirth finds any particular man, all his past sins are then forgiven him, and the guilt he assumed at birth is removed through rebirth. And so true it is that 'the Spirit breatheth where he will'[14] that some men have no experience of the second stage, that of slavery under the

---
10 Rom. 1.17; Gal. 3.11; Heb. 10.38.
11 Wisd. 11.21.
12 John 1.17.
13 Cf. John 1.17.
14 John 3.8.

Law, but along with the commandment begin to enjoy divine assistance. (120) Yet, before a man can receive the commandment, he must live according to the flesh; but, if he has already received the sacrament of rebirth, no harm will come to him if he then passes from this life, 'for to this end Christ died and rose again, that he might be Lord both of the dead and of the living';[15] nor will the kingdom of death have dominion over him, for whom He, who was 'free among the dead,'[16] died.

Chapter 32

(121) All the divine commandments are directed towards charity, of which the Apostle says:[1] 'The end of the commandment is charity, from a pure heart and a good conscience and faith unfeigned.' Accordingly, the end of every precept is charity, that is, every commandment is directed towards charity. For anything that is done, whether through fear of punishment or any carnal motive at all, in such a way as not to be directed towards that charity which the Holy Spirit pours forth in our hearts,[2] is not yet done as it ought to be done, even though it may so appear. This charity embraces both love of God and love of neighbor, 'and on these two commandments depend the whole Law and the Prophets,'[3] and, we may add, the Gospel and the Apostles, for it is from no other source that this voice comes: 'The end of the commandment is charity'[4] and 'God is charity.'[5] Therefore, whatever

---

15 Rom. 14.9.
16 Ps. 87.6.

---

1 1 Tim. 1.5.
2 Rom. 5.5.
3 Matt. 22.40.
4 1 Tim. 1.5.
5 1 John 4.16.

commandment God gives—and one of them is 'Thou shalt not commit adultery,'⁶—and whatever is not ordered but advised as a spiritual counsel—and such is 'It is good for man not to touch a woman,'⁷—are only then rightly carried out when they are directed to the love of God and of one's neighbor for God's sake, both in this world and in the world to come. We now love God through faith; we shall then love Him through sight;⁸ and now we love even our neighbor through faith. For, as mortals, we do not know the hearts of mortals, but then 'the Lord will bring to light the things hidden in darkness and make manifest the counsels of hearts; and then everyone will have his praise from God';⁹ for that will be praised and loved in our neighbor which God Himself will bring to light lest it remain hidden. Moreover, desire is diminished as charity increases, until at length charity comes to that abundance which cannot be surpassed: 'Greater love than this no one has, that one lay down his life for his friends.'¹⁰ For, who will relate how great love will be in the life to come, when there will be no desire to restrain and conquer? For then, health¹¹ will have reached perfection when the struggle with death will be no more.

Chapter 33

(122) But there must be an end somewhere to this volume. It is for you to see whether you ought to call it a

---

6 Matt. 5.27.
7 1 Cor. 7.1.
8 2 Cor. 5.7; cf. 1 Cor. 13.12.
9 1 Cor. 4.5.
10 John 15.13.
11 In the third stage (sect. 118) man's infirmity is not yet healed; here the cure is complete. For other appearances of the figure of health and sickness applied to the human race, see above, sects. 60, 79, 81 and (for the nature of sickness) sect. 11.

handbook or use it as such. As or myself, since I thought that your zeal in Christ was not to be despised, believing and hoping good things for you in the help of our Redeemer, and loving you greatly among the members of His body, I have written for you, as well as I was able, this book on faith, hope, and charity. May it be as useful as it is lengthy.

INDEX

INDEX

Abraham, 28 and *passim;* promise to, 289, 293
Academics, 387f.
Acts, natural and supernatural, 246 n. 7; *see also* Works
Action, the same, may be good or bad, when, 132f.
Activity, source of happiness, 331
Adam, aid and graces received from God by, 240, 280ff.;—constituted in goodness, 254, 277ff.; his freedom of perseverance 277f.; 283ff.; descendants of, 258f., 280; fall of, 254, 278f.; the second, 283; (named or referred to) 380 n. 7, 391f., 408-412, 424, 433, 446, 451-453, 458, 461
Adjutorium = grace, 286 n. 112
Admonition, 248ff.; medical value of, 297f., 301ff.; duty of, 301, 304; —and prayer, 240, 249, 251, 276, 298, 305; —and precept, 249, 305; —and charity, 302, 304f.; —and contrition, 255
Adoptionism, heresy of, 334

Adultery, 51, 385, 390, 436, 471
Aethelstani Psalterium, 399 n. 10
Afflictions as medicine, 38
Africa, North, 310
Agabus, 455
Agar, 206
Ages (stages), the four, 468ff.
agnostici, 310
Agreement, Academic suspension of, 387f.
Aid, divine, two kinds of, 286ff.
Alcuin, 360 n. 21
Allegory, 148
Almsgiving, 425; fruitfulness of, 428; different kinds of, 429ff.; — as thanksgivings, 462
Amasi (1 Par. 12), 300
Ambiguity in Sacred Scriptures, how removed, 117-120, 123
Ambrose, St., 4, 7, 99, 215ff., 218ff.; date of death of, 309
Amen, Alleluia, Raca, Hosanna, 73
Amendment of life, 429, 432

Angels, why happy, 49; —are our neighbors, 49; graces given to, 278ff.; free will of, 278; certainty of perseverance of, 278, 284; good and bad — subject to God, 315, 324, 374; —can be wicked, 379, 387f.; punishment of the wicked, 391ff., 402, 461ff., 444-447, 454f., 463

Anthony, saintly Egyptian hermit, 21

Apollinarism, heresy of, 336

Apollo, 86

Apostolic tradition, 128

Aquila, 177 n. 4

Arabia, 206

Arianism, heresy of, 333; Church persecuted by, 350

Ascension: see Christ

Assyria, 156

Astrologers, 89-91; their work futile, 91

Auctor ad Herennium, 6, 169, 177f., 180, 189f., 192f., 210f., 205, 207, 210, 222

Augustine, Bp. of Hippo, St., *De doctrina Christiana,* translated, 19-235; date of, 4f., purpose of, 3ff.; structure of, 5f.; importance and influence of, 7f.; 359 n. 16
De correptione et gratia, 359 n. 7
translated, 245-305; date of, 204; importance Augustine ascribes to, 241; purpose of, 239; structure of, 240;
De agone Christiano, translated, 315-353; date of, 309f.; origin of title of, 310; scope of, 310; literary value of, 310; purpose of, 310; intended for unlearned, 348; referred to, 5;
Enchiridion de fide, spe et caritate, translated, 369-472; addressee, 357f.; biblical quotations, 361; date of, 357; 358.; imoprtance and influence of, 359ff.; MSS., 360 n. 21; purpose of, 357; structure of 359; variations in title of, 358f.

Confessiones, 176, 190, 196, 201

Contra Academicos, 387

Contra adv. Leg., 190

Contra Crescentium, 189, 193, 196, 222

Contra Faustum, 5

Contra mendacium ad Consentium, 383

De diversis quaestionibus ad Simplicianum, 309

De fide et operibus, 425 n. 1

De genesi ad litteram, 360 n. 20

De haeresibus ad Quodvultdeum, 333, 345
De octo Dulcitii quaestionibus, 357
De Trinitate, 360
Enarrationes in Psalmos, 310
Psalmus contra partem Donati, 348
Retractationes, 3f., 309f., 351, 359 n. 7
Authority, rock of, 170

Babylon, 156
Badcock, F. J., 399 n. 10
Bagua, Donatist council of, 309
Baianism, 241
Baker and Bickersteth, 9
Bamberg MS. of Augustine's *Ench.*, 360 n. 21
Baptism, sacrament of, 128; Donatist concept of, 348; Luciferians' correct notion of, 348; 404, 407-414, 423-425, 429, 433, 449, 462, 469f.; *see* Infants, unbaptized
Barry, M. I., 9
Beatitude, 277f., 286
Beauty,—of style, 210; 371, 376
Belial, children of, 299
Benedictine editors, 7
Bethsaida, 447
Bible: *see* Scriptures
Billiot, L., 328
Birth, spiritual, 74; of twins, 91

Body, never completely annihilated, 40; its interrelation to soul and God, 43; must be subject to the soul, 45; resurrection of: *see* Resurrection
Bonaventure, St., 7
Bourke, V. J., 5 n. 5
Branches, amputated can be grafted again, 349
Breviary, Roman, 391 n. 1
Burn, A. E., 399 n. 10
Byzacene, African province, 239

caesa, 177, 178, 179, 180, 181
Caesar, Julius, 90; Augustus, 90
Called, the, and the Chosen, 270f., 293
Calvin, 270 n. 79
Canticle of Canticles, 65
Carnal minded, 332
Carnal slavery, 127
Carnal pleasures in marriage, 346
Carthage, 95
Cassiodorus, 7, *Commentary on the Psalms*, 360 n. 21
catáchresis, 149
Cataphrygians, 345
Caterva, 224
cathari, 351
Catholic: Catholic faith, its foundation, 371; Catholic faith, rule of, 374; Catholics, 425

Catholic Church, spread all over the world, 320; stronger by victories over heresy, 331; —and unworthy members, 331; forgiveness of sins in, 349-350

Cato, 89

Causes of good and evil, 381

Cavallera, F., 360 n. 20, 362

Cecilian, Bp., 347

Charity, definition of, 130; the laws of, 135; 370-375, 388, 417, 422, 426, 431, 433ff.; 465, 467-471; *see also* Faith, hope and charity

Chastity, 390f.

Children, of God, and perseverance, 268ff.; of Belial, 299

Christ, our physician, 36; His prayer for Peter, 265; His Incarnation, 281f.; as Mediator, 372, 394ff., 406, 410, 412, 420f., 423, 446, 457, 461f., 469, 472; His divine and human natures (the Incarnation), 399ff., 416; the Word, 399-402; the God-man, 461; His baptism by John, 410f.; His crucifixion and death, 373, 385, 407, 411-414, 420f., 439, 455, 470; sinless but called sin, 406, 414; His burial, 414; His resurrection, 407, 412-414, 441, 445, 461, 470; His ascension, 414f.; sits on the right hand of the Father, 373, 414f.; the Judge, 373, 415, 425, 462 (*see also* Judgment); the foundation, 371, 426ff.; His humility, 399f., 411, 461; His obedience, 461; members of His body, 417, 424, 472; *See also* Lord's Prayer

Cham, 163

Christian Combat, The: *see* Augustine, *De agone Christiano*

Christian life, defined, 115

Christian name, 372

Christian teacher, duty of, 172; he should speak wisely rather than eloquently, 173; how eloquence can be attained, 174-175; should pray before preaching, 197-198

Church, the Holy, we should be united with, 22; the Church Christ's body, 38; alluded to as a beautiful woman, 65; as Mother, 217, 350; 400, 416ff., 423-425, 436f.

Cicero, 6, 121, 169, 170, 171, 172, 173, 174, 175, 177, 178, 179, 180, 187, 189, 190, 191, 192, 195, 196, 198, 201, 202, 205, 206, 207, 208, 209, 210, 211, 212, 222, 223, 226, 228, 229, 232

Cities, the two, 463ff. (cf. 394) 209f.
climax, 177
cola, 177
Commandments, three, to love God, 84
commata, 177, 179
Conclusion, *see* Syllogism
Concupiscence: *see* Desires, worldly
'Condemnation', an ecclesiastical penalty, 301
Confession, 390; *see also* Penance
Contraries, dialectical, 379
Cooperation, human, with grace, 247ff.
Cornelius, the centurion, 22
Corozain, 447
Corrective punishment, 430
Corruption and incorruption, 377, 379f., 392, 421, 445f.
Cosmetics, use of, 221
Counsels of perfection, 431, 471
Creatures, all subject to God, 315, 322
Creed (rule of faith), 359, 372f., 374, 375-465 *passim* (esp. 399, 403, 416f., 423, 449, 465)
Cresconius, monk of Hadrumetum, 240

Crime, differs from vice, 130; *see also* Sin(s)
Cross, symbol of Christian life, 115
Crown of victory, a promise, 315
Crucifixion, *see* Christ
'Cry', 438
Cyprian, St., 5, 7, 113, 197, 214f., 217ff.; explanation of the Lord's prayer by, 257.; letter to Quirinus, 260

D'Alès, A., 311, 333
Damnation, justice of, 258ff.; *see* Mass of damnation
David, King, 141, 299f.
'Day', meaning of term, 411
Dead, sacrifice of the Mediator for, 462; offices for, *ibid.*
Death, 309ff., 411, 413, 423, 441ff., 446, 458-463, 470f.
de Bruyne, D., (O.S.B.), 361 n. 24
Deception, 383ff., 420
Definition, 107
Deferrari, R. J., 9
delectatio, 300 n. 163
Denzinger, H., 362, 399 n. 10
Desires, worldly, 391ff., 400, 406, 427f., 440, 468f., 471
Deus, 131

Devil, his influence on us, 22 and *passim*; his beatitude before the fall, 279; free will of, 278; a foe to be conquered, 315; how cast out of world, 316; in what sense a ruler, 316; how to be overcome, 317; not a heavenly dweller, 318;—and his angels, 321; served by creatures, 322; 393f., 411, 446, 461, 463 (*see also* Satan); Devils, 374

Dialectics, helps to interpret Scripture, 102; usefulness of, 108-109

di Capua, F., 358 n. 11

Didactic passages, rule for, 136

dilectio, caritas, amor, 370 n. 6

Docetism, heresy of, 335

Dods, Marcus, 361

Donatists, schism of, 346-348; disunity of, 346-347; 376 n. 3, 382

Donatus, 346, 347

Dulcitius, the tribune, 357f., 359 n. 17

Egypt, 408

Elect, the, effects of predestination on, 260f.; number of, 293ff., 301

Eloquence, its principles true, though sometimes used to persuade what is false, 108;—is joined with wisdom in Scriptures, 175-177; three aims of Roman, 201; to be applied differently for different subjects, 204-205

Emath, the great, 183

enchiridion (handbook), 357 n.5, 358f., 370, 372, 472

Enigma, 148

Enjoyment and use, 29; God alone to be enjoyed, 41; God does not enjoy us, but uses us, 52; how we should enjoy man, 53

Epaphras, a Colossian, 256

Error, and happiness, 331;—and falsehood, 391, 420, 430

Esau, 450f.

Eschatology: eternal life, 371, 383, 385, 388-390, 391f., 394, 420, 422, 424, 426, 428f., 445f., 447f., 460f., 463ff., 466, 467, 471; damnation, 385, 392, 393, 410, 412, 463ff.; *see also* Death, Fire,

Resurrection of the human body
Eskridge, J. B., 9
Esther, Queen, 234
Eucharist, Holy, 128, 215f.
Eugippius, 360 n.21
eusébeia, 370
Eusebius, 111
Evil, foreknowledge of, 290; 373, 376ff., 390ff., 415., 426, 448, 451, 453ff., 458, 466f.
Evodius, St., Bp., 239
Excommunication, 439

Fables, 96
Faith, 239; subjects soul to God, 331; illumined by moral living, 331;—and understanding, 332; 370-465; faith, hope and charity (their inter-relation) 359, 370-374, 396, 465, 467f., 468 n. 4, 470-472
Fall,—of angels, 391 ff. (*see also* Angels);—of man, 254, 391 ff., 459 (*see also* Free will, Judgment, Sin)
Falsehood, defined, 107; two kinds of 107 f.; 381 ff.
Fasting, 84
Fatalism, 249
Faure, J. B., (S.J.) 361, 447 n.3
Fear, 373, 391, 470

Felicianus, Donatist bishop, 309
Felix, monk of Hadrumetum, 239 f.; another monk, 240
Fetuses, abortive, 441 ff.
Figurative expressions, not to be taken literally, 124; how detected, 129; rule to be observed with, 135
Fire, testing, purgatorial, and eternal, 425-429
Fish, a symbol for the just, 343
Flesh, the likeness of sin, 406 f.
Florus, monk of Hadrumetum, 239 f., 245, 247
'Fool,' used of one's brother, 437 f.
Foreknowledge of God: see Predestination, Evil
Forgiveness of sins, 390, 412, 422-424, 429 ff., 440, 466
Fornication and adultery, 436
Fortune-telling, a grave error, 91
Four stages (ages), the, 468 ff.
Free will, and grace, 239 f., 246, 248 n. 14, 265, 291 f., 300 n. 163; two kinds of, 285 ff.; —and sin, 254f.;—of the angels,—of the devil, 278f.;—of Adam, 238ff.; human infirmities for our abuse of, 326-327; condition for merit of, 327; 380, 391, 393, 395ff., 458-460

Fruit and trees, parable of, 380
Futuribles, 268 n. 74

Gedeon, 216
Gehenna, 437
genethliaci (composers of horoscopes), 89
genus and *species*, 155
Geth of the Philistines, 184
Ghost, Holy: *see* Holy Spirit
Gifts, of God, 239f., 267; *see* Grace, Perseverance
Glorification, 273
God, Manichaean notion of, 318-320; Creator (Artificer), 375ff., 392ff., 396, 416, 417, 422, 444; His goodness, 375ff., 391f., 464 (*see also* Grace); His mercy (*see* Grace); His peace, 421f., 469; His omnipotent will, 447-452, 454-460, 465f.; His wrath, 392, 398f., 410, 451, 464; vision of God, 371 (*see also* Eschatology); *see also* Aid, Children, Gifts, Judgment, Mercy, Peace, Predestination, Trinity, Will, etc.
Goldbacher, A., 358 n.14, 400 n.12
Good, 373f., 376ff., 390ff., 415f., 426, 448, 451, 454ff.. 458f.

Grace, special graces to build up the Church, 38; and free will (*see* Free will); early modern controversies on, 241; gratuity of, 239, 260, 280, 296; two kinds of, 280ff., 285ff.; invincible, 292; necessity of, 245ff.; cooperation with, 247ff.;—and Incarnation, 281f.;—and perseverance 255ff., 266ff., 291ff.; mystery of, 266, 372, 393, 395ff., 401f., 405f., 410-412, 421, 429, 433, 435, 440, 447ff., 450ff., 459-461, 463f., 469; *See* Adam, angels, devil, saints
gradatio, 177
Grammatical writers, 373
Greek(s), 369, 375
Gregory, St., of Nyssa, *Oratio catechetica* 324 n. 5

Habit, the power of, 79
Hadrumetum, monastery of, 239f.
Hair, a woman who dyes her— is foolish, 220f.
Happiness, result of knowledge and activity, 331; 371, 381, 388-391, 422, 445f., 464. *See also* Eschatology.
Happy, the good are, 322
Harnack, A., 359 n.18, 362

INDEX

Health, spiritual, 376f., 381, 439, 446, 471
Heaven, *see* Eschatology
'Heavenly body', 351 n.3
Heavenly bodies, are they angels?, 418f.
Hebrew nation, literature of, 99; originated the worship of one God, 99
Hell, *see* Eschatology
Heresies, 360, 370, 371f., 425
Hermeneutics, Biblical, the earliest Latin treatise on, 6
Herod, 408
Hesiod, 86
Hilary, St., 113
Hilberg, I., 442 n.2
Hippo, 239f., 357
History, helps to interpret Scripture, 98
Holy Spirit, 21f., 399, 402ff., 410, 416ff., 423f., 429, 433, 440f., 468f., *passim*; *see also* Trinity
Homiletics, a manual of, 6
Hope, its definition, its rational difference from faith, 374; 370-375, 420, 425, 465-467, 467f.; *see also* Faith, hope and charity
Horoscopes, their composers, 92; their knowledge to be rejected, 92-94

Hrabanus Maurus, 7
Humility, 274f., 294
Hymenaeus (2 Tim. 2), 263
Hyssop, properties of, 115-116

Idols, worship of, 93
Ignorance, 381ff., 388, 391, 419, 439f. (one of the two causes of sin), 468
Immortality, two kinds of, 285.; 459; *see also* Eschatology.
Incarnation, of the Word, how necessary for man's salvation, 328; not injurious to God's inviolability, 340-341; *see also* Christ
Indiculum, 359 n.17, 441 n.7
Inebriation, spiritual, 326
Infants, unbaptized, 259, 266f., 298 n.154
Inheritance of orginal guilt, 393, 398, 423; *see also* Adam, Sin(s)
Intention, 384, 389, 454ff.
Interpretations, may be various for the same passage, 147
interrogatio, 121 n.2
Israel, spiritual and carnal 158f., 408
Israelites, faithful, 127
Itala, 79-80

Jacob, 28, 91, 389, 419, 450f.
Jacquin, A.M., (O.P.), 391 n.1, 458 n.1
Jansenism, 241
Jealousy, 330
Jeremias, 4
Jerome, St., 8; his translation used by Augustine 183; mentions Hebrew meters, 210; '—the priest of holy memory', 357; *Epistula* (72) *ad Vitalem,* 442
Jerusalem, the heavenly, 394, 416
Jersusalem, 125, 449f., 455
Jesus, son of Sirach, 3
Job, the holy, 369
John the Baptist, 338, 410f.
Joseph, spouse of the Virgin Mary, 403
Judas, 262
Judgment, 391-393, 415, 418, 424f., 433f., 445ff., 461ff.
Judgment of God, mystery of, 264ff., 294; and mercy, 259ff. *see also* Damnation, Predestination
Jupiter and Memory, 86
Justification, 273
Just men of old, 469
Justice, 392, 395, 406, 411, 423, 434f., 439f., 459, 467, 469. *For* God's justice *see also* Judgment

Kindness, definition of—,its difference from utility, 130
Knöll, P., 357 n.5, 360 n.21, 387 n.3, 439 n.21
Knowledge, the essence of, 75; general—of animals, stones etc. helpful in interpretation of Scriptures, 83; virtue and, 331;—is a source of happiness, 331; 375, 381ff., 387f.
Krabinger, J.G., 360, 362

Lactantius, 113
Law (God's), no one escapes the law of the Almighty, 322,;—a safeguard, 324; 398, 421, 440, 468ff.
Law, letter of, 246
Lawrence, addressee of Augustine's treatise *Faith, Hope and Charity,* 357f., 369-372, 471f.
Lawsuits, 436f.
'Legitimate numbers', 161
Letters, meaning of, 94; shorthand characters, 97
libertas, and *liberum arbitrium,* 285 n.111
Liberty, 395
Lies, 57, 383ff; the very essence of, 384; *see also* Deception
Life, happy,—consists in enjoying God, 110; eternal, 55;

human, when it begins in the womb, 442
Literature, early Christian, 310
Logic, science of, 107; *see also* syllogism
Lord, the sweetness of, 326; *see* God
Lord's Prayer, 359, 372, 390, 429, 431f., 437, 440, 465-467
Lot, 164
Love, instructions on, 41, 45-46; objects of, 47; God especially, 49; *see* Charity (cf. 370 n.6)
Lowe, E. A., 360 n.21
Lucan, quoted, 373
Luciferians, schism of, 348-349
Lust, definition of, 130; *see* Desires, worldly
Lydda, 442 n.2

Mainz, 7
Man, the image of God, 41; differs from all other created things, 41f.; dignity and importance of, 329; divine aid necessary for 329; *see especially* Death, Eschatology, Fall, Free will, Happiness, Justice, Life, Resurrection of the body, Wisdom
Manes, 345
Manichaeus, origin of name, 345
Manichaeism, cosmogony of, 318-319; sacrilegious character of, 319
Maro, 381;*See also* Virgil
Marriage, its purpose, when good and bad, 435f.
Marrou, H.-I., 7, 9
Mars, 89
Martyrs, 43, 287f., 455
Mary, Bl. Virgin, 282, 399ff.
Mass, of perdition, of the lost, Condemned mass (*massa perditionis, massa damnata*) 259f., 264, 278, 391 n.1, 392, 446, 452, 453, 460; *see* Sacrifice
mathematici (astrologers), 89
Maurist edition of St. Augustine, 358 n.9, 360 n.21, 361, 369 n.4, 448 n.3
Mediator, *see* Christ
Melchisedech, king of Salem, 215
membra, 177, 178, 179, 180, 181, 185, 186, 208
Mercury, deity of literature, 87
Mercy, and judgment, 295ff.; God's *see* Grace; works of, *see* Almsgiving Merit(s),—and grace, 239, 260, 296;—and predestination, 260; 394, 396, 401, 405, 450ff., 460-463; *see* works

Merit(s),—and grace, 239, 260; 394, 396, 401, 405, 450ff., 460-463; *see* Works
Middle Ages, 7
Milk of faith, 352
Mind, characteristics of a depraved, 43
Ministers, God's, 211
Miracles, 447, 456
Miscellanea Agostiniana, 358 n. 11, 359 n. 17, 360 n. 21, 361 n.24, 391 n.1, 441 n.7, 458 n.1
Mitterer, S., (O.S.B.), 8, 358 n.8, 360, 362
Modalism, heresy of, 332
Monsters, 442ff.
Montanus, heresy of, 345
móschos and *moscheúmata*, 75
Moses, 23, 28, 451, 469
mundanos and *mundos*, 351
Muses, origin of, 86
Music, elements of, 85
Mynors, R.A.B., 360 n.21
Mystery,—of grace, 266;—of divine judgment, 264ff., 294

Nature, difference of divine and human, 51; science of, 375, 381;—not defrauded, 442
Neptune, 126-127
Nestorians, 400 n.13

Noah, 163
Noris, Cardinal, 241
Number, of elect, 293ff., 301; *see also* Saved
Numbers, as symbols, 84; their science not invented but discovered by men, 109; 'legitimate', 161

Obediential potency, implied, 340
Obscure passages of Holy Scriptures to be explained by clearer, 146; more safely so explained than by reason, 147-148
Ogilvy, J.D.A., 360 n.21
Ogle, M.B., 380 n.7
Clympiads, 98
Optatus, 113
Orator, ideal, 172 n.2; requisites for Christian, 195; his topics, 197; his speech and his deeds, 225ff.
Oratory, rules of, 169f.
Original sin: *see* Sin(s)

Pain, 391
Paradise, 391f., 458f.
Patriarchs and prophets, spiritual men, 128
Paul, St., revelation to, 252; 345; reprimands St. Peter,

350; permits widows to marry, 351; 455
Peace with God, 301ff.
Pelagianism, 239, 246 n.2, 288 n.117
Pelagianists, 392 n.2
Penance, 409, 424f., 428f., 440, 447, 456
percantatio, 121 n.2
periodos, 178
Perseverance, gift of, 240f., 255ff., 264ff., 291ff.; not given to all, 268ff., 294, 297 n.152;—of the martyrs, 287f.; —of the angels, 278f.; freedom of—in Adam, 277f., 283ff.; two kinds of, 285ff.
Peter, St., 22; denial and repentance of, 252, 275f.; unfailing faith of, 265, 292f.; 347; represents Catholic Church, 349-350; reprimanded by St. Paul, 350; called the 'rock', 350; 386, 388, 440, 455
Peter Lombard, 360, 447 n.3
Pharao, 452
Pharisees, 380 n.7, 432-434, 457
Philemon, 54
Philetus (2 Tim.2), 263
Philosophers, 107
physici, 375
Piety, 369, 462, 469
Plato, 4, 99

Platonists and Christian faith, 112
Plural for singular, 408
Poets, 107
Polyandry, objectionable, 133
Polygamy, was unobjectionable at times, 133, 139
Pope, H., (O.P.), 357 n.2 and 4, 358 n.6, 362
Portalié, E., 361f., 372-468 (footnotes) *passim.*
Possidius, Bp. of Calama, his *Indiculum* of Augustine's writings, 359 n.17, 441 n.7
Prayer, power of, 21; should precede preaching, 234, 235, 240, 247f., 253, 276, 298, 305; the Lord's, 257f.; Christ's — for Peter, 265; 372f., 397f., 429-431, 436, 440, 455-457, 462, 465ff.
Predestination, 239f., 259ff., 293ff., effects of—on the elect, 260ff.; number of the elect a secret, 293ff., 301; God's purpose in, 262f., 271f.; and foreknowledge, 269, 273; 421, 447, 450ff., 454, 458. *see also* Grace, Judgment
Premises, if false, conclusion is false although logical sequence is sound, 105
Pretextatus, Donatist bishop, 309

Pride, 393, 395, 452f., 460f.
Priscilla, 345
Priscillianists, 383 n.2
Prophecy, 469
Prosper of Aquitaine, 241
Providence, divine, 92; embraces all things, 322; how good and evil cooperate with, 322-324; governs according to nature and dignity of creatures, 324-325; extends to lowliest creatures, 325; intellectual creatures, instruments of, 325
Psalms, African text of, 409 n.18
Ptolemy, King, 81
Punctuation, in Scriptures, 118
Punic language, 310
Punishment, salutary effect of, 301
Pythagoras, 99

Quintilian, 6, 121, 177, 178, 180, 187, 188, 189, 190, 191, 202, 205, 206, 207, 208, 209, 210, 222, 223, 229, 230, 232
Quintilis = July, 90

Reason and faith, 370f.
Rebecca, 450
Rebirth: *see* Baptism
Redemption: *see* Christ: Mediator
Repentance: *see* Penance
Responsibility, for sin, 251, 254; for failure to admonish sinners, 304
Resurrection of Christ: *see* Christ
Resurrection of the human body, 441-446, 461, 463, 466, 469
Retractations, referring to *De doctrina Christiana,* 3-4; referring to *De agone Christiano,* 309, 310, 351; referring to the Enchiridion *De fide, spe, et caritate,* 359 n.7
Rhetoric, not the aim of *Christian Instruction,* 168; its use proper for a Christian, 169; when and how to be learned, 169-172
'Right hand of the Father', how to be understood, 342
Rivière, J., 359 n.18, 362, 383 n.1, 441 n.7
Rome, defeat of Donatus at, 347
Rottmanner, O., (O.S.B.), 362, 447 n.3
Rouët de Journel, M.J. (S.J.), 361 n.25, 362, 397-468 (footnotes) *passim.*
Ruhland, A., 360, 362
Rules, mystical, 152
Sabellianism, heresy of, 332

Sacraments, 128, 424f.; *see also* Baptism, Eucharist, Marriage, Penance, Sacrifice
Sacrifice of the Mediator (sacrifice of the altar), 462
Sacrifices under the Law, 398, 406, 421
Sacrilege, 341
Saints, as the teeth of the Church, 65; grace of—different from grace of Adam, 280ff., 291f.; their freedom, 445
Sallust, imitated, 384
Satan, 420, 436, 455; *see also* Devil
Saul, King, 93, 299
Saved, number of the, 394, 421, 449, 453, 456f.
Schaff, P., 361
Scheel, O., 358 n.8, 359 n.18, 360, 362, 406 n.7, 447 n.3
Schism, 425
Scriptures, Holy, norms for expounding, 19-21; two factors in treating, 27; should produce knowledge of God and neighbor in readers, 56; not needed by man of virtue for himself, 59; what kind of reader it requires, 60; its obscurity is useful, 65; canonical books of, 69-71; how we should study, 71; why not understood, 72; knowledge of languages needed for, 73; different translations useful, 74; Itala and Septuagint recommended, 81-99; sciences help to a knowledge of, 98-100; so do other bits of knowledge, 101-102; what dispositions it demands, 114-115; compared with profane literature, 116; rules for, 142-143; its obscure passages to be explained by clearer, 146; more safely so explained than by reason, 147f.; its obscure passages, though eloquent, not to be imitated, 187-188; 371, 410, 452; faulty copies of, 406; misinterpretation of, 463f.
Quotations from or references to Biblical writers or Biblical books
Acts, 21, 22, 23, 93, 113, 126, 135, 198, 257, 345, 386, 405, 433, 455
Amos, 183
Apocalypse, 54, 145, 150, 160, 161, 293, 394, 416, 446
Canticle of Canticles, 65, 153
Deuteronomy, 42, 72, 93, 127, 408
Ecclesiasticus, 3, 69, 103, 137, 139, 140, 229, 369, 376, 424, 427, 429, 433
Esther, 234

Exodus, 23, 28, 52, 83, 112, 115, 408, 451f.
Ezechiel, 157, 158, 304, 409
Genesis, 28, 41, 64, 83, 90, 91, 133, 153, 162, 164, 186, 215, 322, 376, 380 n.7, 389, 391, 419, 438
Habacuc, 387
Hebrews, 30
Isaias, 67, 74, 152, 153, 165, 273, 294, 299, 302, 332, 350, 378f., 385, 394, 438
James, 52, 143, 173, 255, 295, 374, 426, 437
Jeremias, 41, 131, 161, 196, 233, 452, 465,
Job, 268, 291, 369, 398
Joel, 372
John, 24, 35, 36, 37, 41, 54, 55, 63, 81, 85, 96, 98, 99, 118, 122, 125, 132, 136, 139, 145, 146, 164, 214, 229, 246, 247, 253, 257, 259, 259, 270, 271, 272, 273, 274, 275, 288, 294, 296, 304, 326, 327,, 334 342, 343, 344, 349, 395, 398-400, 402-405, 410f., 415, 417f., 423, 429, 431
Josue, 380
Jude, 257,
Judges, 216
Kings, 83, 93, 116, 141, 142, 299, 380
Leviticus, 42, 258
Luke, 50, 51, 98, 126, 133, 143, 160, 164, 165, 202, 217, 252, 256, 265, 276, 282, 293, 302, 329, 341, 345, 378, 394, 398, 402, 422f., 430-435, 437, 440, 445, 457, 466f.
Machabees, 204, 295
Malachias, 450,
Mark, 160
Matthew, 24, 27, 39, 40, 42, 47, 50, 63, 67, 82, 83, 84, 114, 137, 144, 145, 153, 154, 160, 161, 165, 198, 199, 204, 220, 230, 233, 234, 257, 260, 262, 264, 279, 288, 293, 305, 318, 325, 335, 341, 344, 346, 349, 351, 352, 378, 380, 382, 390, 394, 397f., 403, 405, 408, 410f., 415, 419, 422, 428-432, 434, 437f., 440f., 447, 449, 455, 464-468, 470f.
Numbers, 77, 216, 407
Osee, 133, 406
Paralipomenon, 142, 300
Paul, quotations from his work, 22, 23, 24, 27, 28, 30, 32, 35, 38, 39, 40, 43, 44, 45, 47, 49, 50, 52, 53, 54, 55, 56, 57, 58, 59 60, 6ª, 72, 74, 75, 77, 78, 82, 87, 93, 99, 103, 114, 115, 118, 120, 121, 122, 123, 124, 125, 126, 127, 131, 132, 135, 136, 137, 138, 139, 143, 145, 146, 152, 153, 154, 155, 157, 158, 159,

165, 177, 178, 181, 182, 199, 200, 201, 203, 205, 206, 207, 208, 209, 212, 213, 216, 217, 220, 229, 230, 231, 232, 235, 246, 247, 248, 249, 252, 253, 255, 256, 257, 258, 259, 260, 261, 263, 264, 267, 268, 270, 272, 273, 274, 275, 276, 280, 281, 287, 288, 289, 290, 291, 294, 296, 298, 301, 302, 303, 304, 310, 315, 317, 318, 321, 322, 323, 325, 326, 335, 343, 344, 348, 349, 351, 352, 353, 369, 370, 371, 373-375, 387-389, 392, 394-401, 404, 406, 408, 410-418, 420-423, 425-430, 433, 435-440, 445f., 449-453, 456f., 460-463, 467-471;
Peter, 38, 57, 143, 145, 305, 395, 418, 468
Proverbs, 55, 136, 143, 145, 167, 177, 265, 295, 396, 460
Psalms, 32, 43, 51, 52, 69, 75, 77, 83, 85, 115, 122 145, 146, 159, 161, 166, 189, 196, 200, 215, 227, 246, 247, 248, 263, 274, 275, 289, 290, 293, 295, 299, 301, 318, 326, 344, 346, 396-398, 409, 411, 415-418, 424, 435, 438, 440, 447-449, 454, 456, 458, 463f., 470
Wisdom 3, 22, 76, 90, 174, 198, 235, 267, 268, 327, 369, 394, 423, 469
Zacharias, 419

Seeberg, R., 359 n.18, 362
Sem, 163
Semipelagianism, 241
Senses, human, 371, 374, 386ff., 419f.
Septuagint, 80-81, 183
Serpent, the, 317
Servius, grammarian, 373 n.6, 407 n.8
Seven, the number, 84
Sextilis = August, 90
Shame, 440
Shaw, J. F. 8, 360, 361, 445 n.4
Sickness, spiritual, 420, 437f., 461, 469, 471 n.11
Sidon, 447
Signs, 28; different from things, 28-9; definition of, 61; natural and convenutal, 61f.; words are the most important, 63; when unknown or obscure they impede a knowledge of Scripture, 72; knowledge of languages and things helps to understand figurative signs, 81; slavery of the Jews unclear, 125; of pagans, 126; Jews and Gentiles freed differently from slavery to, 127-128; who is oppressed by slavery to, 128
Siloe, 81

Simplicianus, Bishop, successor to Ambrose, 309

Sin, ultimate cause of, 253ff.; responsibility for, 251, 254; domination of, 246f.; venial, 288; two kinds of freedom from, 285ff.; original, 254, 258, 278, 297, 392, 394, 398, 400, 406f., 408 (compounded of many sins), 409-413, 423, 433, 446, 452f.; actual sin, 394, 398, 407-409, 411f., 423, 446, 459; trivial sins, 429, 435, 437f.; crimes (grave sins), 423f., 428f., 435, 437f.; customary sins, 438f.; two causes of sin, 439; license to sin, 429, 435; *see also* 372, 383, 387-390, 391ff., 395, 405, 414, 422, 424-426, 432, 434, 436, 440f., 454, 458, 460f., 463, 466, 468f.

Sinai, Mount, 4

Singular for plural, 407

Sixtus III, Pope, 239

Son, meaning of term, 404f.

Son of God, medicine for spiritual ills, 330

Sophisms, 103

Soul, human, essentially different from God, 327; principle of life, 337; subject to God by faith, 331; some souls are like dampened pieces of wood, 334

Speaker, aim of eloquent, 193

species and *genus,* 153

Speech, human, 389

Stages (ages), the four, 468ff.

Statue: analogically used to explain resurrection of the body, 443f.

Stealing, 390, 408

Strassburg, 7

Style, of eloquent orator threefold 201; should be different for different subjects, 204-205, 221; styles should be intermingled, 223; subdued, 205-207, 214-217; moderate, 207-208, 217, 219; its proper purpose, 225-227; grand, 210-213, 219-221; its effect, 224-225

Substance, God's, unchangeable, 340

Sullivan, M. T., 6 n.8, 7, 8

Summa Theologica, 328

Superstition, 88ff.

Syllogism, false and true, 104; when illogical, 105f.

Symbols, 63; *see also* Signs

Syriac, 111

Temple of God, 417f.

Temporal punishment for sin, 425

Temptation, 466f.
Ten, the number, 84
Terence, 111
Theatres, places of wickedness, 48
theosébeia, 369f.
Things, 28; to be enjoyed or used, 29; God's use of, 52; our use of, 52; love of, 56; in their superstitious use is an alliance with demons, 94
Thomas Aquinas, St., 7, 328, 359
Time, its intervals, 84
Times and seasons, misuse of, 438
Timothy, 263
Topics of Christian orator, 197
tractio, 300 n.163
Tradition, apostolic, 128
Translation, difference between ambiguous and erroneous, 75
Trees and fruit, parable of, 380
Trinity, Holy, three persons in, 30f.; 54, 376, 399ff., 404, 416, 417f.
Tritheism, heresy of, 333
Tropes, knowledge of—is essential, 148
Truth, not instituted by men, but only observed, 104-5; should be our aim, rather than words, 231-232; unchangeable—332; 381ff., 387f.

Two cities, the, 463ff. (cf. 394)
Twins, and the constellation at the time of their birth, 91
Tyconius, 6; his rules considered, 150-152; first rule of, 152; second rule of, 153; third rule of, 154; fourth rule of, 155; fifth rule of, 160; sixth rule of, 162; seventh rule of, 165
Tyre, 447

Unforgiveable sin, 440f.
Unwillingness to be admonished, 251
Utility, what it is and its difference from kindness, 130
Uzale, Monastery of 239

Valentine, superior of monastery of Hadrumetum, addressee of St. Augustine's *Admonition and Grace,* 239f., 245
Various Questions to Simplicianus, 309
Varro, 86f.
Venus, 89
Verona Psalter, *MS. Capit. I(1),* 409 n.18
'Vessels of mercy,' 463
Vice, definition of, 130; its difference from crime, 130
Victorinus, 113

Virgil, 90, 109, 211; quoted, 373, 376, 381, 382, 387f., 407
Virgins, good, their nobility, 217
Vogels, H. J., 8
Volusianus, 400

Weakness, aids to, 290ff.; one of the two causes of sin, 439f.
Weapons of a brave man, 211
Wicked, the, qualities of, 331 f.
Will, freedom of: *see* Free will; —of God, 240, 298ff., 302f.; supernatural goodness of, 247 n.10
Wilmart, A., (O.S.B.), 359 n. 17, 441 n.7

Wisdom, absolute and participated, 336-338; man's, 369f., 387f.
Words, figurative, 124
Works, 246 n.7, 247, 394ff., 401, 426, 450f., 460, 465: *see also* Almsgiving, Merit
Worship of God, 369f., 383, 384, 417
Wrath of God: *see* God

X, the letter, different meaning of, 94

Zycha, J., 311, 380 n.7, 425 n.1

www.ingramcontent.com/pod-product-compliance
Lightning Source LLC
Chambersburg PA
CBHW032021290426
44110CB00012B/623